# Edmund Spenser and the romance of space

Manchester University Press

# The Manchester Spenser

The Manchester Spenser is a monograph and text series devoted to historical and textual approaches to Edmund Spenser – to his life, times, places, works and contemporaries.

A growing body of work in Spenser and Renaissance studies, fresh with confidence and curiosity and based on solid historical research, is being written in response to a general sense that our ability to interpret texts is becoming limited without the excavation of further knowledge. So the importance of research in nearby disciplines is quickly being recognised, and interest renewed: history, archaeology, religious or theological history, book history, translation, lexicography, commentary and glossary – these require treatment for and by students of Spenser.

The Manchester Spenser, to feed, foster and build on these refreshed attitudes, aims to publish reference tools, critical, historical, biographical and archaeological monographs on or related to Spenser, from several disciplines, and to publish editions of primary sources and classroom texts of a more wide-ranging scope.

The Manchester Spenser consists of work with stamina, high standards of scholarship and research, adroit handling of evidence, rigour of argument, exposition and documentation.

The series will encourage and assist research into, and develop the readership of, one of the richest and most complex writers of the early modern period.

*General Editors* Joshua Reid, Kathryn Walls and Tamsin Badcoe
*Editorial Board* Sukanta Chaudhuri, Helen Cooper, Thomas Herron, J. B. Lethbridge, James Nohrnberg and Brian Vickers

*Also available*
*Literary and visual Ralegh* Christopher M. Armitage (ed.)
*The art of* The Faerie Queene Richard Danson Brown
*A Concordance to the Rhymes of* The Faerie Queene Richard Danson Brown & J.B. Lethbridge
*A Supplement of the Faery Queene: By Ralph Knevet* Christopher Burlinson & Andrew Zurcher (eds)
*A Companion to Pastoral Poetry of the English Renaissance* Sukanta Chaudhuri
*Pastoral poetry of the English Renaissance: An anthology* Sukanta Chaudhuri (ed.)
*Spenserian allegory and Elizabethan biblical exegesis: A context for* The Faerie Queene Margaret Christian
*Monsters and the poetic imagination in* The Faerie Queene*: 'Most ugly shapes and horrible aspects'* Maik Goth
*Celebrating Mutabilitie: Essays on Edmund Spenser's Mutabilitie Cantos* Jane Grogan (ed.)
*Spenserian satire: A tradition of indirection* Rachel E. Hile
*Castles and Colonists: An archaeology of Elizabethan Ireland* Eric Klingelhofer
*Shakespeare and Spenser: Attractive opposites* J.B. Lethbridge (ed.)
*Dublin: Renaissance city of literature* Kathleen Miller and Crawford Gribben (eds)
*A Fig for Fortune: By Anthony Copley* Susannah Brietz Monta
*Spenser and Virgil: The pastoral poems* Syrithe Pugh
*The Burley manuscript* Peter Redford (ed.)
*Renaissance psychologies: Spenser and Shakespeare* Robert Lanier Reid
*European erotic romance: Philhellene Protestantism, renaissance translation and English literary politics* Victor Skretkowicz
*Rereading Chaucer and Spenser: Dan Geffrey with the New Poete* Rachel Stenner, Tamsin Badcoe and Gareth Griffith (eds)
*God's only daughter: Spenser's Una as the invisible Church* Kathryn Walls
*William Shakespeare and John Donne: Stages of the soul in early modern English poetry* Angelika Zirker

# Edmund Spenser and the romance of space

TAMSIN BADCOE

Manchester University Press

Copyright © Tamsin Badcoe 2019

The right of Tamsin Badcoe to be identified as the author of this work has been asserted by her in accordance with the Copyright, Designs and Patents Act 1988.

Published by Manchester University Press
Oxford Road, Manchester M13 9PL
www.manchesteruniversitypress.co.uk

*British Library Cataloguing-in-Publication Data is available*

ISBN 978 1 5261 3967 2 hardback
ISBN 978 1 5261 6400 1 paperback

First published by Manchester University Press in hardback 2019

This edition published 2022

The publisher has no responsibility for the persistence or accuracy of URLs for any external or third-party internet websites referred to in this book, and does not guarantee that any content on such websites is, or will remain, accurate or appropriate.

Typeset by Servis Filmsetting Ltd, Stockport, Cheshire

I seeke the fields with her late footing synd,
    I seeke her bowre with her late presence deckt,
    yet nor in field nor bowre I her can fynd:
    yet field and bowre are full of her aspect,
But when myne eyes I thereunto direct,
    they ydly back returne to me agayne,
    and when I hope to see theyr trew obiect,
    I fynd my selfe but fed with fancies vayne.
(Edmund Spenser, *Amoretti* (1595), from 'Sonnet LXXVIII')

# Contents

| | |
|---|---:|
| List of illustrations | *page* viii |
| Textual note | x |
| Acknowledgements | xi |
| List of abbreviations | xiii |
| Introduction | 1 |

**Part I: Orientations**

| | | |
|---|---|---:|
| 1 | Strange paths and perspective glasses | 25 |
| 2 | Movement and measurement | 61 |
| 3 | Feyned no where acts | 97 |
| 4 | Compassing desire: cosmography and chorography | 133 |

**Part II: Environments**

| | | |
|---|---|---:|
| 5 | Seamarks and coastal waters | 163 |
| 6 | Wetlands and Spenser's 'personal curvature' | 202 |
| 7 | Spenser's insular fictions | 241 |
| | Afterword | 276 |
| | Bibliography | 281 |
| | Index | 323 |

# Illustrations

1 William Cuningham. *The Cosmographical Glasse* (London, 1559), fol. 53ʳ. Call #153493: STC 6119. Used by permission of the Folger Shakespeare Library. 33
2 William Cuningham. Title page from *The Cosmographical Glasse* (London, 1559). Call #042054: STC 6119. Used by permission of the Folger Shakespeare Library. 34
3 Lucas Janzoon Waghenaer. Title page from *The Mariners Mirrour*, trans. Anthony Ashley (London, 1588). 69788. The Huntington Library, San Marino, California. 48
4 Hans Holbein the Younger. Inked illustration of a pilgrim from a single copy of Erasmus's *Moriae Encomium* (Basel, 1515), sig. M4ʳ. Kunstmuseum Basel – Amerbach Kabinett. 66
5 Lucas Janzoon Waghenaer. Northern Europe from 'A Generall Carde, and Description of the Sea Coastes of Europe', in *The Mariners Mirrour*, trans. Anthony Ashley (London, 1588). 69788. The Huntington Library, San Marino, California. 134
6 John Dee. Title page from *General and Rare Memorials Pertayning to the Perfect Arte of Navigation* (London, 1577). 82497. The Huntington Library, San Marino, California. 177
7 Lucas Janzoon Waghenaer. Southern Europe from 'A Generall Carde, and Description of the Sea Coastes of Europe', in *The Mariners Mirrour*, trans. Anthony Ashley (London, 1588). 69788. The Huntington Library, San Marino, California. 200
8 Flavius Vegetius Renatus. 'Submarine Knight', in *Du Fait de Guerre* (*De Re Militari*) (Paris, 1536), p. cxiv. Call #064409: U101.V3 F7 1536 Cage Fo. Used by permission of the Folger Shakespeare Library. 227

9  Geffrey Whitney. 'The Raging Sea', in *A Choice of Emblemes* (Leiden, 1586), fol. 129ᵛ. Call #054118: STC 25438 copy 1. Used by permission of the Folger Shakespeare Library.       260

# Textual note

All quotations from *The Faerie Queene* are taken from the edition by A.C. Hamilton, revised and edited by Hiroshi Yamashita and Toshiyuki Suzuki (Harlow: Longman, 2001), and are cited by book, canto, and stanza number. The poem's accompanying paratexts are also taken from this edition.

All quotations from Spenser's shorter poems are taken from *Edmund Spenser: The Shorter Poems*, ed. Richard A. McCabe (London: Penguin, 1999).

Quotations from Spenser's prose work, namely *A View of the Present State of Ireland*, are taken from *The Works of Edmund Spenser: A Variorum Edition, X: The Prose Works*, ed. Rudolf Gottfried (Baltimore: Johns Hopkins University Press, 1949). All references are given by page number. I also take quotations from *A Brief Note of Ireland* from this edition.

All quotations from Geoffrey Chaucer's works are taken from *The Riverside Chaucer*, ed. Larry D. Benson and F.N. Robinson, 3rd edn (Oxford: Oxford University Press, 1987; repr. 2008).

Where I have quoted from early modern sources I have silently expanded contractions, removed unnecessary italicisation, and regularised the alphabetic conventions i/j and u/v.

# Acknowledgements

The project that provided the foundation for this book began under the auspices of the Centre for Renaissance and Early Modern Studies at the University of York, and my heartfelt thanks are owed to the academics and postgraduates of this scholarly community. I am particularly indebted to Patricia Palmer and William Sherman, who provided constant and good-humoured guidance, and I am also grateful to David Attwell, Mike Jones, Nicola McDonald, Nick Moon, Varsha Panjwani, Regina Papachlimitzou, Kate Pond, Chloe Preedy, John Roe, Helen Smith, Louise Wilson, Rachael Williamson, and Rachel Willie, for stimulating conversations along the way. Two early readers, Andrew Hadfield and Kevin Killeen, gave valuable feedback and constructive criticism, and I am grateful to the AHRC, whose financial assistance enabled my travails.

Nick Davis, Hester Jones, Brian Nellist, and Simon Palfrey shaped my first encounters with Edmund Spenser at the University of Liverpool, and I thank them for fostering my love of early modern literature. I am also grateful for the interest taken in my Spenser project while I was at work on other tasks during postdoctoral years, in particular by Lukas Erne and Martin Leer at the University of Geneva, and by Matthew Woodcock at the University of East Anglia.

At the University of Bristol, the growing early modern community continues to energise my thinking and I would like to thank John Lee and Lesel Dawson, in particular, for their collegial support and friendship. I am grateful to Julian Lethbridge and Joshua Reid of The Manchester Spenser, and Matthew Frost at Manchester University Press, for helping see this project through to completion. The two anonymous readers provided generous and insightful advice at a vital time, saving me from myself on several occasions. In a book that takes a particular interest in errors and occlusions, any of these remaining are of course my own.

## Acknowledgements

Some of the arguments that appear here have been rehearsed in other guises and I am grateful to the publishers and editors in each case for permission to reproduce this material. An early draft of part of the Lucas Waghenaer section in Chapter 1 appeared as 'Mariners, Maps, and Metaphors: Lucas Waghenaer and the Poetics of Navigation' in a volume of *Swiss Papers in English Language and Literature*, and an early draft of part of Chapter 7 appeared in *Renaissance Studies* as '"The Compasse of That Islands Space": Insular Fictions in the Writing of Edmund Spenser'. Some of my thoughts concerning Spenser, romance, and landscape appeared in embryonic form in '"The Porch of that Enchaunted Gate": Spenserian Influences and the Romance of Place in *Lamia* by John Keats' in *Romanticism*.

My literary thinking has been shaped by several environmental encounters and thanks are owed to Richard Morris for leading a group of us in the footsteps of Gawain on a frozen New Year's Day, and to Jane Grogan, and especially to Mark Rasmussen and Jennifer Lewin, who became travelling companions along uncertain roads to Kilcolman. Most recently, my thanks are owed to the members of the University of Bristol's Centre for Environmental Humanities with whom I travelled to the island of Lundy.

Finally, I would like to thank Laurence Publicover, for his kindness and for his unfaltering belief in the end of this work being in sight, and my mother, Imelda Badcoe, for her support in this and in everything that has preceded it.

# Abbreviations

| | |
|---|---|
| ELH | *English Literary History* |
| ELR | *English Literary Renaissance* |
| EMLS | *Early Modern Literary Studies* |
| FQ | *The Faerie Queene* |
| IUR | *Irish University Review* |
| JMEMS | *Journal of Medieval and Early Modern Studies* |
| 'A Letter of the Authors' | Edmund Spenser, 'A Letter of the Authors', in *Edmund Spenser: The Faerie Queene*, ed. A.C. Hamilton, Hiroshi Yamashita, and Toshiyuki Suzuki (Harlow: Longman, 2001), pp. 714–18 |
| MLN | *Modern Language Notes* |
| NLH | *New Literary History* |
| OED | *Oxford English Dictionary Online* |
| PMLA | *Publications of the Modern Language Association of America* |
| RES | *Review of English Studies* |
| RQ | *Renaissance Quarterly* |
| SC | *The Shepheardes Calender* |
| SEL | *Studies in English Literature, 1500–1900* |
| SEnc | *The Spenser Encyclopedia* |
| SQ | *Shakespeare Quarterly* |
| TRHS | *Transactions of the Royal Historical Society* |
| A View | *A View of the Present State of Ireland* in *The Works of Edmund Spenser: A Variorum Edition, X: The Prose Works*, pp. 43–231 |

# Introduction

Space melts like sand running through one's fingers. Time bears it away and leaves me only shapeless threads:

To write: to try meticulously to retain something, to cause something to survive; to wrest a few precise scraps from the void as it grows, to leave somewhere a furrow, a trace, a mark or a few signs.[1]

is there a system? What is the centre of it? What the depth? What the connexion? And what the order of the position of the parts?[2]

In his essay, 'Species of Spaces', Georges Perec offers a system for classifying the relationship between space, writing, and the imagination. Perec's own prose, which is sensitive to the practices of geography and the mutability of worldly experience, seeks to find a series of expressions for the provisional quality implicit in textual and spatial encounters. In the epigraph quoted above, he describes the capacity of the written word to retain something of the world: a process that can be recognised in the various literary geographies of Edmund Spenser's work.[3] It has long been acknowledged, for example, that when Spenser 'wants to discuss principles or concepts', as Humphrey Tonkin writes, 'he organizes them spatially';[4] yet, the poet's images have a characteristic tendency to defy the

---

1 Georges Perec, *Species of Spaces* in *Species of Spaces and Other Pieces*, ed. and trans. John Sturrock (London: Penguin, 1997; repr. 1999), pp. 1–96 (pp. 91–2).
2 Francis Bacon, *A Description of the Intellectual Globe*, in *The Philosophical Works of Francis Bacon*, ed. John M. Robertson (Oxford: Routledge, 1905; repr. 2011), pp. 670–702 (p. 689).
3 For the range of methods encompassed by 'literary geography' see Angharad Saunders, 'Literary Geography: Reforging the Connections', *Progress in Human Geography*, 34.4 (2010), 436–52. For a classic introduction to the landscapes of poetry see Ernst Robert Curtius, 'The Ideal Landscape', in *European Literature and the Latin Middle Ages*, trans. Willard R. Trask (London: Routledge and Kegan Paul, 1953), pp. 183–202.
4 Humphrey Tonkin, 'Spenser's Garden of Adonis and Britomart's Quest', *PMLA*, 88.3 (1973), 408–17, p. 409. See also R. Rawdon Wilson, 'Space', in *SEnc*, pp. 666–7.

reader's grasp. The purpose of this study is not to make another attempt to find unity in Spenser's fictions or to 'map' the spaces of his longest poem: objectives that are, as Matthew Woodcock observes, a 'perennial feature of Spenser criticism'.[5] Instead, my interest lies in how Spenser's writings are preoccupied by moving forms: writing space, it seems, asks the poet both to create and confront contours that outline the relationship between the subject and the changing textures of the geographies in which they dwell.[6]

The readings and analyses I present attend to both the spaces of Spenser's writings and the poetics of geographical thinking.[7] My focus rests in the main on *The Faerie Queene* but also considers the strategies that are shared across Spenser's poetry and prose, demonstrating how spatial motifs travel across literary forms and take on distinct resonances that depend on circumstance and framing. Taken as a whole, my approach brings together two complementary methodologies: the first considers Spenser's use of figurative language and his adaptation of literary modes and genres, and the second draws upon interdisciplinary perspectives found in the work of cultural and historical geographers, who engage directly with questions of representation and, more specifically, the roles that aesthetic subjectivity and the imagination play in early modern spatial practices. While no single monograph could claim to be sufficiently capacious to contain a unified field theory of the spaces of Spenser's writings, the selective approach taken by this study offers a partial view of their variegated qualities.[8] In the readings that follow, I focus on the relationship between figurative language, genre, and the shaping hand implicit in the writing of geography, reflecting on how these features of Spenser's work are continually realigned as his longest poem progresses.

5 Matthew Woodcock, *Fairy in The Faerie Queene: Renaissance Elf-Fashioning and Elizabethan Myth-Making* (Aldershot: Ashgate, 2004), p. 78 (see also pp. 76–80).
6 The meaning of the word *geography* is, as Trevor J. Barnes and James S. Duncan observe, 'literally "earth writing" (from the Greek *geo*, meaning "earth", and *graphien*, meaning "to write")'. See 'Introduction: Writing Worlds', in *Writing Worlds: Discourse, Text, and Metaphor in the Representation of Landscape* (London: Routledge, 1992), pp. 1–17 (p. 1).
7 For analysis of Giambattista Vico's concept of 'poetic geography' see John Gillies, *Shakespeare and the Geography of Difference* (Cambridge: Cambridge University Press, 1994), p. 39.
8 For the 'manifold capacity' of the *FQ* see James Nohrnberg, *The Analogy of The Faerie Queene* (Princeton: Princeton University Press, 1976). 'Each book', as Thomas P. Roche, Jr. has observed, 'has a life of its own'. See *The Kindly Flame: A Study of the Third and Fourth Books of Spenser's Faerie Queene* (Princeton: Princeton University Press, 1964), p. 32.

As has been frequently acknowledged, *The Faerie Queene*'s heterogeneous landscapes encompass the local places of antiquarian study as well as the 'new worlds' of the Americas; fragments of Ireland jostle against Elizabeth's England, although most of the time we are somewhere far beyond the margins of any sixteenth-century chart.[9] Mirroring the reader's lack of bearings, Spenser's questing knights, who provide fluctuating focal points within *The Faerie Queene*'s six complete books, generally travel without the instrumental aids available to sixteenth-century travellers, preferring a course plotted 'withouten compasse, or withouten card' (III.ii.7). The most basic tools of navigation are unworkable in spaces shaped by the imagination, cultural memory, and the conscience, or where, as Harry Berger, Jr. has observed, 'psyche is scarcely separable from nature, inscape from landscape'.[10] Instead, Spenser's knights, questing in pursuit of holiness, temperance, chastity, friendship, justice, and courtesy, seem to be guided by the exercise of their hidden virtue as if it were a compass needle pointing homewards. The complete path remains occluded, its endpoint as problematic to fix as true north.

I describe *The Faerie Queene* in these terms in order to give a sense of why Spenserian criticism, as demonstrated by the work of Wayne Erickson, Bernhard Klein, Joanne Woolway Grenfell, and Christopher Burlinson, amongst others, has long been fascinated by the geographical, generic, conceptual, and structural landscapes of the poem. At the time of their publication in 1590, the first three books of Spenser's epic allegorical romance constituted the longest printed poem written in the English language, making the work an impressively spacious production even without the publication of an additional three books in 1596.[11] Famously, the poem begins *in medias res*, and, without Ariadne's yarn to ensure safe passage, the task of following its many interlaced narratives, shaped by chance encounters, misrecognitions, and acts of abandonment and deception, is often disorientating. The poem's labyrinthine qualities are produced by narrative deferrals as well as an aesthetic interest in the

---

[9] More literal mapping exercises such as those carried out by Terence Clifford-Amos may work in limited localities but as a whole the poem resists and undermines such attempts. See '"Certaine Signes" of "Faeryland": Spenser's Eden of Thanksgiving on the Defeat of the "Monstrous" "Dragon" of Albion's North', *Viator*, 32 (2001), 371–415. See also Philip Edwards, *Sea-Mark: The Metaphorical Voyage, Spenser to Milton* (Liverpool: Liverpool University Press, 1997), p. 27.
[10] Harry Berger, Jr., *Revisionary Play: Studies in the Spenserian Dynamics* (Berkeley: University of California Press, 1990), p. 107.
[11] See Andrew Zurcher, 'Printing *The Faerie Queene* in 1590', *Studies in Bibliography*, 57 (2005), 115–50.

creation of a landscape of quest and 'straunge aduentures' (I.i.30). The poet ultimately offers readers an interpretive challenge which is shared by the poem's protagonists, inviting them to contemplate the relationship between, and nature of, the mobile spaces of his fiction. Such spaces are sufficiently capacious to contain not only echoes of the wanderings of biblical and classical archetypes and exiles, the pilgrimages of saints, the errancy of native and continental romance, but also reflections on the expeditions and discoveries of the early modern navigators, for whom the prize always seemed to lie further away.[12]

Various forms of travel invite the contemplation of different kinds of epistemological horizon, from the historical and the spiritual, to those of conquest, both erotic and territorial. When Spenser uses the word 'space' in *The Faerie Queene*, it is almost always to convey either the passage of time or 'the interval between objects',[13] where events can be seen to happen 'Some in short space, and some in longer yeares' (VII.vii.55); only during the final complete book does the narrator take the opportunity to look back over the 'exceeding spacious' (VI.pro.1) qualities of the poem he has fashioned. In *The Faerie Queene* the experience of space unfurls in time: the time in which the reader dwells within the poem's unfolding stanzaic progress and in the shifting temporal patterns of the poem's interlaced narratives. Spenser uses the allegorical motion of bodies travelling at different speeds to suggest the cognitive elision of the spatial and the temporal.[14] Throughout these travails, the representation of duration, velocity, and labour is complicated by the changing scales of human history, by moments of transformation and recurrence, and even, finally, by recognition, revelation, and the contemplation of apocalypse.

A reader of *The Faerie Queene* is thus tasked with finding a way through the poem that allows for meaningful interpretation to occur without shutting down the work's capacity for generating perplexity. Spenser's purpose in his longest poem may ultimately be didactic but it is a curiously provisional type of knowledge that he advances. As a writer of romance, he delights in deferral, and the cumulative refusal to provide readers with oversight generates writing, both poetic and political, that is characterised by the figuration of error, ignorance, folly, and testing

12 See, for example, Mary C. Fuller, 'Ralegh's Fugitive Gold: Reference and Deferral in *The Discoverie of Guiana*', *Representations*, 33.1 (1991), 42–64.
13 See Alastair Fowler, *Renaissance Realism: Narrative Images in Literature and Art* (Oxford: Oxford University Press, 2003; repr. 2009), pp. 4–7 (p. 4).
14 See Rafael Núñez and Kensy Cooperrider, 'The Tangle of Space and Time in Human Cognition', *Trends in Cognitive Sciences*, 17.5 (2013), 220–9.

travail.¹⁵ Owing to its fusion of romance with epic and allegory, *The Faerie Queene* contains a multitude of potential trajectories: within such a generic welter, distinct spatial imaginaries mobilise divergent itineraries. The 'romance quester', as James Nohrnberg has observed of Spenser's challenging combination of literary models, 'is typically sent *away* from his homeland, in order to find his way back to it, while the epic quester migrates *towards* a homeland, in order to leave a past behind'.¹⁶ In addition, the allegorical frame, and the inclusion of metaphysical vanishing points such as heaven and the New Jerusalem, cause obvious problems for anyone trying to conceive of the poem's dimensions.¹⁷ For Christopher Burlinson, the representations of physical places in Spenser's poetry, such as fortifications, forests, and hovels, retain the memory of the social and political structures that shaped them; because of this, the cognitive abstractions of allegory are complicated by 'a physical presence ... that fits awkwardly with the idea of allegorical narrative as a transcendence of the material'.¹⁸ Furthermore, the earthiness of much of Spenser's imagery, and the residual implications of his interests in the relationships existing between environment, labour, and stasis, invite considerations of the pastoral and georgic:¹⁹ modes that have received recent energising attention from literary ecologists, whose writing on the subject of literature and territory has been particularly generative in recent years.²⁰

With the poem's disparate and turbulent elements in mind, I am particularly interested in how its geographical forms invite an appreciation of how the poet imagines change and movement. For Spenser, protagonists

---

15 For the intrinsic play of literature and ignorance see Andrew Bennett, *Ignorance: Literature and Agnoiology* (Manchester: Manchester University Press, 2009), pp. 9–32. See also the chapters on Spenser in Susanne Lindgren Wofford, *The Choice of Achilles: The Ideology of Figure in the Epic* (Stanford: Stanford University Press, 1992).
16 James Nohrnberg, 'Britomart's Gone Abroad to Brute-land, Colin Clout's Come Courting from the Salvage Ire-Land: Exile and the Kingdom in Some of Spenser's Fictions for "Crossing Over"', in *Edmund Spenser: New and Renewed Directions*, ed. J.B. Lethbridge (Madison: Fairleigh Dickinson University Press, 2006), pp. 214–85 (p. 215).
17 See Marco Nievergelt, *Allegorical Quests from Deguileville to Spenser* (Cambridge: D.S. Brewer, 2012), p. 13.
18 Christopher Burlinson, *Allegory, Space and the Material World in the Writings of Edmund Spenser* (Cambridge: D.S. Brewer, 2006), p. 15. Burlinson draws on the work of the philosopher and sociologist Henri Lefebvre.
19 See Thomas Herron, *Spenser's Irish Work: Poetry, Plantation and Colonial Reformation* (Aldershot: Ashgate, 2007) and Linda Gregerson, 'Spenser's Georgic: Violence and the Gift of Place', *Spenser Studies*, 22 (2007), 185–201.
20 See Benjamin P. Myers, 'The Green and Golden World: Spenser's Rewriting of the Munster Plantation', *ELH*, 76.2 (2009), 473–90 and Alfred K. Siewers, 'Spenser's Green World', *Early English Studies*, 3 (2010), 1–34.

typically occupy states of suspension, searching for lost loves, homes, and identities; as exiles moving 'in the wide deepe wandring' (I.ii.1), which may manifest as forest or sea, or other desert waste on the margins of cultivation, they move through spaces in which conclusive knowledge and fulfilment is deferred. As Kenneth Gross has observed of Spenser's labyrinthine work: 'to be "in place" is no simple thing …, where any site is likely … to be other than itself, a surface to be fallen through, a where that is also an elsewhere'.[21] And indeed, as Britomart discovers when her bed falls through a false floor at the house of Dolon, the ground on which one stands is not always *terra firma*: an example of Spenser's plotting that also comments on the experience of attempting to interpret the poet's images. Such sites are meta-fictions, self-referential in their ability to give form to the poet's meanings.

By building on Wayne Erickson's sense of Spenser's 'multiform narrative world' in the chapters that follow, I explore the ways in which Spenser's spaces are produced by the conceptual blends that occur alongside and across expected boundaries;[22] the literary geographies he creates can, I suggest, be thought of as *ecotonal*, to borrow a term from environmental science, in that they occupy the fertile imaginative ground that emerges when the distinct spatial imaginaries associated with the 'rhetorical ecosystems' of particular genres and traditions converge and interact.[23] An ecotonal reading of Spenser, whose deft handling of the meeting of modes delights in in-betweenness, offers a way of thinking about the vagrant qualities of Spenser's work without needing to solve or reconcile them: for Spenser, occupying the ground between distinct literary habitats frequently results in imaginative fecundity rather than wreck.[24] It is perhaps no coincidence that Spenser's imagination, in a

---

21 Kenneth Gross, *Spenserian Poetics: Idolatry, Iconoclasm, and Magic* (Ithaca: Cornell University Press, 1985), p. 219.
22 Wayne Erickson, *Mapping The Faerie Queene: Quest Structures and the World of the Poem* (New York: Garland, 1996), p. 7. For Spenser's ability to create 'one vast composite' from disparate components see Colin Burrow, *Epic Romance: Homer to Milton* (Oxford: Clarendon, 1993), p. 100.
23 See Anis S. Bawarshi, 'Genres as Rhetorical Ecosystems', in *Genre and the Invention of the Writer: Reconsidering the Place of Invention in Composition* (Logan: Utah State University Press, 2003), pp. 80–6. See also *Biodiversity in Land-Inland Water Ecotones*, ed. Jean-Bernard Lachavanne and Raphaëlle Juge (Paris: UNESCO; New York and Carnforth: Parthenon, 1997), and John R. Gillis, 'Not Continents in Miniature: Islands as Ecotones', *Island Studies Journal*, 9.1 (2014), 155–66. I am grateful to Keith Botelho for introducing me to the concept of the ecotone in relation to my work on Richard Carew's *Survey of Cornwall* (1602).
24 Catherine Bates argues that Spenser's competing narrative desires end in 'a veritable wreck'. See *Masculinity and the Hunt: Wyatt to Spenser* (Oxford: Oxford University

complementary movement, is drawn instinctively to the representation of places in the natural world where ecotonal transitions occur: an open plain becoming a wandering wood, wetlands and islands, or freshwater channels that lose distinction at the saline margins of the sea.[25] Such interstitial dwelling places for the imagination cease being static literary *topoi*, or common places, in Spenser's writings and instead perform the self-conscious activity of the poet, imitative of both world and creative process: the poet's gestures towards the familiar, the grounded, and the proximate are typically distanced or undermined by habits of thought that rely on figurative language to turn, or move, from one place to somewhere else entirely, thus testing the limits of the credible.[26] Underlying these complex allegorical geographies is the poem's deep concern with the fixity of knowledge; the positive, generative energy of Spenser's advancing knights is pitched against the deconstructive motion of the endless quests. In a poem where appearances are often deceptive, the author, as Nick Davis observes, refuses to answer the question 'of whether fixity of structure is to be encountered by human beings in the cosmos they inhabit'.[27] As the author and architect of the fiction, Spenser writes of the impossibility of representing his subject truthfully; his craft is subject to error and frailty, suggesting that the travail of building the world of the work is a task that mirrors the complexity of its navigation. Landmarks often only 'seemd to bee' (II.xi.35) and the guiding 'stedfast starre' is frequently occluded by 'foggy mistes, or cloudy tempests' (II. vii.1). Within a poem whose spatial master-trope takes the form of an urban centre of 'idealized government ... which no one ever visits', as Michael J. Murrin writes, the poet's labours often consciously seem to undo themselves:[28] without a sense of centre, an exile has nowhere to

---

Press, 2013), p. 324. Conversely, Andrew Fichter argues that 'romance and epic are best viewed as two aspects of a single undertaking', where both components are vital to 'what has been conceived as a new entity, the Christian epic'. See *Poets Historical: Dynastic Epic in the Renaissance* (New Haven: Yale University Press, 1982), p. 17.

25 See Susanne Lindgren Wofford, 'Britomart's Petrarchan Lament: Allegory and Narrative in *The Faerie Queene* III, iv', *Comparative Literature*, 39.1 (1987), 28–57, pp. 55–6 in particular.

26 For the generative relationship between the commonplace and the far-fetched in early modern rhetoric see Catherine Nicholson, *Uncommon Tongues: Eloquence and Eccentricity in the English Renaissance* (Philadelphia: University of Pennsylvania Press, 2014), pp. 45–71 and '*Othello* and the Geography of Persuasion', *ELR*, 40.1 (2010), 56–87.

27 Nick Davis, *Stories of Chaos: Reason and its Displacement in Early Modern English Narrative* (Aldershot: Ashgate, 1999), p. 79.

28 Michael J. Murrin, 'Faerie Land', in *SEnc*, pp. 296–8 (p. 297). Elizabeth J. Bellamy describes Cleopolis as 'the city not seen' in *Translations of Power: Narcissism and the*

return. And yet, it is a testimony to the poet's skill that the questions asked by Francis Bacon in his *Descriptio Globi Intellectualis* concerning the order of the heavens – questions which seek to fathom, to compass, to orientate, and finally, to understand – can also be asked, if not satisfactorily answered, of Spenser's 'continued Allegory, or darke conceit' ('A Letter of the Authors', p. 714).

### Spenser and the poetics of space

It has been claimed that 'space appears to have lost its poetry' in the seventeenth century, thereby unshackling itself from the interventions of myth, theology, visual language, and allegory.[29] Yet, for Spenser at the close of the sixteenth century, both life and work coincided with a wider cultural fascination for the discovery of 'new worlds' and the aesthetic and ideological repercussions prompted by the writing and re-writing of cosmos and nation.[30] This study argues that the imaginative literature of the late sixteenth century is shaped by a shifting epistemological moment, in which the wanderings of romance, and its relationship to allegory, were called into question by new ways of making knowledge. This is nowhere more evident than in Spenser's unfinished attempt at writing what should have been, by his own account, a national epic. Spenser's poetry reached print at a time when the book trade was saturated with practical guides concerning how to direct a ship's course, descriptions of the regional landscape and the cultural memories embedded therein, collections of maps which offered the beholder mastery over the spaces they portray, and translations of technical manuals made available for the first time in vernacular English.[31] In a marginal annotation located in his copy of Thomas Twyne's translation of Dionysius Periegetes's *The Surveye of*

---

*Unconscious in Epic History* (Ithaca: Cornell University Press, 1992), p. 190. A parallel can perhaps be made with how the Garden of Eden is given a physical location on some medieval maps. See Alessandro Scafi, *Mapping Paradise: A History of Heaven on Earth* (Chicago: University of Chicago Press, 2006).

29 See Jeffrey N. Peters, *Mapping Discord: Allegorical Cartography in Early Modern French Writing* (Newark: University of Delaware Press, 2004), p. 18.

30 See, for example, Mary B. Campbell, *Wonder and Science: Imagining Worlds in Early Modern Europe* (Ithaca: Cornell University Press, 1999) and Richard Helgerson, *Forms of Nationhood: The Elizabethan Writing of England* (Chicago: University of Chicago Press, 1992).

31 See Lesley B. Cormack, *Charting an Empire: Geography at the English Universities, 1580–1620* (Chicago: University of Chicago Press, 1997) and Adam Max Cohen, *Shakespeare and Technology: Dramatizing Early Modern Technological Revolutions* (New York: Palgrave Macmillan, 2006).

*the World* (1572), for example, Spenser's friend Gabriel Harvey reflected on his wonder that 'Chaucer and Lydgate were such good astronomers' and also revealed that 'Spenser himself is ashamed, though he is not completely ignorant of the globe and astrolabe, of the difficulty he has with astronomical rules, tables, and instruments'.[32] If this brief insight into Spenser's intellectual predilections does not demonstrate the poet's mastery of spatial *techne*, it does at least signal his engagement with the challenges of spatial measurement and representation.[33] It is no coincidence that *The Faerie Queene* continually addresses the topic of how to approach unseen, unknown, or unconquered terrain; generic forms that were developed, if not perfected in the Middle Ages, were met head-on in the sixteenth century by new epistemological perspectives, which became increasingly invested in the relationship between abstraction and experience.[34]

Medieval constructions of the inhabited world, which fixed Jerusalem and the contemplation of salvation at their centre, contrast starkly with those visualised by the likes of Abraham Ortelius, author in 1570 of the world's first atlas. In his world maps, the centralisation of the Atlantic Ocean displaces the viewer's sense of focus, as John Gillies explains: in 'place of the comfort of the medieval map we find restlessness, in place of stasis: dynamism'.[35] The beholder's gaze, unnaturally beholding an expanding world, as Gillies writes, privileges the 'unknown and unpossessed over the known and possessed', and thus authorises a 'semiosis of desire'.[36] For Jonathan Goldberg, a similar driving principle can be

32 See *Gabriel Harvey's Marginalia*, ed. G.C. Moore Smith (Stratford-Upon-Avon: Shakespeare Head Press, 1913), p. 162. The translation is taken from *Spenser: The Critical Heritage*, ed. R.M. Cummings (London: Routledge and Kegan Paul, 1971), p. 50. For Harvey's own reading practices see Virginia F. Stern, *Gabriel Harvey: His Life, Marginalia and Library* (Oxford: Clarendon Press, 1979).
33 See Davis, *Stories of Chaos*, pp. 75–120 (p. 76 in particular). See also Sarah Powrie, 'Spenser's Mutabilitie and the Indeterminate Universe', *SEL*, 53.1 (2013), 73–89.
34 For classic studies see C.S. Lewis, *The Discarded Image: An Introduction to Medieval and Renaissance Literature* (Cambridge: Cambridge University Press, 1964); Marjorie Hope Nicolson, *The Breaking of the Circle: Studies in the Effect of the 'New Science' upon Seventeenth-Century Poetry* (New York: Columbia University Press, 1960); and Frank Lestringant, *Mapping the Renaissance World: The Geographical Imagination in the Age of Discovery*, trans. David Fausett (Cambridge: Polity, 1994). See also Denise Albanese, *New Science, New World* (Durham: Duke University Press, 1996) and Robert Appelbaum, 'Anti-Geography', *EMLS*, 4.2 (1998), 12.1–17.
35 Gillies, *Shakespeare and the Geography of Difference*, p. 62.
36 Ibid., p. 62. For how the strategies of erotic poetry are appropriated by geopolitical discourses see Roland Greene, *Unrequited Conquests: Love and Empire in the Colonial Americas* (Chicago: University of Chicago Press, 1999) and Lowell Duckert, 'Water Ralegh's Liquid Narrative: The Discoverie of Guiana', in *Literary and Visual Ralegh*,

identified in Spenser's longest poem: in the shared responsibility of author and reader to make meaning, the poem holds together 'an "endlesse worke" of substitution' characterised by 'sequences of names in place of other names, structures of difference, deferred identities'.[37] As the following chapters discuss in more detail, the deconstructive fluidity Goldberg observes in Spenser's writing is at work in the cartographic, navigational, and cosmographical enterprises of his contemporaries.[38] As provisional products, their crafted surfaces are open to transformation by brief and often contradictory eddies of mutable space. By reading Spenser's poem alongside such writings, I explore what is involved in the translation of world to word and image and back again: a legacy of the longstanding history of connection between cosmography and epic.[39]

In the following chapters I investigate more fully how the skilled craftsmanship associated with the spatial arts also relies on the writerly techniques of persuasive rhetoric in order to assert authority.[40] Acts of making, or *poiesis*, are aspects of geographical practice which have received increasing critical attention in recent years owing to a new critical emphasis placed on how the ethical significance of spatial representation coexists with the performativity and materiality of the geographer's labour. At the heart of such processes, Denis Cosgrove argues, is 'a philosophy and vision of a perfectable world' that finds its origin in textual practices.[41] As a consequence of his employment in Ireland as part of Elizabeth I's administration, Spenser's geographical imagination is inflected by the compromised views of late sixteenth-century colonialism: an activity which defined ideas of reformation and perfection

  ed. Christopher M. Armitage (Manchester: Manchester University Press, 2013), pp. 217–41.
37 Jonathan Goldberg, *Endlesse Worke: Spenser and the Structures of Discourse* (Baltimore: Johns Hopkins University Press, 1981), p. 11.
38 See J.B. Harley, 'Deconstructing the Map', in *Writing Worlds*, pp. 231–47.
39 See Philip R. Hardie, *Virgil's Aeneid: Cosmos and Imperium* (Oxford: Clarendon Press, 2003).
40 See David N. Livingstone, *The Geographical Tradition: Episodes in the History of a Contested Enterprise* (Oxford: Blackwell, 1993); *Writes of Passage: Reading Travel Writing*, ed. James Duncan and Derek Gregory (London: Routledge, 1999); Michael R. Curry, *The Work in the World: Geographical Practice and the Written Word* (Minneapolis: University of Minnesota Press, 1996); and *Place / Culture / Representation*, ed. James Duncan and David Ley (London: Routledge, 1993).
41 Denis Cosgrove, 'Prologue: Geography within the Humanities', in *Envisioning Landscapes, Making Worlds: Geography and the Humanities*, ed. Stephen Daniels, Dydia DeLyser, J. Nicholas Entrikin, and Douglas Richardson (Oxford: Routledge, 2011), pp. xxii–xxv (p. xxiii).

through a set of subjective and strategic perspectives.⁴² In the mind of the Anglo-Irish poet W.B. Yeats, for example, Spenser was blinded by Elizabeth's colonial agenda, seeing only what was required of him:

> he wrote as an official, and out of thoughts and emotions that had been organised by the State. He was the first of many Englishmen to see nothing but what he was desired to see. Could he have gone there as a poet merely, he might have found among its poets more wonderful imaginations than even those islands of Phaedria and Acrasia. He would have found among wandering story-tellers, not indeed his own power of rich, sustained description, for that belongs to lettered ease, but certainly all the kingdom of Faery, still unfaded, of which his own poetry was often but a troubled image.⁴³

In passing judgement on the nature of Spenser's 'sustained description', Yeats highlights the burden of responsibility that falls upon writers of imaginative literature; it is telling that Arcadian spaces of potential ease are characteristically invaded, dismantled, and abandoned in Spenser's work.⁴⁴ For Yeats, Spenser could have encountered an island space capable of surpassing even his own most seductive fictions; had he so wished, Yeats speculates, this impossible Spenser could have enacted and recorded an encounter of a different order, one of both island and self. It is a fiction perhaps as misrepresentative as Spenser's own, but out of which a dream of a lost literary geography emerges: a geography that had the potential to be ethically and poetically superior to that of Spenser's own 'troubled image'. For a modern reader, it is impossible to see how the cultural imagination of the early modern period could ever have been situated outside the cross-currents of imperial desire; after all, no poet went anywhere during this period as 'a poet merely'.⁴⁵

To search for space in Spenser's writing, then, is to find it subject to multiple forms of fabrication and speculation.⁴⁶ Critics such as Rhonda

---

42 Edward W. Said identifies the importance of 'imaginative geography' to the colonial mind-set. See *Orientalism* (London: Penguin, 1978; repr. 2003), pp. 54–5. See also *Culture and Imperialism* (London: Vintage, 1994), p. 5 and Leif Jerram, 'Space: A Useless Category for Historical Analysis?', *History and Theory*, 52.3 (2013), 400–19.
43 W.B. Yeats, *The Cutting of an Agate*, in *Essays and Introductions* (London: Macmillan, 1961; repr. 1980), p. 372.
44 See Chris Fitter, *Poetry, Space, Landscape: Toward a New Theory* (Cambridge: Cambridge University Press, 1995), p. 295.
45 See Bruce McLeod, *The Geography of Empire in English Literature, 1580–1745* (Cambridge: Cambridge University Press, 1999; repr. 2009).
46 For the challenges of literary 'space' see Henri Lefebvre, *The Production of Space*, trans. Donald Nicholson-Smith (Oxford: Blackwell, 1991), p. 15 and Burlinson, *Allegory, Space and the Material World*, pp. 37–42.

Lemke Sanford, Mercedes Camino, and Donald Kimball Smith, for example, have looked to Spenser's work for an intellectual engagement with particular kinds of early modern spatial practices such as cartography.[47] Smith, for one, elegantly argues that *The Faerie Queene* incorporates the transformations implicit in moving from medieval to early modern conceptions of space; however, his sense that the poem ultimately functions as a memory theatre in which the protagonists' wanderings accrue in the reader's mind 'in the coherent and comprehensive way that a map allows' is more problematic.[48] Tellingly, his argument rests on examples taken from the first three books of the poem and makes little mention of Spenser's involvement in Ireland. If the later books of *The Faerie Queene* and *A View of the Present State of Ireland* (c. 1596; pub. 1633) suggest anything, it is that memory, like cartographical representation, can be manipulated.[49]

A more successful model of the relationship between mapping and the arts of memory, this study suggests, would allow for a more heightened awareness of the generative potential of mobility, strategy, and fallibility:[50] the 'pervasive metaphorics of navigation' in early modern texts suggest that readers were highly attuned to the epistemological challenges of charts.[51] Bernhard Klein's work on the 'anti-cartographic' nature of *The Faerie Queene*'s terrain, for example, decisively concludes that 'the crucial point is not how much "real" geography finds its way into the poem ...; rather, the poem undertakes to question the epistemological significance of space as such, and to describe its power to define the existential state of the fictional characters moving through it'.[52] In

47 See Rhonda Lemke Sanford, *Maps and Memory in Early Modern England: A Sense of Place* (New York: Palgrave, 2002) and Mercedes Camino, '"Methinks I See an Evil Lurk Unespied": Visualizing Conquest in Spenser's *A View of the Present State of Ireland*', *Spenser Studies*, 12 (1990), 169–94.
48 Donald Kimball Smith, *The Cartographic Imagination in Early Modern England: Rewriting the World in Marlowe, Spenser, Raleigh and Marvell* (Aldershot: Ashgate, 2008), p. 79. See also pp. 85–94.
49 See Mark S. Monmonier, *How to Lie with Maps* (Chicago: University of Chicago Press, 1991) and Zbigniew Bialas, 'Ambition and Distortion: An Ontological Dimension in Colonial Cartography', in *Borderlands: Negotiating Boundaries in Post-Colonial Writing*, ed. Monika Reif-Hülser (Amsterdam: Rodopi, 1999), pp. 17–28.
50 Importantly, Mary Carruthers frames her discussion of the relationship between space and memory by criticising Frances Yates's emphasis on stasis in *The Art of Memory* (Chicago: University of Chicago Press, 1966). See Carruthers, *The Craft of Thought: Meditation, Rhetoric, and the Making of Images, 400–1200* (Cambridge: Cambridge University Press, 1998; repr. 2008), p. 9.
51 Davis, *Stories of Chaos*, p. 85.
52 Bernhard Klein, *Maps and the Writing of Space in Early Modern England and Ireland*

addition, a consideration of the inherently provisional quality of cartographical enterprises allows for a more nuanced recognition of performativity and dynamism in spite of the pretence of two dimensional stasis. Joanne Woolway Grenfell, for example, has shown how Spenser's choice not to include maps in *The Faerie Queene* is to make the point that 'real knights don't need maps – because … Spenser was also charting a course through representational boundaries which had suddenly become fluid'.[53] Her own use of metaphorical language is suggestive of the contingencies implicit in sea travel: where land maps implicitly invite a mobile eye and intellect, the art of navigation explicitly emphasises process over completion and also assumes a mobile self or body, moving within an environment that is itself unpredictable and in flux.

Spatial metaphors provide both a useful model for negotiating the relationship between abstraction and experience and a series of analogies for the active reading that *The Faerie Queene* requires. As this study argues, Spenser's writing, both poetry and prose, participates in wayward movements that are shared by both early modern cosmographical discourse and by fiction-making.[54] When Roland Greene suggests that *The Faerie Queene* 'everywhere displays multiple, partial, and emergent worlds', for example, he mobilises a way of thinking that relates not only to the practices of early modern geography but also to the relationship between the self and the other, between social and political reality, and between cultural history and the creation of an individual literary reputation.[55] For my purposes, the activities Greene outlines are constantly shaped by the contours of the natural environment, which are sometimes complicit in and sometimes resistant to 'worldmaking' as a purely intellectual process. More recently, Patrick Cheney has argued that poets of the early modern period 'use their world-making invention to invite readers to

(Basingstoke: Palgrave Macmillan, 2001), p. 74 and p. 167. For a discussion of maps and Ireland see pp. 112–30.

53 Joanne Woolway Grenfell, 'Do Real Knights Need Maps? Charting Moral, Geographical and Representational Uncertainty in Edmund Spenser's *The Faerie Queene*', in *Literature, Mapping and the Politics of Space in Early Modern Britain*, ed. Andrew Gordon and Bernhard Klein (Cambridge: Cambridge University Press, 2001), pp. 224–38 (p. 230).

54 See Constance C. Relihan, *Cosmographical Glasses: Geographic Discourse, Gender, and Elizabethan Fiction* (Kent, OH: Kent State University Press, 2004), p. xii.

55 Roland Greene, 'A Primer of Spenser's Worldmaking: Alterity in the Bower of Bliss', in *Worldmaking Spenser: Explorations in the Early Modern Age*, ed. Patrick Cheney and Lauren Silberman (Lexington: University Press of Kentucky, 2000), pp. 9–31 (p. 10). See also Nelson Goodman, *Ways of Worldmaking* (Hassocks: Harvester, 1978).

*remake* objective reality in light of imaginative vision'.[56] The relationship he describes between the activity of the author and the engagement of the reader is a vital one; yet, as this study argues, it is frequently 'objective' vision itself that is questioned.[57]

The spaces under discussion here are typically those that do not yet present a continuous or 'objective' reality to the person perceiving them, such as islands and other littoral spaces. The fragments of worlds that pass in and out of view in the following chapters – spaces such as the cosmos, the coastline, 'elsewhere', 'nowhere', and finally, and most problematically, England and Ireland – do not retain ideal forms.[58] Each space tests the limits of the author's skill as imitator and inventor and illuminates an aspect of what Ayesha Ramachandran has recently identified as the 'increasing emphasis in the late sixteenth and seventeenth centuries on worldly plurality, contingency, and the limitations of human perception and knowledge'.[59] In Spenser's longest poem the spatial imagination may temporarily inhabit open plains and 'desert wildernesse' (II. vii.2) but it returns repeatedly to horizons, edges, and impasses, offering a topological account of intellectual complexity and how this is shaped by a lived environment.[60]

The relationship between the local and the global, and the conception of 'world' itself, is receiving increasing attention in the comparative study of early modern literature;[61] however, an academic interest in the relationship between geography and the imagination is not new. As John K. Wright observed in his presidential address to the Association of American Geographers in 1946, anticipating many of the thinkers and writers acknowledged above, 'the most fascinating *terrae incognitae* of

---

56 Patrick Cheney, *Reading Sixteenth-Century Poetry* (Chichester: Wiley-Blackwell, 2011), p. 68.
57 See Harry Berger, Jr., 'The Ecology of the Mind', in *Second World and Green World: Studies in Renaissance Fiction-making*, ed. John Patrick Lynch (Berkeley: University of California Press, 1988), pp. 41–62. See also Jon A. Quitslund, *Spenser's Supreme Fiction: Platonic Natural Philosophy and The Faerie Queene* (Toronto: University of Toronto Press, 2001).
58 For the discontinuity of *The Faerie Queene*'s spaces see John B. Bender, *Spenser and Literary Pictorialism* (Princeton: Princeton University Press, 1972).
59 Ayesha Ramachandran, *The Worldmakers: Global Imagining in Early Modern Europe* (Chicago: University of Chicago Press, 2015), p. 6.
60 See Angus Fletcher, *The Topological Imagination: Spheres, Edges, and Islands* (Cambridge, MA: Harvard University Press, 2016). Fletcher's earlier work on labyrinthine and templar space also informs my arguments throughout. See *The Prophetic Moment: An Essay on Spenser* (Chicago: University of Chicago Press, 1971).
61 See Roland Greene, 'World', in *Five Words: Critical Semantics in the Age of Shakespeare and Cervantes* (Chicago: University of Chicago Press, 2013), pp. 143–72.

all are those that lie within the minds and hearts of men'.⁶² After musing on the imaginative power held latent in cartographical regions marked as *terra incognita* on antique maps, Wright contemplated the role that aesthetic subjectivity plays in the development of geographical knowledge. Designed predominantly as an early appeal for more interdisciplinary exchange between geographers and humanities scholars, his speech called to mind Odysseus, bound securely to the mast of his ship: ears open to the sound of the Sirens' song, the mariner, a figure for the geographer himself, allows his imagination to be kindled by the sound. The myth functions for Wright as a way of figuring epistemological limits and, as he would later observe, it is 'the errors of an age' that are 'as characteristic as the accurate knowledge which it possesses – and often more so'.⁶³ His words give further emphasis to the notion that 'situated knowledge', as Derek Gregory writes, 'is not a barrier to understanding but rather its very condition'.⁶⁴

Spenser's halting errant knights are situated knowers. Samuel Taylor Coleridge famously remarked that the world Spenser created in his longest poem 'is the domain neither of history or geography; it is ignorant of all artificial boundary, all material obstacles; it is truly a land of Fairy, that is, of mental space'; however, this study suggests that the distinction he implies is a false one.⁶⁵ Spenser is a spatial maker whose imaginative and epistemological horizons were shaped by his lived and literary experiences, and these in turn shaped the travails of his protagonists. For writers of the sixteenth century, the perception of *terra incognita* may have been a necessary condition for the construction of

62 John K. Wright, '*Terrae Incognitae*: The Place of the Imagination in Geography', *Annals of the Association of American Geographers*, 37.1 (1947), 1–15, p. 15. See also Stephen Daniels, 'Geographical Imagination', *Transactions of the Institute of British Geographers*, 36.2 (2011), 182–7, p. 184.
63 John K. Wright, *The Geographical Lore of the Time of the Crusades: A Study in the History of Medieval Science and Tradition in Western Europe* (New York: American Geographical Society, 1925), p. 2. Wright coined the term *geosophy* to express the study of subjective 'geographical ideas, both true and false, of all manner of people' (see '*Terrae Incognitae*', p. 12). For the reception of Wright's ideas see Innes M. Keighren, 'Geosophy, Imagination, and *Terrae Incognitae*: Exploring the Intellectual History of John Kirtland Wright', *Journal of Historical Geography*, 31.3 (2005), 546–56.
64 Derek Gregory, 'Imaginative Geographies', *Progress in Human Geography*, 19.4 (1995), 447–85, p. 474. Gregory writes with reference to Donna Haraway's 'Situated Knowledges: The Science Question in Feminism and the Privilege of Partial Perspective', *Feminist Studies*, 14.3 (1988), 575–99 (p. 579 in particular). For a case study along these lines, see Valerie I.J. Flint's *The Imaginative Landscape of Christopher Columbus* (Princeton: Princeton University Press, 1992).
65 Samuel Taylor Coleridge, *Coleridge's Miscellaneous Criticism*, ed. Thomas Middleton Raysor (London: Constable, 1936), p. 36.

the utopian text;[66] yet, for Spenser, early modern Ireland, where he spent most of his adult working life as both poet and planter, was far from deserted, even if non-native textual representations frequently attempted to make it appear so.[67] To consider the complexities of 'mental space', then, is to consider that which Coleridge seeks to erase: namely, the intentions and agendas in which Spenser was complicit, and the ways in which these informed the depiction of temporal and spatial relations between subjects and objects.[68] In seeking to complicate Coleridge's dismissal of geography and its cognate disciplines in order to reanimate the poetry that contributes to geographical, hydrographical, chorographical, and cosmographical ways of thinking in the late sixteenth and early seventeenth centuries, this study addresses the speculative undertakings of those tasked with representing the spaces through which minds and bodies move.

## Structure

Reading Spenser's work invites an understanding of how particular spatial practices are already shaped and mediated by literary forms, figures, and fictions. In the writing of world, place, and waters, authors fashion textual spaces that connect memory and desire to knowledge claims and intellectual, but subjective, processes. This study is divided into two parts: the first addresses the issue of thinking spatially through a focus on literary matters such as representation, rhetoric, and genre; the second, through its readings of particular terrains, moves towards furthering our understanding of how the writing of space, even in fiction, is never a politically neutral act. The first part takes most of its examples from Books I, II, and III of *The Faerie Queene*; the second part reads across the rest of the poem and a selection of Spenser's shorter poems and prose, which have been chosen because they complement the readings of *The Faerie Queene* directly. A longer book would have the space to address the shorter poems more generously, but for my purposes here they lie just beyond the horizon.

---

66 See Jeffrey Knapp, *An Empire Nowhere: England, America, and Literature from Utopia to The Tempest* (Berkeley: University of California Press, 1992), p. 1.
67 For the persistent trope of Ireland as wasteland see Elizabeth L. Rambo, *Colonial Ireland in Medieval English Literature* (Selinsgrove: Susquehanna University Press, 1994).
68 See David Galbraith, *Architectonics of Imitation in Spenser, Daniel and Drayton* (Toronto: University of Toronto Press, 2000), pp. 11–17 and pp. 52–74 in particular.

## Part I: Orientations

In order to frame the readings of the curious spaces of Edmund Spenser's generically hybrid *Faerie Queene*, the first part of this study explores the use of spatial images to perform, describe, and interrogate the accrual of knowledge: a technique Spenser inherits from writers and thinkers from the Middle Ages and antiquity. Extracts from two major works concerning cosmography and navigation are examined alongside the first part of Spenser's *Faerie Queene* in order to provide analogous models for the aesthetics and function of Spenser's spaces; the imaginative travail Spenser asks of his readers finds parallels in the perceptual travail demanded by early modern authors of non-fiction. These voices are more than contextual aids: reading Spenser's poetry and prose also helps us to appreciate their knowledge-making processes more fully. The literary making that happens at Spenser's hands is no less present in the work of his practically-minded contemporaries; their imaginations chase the promise of an ordered cosmos, chartable oceans, and clearly labelled insular and coastal maps, and the figurative language they use to accomplish their pursuits often resorts, like that of modern critics, to what Michael Booth describes as 'a spatial vocabulary as [the] ultimate grounds of argument'.[69] The rhetorical practices they have in common would even have been considered spatial practices in their own right, as the work of Mary Carruthers suggests: 'cognitive craft', she explains, is bound to conceptions of *inventio* or 'invention', which pertains to both the art of creation and the act of imposing structure, as well as to the production of 'locational memory'.[70]

In the first chapter, I introduce the ways in which early modern works of cosmography and navigation employ literary techniques for didactic purposes and examine the ways in which reading their strategic rhetoric offers a parallel project to reading Spenser's own fashioning of space and myth. The chapter focuses on self-consciously literary moments found in two works that deal with spaces that are particularly difficult to imagine, namely the cosmos in William Cuningham's *The Cosmographical Glasse* (1559) and the sea and shore in Lucas Janzoon Waghenaer's *The Mariners Mirrour* (1584; trans. 1588). The chapter establishes the role that inherently spatial motifs and metaphors, including the figure of the labyrinth and the perspective glass, play in questions of interpretative

---

69 Michael Booth, '"Moving on the Waters": Metaphor and Mental Space in Ralegh's *History of the World*', in *Literary and Visual Ralegh*, pp. 200–16 (p. 200).
70 Carruthers, *The Craft of Thought*, p. 5 and pp. 10–14.

difficulty, and this informs my approach to Spenser's use of allegory, and his interest in error in particular. Identifying the contrasting approaches of Cuningham and Waghenaer to their subjects also opens up a debate concerning the relative values of abstraction and experience, and hints at the participation of technical writing in a spatial imaginary shaped by the epic mode. In an age that increasingly prided itself on cartographical literacy and purposeful travel, deliberate wandering, even by characters in fiction, is called into question precisely because they should know better.

Chapter 2 expands the first chapter's interest in the rhetoric of error and considers the ways in which *The Faerie Queene* constantly questions the nature of directive authority: in Spenser's poem, a succession of figures representing false and true guidance results in the creation of an epistemological geography concerned with measurement, orientation, and memory. The chapter focuses on the relationship between the body and the determination of whereabouts in order to think about how Spenser uses 'moving metaphor' to model states of virtue and knowing,[71] and tests the premise that Spenser's allegories engage in debates concerning not only the mode's efficacy but also the extent to which man, to borrow the formulation of Protagoras, can truly be considered as 'the measure of all things'.[72]

Chapter 3 moves the discussion from allegory into new generic terrain and attends to the spatial paradoxes and utopian drives of romance, paying particular attention to the relationship between the natural environment and the landscape of chivalry. Romance is traditionally associated with marvellous settings and the traversal of impossible distance; yet, in the late sixteenth century, the mode was also associated with inertia, passivity, and the petrifaction of knowledge. It is famed for its dilatory qualities and its tendency to postpone endings for the delight and entertainment of an audience; however, as critics such as Andrew King have observed, Spenser's *Faerie Queene* offers a radical reassessment of the mode.[73] In Spenser's hands, the epistemological strategies of

---

71 I am indebted throughout to Judith H. Anderson's work on allegory. See, in particular, *Reading the Allegorical Intertext: Chaucer, Spenser, Shakespeare, Milton* (New York: Fordham University Press, 2008), p. 5. See also Maureen Quilligan, who emphasises how allegory is distinguished 'from other sophisticated forms of self-reflexive fiction' by 'the part the reader must play in order for the fiction to be perfected'. See *The Language of Allegory: Defining the Genre* (Ithaca: Cornell University Press, 1979; repr. 1992), p. 226.
72 See Plato, *Theaetetus*, trans. M.J. Levett and Myles Burnyeat, in *Plato: Complete Works*, ed. John M. Cooper (Indianapolis: Hackett, 1997), pp. 157–234 (p. 152a, p. 169).
73 See Andrew King, *The Faerie Queene and Middle English Romance: The Matter of Just Memory* (Oxford: Clarendon, 2000), p. 212.

romance allow for both deliberate plotting and regressive drift, and the chapter places particular emphasis on the capacity of imaginative literature to confront conditions of uncertainty and ignorance. The reading of romance landscapes provides context for Britomart's encounter with Merlin, which provides the focus of Chapter 4. At the heart of this chapter is a reading of Merlin's glass: a perspectival object that acts as a focus for the critical perspectives put in motion throughout the first part of the study. The chapter thinks about how to gauge the changing scales of Britomart's journey by reading her quest alongside the spatial arts of cosmography and chorography, and looks back to the readings of Cuningham and Waghenaer established in Chapter 1. In seeking out the maker of her vision, Spenser's lady-knight makes the transition from speculative armchair traveller to practical wayfarer.

## Part II: Environments

The second part of the study draws more substantially on lines of enquiry proposed by the arguments of cultural and historical geographers, whose work considers the thought, language, and speculations of early modern literature in ways that are historically and materially located. The rhetorical strategies and aesthetics of historical practices have implications for literary depictions of travel and geography, particularly those that invest in what Paul Carter has described as 'the spatial forms and fantasies through which a culture declares its presence'.[74] Authors of the late sixteenth century, it seems, grapple in highly imaginative ways with problems that are still encountered by modern theorists and critics when attempting to define space, place, and landscape as categories of analysis;[75] as such, an ever-expanding body of work by cultural historians and literary critics has been responsive to the textual practices of geography and the spaces that shape, and are produced by, the early modern imagination.[76]

---

74 Paul Carter, *The Road to Botany Bay: An Exploration of Landscape and History* (New York: Knopf, 1988), p. xxii.
75 See, in addition to Lefebvre's *The Production of Space*, Gaston Bachelard, *The Poetics of Space*, trans. Maria Jolas (Boston: Beacon, 1964; repr. 1994); Michel De Certeau, *The Practice of Everyday Life*, trans. Steven Rendall (Berkeley: University of California Press, 1984); Michel Foucault, 'Of Other Spaces', trans. Jay Miskowiec, *Diacritics*, 16.1 (1986), 22-7; W.J.T. Mitchell, 'Spatial Form in Literature: Toward a General Theory', *Critical Inquiry*, 6 (1980), 539-67; and 'Preface to the Second Edition of *Landscape and Power*: Space, Place and Landscape', in *Landscape and Power*, ed. W.J.T. Mitchell (Chicago: University of Chicago Press, 2002), pp. vii-xii.
76 See James M. Sutton, *Materializing Space at an Early Modern Prodigy House: The Cecils at Theobalds, 1564-1607* (Aldershot: Ashgate, 2004); Henry S. Turner, *The English*

The contemporary challenge issued by the geographer Doreen Massey to the assumption that space acts as 'a surface, continuous and given', for example, offers a particularly vital way of framing Spenser's geopolitical allegories; thinking about space as a dynamic 'meeting up of histories' and a 'simultaneity of stories-so-far', as she advocates, serves to illuminate the fissures created by ideological divergence.[77] In Spenser's case, this manifests most perceptively in his writing about Ireland: both *The Faerie Queene* and *A View of the Present State of Ireland* illuminate the challenges of constructing a single coherent narrative, and both occupy forms that rely on increasingly strained polyphony. Acquiring a sense of geographical complexity undoes any trust in allegorical fixity.

In recent years, in order to address the impact of the mapping, plotting, navigating, illustrating, and surveying undertaken by numerous printed and manuscript works on the creative literature of the period, critics have striven to develop new terminologies and interdisciplinary methodologies with which to discuss concepts of space, place, geography, landscape, and language.[78] In Chapter 5, I consider the work done by a tidal, hydrographical imagination, reading the coastal imaginaries of *The Faerie Queene*'s middle books alongside works by John Dee and Sir Walter Ralegh. The tideline is considered as an emblematic space, characterised by recurrent images of gain and loss, in which personal desire is put under pressure by nationalistic dreams of empire. Chapter 6, which addresses Spenser's 'personal curvature', borrows a term used by the historical geographer J.H. Andrews to describe 'the subjective element in a cartographer's linework' in order to suggest that analogous distortions can be seen in writings by Spenser and other Englishmen to cross the Irish Sea.[79] Focusing on the fifth and sixth books of *The Faerie Queene* and moments from a variety of prose texts, this chapter considers

---

*Renaissance Stage: Geometry, Poetics, and the Practical Spatial Arts 1580–1630* (Oxford: Oxford University Press, 2006; repr. 2010); and Jess Edwards, *Writing, Geometry and Space in Seventeenth-Century England and America: Circles in the Sand* (London: Routledge, 2006).

77 Doreen Massey, *For Space* (London: Sage Publications, 2005), p. 4 and p. 9.
78 Tom Conley, for example, coins the term 'cartographic literature' to describe the hybrid works produced alongside the new spatial contexts of the early modern period. See *The Self Made Map: Cartographic Writing in Early Modern France* (Minneapolis: University of Minnesota Press, 1996), p. xi. See also Fabienne L. Michelet, *Creation, Migration, and Conquest: Imaginary Geography and Sense of Space in Old English Literature* (Oxford: Oxford University Press, 2006), p. 8 and pp. 19–21 for a discussion of historical terms and vocabularies.
79 J.H. Andrews, *Shapes of Ireland: Maps and their Makers 1564–1839* (Dublin: Geography Publications, 1997), p. 31.

the perceived textures of the Irish environment, including its wandering coastlines and unstable wetlands, in order to argue that the westward gaze of Spenser and his fellow literary strategists struggled to find a rhetoric of discovery that could also acknowledge the frustrations of partial and provisional knowledge. The final chapter connects the threads of previous readings and explores Spenser's intertextual blend of genres through the perspective of insularity. By reading the manipulation of 'mental space' as a tool of propaganda, this chapter considers the role of insularity in the early modern colonial imaginary and examines the irreconcilable perspectives found in 'Colin Clouts Come Home Againe' (1595), *A View of the Present State of Ireland*, and the last books of *The Faerie Queene*, including the Mutabilitie Cantos (1609). By moving between and across coastlines, wetlands, and islands I thus offer ways of navigating the shifting, ecotonal spaces of Spenser's fictions.

# PART I

# Orientations

# 1

# Strange paths and perspective glasses

Excuse me, gentle reader if oughte be amisse, straung paths ar not troden al truly at the first: the way muste needes be comberous, wher none hathe gone before.[1]

all geographies are imaginative geographies – fabrications in the literal sense of 'something made' – and our access to the world is always made through particular technologies of representation.[2]

The constructions of space that occur in Renaissance literature can be related to Sir Philip Sidney's argument in *The Defence of Poesy* that the poet is capable of creating a second nature, or golden world: as Sidney explains, the title of poet 'cometh of this word *poiein*, which is, to make'.[3] Central to this study is the idea that Spenser's *Faerie Queene* aims to foster a particularly active kind of reading through the poet's strategies of 'making', and that fundamentally, as Isabel MacCaffrey observes, the poem 'is about processes of coming to know'.[4] In his paratextual letter addressed to Sir Walter Ralegh, Spenser explains that the proposed twelve books of his poem will offer a model of virtuous thought and action, embodied in the figure of Prince Arthur, a 'braue knight, perfected in the twelue priuate morall vertues' ('A Letter of the Authors', p. 715). In order to make sure that his readers recognised the ingenuity of his poem's complex moral and allegorical structure,

---

1 Robert Recorde, 'To the Gentle Reader', in *The Pathway to Knowledge* (London, 1551), sig. ¶ii$^r$.
2 James Duncan and Derek Gregory, 'Introduction', in *Writes of Passage: Reading Travel Writing* (London: Routledge, 1999), pp. 1–13 (p. 5).
3 Sir Philip Sidney, *The Defence of Poesy*, in *The Oxford Authors: Sir Philip Sidney*, ed. Katherine Duncan-Jones (Oxford: Oxford University Press, 1989; repr. 1992), pp. 212–50 (p. 215). See R. Rawdon Wilson, 'Space', in *SEnc*, pp. 666–7 (p. 666).
4 Isabel G. MacCaffrey, *Spenser's Allegory: The Anatomy of Imagination* (Princeton: Princeton University Press, 1976), p. 8. See also Kenneth Gross, 'Green Thoughts in a Green Shade', *Spenser Studies*, 24 (2009), 355–71.

Spenser draws attention to the latent epistemological challenge it presents: namely, 'to discouer' the veiled 'intention and meaning' of the adventures as they unfold via a combination of 'Accidents' and 'intendments' (p. 714 and p. 718). For Spenser, the crafted fiction contains not only a model of virtue but a model of the means of attaining it; the hypothetical journeys it outlines require sustained readerly investment as well as consent.[5]

Spenser's poem invites a consideration of the radical contingencies implicit in gauging the relationship between self, world, and text: a relationship addressed in this chapter by considering the mental and manual labour implicit in describing, representing, and interpreting non-objective reality. *The Faerie Queene* may be, in A.C. Hamilton's mind, 'the most deliberate artifact in our language' but it is also a monument to the art of provisional knowledge.[6] By close reading some of the paradigmatic spaces of the first book of Spenser's poem alongside the knowledge-making practices of William Cuningham's *The Cosmographical Glasse* (1559) and Lucas Janszoon Waghenaer's *The Mariners Mirrour* (1584; trans. 1588), which deal with the writing of cosmography and navigation respectively, the chapter considers the figurative modes required to encompass spaces that stretch the limits of the author's skill to gauge and represent them.[7] Throughout, my focus comes to rest on the relationship between spatial metaphors and cognition: mirrors, labyrinths, and impossible journeys to heights and depths are seen to give shape to ways of thinking and habits of mind that are as complex as they are beautiful.[8] Spenser's claim that his epic allegorical romance will 'fashion a gentle-

---

5 For the 'knowledge practices that define early modern science and imaginative fiction' (p. 3) and the making of 'virtuous knowledge' in particular, see Elizabeth Spiller, *Science, Reading, and Renaissance Literature: The Art of Making Knowledge, 1580–1670* (Cambridge: Cambridge University Press, 2004; repr. 2007). For the 'world-making capacity of figure', which the author calls '*indecorous*', see Colleen Ruth Rosenfeld, *Indecorous Thinking: Figures of Speech in Early Modern Poetics* (New York: Fordham University Press, 2018), quotations from p. 12 and p. 26.
6 A.C. Hamilton, *The Structure of Allegory in The Faerie Queene* (Oxford: Clarendon, 1961), p. 207. See also Paul J. Alpers, 'Narration in *The Faerie Queene*', *ELH*, 44.1 (1977), 19–39, p. 27.
7 For the broader cultural and cosmographical dynamics 'emerging from a renewed celebration of *homo faber*' see Ayesha Ramachandran, *The Worldmakers: Global Imagining in Early Modern Europe* (Chicago: University of Chicago Press, 2015), p. 10.
8 For the role of spatial metaphors in cognition see George Lakoff and Mark Johnson, *Metaphors We Live By* (Chicago: University of Chicago Press, 1980), p. 3 and p. 29. See also Mary Thomas Crane, 'Analogy, Metaphor and the New Science: Cognitive Science and Early Modern Epistemology', in *Introduction to Cognitive Cultural Studies*, ed. Lisa Zunshine (Baltimore: Johns Hopkins University Press, 2010), pp. 103–14.

man or noble person in vertuous and gentle discipline' ('A Letter of the Authors', p. 714) can also be applied to these mirror works, which seek to fashion their readers in similarly testing and generative ways. To consent to their logic is to invest in the idea that there is something magnificent to be attained in acquiring the ability to navigate: the ability to recover from being cast adrift is praised as a skill most requisite for 'al men', even those whose seas are made only of paper and the imagination.[9]

Like *The Faerie Queene*, which invites Elizabeth I to recognise the realm over which she governs in Spenser's 'fayre mirrhour' (II.pro.4), the treatises by Cuningham and Waghenaer rely on the metaphor of the perspective glass to organise a complete, yet condensed, vision of a wider world.[10] The pressure exerted on the mirror trope is indicative of the role played by the imagination in the spatial arts and the distortion inherent in acts of *poiesis*.[11] As Rayna Kalas importantly observes, Renaissance texts frequently drew attention to how 'tempered' or 'framed' language 'emphasized poetic invention as *techne*, a conjoining of artful manipulation and imaginative invention'.[12] Cuningham's work, for example, which was dedicated to Sir Robert Dudley, delights in its use of the dialogue form; and Waghenaer's compilation of sea charts, which was originally dedicated to William I, Prince of Orange and to Sir Christopher Hatton in the English edition, is notable for its inclusion of poetry alongside its prose prefaces. Although I present the works here as aids for thinking about Spenser's figurations of contingency, they also require reading in their own right. They illuminate how the early modern writing of space relies upon the relationship between *techne*, or technical knowledge or skill, and *poiesis*, the productive kind of knowing that comes from imitating and shaping nature through acts of 'making'.[13] The implied ideal

---

9   See William Cuningham, *The Cosmographical Glasse* (London, 1559), sig. P2$^v$. All subsequent references are placed in the text.
10  See Herbert Grabes, *The Mutable Glass: Mirror-Imagery in Titles and Texts of the Middle Ages and English Renaissance*, trans. Gordon Collier (Cambridge: Cambridge University Press, 1973; repr. 1982), p. 43.
11  See Michel Foucault, 'Of Other Spaces', trans. Jay Miskowiec, *Diacritics*, 16.1 (1986), 22–7, p. 24.
12  Rayna Kalas, *Frame, Glass, Verse: The Technology of Poetic Invention in the English Renaissance* (Ithaca: Cornell University Press, 2007), p. 54.
13  For the cognate concept of *metis* see Jessica Wolfe, *Humanism, Machinery, and Renaissance Literature* (Cambridge: Cambridge University Press, 2004), pp. 125–6. See also Henry S. Turner, *The English Renaissance Stage: Geometry, Poetics, and the Practical Spatial Arts 1580–1630* (Oxford: Oxford University Press, 2006; repr. 2010), pp. 66–76. In a maritime context, Steve Mentz glosses *metis* as a suggestive conjunction between 'technical labors ... and the formal labor that shapes poems' in *Shipwreck Modernity: Ecologies of Globalization, 1550–1719* (Minneapolis: University of Minnesota Press,

reader also contributes a politicised and interpersonal charge to the image reflected.

In a classic essay on the Renaissance imagination, Harry Berger Jr.'s reflections on the distinctions between green worlds and second worlds, or heterocosms, introduced the paradigmatic idea that the act of holding a mirror up to nature is impossible,

> unless we have first framed a reflecting or refracting surface which is different and at a distance from whatever nature we have in mind, a surface which can admit the image only on condition that it keep out the original. This condition was felt as a necessary defect in the medieval speculum, a reflector valued more for its likeness than for itself. But the Renaissance glass was invested with dioptric and prismatic powers deriving from the interpretive activity of the human mind. Its exclusiveness was therefore prized as a guarantee of the mind's freedom from the tyranny of the actual world.[14]

Berger captures the agility of the Renaissance imagination but perhaps overestimates its liberty. By reading across genres and by putting pressure on the figurative impulses of two 'non-fiction' Renaissance glasses, this chapter identifies some of the pressures placed upon Spenser's poem by what Berger terms 'the actual world'. For the purposes here, the mirror works are used to think about the substitutions, deferrals, and sleights of hand required to make meaningful spatial imitations: to bridge the void between what Jonathan Goldberg has described as the 'writerly text' and the active mind of the reader.[15]

Both *The Cosmographical Glasse* and *The Mariners Mirrour* use figurative language to think not only about the formal shapes of the cosmos and the sea respectively, but also about how such impossible spaces can be placed on printed pages and held within a reader's grasp.[16] In both

---

2015), pp. 77–128 (p. 83 in particular). For the goddess Metis, 'Jove's first wife', as governor over the borders of the 'vast world of conjectural knowledge' see Carlo Ginzburg, *Clues, Myths, and the Historical Method*, trans. John and Anne C. Tedeschi (Baltimore: Johns Hopkins University Press, 1989), p. 105.

14 Harry Berger, Jr., 'The Renaissance Imagination: Second World and Green World', in *Second World and Green World: Studies in Renaissance Fiction-making*, ed. John Patrick Lynch (Berkeley: University of California Press, 1988), pp. 3–40 (p. 15).

15 Jonathan Goldberg, *Endlesse Worke: Spenser and the Structures of Discourse* (Baltimore: Johns Hopkins University Press, 1981), p. 11.

16 As Steve Mentz writes, this is 'the basic challenge the ocean always poses: to know an ungraspable thing'. See *At the Bottom of Shakespeare's Ocean* (London: Continuum, 2009), p. ix. For the challenge in relation to astronomy see Ladina Bezzola Lambert, *Imagining the Unimaginable: The Poetics of Early Modern Astronomy* (Amsterdam: Rodopi, 2002).

volumes, paratexts play an important strategic role by offering a discursive threshold across which the reader must pass.[17] As Helen Smith and Louise Wilson explain, paratextual elements 'work upon our imagination' and provide 'a way of approaching the world which is structured by the physical forms in which it is described'.[18] As addressed more explicitly in subsequent chapters, the spaces attended to by Cuningham and Waghenaer are also particularly generative for Spenser. The cosmos towards which Spenser most fully gestures in the unfinished 'Cantos of Mutabilitie' allows the author to juxtapose microcosm with macrocosm, island with world. The sea, the marine site of 'endlesse worke' that Spenser tries to fathom 'in hand' (IV.xii.1), and where he ultimately admits defeat, has, of course, become freighted with meaning in relation to the poem as a whole.[19] The desire to possess knowledge, whether grasped 'in hand' or perceived from a privileged vantage point, is a recurrent feature in each case. All three works invite the percipient reader to grapple with their textual spaces in self-reflexive ways, requiring complicit labour in order to be perfected.

## William Cuningham and the performance of space

The invitation to peruse the prefatory pages of Cuningham's *The Cosmographical Glasse* is accompanied by a kind of leave-taking, as if the reader is imagined departing from familiar shores: 'from this perigrination, thy wife with sheadinge salte teares, thy children with lamentations, nor thy frendes with wordes shal dehort and perswade the'. There is nothing to be feared, for the intellectual journey Cuningham promises names the 'pleasaunte house, or warme study' as its site of engagement. His words seek to mobilise an audience of armchair travellers whose initial encounter with the sea and stars will be from a place of contemplative domesticity, far from the discomforts of actual travel. By submitting to the preface's logic, readers are promised that they 'in travailing, ... shalt not be molested with the inclemencye of th' Aere, boysterous windes, stormy shoures, haile, Ise, and snow' and 'in sayling ... shalt not dread Pirates ... and greate windes, or have a sicke stomacke through unholsome smelles' (sig. A6$^r$). Like many before him, Cuningham appropriates

---

17 See Gérard Genette, *Paratexts: Thresholds of Interpretation*, trans. Jane E. Lewin (Cambridge: Cambridge University Press, 1997).
18 Helen Smith and Louise Wilson, 'Introduction', in *Renaissance Paratexts* (Cambridge: Cambridge University Press, 2011), pp. 1–14 (p. 7).
19 See Mentz, *Shipwreck Modernity*, p. xix.

the language of physical experience to model the mobile capacity of the intellect, privileging an unburdened mental encounter over one mediated by the frailties of the weakened body and its confused senses.[20] By figuring his didactic work as a prolonged journey, he introduces the reader to the linguistic and conceptual agility required to navigate the material that follows.

Cuningham also draws on classical predecessors. In the dialogue *Timaeus* Plato addresses the idea that to speak of a *kosmos* is to articulate something that is aesthetically shaped. In this work, as Donald J. Zeyl explains, Plato 'introduces a creator god, the "demiurge" (Greek for "craftsman"), who crafts and brings order to the physical world by using the Forms as patterns'.[21] In his translation, Zeyl glosses the Greek term *kosmos* as 'world order', evoking the etymological play that suggests something both ordered and ornamental:[22] an ambiguity with which Cuningham also happily engages. Cuningham ostentatiously presents his reader with a physically attractive work, and, as S.K. Heninger observes, its pages 'reveal a variety of handsome types, elegant illustrations in profusion, mathematical tables and marginal glosses and foldout maps – everything to draw attention and win respect'.[23] The study of cosmography may have primarily been intended as a way to marshal and order thought; yet, as Cuningham's work demonstrates, it had always an eye to aesthetics and design. At the time of its publication in 1559, *The Cosmographical Glasse*'s contents were superseded by authors more willing to embrace, or at least acknowledge, the existence of the theories of Copernicus, for example, but its literary qualities are outstanding.[24] Without a longstanding vernacular tradition behind him, Cuningham delights in his own intellectual inventiveness; anticipating Sidney, he ranges freely 'within the zodiac of his own wit'.[25]

Famously, Sidney would later discuss the reputation of gifted and responsible poets in terms that describe their work as the making of per-

---

20 See Jess Edwards, *Writing, Geometry and Space in Seventeenth-Century England and America: Circles in the Sand* (London: Routledge, 2006), pp. 12–13.
21 See Plato, *Timaeus*, trans. Donald J. Zeyl, in *Plato: Complete Works*, ed. John M. Cooper (Indianapolis: Hackett, 1997), pp. 1224–91 (p. 1224).
22 Ibid., 28b–c (p. 1235).
23 S.K. Heninger, Jr., *The Cosmographical Glass: Renaissance Diagrams of the Universe* (San Marino: Huntington Library, 1977; repr. 2004), p. 1.
24 See John L. Russell, 'The Copernican System in Great Britain', in *The Reception of Copernicus' Heliocentric Theory*, ed. Jerzy Dobrzycki (Dordrecht: Reidel, 1972), pp. 189–239 (p. 198).
25 Sidney, *The Defence of Poesy*, p. 216.

fected worlds; however, Cuningham's imagination is increasingly drawn to how the knowledge of poets can itself be perfected. His cosmographical interests are as much invested in literary representation as they are in the relationship between speculation and practical know-how. As he observes in the preface addressing Sir Robert Dudley, the uses of cosmography range from the civic to the medicinal, and furthermore, even the serious reader of imaginative literature should be able to understand cosmographical references, from the mundane to the extraordinary:

> Grammarians also, can not fullye understand the pleasaunte invention and perfite sense of the witty Poetes, but by Cosmographies aide, because of the names of Regions, Cities, Townes, waters, fluddes, mountaines, ceremonies, people and monsters, which every Poet do commenlye introduce, in all theyr writings. (sig. A5$^r$)

Cuningham's argument rehearses the idea that geography, as Denis Cosgrove observes, was 'the "eye" of history' and provided 'the necessary knowledge of the physical earth and its spaces without which the human record cannot be understood'.[26] In the world of words Cuningham imagines, the monsters that commonly populate cartographical peripheries jostle with implicitly geopolitical endeavours to name and divide terrain: that which is 'commenlye' introduced sits alongside a capacity for strangeness and invention. The categorising drive of cosmography is thus credited with containing an ordered and encyclopaedic sense of the world within its limits, encompassing nature as well as culture. Tellingly, Cuningham takes it for granted that the makers of such poetry would be learned enough to incorporate accurate and up-to-date cosmographical material in their writings in the first place.

In the dialogue that follows, the authoritative interlocutor Philonicus tells his companion of the correct use of charts and tables, of the applications of geometry, of climates, and of the errors of the magnetic compass. In response, Spoudaeus, an armchair traveller keenly in search of knowledge, displays a mind replete with delight in the imaginative potential of the material. After musing on 'the Race that every man in this his transitory life have to runne' (sig. B1$^r$), Spoudaeus declares his thirst for 'vertuouse travell' and seems to conjure a green world into being as a place to stage the reviving educational encounter: 'But whom do I se walking

---

26 Denis Cosgrove, 'Prologue: Geography within the Humanities', in *Envisioning Landscapes, Making Worlds: Geography and the Humanities*, ed. Stephen Daniels, Dydia DeLyser, J. Nicholas Entrikin, and Douglas Richardson (Oxford: Routledge, 2011), pp. xxii–xxv (p. xxiii).

in yonder grene place, among the pleasaunt byrdes, flowers, and trees, is it not Philonicus? It is he: I will go and salute him' (sig. B1ᵛ). At the end of the discussion on the first day he is so inspired by Philonicus's teachings that his mind refuses to stop moving, even in sleep. In the company of Morpheus, he explains, he began to take flight through the heavens, and is only halted by an intervention from the messenger-god Mercury, heralding the dawn:

> Morpheus the God of dreames, with his slepie rodde, so much this last night frequented my companie, that (my bodye taking rest) my mind was much more busilie traveling in such conclusions as I had learnid of Philonicus, then it was in the time of his teaching. ... But as he wold have carried me about the heavens, to have shewid me the North Crowne, stronge Hercules, Cassiopeia, th'Egle, the flieng Horse, mightie Orion, the two Dogges, and the famous, and great shippe Argo etc. Mercury the messenger of the Godes came to my bedde side, and saide, Aurora did appeare, and Phebus with his golden beames, was entred his chariot, minding to finishe his diurnall Arcke: so that it was a reproche for me, any longer to play the sluggard: declaringe more over that Philonicus was in the fildes. And surely I suppose no lesse, but I shall not from him be longe absent. I am justly reprehended of Mercury, because the time that is consumed with slepe more then nature requireth, is all lost: for ther spring no profit therof, but sicknes and disquietnes, both of body and minde. But what is he that calleth Spoudaeus, and beckneth with his hand? It is Philonicus. I will make spede to mete him. (sig. F3ʳ⁻ᵛ)

The ornate initial letter M that marks the start of the literary set-piece illustrates the katascopic flight, which in turn functions as an allegory of the ways in which the engaged mind processes the knowledge the pupil has accrued (see Figure 1). Cuningham's mercurial inventiveness allows his human interlocutors to cross paths with divine spectators, and with the body at rest the mind still travails, exceeding the discipline of study.

Mercury himself appears prominently on Cuningham's title page as a threshold figure, who navigates between the domestic scene of reading and the world beyond (see Figure 2),[27] and by including him within Spoudaeus's dream, Cuningham suggests the ways in which the identities of the god and the knowledgeable Philonicus, himself an educator

---

27 For the dialectic of Hestia, goddess of hearth and centre, and Hermes, god of mobility and exchange, see Jean-Pierre Vernant, *Myth and Thought Among the Greeks*, trans. Janet Lloyd with Jeff Fort (New York: Zone, 2006), pp. 157–96. See also John Gillies, *Shakespeare and the Geography of Difference* (Cambridge: Cambridge University Press, 1994), pp. 7–8.

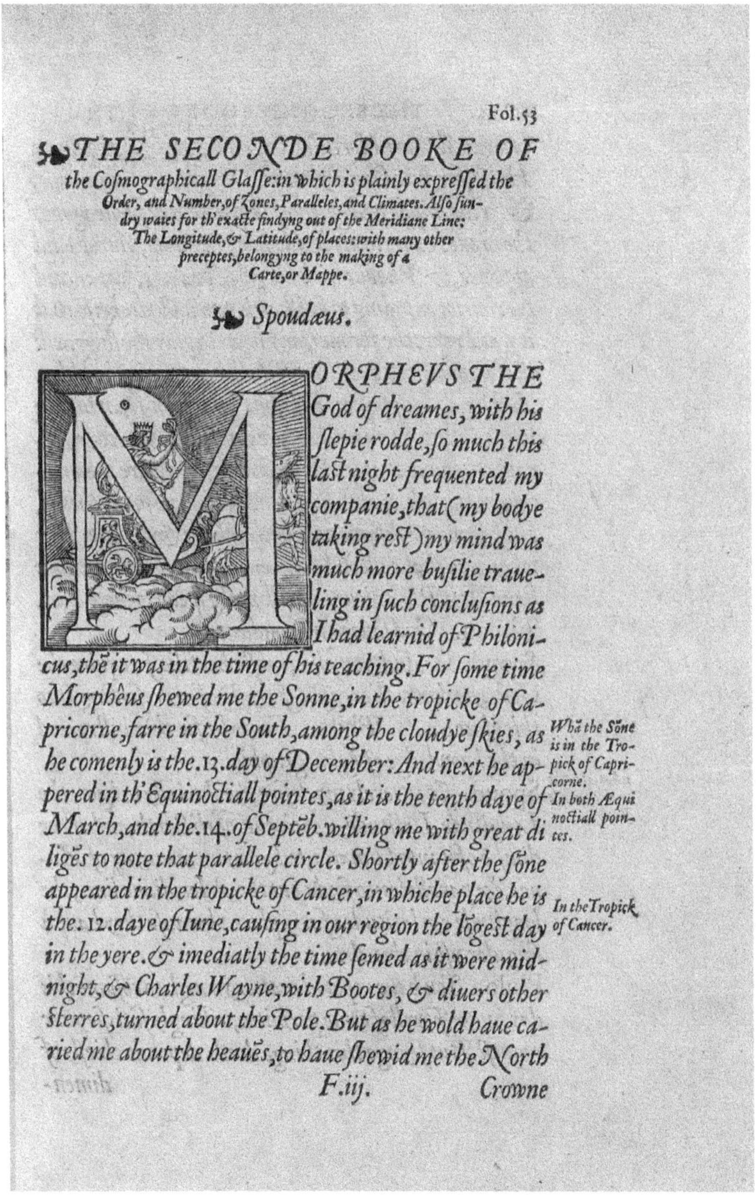

Fol. 53

# ❧ THE SECONDE BOOKE OF
the Cosmographicall Glasse: in which is plainly expressed the
Order, and Number, of Zones, Paralleles, and Climates. Also sundry waies for th' exacte findyng out of the Meridiane Line:
The Longitude, & Latitude, of places: with many other
preceptes, belongyng to the making of a
Carte, or Mappe.

❧ Spoudæus.

ORPHEVS THE God of dreames, with his slepie rodde, so much this last night frequented my companie, that (my bodye taking rest) my mind was much more buſilie traue-ling in such conclusions as I had learnid of Philoni-cus, thē it was in the time of his teaching. For some time Morpheus shewed me the Sonne, in the tropicke of Ca-pricorne, farre in the South, among the cloudye skies, as *Whā the Sōne is in the Tro-*he comenly is the .13. day of December: And next he ap-*pick of Capri-corne.* pered in th' Equinoctiall pointes, as it is the tenth daye of *In both Æqui-*March, and the .14. of Septēb. willing me with great di-*noctiall poin-tes.* liges to note that parallele circle. Shortly after the ſone appeared in the tropicke of Cancer, in whiche place he is *In the Tropick* the .12. daye of Iune, causing in our region the logest day *of Cancer.* in the yere. & imediatly the time semed as it were mid-night, & Charles Wayne, with Bootes, & diuers other sterres, turned about the Pole. But as he wold haue ca-ried me about the heaūēs, to haue shewid me the North

F.iij.                                   Crowne

*Figure 1* William Cuningham. *The Cosmographical Glasse* (London, 1559), fol. 53ʳ.

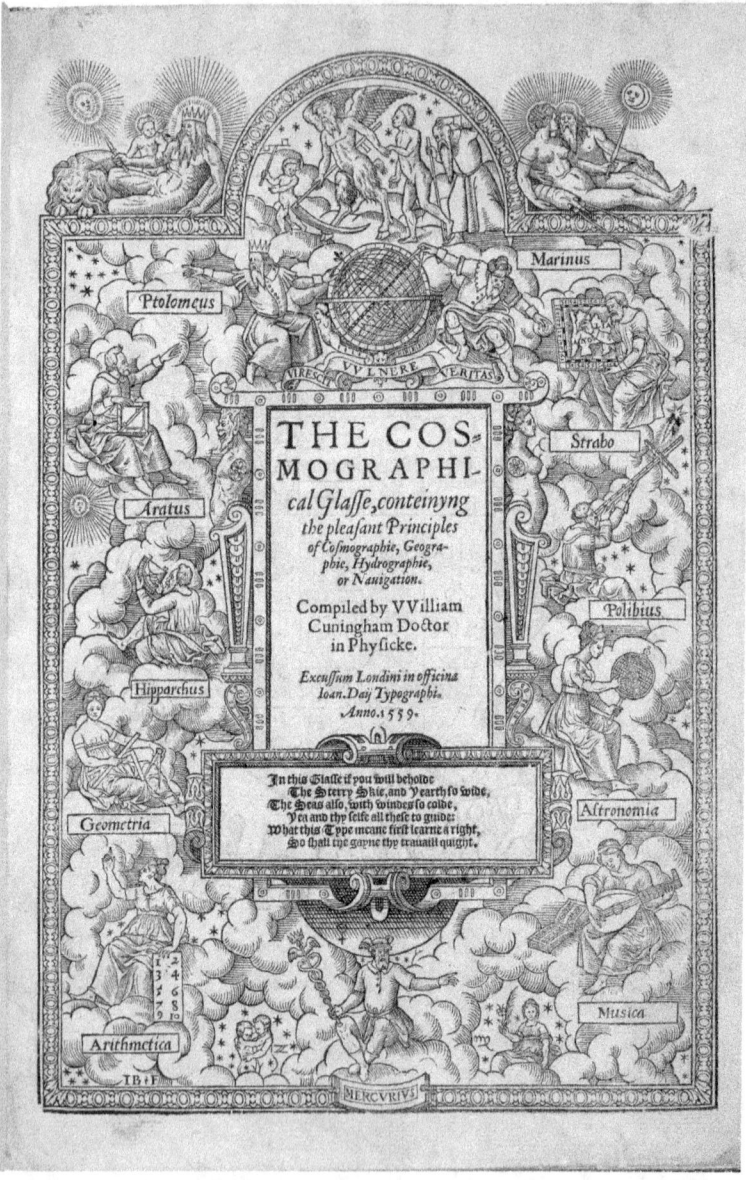

*Figure 2* William Cuningham. Title page from *The Cosmographical Glasse* (London, 1559).

and messenger, are briefly elided. On the cusp of sleep and waking, Spoudaeus's elevated awareness acknowledges both Mercury's awakening reproach and the arrival of his tutor, who beckons from the fields outside. The sleepy pupil may come back to earth abruptly, with the self-cautioning reminder not to get too ahead of himself, and that too much repose leads to ill-health, but the movement playfully manages the changes in scale required to translate the vastness of the cosmos into the spaces provided by the pages of Cuningham's book. There is ultimately no rest for the pupil who must 'make spede' if he is to make progress through all the material on offer. With his mind in transit, perception and celerity are imagined as coexistent, granting Spoudaeus the capacity to move between the labours of the study and the cosmos beyond.

Cosmography was a privileged science in the sixteenth century, Cosgrove explains, because it could contemplate 'the implications of this revolutionary relocation of a human individual liberated to soar imaginatively above the earth through the spheres of creation'.[28] By including the dream vision, Cuningham allows Spoudaeus to engage in a spatial fantasy, which his 'glasse', the revelatory device that epitomises the cosmos, offers to his readers via visual and textual allegory. For Cuningham, the figurative mirror negotiates the process whereby the faculty of sight is elevated to divine vision, linking man to the whole of creation itself. As the poem that is prominently positioned on the title page of *The Cosmographical Glasse* proposes:

> In this Glasse if you will beholde
> The Sterry Skie, and th'earth so wide,
> The Seas also, with windes so colde,
> Yea and thy selfe all these to guide:
> What this Type meane first learne a right,
> So shall the gayne thy travaill quight.

The paratextual poem announces the scale and limits of Cuningham's project; not only will readers observe the relationship between the sky, the earth, and the sea, but they will also contemplate the relationship between world and self, microcosm and macrocosm. And with the 'selfe' rather than the author as guide, it is only by learning to read correctly that the travail will be a success. The reader of Cuningham's 'glasse' must thus also learn to parse the relationships between the imitative realm, the world, and the self, where the use of the word 'type' is inherently

---

28 Denis Cosgrove, *Apollo's Eye: A Cartographic Genealogy of the Earth in the Western Imagination* (Baltimore: Johns Hopkins University Press, 2001), p. 118.

ambiguous, covering both the poem's printed letters and the typologies put in play by the brief allegorical turn. The idea of 'travaill' places particular emphasis on mental toil: an early warning that Spoudaeus's somewhat whimsical vision should be kept framed within the methodical progress outlined by the rest of the volume, which aims to restructure the cosmographical imagination through the technology of the printed page.

Cuningham's rhetorical methods typically aim to create the necessary conceptual scaffolding by which his readers can safely approach vertiginous perspectival encounters, and one of his main strategies involves indulging in literary criticism. When introducing the importance of the art of navigation, for example, he illustrates the lesson on 'howe to directe anye shippe, from place to place, from Port to Port, exactly by Art' using a discussion of case studies taken from classical literature. During the expository dialogue, Spoudaeus exclaims with exaggerated incredulity:

> If Ulisses had knowne this art, he shoulde not have bene so long tossed on the troublous seas. If Diomedes, or Aeneas, had bene herein learned, they had not so manye yeares bene driven from place to place: knowinge not by what meanes, to attaine to their so longe desired region. (sig. P2$^v$)

Spoudaeus's sense of wonder helps to translate the technical information proffered by Philonicus to Cuningham's readers; yet, the literary intervention also provides a critique of the conventions used by authors of imaginative literature in the creation of their fictions. Spoudaeus invokes the works of Homer and Virgil in order to criticise the navigational skills of their protagonists, as if the seas sailed by Ulysses, Aeneas, and Diomedes could be matched to a corresponding sixteenth-century material reality. Of course, the Ionian, Aegean, Tyrrhenian, and Mediterranean seas can be seen measured and plotted on early modern maps. Abraham Ortelius, for example, producer of the world's first atlas (*Theatrum Orbis Terrarum*, 1570), even included maps depicting the travels of Aeneas, the Argonauts, and Ulysses in later editions of the work within a section that dealt with historical geography, which suggests a growing intellectual investment in the relationship between narrative and place (see the cover of this book for the inset map of 'Ulyssis Errores', 1608). In his detailed charting of 'The Peregrination of Ulysses', for example, Ortelius was keen to distinguish between the improbable challenges of navigating an open ocean – a type of travel avoided by Greek mariners – and plausible wandering within an inland sea:

> If any man shall againe object (with Ovid in the first booke of his Tristium, who saith that *illius pars maxima ficta laborum est*: The most part of

Ulysses toile, was forged in Poets braine) and say that this whole history, and not only this navigation upon the Maine Ocean, was but a feined tale. I answer, that all the story, except this part of his navigation by the vast Ocean only, is somewhat probable, and nothing in it impossible but might have beene done.[29]

Importantly, Ortelius makes his argument with reference not only to classical authorities but also to technological horizons, anchoring his discussion in methods of ship building and navigational techniques. In anticipation of such endeavours, then, Spoudaeus's new-found enthusiasm for empiricism casts doubt not only on the prowess of the classical heroes but also on the status of defined purpose and direction in narrative fictions that have voyaging at the heart of their structure. As Spoudaeus concludes at the end of the discussion of navigational concerns: 'what thing more commodious for Princes, was there ever invented: more profitable for a comon weale: and more necessary for al men?' (sig. P2ᵛ). In the midst of his quest to seek out Gloriana, *The Faerie Queene*'s Prince Arthur would probably agree.

Although most likely intended as a rich imaginative hook for what could otherwise have been a dry exposition of advice, Spoudaeus's comment also hints at a major shift in readerly expectations. In the second half of the sixteenth century, it was perhaps no longer good enough for fictional heroes to wander undirected, and for fragmentary imagined worlds to be left unchallenged: for readers with maritime ambitions, it appears that the speculations of classical epic felt newly charged with a contemporary immediacy.[30] Furthermore, although many early modern readers may not have been as discerning, or even as literal-minded, as Spoudaeus, the point he raises illustrates an interesting conundrum. If Ulysses had not 'bene so long tossed on the troublous seas' there would have been no *Odyssey*, only a sailing manual void of the marvellous, the unexpected, the truly perilous, and the chance encounter. The weaving of Penelope would have had to wait for another opportunity; there would have been no story.[31] It would seem, therefore, that Spoudaeus puts his finger on a particularly slippery moment, in which the wanderings of romance, and its relationship to epic, were called into question by new ways of making knowledge: advances made in practical attitudes towards

---

29 Abraham Ortelius, *Theatrum Orbis Terrarum*, trans. William Bedwell (London, 1606[08]), fol. xxxiiii.
30 For the relationship between epic poetry and cosmography in Camões's *Os Lusíadas* and *The Faerie Queene* see Ramachandran, *The Worldmakers*, pp. 106–46.
31 See Patricia A. Parker, 'Romance', in *SEnc*, pp. 609–18 (p. 610).

space and movement created a challenge for authors of narrative fiction, limiting their capacity to craft deferral in a credible way.

## Edmund Spenser and the space of error

There is more at stake in Spoudaeus's observation than a concern with the literal ability to orientate oneself, and his words anticipate an issue familiar to critics of Spenser. The process of reading an epic allegorical romance, like the art of navigation, requires the ability to read signs; tides, stars, and coastal seamarks stand in for the markers of interior landscapes and geopolitical debates. As Philip Edwards writes in his discussion of the renewed vitality of the voyaging metaphor at the hands of sixteenth-century authors, the 'prolonged battle for dominance ... between wandering and purposeful self-direction' is imaged in Spenser's poem as though 'they were two of his own allegorical knights'.[32] From a writer of a Protestant epic, owing to the ever-attendant suspicion of overwrought image-making, an audience might expect to find characters with a better sense of direction;[33] yet, in the words of Angus Fletcher, 'there is a little of Odysseus in many of Spenser's protagonists, especially insofar as they are seeking to respond to the transformations of an endlessly shape-shifting scene'.[34] The latent problem Spoudaeus identifies in classical epic is appropriated and exploited by Spenser in the development of his own poetic method whereby the deliberate avoidance of having 'good discipline deliuered plainly in way of precepts' ('A Letter of the Authors', p. 716) invigorates an allegorical mode that becomes ever more freighted with epistemological concerns.

In *The Arte of English Poesie* (1589), George Puttenham defined allegory as a rhetorical device that can be used to convey 'duplicity of meaning or dissimulation under covert and dark intendments'.[35] His own ironic poetics insist on duplicity, Englishing *Allegoria* as both 'the Courtier or Figure of Fair Semblant' and 'the Figure of False Semblant'.[36] For Puttenham, 'allegorie' provides shifting semblance rather than stable

---

[32] Philip Edwards, *Sea-Mark: The Metaphorical Voyage, Spenser to Milton* (Liverpool: Liverpool University Press, 1997), p. 4.
[33] See Linda Gregerson, *The Reformation of the Subject: Spenser, Milton, and the English Protestant Epic* (Cambridge: Cambridge University Press, 1995).
[34] Angus Fletcher, *The Prophetic Moment: An Essay on Spenser* (Chicago: University of Chicago Press, 1971), p. 37.
[35] George Puttenham, *The Art of English Poesy: A Critical Edition*, ed. Frank Whigham and Wayne A. Rebhorn (Ithaca: Cornell University Press, 2007), p. 238.
[36] Ibid., p. 379 and p. 241 (marginal note).

identity: it is a mode that operates somewhere between the creation of fair resemblance and the image perpetuated by the false perspective glass, and thus appeals to the efficacy of the mental faculties in acts of recognition and judgement. Anticipating Spenser's expansive allegorical vision, Puttenham uses the image of the perspective glass to test the diligence of the inventing mind, which itself 'may be resembled to a glass, as hath been said, whereof there be many tempers and manner of makings, as the perspectives do acknowledge'. Those 'illuminated with the brightest irradiations of knowledge and of the verity and due proportion of things' Puttenham terms *euphantasiote*, a category that encompasses makers of very different disciplinary strengths, from 'cunning artificers and enginers' to 'all legislators, politicians, and counselors of estate' most reliant on 'the inventive part'.[37]

In the first pages of *The Cosmographical Glasse*, William Cuningham appeals directly to this 'inventive part'. He opens the prefatory letter to Sir Robert Dudley by appropriating the myth of Daedalus, in order to present an image of the architect initially bound within the labyrinth of his own making:

> Daedalus that excellent Geometrician (right honourable) whan as with the eyes of knowledge, he did beholde that horrible Monster Ignorance, he therwith praesently conceived suche intollarable griefe, that he daily sought occasion ether how to banish hir his praesence and companye: or els by what means to escape, oute of her loathsome Labyrinthe. At lengthe, perceivinge she coulde not be banished, he praepared winges (throughe Science aide) and so did flye oute of his mooste filthy Prison. (sig. A2ʳ)

Cuningham writes in a tradition that recognised Daedalus as an emblem for the potential of invention and the labyrinth as an emblem of complexity, both intellectual and aesthetic.[38] As a figure for both the world and the unknowing mind, the labyrinth stands in for two abstractions: one inside and one outside the self. Instead of facing the expected Minotaur at the centre of the labyrinth in Cuningham's image, Daedalus is confronted with the feminine monster 'Ignorance', his winged ascent offering an emblem of the artful application of science.[39] Anticipating Spenser's labyrinthine poetics of wondering and wandering, injured virtue and amazement, the Latin motto included on the work's title page, located

---

37 Ibid., p. 110. See Turner, *The English Renaissance Stage*, pp. 118–19.
38 See Wolfe, *Humanism, Machinery, and Renaissance Literature*, p. 190.
39 For comparison with Ariosto see Patricia A. Parker, *Inescapable Romance: Studies in the Poetics of a Mode* (Princeton: Princeton University Press, 1979), p. 21.

under the central globe, is 'virescit vulnere veritas' ('truth flourishes by its oppression or wounding'). When juxtaposed with Cuningham's use of the myth of Daedalus, whose labyrinth was of his own making and whose flight was accompanied by personal loss,[40] the motto suggests that it is only within hostile spaces that knowledge is produced. The labour of the author-craftsman creates 'mental spaces', not only of the cosmos itself, but also of the necessary intellectual processes that must be undertaken in order to perceive it.

For Spenser, the relationship between truth and labour comes into focus in the proem to Book III of *The Faerie Queene*, in which the narrator reflects on the intellectual and aesthetic challenges of constructing a labyrinth of refracted images, transforming abstract virtue into the play of form and light:

> It falls me here to write of Chastity,
>   That fayrest vertue, far aboue the rest;
>   For which what needes me fetch from *Faery*
>   Forreine ensamples, it to haue exprest?
>   Sith it is shrined in my Soueraines brest,
>   And formd so liuely in each perfect part,
>   That to all Ladies, which haue it profest,
>   Neede but behold the pourtraict of her hart,
> If pourtrayd it might bee by any liuing art.
>
> But liuing art may not least part expresse,
>   Nor life-resembling pencill it can paynt,
>   All were it *Zeuxis* or *Praxiteles*:
>   His daedale hand would faile, and greatly faynt,
>   And her perfections with his error taynt:
>   Ne Poets witt, that passeth Painter farre
>   In picturing the parts of beauty daynt,
>   So hard a workemanship aduenture darre,
> For fear through want of words her excellence to marre.
>
> How then shall I, Apprentice of the skill,
>   That whilome in diuinest wits did rayne,
>   Presume so high to stretch mine humble quill?
>   Yet now my lucklesse lott doth me constrayne
>   Hereto perforce. But O dredd Souerayne
>   Thus far forth pardon, sith that choicest witt

---

40 See Edwards, *Writing, Geometry and Space*, p. 13 and pp. 45–54. See also Mary Carruthers, *The Craft of Thought: Meditation, Rhetoric, and the Making of Images, 400–1200* (Cambridge: Cambridge University Press, 1998; repr. 2008), p. 22.

Cannot your glorious pourtraict figure playne,
That I in coloured showes may shadow itt,
And antique praises vnto present persons fitt. (III.pro.1–3)

Critics have long observed how Spenser's poetry draws attention to its own status as created artefact. In an allusion to the labours of Daedalus, the poet draws attention to the work of the master painter's 'daedale hand', which anticipates the poet's betrayal of his subject; perfection cannot be shadowed by the brush or quill, but manifests in the space between object and trace, which retains the clumsy action, and even trickery, of the workman's 'aduenture'.[41] In the play of false and true perspectives it is Spenser's delight in multiplicity that allows the subject to emerge; within the wider poem, a product made by an architect of labyrinthine space, the vestigial traces of master craftsmen coexist with those of 'antipoets', whose labours draw attention, as Berger observes, to 'their own powers and limitations'.[42] When framed thus, the appeal made to the poem's ideal reader Elizabeth I, in the form of an invitation to recognise her refracted image in 'mirrours more then one' (III.pro.4), is also a challenge to recuperate that which has been displaced by its representation.[43]

Spenser, of course, perversely delights in misdirection; the reader must be aware that his or her own perspective, or way of 'looking through' the poem, is constantly being manipulated.[44] This dynamic persists throughout *The Faerie Queene* and is enacted and re-enacted at a local level by individual characters, as well as by the narrator, whose voice is capable of both merging with, and separating itself from, the words and thoughts of his protagonists.[45] For the Redcrosse Knight, who appears to stand at a perpetual crossroads, the ability constantly to reframe and re-orientate his perspective is the first lesson to be learned. In the first canto of the first book of the poem, the allegory of the 'wandring wood' introduces the motif of directional confusion that underlies the travels of all subsequent

---

41 See Harry Berger, Jr., 'The System of Early Modern Painting', *Representations*, 62 (1998), 31–57.
42 Berger, 'The Renaissance Imagination: Second World and Green World', p. 25. See also Stephen Greenblatt, *Renaissance Self-Fashioning from More to Shakespeare* (Chicago: University of Chicago Press, 1980), p. 190.
43 See Gregerson, *The Reformation of the Subject*, p. 20. See also Michael Murrin, *The Allegorical Epic: Essays in its Rise and Decline* (Chicago: University of Chicago Press, 1980), p. 136.
44 See James Elkins, *The Poetics of Perspective* (Ithaca: Cornell University Press, 1994; repr. 1996), p. 45.
45 See Jerome S. Dees, 'The Narrator of *The Faerie Queene*: Patterns of Response', *Texas Studies in Literature and Language*, 12.4 (1971), 537–68, p. 547.

knights. From this paradigmatic allegorical locus, a false 'faire harbour' and 'couert' space hidden from divine witness, the poet takes his knights on ever-stranger journeys:

> Enforst to seeke some couert nigh at hand,
>   A shadie groue not farr away they spide,
>   That promist ayde the tempest to withstand:
>   Whose loftie trees yclad with sommers pride,
>   Did spred so broad, that heauens light did hide,
>   Not perceable with power of any starr:
>   And all within were pathes and alleies wide,
>   With footing worne, and leading inward farr:
> Faire harbour that them seemes, so in they entred ar. (I.i.7)

The final words of the stanza imply that Spenser's initial protagonists, the prideful youth, mysterious lady, and heavily burdened dwarf, cross a threshold into a treacherous fictional domain; hermetically sealed, its interior world consists of tracks, passages, and thresholds that only reveal themselves in or after the moment of encounter.[46] In spite of the implied movement, there is an unnerving stillness that suspends the moment of entrance.[47] Entrance implies consent, and once 'in', Una and Redcrosse have no choice but to put their uncertain trust in the apparent knowledge of others:

> At last resoluing forward still to fare,
>   Till that some end they finde or in or out,
>   That path they take, that beaten seemd most bare,
>   And like to lead the labyrinth about. (I.i.11)

For Redcrosse it conveys 'shame to reuoke,/ The forward footing' (I.i.12); yet, as his quest progresses, he must depart from the well-trodden paths that 'beaten seemd most bare' to tread a new path, which has both its origin and ending in revelation. Like Cuningham's cosmographical readers, he must learn to read 'a right'.[48]

---

46 For the aesthetics of labyrinthine space in *The Faerie Queene* see William Blissett, 'Caves, Labyrinths, and *The Faerie Queene*', in *Unfolded Tales: Essays on Renaissance Romance*, ed. George M. Logan and Gordon Teskey (Ithaca: Cornell University Press, 1989), pp. 281–311 (pp. 298–9 in particular).

47 For the evocative idea that the Spenserian stanza appears to '*stand*, fixed for the moment as a globe for our contemplation, or as a painting to be read in spatial terms' see Hamilton, *The Structure of Allegory*, p. 14.

48 For 'the Christian ... imperative to right reading' see Hester Lees-Jeffries, 'From the Fountain to the Well: Redcrosse Learns to Read', *Studies in Philology*, 100.2 (2003), 135–76, p. 136.

When the confrontation with the monstrous form at the conceptual centre of the wood finally occurs, the moment of recognition is acknowledged by Una, the veiled personification of truth:

> Yet wisdome warnes, whilest foot is in the gate,
> To stay the steppe, ere forced to retrate.
> This is the wandring wood, this *Errours den*,
> A monster vile, whom God and man does hate:
> Therefore I read beware. (I.i.13)

Una reveals her nature only when Errour's threat becomes palpable, opening, as it were, what Cuningham refers to as the 'eyes of knowledge'. A misshapen descendent of 'that horrible Monster Ignorance', Spenser's monstrous 'Errour' is grotesquely generative, both located at the heart of the labyrinthine wood and immanent in its every misleading path.[49] Errour and her inky offspring may vanish but, as Patricia A. Parker explains, she leaves 'her trace in the serpentine progress of the poem itself, the *vestigia* the reader must follow in order to thread the labyrinth'.[50] As Parker continues, Spenser's appropriation of Ariosto's fascination with error suggests 'not ignorance but rather a highly deliberate choice … whose implications turn a possible criticism of the poem into a perspective on the nature of all fictions'.[51] The 'possible criticism' of perverse waywardness, to which Parker alludes, of course, shares the same impulse that drives Cuningham's interlocutor Spoudaeus when he decries the inconstant art of Ulysses and his fellow navigators.

For one particular early reader of *The Faerie Queene*, as Stephen Orgel has shown, the ambiguity of Spenser's allegory was cause for frustration and, where the antagonistic play between hypocrisy and truth in Book I proved especially provocative, prompted a refusal to consent to the poem's logic. Commenting anonymously in the margin near the image of Errour's disgorging of various matters, the Puritanical reader observes pithily that 'A part of this book was there'.[52] Although this particular reader's ire is directed specifically at Spenser's representation of theological matters, it reveals the difficulty of differentiating between the agencies

---

49 See Peter Remien, 'Silvan Matters: Error and Instrumentality in Book I of *The Faerie Queene*', *Spenser Studies*, 27 (2013), 119–43.
50 Parker, *Inescapable Romance*, p. 69.
51 Ibid., p. 20.
52 See Stephen Orgel, 'Margins of Truth', in *The Renaissance Text: Theory, Editing, Textuality*, ed. Andrew Murphy (Manchester: Manchester University Press, 2000), pp. 91–107 (p. 103). See also Andrew Fleck, 'Early Modern Marginalia in Spenser's *Faerie Queene* at the Folger', *Notes and Queries*, 55.2 (2008), 165–70.

of Archimago and Una.[53] Even in the words used by Una to congratulate Redcrosse after his defeat of Errour there is a duplicity that evokes the unavoidability of constant movement:

> ... Faire knight, borne vnder happie starre,
> Who see your vanquisht foes before you lye:
> Well worthie be you of that Amory,
> Wherein ye haue great glory wonne this day,
> And proou'd your strength on a strong enimie,
> Your first adventure: many such I pray,
> And henceforth euer wish, that like succeed it may. (I.i.27)

Una's words are offered in praise, but the emphasis put by her prayer on the repetition of 'like' adventures suggests both curse and blessing. If Redcrosse's initial adventure serves as a forerunner for all that follows, he will find himself forever trapped in '*Errours* endlesse traine' (I.i.18), fighting the same uncanny battles for all the time to come. Like Cuningham's Ulysses, Redcrosse fails to master the art of defeating error and he is drawn, and Una with him, into further misread and misrecognised terrain, where both are bound by 'knowinge not by what meanes, to attaine to their so longe desired region' (*The Cosmographical Glasse*, sig. P2ᵛ). By definition, Archimago, whom Linda Gregerson elegantly categorises as one of Spenser's 'villainous avatars of craven poesis',[54] and Una, as indivisible religious and philosophical truth, should figure concepts that are in essential opposition with each other; however, they operate in cognate ways, offering figures for different stages in the pursuit of knowledge-making.[55] For Spenser, as for Cuningham, the coupling of 'the inventive part' with the 'daedale hand' traces a fine line between what Puttenham describes as the creation of 'false glasses' that 'show things otherwise than they be indeed' and those, 'right as they be indeed', which contain no exaggeration or distortion.[56]

---

53 See James A. Knapp, *Image Ethics in Shakespeare and Spenser* (New York: Palgrave Macmillan 2011), pp. 76–9 and Kenneth Gross, *Spenserian Poetics: Idolatry, Iconoclasm, and Magic* (Ithaca: Cornell University Press, 1985), p. 69.
54 See Linda Gregerson, 'Protestant Erotics: Idolatry and Interpretation in Spenser's *Faerie Queene*', *ELH*, 58.1 (1991), 1–34, p. 11.
55 The 'uncertainties' that attend Una's role in the narrative, as indicated by her 'various namings', are expertly surveyed by Alpers in 'Narration in *The Faerie Queene*', p. 28. See also Gordon Teskey, 'From Allegory to Dialectic: Imagining Error in Spenser and Milton', *PMLA*, 101.1 (1986), 9–23.
56 Puttenham, *The Art of English Poesy*, p. 110.

## Lucas Waghenaer and learning to navigate

In order to address the nature of purposeful, generative, and even corrective error, *The Faerie Queene*'s narrator explains that the poem acts as an imaginative transport for the reader. He wearily likens the motions of the poem to those of a ship, which casts the author in the role of a pilot, or skilled navigator.[57] In the first canto of Book VI, for example, the narrator attempts to account for the labyrinthine journeys and deliberate delays of previous books:

> Like as a ship, that through the Ocean wyde
>   Directs her course vnto one certaine cost,
> Is met of many a counter winde and tyde,
>   With which her winged speed is let and crost,
>   And she her selfe in stormie surges tost;
> Yet making many a borde, and many a bay,
>   Still winneth way, ne hath her compasse lost:
> Right so it fares with me in this long way,
> Whose course is often stayd, yet neuer is astray. (VI.xii.1)

The ebb and flow of the syntax mirrors the stanza's conceit, embodying a vessel cast off course and at the mercy of the elements. Progress is stayed, stopped, or temporarily deferred, but never truly lacking in purpose. The metaphor is not unique to Spenser and, as Ernst Robert Curtius observes, nautical images were frequently used in classical literature to describe the process of composition: 'the poet becomes the sailor, his mind or his work the boat'.[58] Although Spenser's use of navigational terms originate within an ancient tradition, they retain a vital sense of how the author and his work are susceptible to, but capable of mastering, radical contingency. As the Renaissance polymath John Dee explains in his *Mathematicall Praeface* (1570), the 'Arte of Navigation' incurs a trade-off between purposeful movement and the vigilant righting of unavoidable error. The art demonstrates, he writes:

> how, by the shortest good way, by the aptest Direction, and in the shortest time, a sufficient Ship, betwene any two places (in passage Navigable,)

---

57 For the use of the motif throughout Spenser's poem see Jerome S. Dees, 'The Ship Conceit in *The Faerie Queene*: "Conspicuous Allusion" and Poetic Structure', *Studies in Philology*, 72 (1975), 208–25.
58 Ernst Robert Curtius, *European Literature and the Latin Middle Ages*, trans. Willard R. Trask (London: Routledge and Kegan Paul, 1953), p. 129. See also Hans Blumenberg, *Shipwreck with Spectator: Paradigm of a Metaphor for Existence*, trans. Steven Rendall (Cambridge, MA: MIT Press, 1997).

assigned: may be conducted: and in all stormes, and naturall disturbances chauncyng, how, to use the best possible meanes, whereby to recover the place first assigned.[59]

If the image of a 'sufficient Ship' sailing 'by the aptest Direction' accords with Spoudaeus's idealised sense of what epic poetry should also accomplish, the language of 'chauncying' accrues familiarity as the language of romance. As Britomart boldly declares to the wavering Scudamour, following a declaration of despair prompted by the loss of his beloved wife Amoret:

> ... for shamefull thing
> Yt were t'abandon noble cheuisaunce,
> For shewe of perill, without venturing:
> Rather let try extremities of chaunce,
> Then enterprised praise for dread to disauaunce. (III.xi.24)

The art of prospecting for items and persons of value, Britomart argues, should not be foregone for an excess of what Spenser elsewhere terms 'Accidents' ('A Letter of the Authors', p. 718). Following the earlier discussion of Cuningham's imaginative engagement with the navigations of Ulysses, I now turn to a work that explicitly addresses the conceptual and imaginative pursuits of an increasingly maritime culture and further investigate the art of navigation as a model for the kind of active reading practices that Spenser's poem demands.

The sea is a difficult kind of space to place within a reader's hands. As a result, texts about navigational theory often have strange cosmographies, typically describing mere fragments of a coastal world under skies populated with unfamiliar constellations. Like *The Faerie Queene*, they are themselves difficult to navigate; they use their physical spaces, particularly their paratextual materials, to confront the troubling experiential gap that exists between a printed account and an encounter with wide waters. In one of the best known navigational treatises from the period, *The Mariners Mirrour*, both the Dutch author, Lucas Janszoon Waghenaer, and the English translator, Anthony Ashley, use prefaces and dedicatory letters to prepare and orientate their readers. Owing to its innovative content, the work constantly meditates on the difficulties of communication and representation, asking its audience to imagine that which cannot be seen, or grasped, in simultaneity, and to conceive of pro-

---

59 John Dee, *Mathematicall Praeface* in *The Elements of Geometrie of the Most Auncient Philosopher Euclide of Megara*, trans. Henry Billingsley (London, 1570), sig. D4ᵛ. All subsequent references are placed in the text.

cesses which, to ensure the survival of its users, have to remain fluid. The reader is orientated from the outset so that their way of looking though subsequent pages is alert to mobility; not all can be mastered from the comfort of the study.

The English translation of Waghenaer's *The Mariners Mirrour* was published in 1588 following the defeat of the Spanish Armada: an event to which it makes celebratory reference. Originally printed in Leiden in 1584 by Christophe Plantin as the *Spieghel der Zeevaerdt* and dedicated to William I, Prince of Orange, the work is usually credited with being the first of its kind, due to its presentation of both written sailing directions and lavish coastal charts, which had previously existed as separate hydrographic traditions.[60] In testimony to the popularity of the work, Ashley's English vernacular translation gave rise to the use of the colloquial anglicised name 'waggoner' for all subsequent sea atlases published in England (see Figure 3).[61]

The way in which the English, or 'Englished' paratexts create a dialogue involving the translator, author, and imagined reader, suggests that the work constantly and consciously demands an active reception.[62] Dedicatory epistles and letters to readers are accompanied, for example, by a Latin panegyric attributed to the Dutch humanist Janus Dousa (Johan van der Does), which incorporates a variety of classical references to the sea. When read together, the paratexts reflect on the unique cognitive practices required for the transmission and exchange of navigational theory and information. As a group, they provide a range of social contexts for an exchange of ideas performed across geographical, generic, and linguistic borders.

In his 'Authors Admonition to the Reader', Waghenaer concerns himself with problems of legibility and asks his audience to question the nature of the representations his atlas contains, demanding that his reader practice a process of mental translation that can hold the movement between the literal and figurative in constant suspension. In an attempt to get the reader to question what they do when they look at a marine map, he points out something fairly obvious, though perhaps easily forgotten: 'Freendly Reader', he writes, 'forasmuch as all skilfull

60 See Günter Schilder, *The Netherland Nautical Cartography from 1550 to 1650* (Lisboa: Instituto de Investigação Científica Tropical, 1984), pp. 99–102.
61 See *The Cambridge History of the Book in Britain Volume 4: 1557–1695*, ed. John Barnard, D.F. McKenzie, and Maureen Bell (Cambridge: Cambridge University Press, 2002), p. 233.
62 For the importance of shared knowledge production in the period see Spiller, *Science, Reading, and Renaissance Literature*, p. 3.

*Figure 3* Lucas Janzoon Waghenaer. Title page from *The Mariners Mirrour*, trans. Anthony Ashley (London, 1588).

and experienced in the art of Navigation, do well know, that certein of the sandy coastes and shoares ... are moveable, and have not alwaies their being in one self place, as in these Tables or Chartes'.[63] His charts are faithfully set down but subject to contingency: a distinction made not on the basis of observational inaccuracy but as a concern with the technology used to share information with readers. Noting how landmasses are liable to shift owing to surrounding currents and the susceptibility of sandy shores to violent storms, he continues to draw attention to the cognitive breach that occurs when the pages of a book are asked to compass the seas of Europe and beyond:

> First, that by these examples, thou mightest understand, that upon the like causes, the like chaunges may happen: next that the unskilfull and especially the envious backbiter and carper, may have no matter to cavill, nor occasion to carp: seeing that things to come, and uncerteine, can by no meanes possible, bee perfectly described. (sig. ¶2ʳ)

With no hope of attaining the impossible ideal of perfect description the author defends himself against the 'backbiter and carper', whose jealous minds are incapable of unravelling the delicate process he seeks to promote.

Waghenaer is defending a feature of all representations, of course, which Spenser himself confronts in *The Faerie Queene*'s sixth book through the destructive actions of the Blatant Beast; it is just that the challenges posed by coastal spaces and their movements make the issue more immediately and life-threateningly apparent. As Ulrich Kinzel observes, 'navigation cannot be regarded as an *episteme*, knowledge aiming at unchangeable objects or the representational mode of being', and 'rather has to be seen as *techne*, knowledge that relates to changing objects or the operative mode of formation'.[64] For Spenser, the changeable nature of multitudinous waters prompts *The Faerie Queene*'s own famous acknowledgement of the 'endlesse worke' the poet has 'in hand' and the distorting capacity of the poem-as-mirror:

> Then blame me not, if I haue err'd in count
> Of Gods, of Nymphs, of riuers yet vnred:
> For though their numbers do much more surmount,
> Yet all those same were there, which erst I did recount. (IV.xii.2)

---

63 Lucas Janzoon Waghenaer, *The Mariners Mirrour*, trans. Anthony Ashley (London, 1588), sig. ¶2ʳ. All subsequent references are placed in the text.
64 Ulrich Kinzel, 'Orientation as a Paradigm of Maritime Modernity', in *Fictions of the Sea: Critical Perspectives on the Ocean in British Literature and Culture*, ed. Bernhard Klein and Gesa Mackenthun (Aldershot: Ashgate, 2002), pp. 28–48 (p. 30).

As an instrument of the imagination, Spenser's poem, like the mirror work imagined for the mariner's use, falls short of complete spatial mastery: that which lies beyond the author's field of vision remains 'yet vnred'.

In the dedicatory letter addressed to Sir Christopher Hatton, which introduces *The Mariners Mirrour* in English, the translator Anthony Ashley also raises the issue of representational finality. He helpfully explains that in most cases the sea charts and maps have been designed for individual completion and have been left unfinished and therefore suitable for additions as befitting each user:

> in most of the Plots, the Sea is purposly left in blanc, because the Traveiler, finding perchance some poynt of the Compasse, risings of Lands, Depths, Soundings, or ought els mistaken; or some Rocke, Sand, or other danger left out, or not rightly expressed (for nothing so perfect but hath his fault) may as he traveileth set downe and correct the same with his owne hand, as it shall best like him selfe; which doubtles wilbe no smale furtherance and contentment even to the best Docters in this science. (sig. ¶1ʳ)

In charts such as these, produced as the known world gradually expanded and the knowledge of antiquity was outgrown, the cartographer's *terrae incognitae* are still seen filled with monsters, and other hybrid creatures. Such spatial markers, representative of the anxiety of the unknown, compete with compass roses and cartouches denoting patronage and authority, more rational markers of empire and influence.[65] Yet, the decision made in the English edition to leave the seas blank, rather than texturing them with decorative inky waves, marks an interesting choice; it is a rational acknowledgement that the known world is not continuous but filled with lacunae, advertised here to encourage participation and amendment.[66] Consequently, owing to Ashley's disclaimer, which henceforth functions as an advertisement and invitation, the charts do not claim totalising divine perspective but fully acknowledge their status as provisional human artefacts. The ideal reader is invited by Ashley to contribute his own knowledge to the work, 'with his owne hand', and to complete the task that the chart makers purposefully left unfinished. The blank space, networked by rhumb lines, lies waiting; it is a legitimate place for the reader to improvise, 'as it shall best like

---

65 For the aesthetics of navigational charts see Richard W. Unger, *Ships on Maps: Pictures of Power in Renaissance Europe* (Basingstoke: Palgrave Macmillan, 2010). For Waghenaer's charts see pp. 147–50.
66 See David W. Waters, *The Art of Navigation in England in Elizabethan and Early Stuart Times* (New Haven: Yale University Press, 1958), p. 175.

him selfe'.⁶⁷ The provisional representation of an incomplete world actively welcomes readers to participate in the exploration of the territories represented: absence is privileged over excess.⁶⁸ The unfinished charts invite collaboration and exchange, even if the users never meet in person.

In a subsequent section of *The Mariners Mirrour* printed under the heading 'Of the Use and Practise of this Booke', the reader is once again asked to collaborate in the attempts of the author and editor to grasp the ungraspable:

> And let it not seeme straunge to any if peradventure some of the sea coastes, havens, countries, etc., appeare not so fully and plainely, and shewe themselves as indeed they are, and as they are pourtraied in our severall Chartes. For albeit (besides mine owne skill and experience) I have conferred and shewen whatsoever is contained in this booke to divers Shipmasters and expert Pilots, and have corrected the same by their notes, who according to their severall experience and judgement, have praised and allowed all these severall Chartes: which since that I have published in the same forme; yet because it is naturall for men to be deceaved, and for that divers men have not only divers opinions, but also evident faults: perhaps many errors wilbe found in this booke, which a painfull and diligent Pilot will easely amend, seing as it is farre easier to correct that which is already invented, then to frame a new. (sig. A1ʳ)

The author reflects on the value of his endeavour, concluding with an acknowledgement of unavoidable error. He reminds the reader of the frailties of perception, 'because it is naturall for men to be deceaved', suggesting that it is only through further trial that his atlas of the sea can be augmented and amended. 'To correct' rather than 'to frame a new' is the challenge offered, implicating its readers in its travails, where imagery of 'framing', as Kalas observes, typically 'did not connote conscious mastery but, rather, technologies of human making'.⁶⁹ When dealing with mutable spaces, a theory of process must be privileged over claims of mastery, making *The Mariners Mirrour* ultimately only as effective as its users.

---

67 When exploring the shared spatialities of early modern navigational literature and the Portuguese epic poem, *The Lusiads*, Bernhard Klein playfully evokes Lewis Carroll's nonsense poem *The Hunting of the Snark* and its accompanying blank 'map'. See 'Mapping the Waters: Sea Charts, Navigation, and Camões's *Os Lusíadas*', *Renaissance Studies*, 25.2 (2011), 228–47, p. 239.
68 For contrast compare André Thevet's excessive description in his *Cosmographie Universelle* (1575). See Jeffrey N. Peters, *Mapping Discord: Allegorical Cartography in Early Modern French Writing* (Newark: University of Delaware Press, 2004), pp. 50–2.
69 Kalas, *Frame, Glass, Verse*, p. 77.

Waghenaer's refusal to commit to the creation of a treatise in which the coasts of Europe 'shewe themselves as indeed they are' demonstrates an acute awareness of the limits of how his charts function. Rather than standing as inert reflections of objective reality, they require dynamic interpretation and use a graphic mode that complicates commonplace metaphorical associations between maps and mirrors.[70] Although he stops his reading at the volume's title page, for example, Dan Brayton notes that there is something inherently performative about its composition, which he describes as depicting 'mariners as actors in a *naumachia*, or nautical drama, and a group of cartographers assembled around a blank globe as playwrights of a sort'.[71] The part of the image to which he refers could be a blank globe but it is more likely to be a mirror, where the speculative elision between global surface and perspective glass echoes the metaphors used elsewhere in the period. The figurative prose used to introduce Mercator's atlas *Historia Mundi*, for example, theorises its own cartographical project in similar terms:

> it presenteth to our sight the whole Globe of the Earth as it were in a Mirrour or Looking-glasse, and doth shew the beautie and ornaments of the whole Fabricke of the world, and containeth all things in her ample and spacious bosome, and like the vaste Sea, it does not onely open and lay forth the hidden and remote Islands, but also all other Countries.[72]

Seductively, the task of Mercator's 'Looking-glasse' is to expose: to 'open and lay forth' a feminised form to the encompassing gaze of the atlas's possessor. The imagined actions of receding tides reveal the contours of the land, made passive and naked before such penetrating observation.

The mutable mirror trope that frames the image of the world is itself notorious for its protean ability to distort, refract, and transform. As Herbert Grabes observes, a 'mirror shows an image only so long as the original is present, only so long as mirror and original are juxtaposed';[73] however, to look at Waghenaer's sea atlas is to face ambiguity. The mirror-globe's empty sheen contrasts with the busy lines of longitude and latitude networking the sphere that occupies a similar position on the title page of Cuningham's work. Waghenaer's original, this emblem

---

70 See J.B. Harley, *The New Nature of Maps: Essays in the History of Cartography*, ed. Paul Laxton (Baltimore: Johns Hopkins University Press, 2001), p. 36.
71 Dan Brayton, *Shakespeare's Ocean: An Ecocritical Exploration* (Charlottesville: University of Virginia Press, 2012), p. 2.
72 Gerhard Mercator, 'The Preface to the Courteous Reader', in *Historia Mundi: Or Mercator's Atlas* (London, 1635), sig. A3ᵛ.
73 See Grabes, *The Mutable Glass*, p. 113.

suggests, is not a singular object but a subject as changeable as water. Rather than being read as a frame though which the reader is supposed to behold the mutable coasts of Europe, or a sea made as transparent to the viewer as tempered glass, then, the mirror is instead most consistent when being held up to the mariner himself, refracting the ideal qualities that he is supposed to possess.

This reading of Waghenaer's sea atlas demonstrates the complex nature of the discussions concerning chart-making in the sixteenth century. The highly rhetorical prefaces stress how the apparent coherence of cartographic representations has the dangerous ability to promote carelessness. With this hazard in mind it is productive to compare the prefaces produced by the author and translator with the poem that appears on the pages immediately following Waghenaer's 'Admonition': a Latin panegyric entitled 'Operis Commendatio' and attributed to Janus Dousa, which appears in the English edition with a facing page translation.[74] Its rich images complement but also further trouble the cautious advice of the prose prefaces, offering both a metaphorical transformation of Waghenaer's labours and images that self-reflexively address the chart-maker's processes of figuration. As Jeffrey N. Peters observes, 'maps succeed not only because they are science, but also because they are metaphors', and this poem, it seems, finds a way into thinking about what maritime maps might be a metaphor for.[75]

Waghenaer's charts, the poem suggests, enter into metaphorical relationships that speak of motion, subjective discovery, possibility, and measurement; as such, a reader must be aware of how their rhetoric and figuration operates. The poem offers yet another reframing of Waghenaer's endeavour, casting the author's travails both alongside and in opposition to the epic voyage of the Argonauts: put thus, the work done by *The Mariners Mirrour* takes on a kind of epic quality. The poet makes it clear that *The Mariners Mirrour* is a work proudly produced in Northern Europe, distinct from the efforts of the Spanish and Portuguese:

> ... Ile none of your *Argos* adventurs
> Western discoverers: tis enough for mee t'have a corner
> In this swift caravell to behold these Tables in order:

---

74 The Dutch edition contains substantially more poetry, including a poem by the Leiden author Jan van Hout; this does not appear in Ashley's translation and the single poem that is present bears only a passing resemblance to the earlier panegyric on which it was modelled. See Cornelis Koeman, *The History of Lucas Janszoon Waghenaer and his Spieghel der Zeevaerdt* (Lausanne: Sequoia, 1964), pp. 43–7.

75 Peters, *Mapping Discord*, p. 35.

And learne how *Northern Nereus* hath spread many braunches. (sig. ¶3ʳ,
34–7)

In addition to the worldliness of its northern orientation, which proposes to direct the reader to places where 'no star, nor lead, hath led any *Spaignard*' (41), the poem also conveys an idealised sense of Waghenaer's project. The poem speaks of surfaces, where the reader will behold the ocean regions as if in a glass, and also of depths. The penetrating alien presence of the author's gaze has astonished the sea-calves and other, more mythical, creatures of the deep. The knowledge offered by the work provides entrance to 'the secreat closet of Seagoddeses' (22) and access to 'th'hidden secreats of th'old *Lady Tethys*' (30). Its praise of the author is great indeed:

> Now Mariners henceforth at Sea may ye live very carelesse,
> For that a saulfe journey cleered from dangerous extreames,
> Is for ye prepared. For now may ye into good harbour
> Hale even at pleasure. Now doth to the forme o the mayn-deepe,
> And all shoalds proffer themselves to be cleerly beholden.
> All this prayse is dew to thy witt, to thy paines, to thy charges,
> Ingenious *Wagener*, which hast so worthily guyded,
> That Wagon on Mayn-sea which winds cause flie to the compasse:
> As if upon thy both hands and knees with curious insight
> Strongly thy selfe hadst crept, and search out th'*Ocean* althrough.
> Moreover unlesse that peradventure a Searcher of East-seas,
> Or Northern passage, should want any thing that he searcheth:
> Thou shewst each Region farr of, what sort it ariseth.
> Nor *Venus* in Mirrour could view her selfe any cleerer,
> Then *Tethys* in this Glasse may well discerne her apeeraunce. (6–20)

Produced in the wake of experiments at sea, the poem is characterised by a vocabulary of elevations, breadths, and depths or soundings, of impossible and fantastic spatial and conceptual mastery. The 'mayn-deepe' is given 'forme', fashioned into something transparent in which its riches can be 'cleerly beholden'. The translator of the poem even allows himself to indulge in making a pun on Waghenaer's name, where the imagined ship guided by the author is refashioned as a 'Wagon', implicitly finding sea roads to traverse. Even the sea-born goddess Venus, mirror in hand, is outdone by Waghenaer's apparent performance. As in Spenser's *Faerie Queene*, the creative capacity of *Venus Genetrix* informs the presentation of the author's craft. Here, Dousa's poem makes the claim that Waghenaer's atlas gives shape to *Tethys*, the Titan mother of waters, providing limits to what would otherwise be endless, generative, liquid abundance.[76]

If, as Steve Mentz has implied, there is a difference between sea-based and land-based ways of knowing, the translation of Dousa's poem conflates the two, imagining a solid bottom to the ocean's murky depths which can support the crawling, yet undaunted, body of the author.[77] Waghenaer, breathing miraculously among the fishes, suffers only the discomfort caused by his travail, not the inhuman transgression of elements. His imagined body is contorted in order to make maximum contact with the sea floor; fathoming his subject, his hands and knees are loaded with the same intent as the mariner's lead and line. What is usually only perceived using instrumental means is here passed through Waghenaer's imagined fingers, his 'curious', or attentive, insight allowing him both visual and tactile experience of an untouchable space. Put in such terms, the sea made by the poem requires the reader to imagine an empirical encounter through the medium of a cultural fantasy. To evoke a metaphor used by Gérard Genette, this poem-as-paratext acts as a very particular kind of threshold: an 'airlock that helps the reader pass without too much respiratory difficulty from one world to the other'.[78] In *The Mariners Mirrour*, the poem functions as a conceptual airlock in a very immediate sense, establishing a sea road between the study of the humanist scholar and a fathomable ocean; simultaneous land-based and sea-based perspectives are thus made possible. The sea of the poem is not a bottomless depth but a place of transparent exchange that appears illuminated from within. It is perhaps no coincidence that Waghenaer's instructions for 'How to Draw and Use a True and Perfect Sea Carde' specify the use of a 'table of glasse' that should be lit from behind in order to render the inscribed surfaces translucent (sig. B4$^v$).

To return to dry land, what the poem imagines is, of course, an impossible ideal. The impossible image of Waghenaer crawling along the sea floor dangerously obscures the single most vital piece of information both he and Ashley otherwise seek to emphasise: forgetting that a map or chart is non-identical to the place it represents effects a loss, as Theodore Roszak writes, of the 'intelligent plasticity and intuitive judgement that

---

76  For this dynamic in *The Faerie Queene* see Balachandra Rajan, *The Form of the Unfinished: English Poetics from Spenser to Pound* (Princeton: Princeton University Press, 1985), pp. 55–6.
77  See Mentz, *At the Bottom of Shakespeare's Ocean*, p. 3. For discussion of what Mentz terms 'the aquaman fantasy' see pp. 44–7.
78  Genette, *Paratexts*, p. 408.

every wayfarer must preserve'.⁷⁹ No mariner can ever 'live very carelesse' as long as the sea and coast behave in the changeable way that is natural to them. The layering of perspectival frames thus serves to sound the limits of the printed book as a piece of navigational technology and produces the reader as the site where knowledge is finally made. The poem may encourage the reader to dream, to fantasise about the possession of an oceanic epistemology, and to share in the ambition of Waghenaer's project, but it will not aid survival. It offers a different mode of knowing and understanding, in opposition to the rhetoric of the cautious prose prefaces which situate navigation as a field of knowledge that fully belongs to the *technai*, the knowledge arts categorised by, in Paul Stern's words, 'their ability to manipulate the world, exercising some control over forces that otherwise might lead to our ruin'.⁸⁰ What the poem provides instead is an interrogation of the process of thinking hydrographically, which complements the construction, by both author and translator, of an active reader – an 'Apprentice of the Art of Navigation' – who must 'exerciseth, searcheth out and observeth' for himself (sig. A2ʳ).

## Making safe harbours

In the works by Cuningham and Waghenaer, the reader is regularly reminded of the limits of the body and must extrapolate the matter available for practical use from fantastical images. The katascopic voyage of Spoudaeus through the firmament, and the submarine portrait of Waghenaer touching the seabed, represent the two most notable examples: as self-consciously spatial moments, both the flight and the submergence offer allegories of discovery. Both treatises share an interest in the capacity of figurative practices not only to confront expanding world geographies, but also to chart the necessary conceptual processes that must be undertaken in order to perceive them. From the depths of the ocean to the heights of the heavens, *The Cosmographical Glasse* and *The Mariners Mirrour* offer readers not just the physically possible but idealised augmentations of human perception. That which is unseen and ungraspable is made navigable by figurative language. For the purposes of framing my readings of Spenser's *Faerie Queene*, the works of nonfiction considered in this chapter prompt ways of thinking about how the

---

79 Theodore Roszak, *Where the Wasteland Ends: Politics and Transcendence in Postindustrial Society* (Berkeley: Celestial Arts, 1989), p. 408.
80 Paul Stern, *Knowledge and Politics in Plato's Theaetetus* (Cambridge: Cambridge University Press, 2008), p. 50.

author's 'daedale hand' gives shape to mental processes and the writing of space: a dynamic that, as this study progresses, increasingly fuses the expectations set up by particular genres and literary modes with the challenges of representing terraqueous environments.

When concluding his preface to the reader, William Cuningham draws on images of errancy and wished-for safe harbours once again in order to remind his audience that his labour has been performed for the benefit of others:

> And if for the difficultie of the worke, any errour escape: remember I am the firste that ever in oure tongue have written of this argument, and therfore am constrained, to finde out the pathe. Whiche if it be not at this time made plaine, smothe and pleasaunt: if God graunt life, and leisure, I trust so to treade it againe, that both night and day (walking in the same) thou shalt not misse of the desired Port. (sig. A6$^v$)

Cuningham imagines the knowledge exchange as a journey-space, which requires the reader to recollect and imagine the full dimensions of physical experience whilst contemplating a variety of abstractions. Mixing his metaphors, Cuningham imagines himself on foot, and his reader at sea; he is a pioneer in whose wake, or footsteps, others can follow. Such pleasurable motions are perhaps reminders that his performance of cosmographical and conceptual space ought to delight as much as it teaches. However, for all their rhetorical performativity, the arts with which both Cuningham and Waghenaer engage, namely cosmography and navigation, are essentially practical; literary engagement is not meant to replace practical engagement, and the material world continually re-asserts itself. As we have seen, the ways in which Waghenaer and Ashley confront the contingent nature of hydrography in *The Mariners Mirrour* are one of the most impressive features of the work. If Waghenaer's sea charts offer the viewer what is essentially an allegorical representation, owing to the way that they attempt to fix something that is in constant motion, they do so in a way that constantly privileges the mariner's material and temporal concerns. As Cuningham, Waghenaer, and Spenser all demonstrate, the hostile textual spaces created by the acknowledgement and confrontation of error yield generative rather than merely monstrous results.[81]

The act of reading Cuningham and Waghenaer alongside Spenser helps to destabilise critical desires to 'map' Spenser's poem; that such

---

81 See François Rigolot, 'The Renaissance Fascination with Error: Mannerism and Early Modern Poetry', *RQ*, 57.4 (2004), 1219–34.

a drive exists can perhaps be thought of in relation to what Jeffrey N. Peters has identified as the reductive product of 'a foundational chiasmus: maps are always allegorical; allegory is always cartographic'.[82] Mary Thomas Crane, for one, has argued that the spatial relationships typically suggested by the use of allegory, such as veiling, imply that Spenser conceived of writing his poem 'as a journey over a flat surface', whereby the poem 'lacks a sustained sense of textual depth'.[83] Yet, to create a map-like analogy using such terms does the mobile and palimpsestic qualities of both chart-making and allegory something of a disservice. For Spenser's narrator, the meaning of the poem can only be found in the sedimentary interrelation of its parts: in every moment there is an implied extension that reaches beyond the immediate scene. And for Redcrosse, of course, the threat of error is often a submerged one, as he discovers on his hasty exit from the House of Pride:

> As when a ship, that flyes fayre vnder sayle,
>   An hidden rocke escaped hath vnwares,
> That lay in waite her wrack for to bewaile,
>   The Marriner yet halfe amazed stares
>   At perill past, and yet in doubt ne dares
> To ioy at his foolehappie ouersight:
>   So doubly is distrest twixt ioy and cares
> The dreadlesse corage of this Elfin knight,
> Hauing escapt so sad ensamples in his sight. (I.vi.1)

The aporia that underlies the mariner's mixed emotional state in the simile captures Redcrosse's incomplete understanding of the peril he has just survived; as an experience that has not been fully processed, the escape from the visibly carcass-strewn walls of the House of Pride is refigured in the gap between cantos as a submerged hazard that is not easily descried. Any chart maker can mark a rock but it is impossible to predict how the light, the wind, the swell of the sea, and the temperament of the crew will interact on any specific, or future, occasion; for Redcrosse, the

---

82 Peters, *Mapping Discord*, p. 33. Andrew Zurcher takes 'mapping' as a productive metaphor for interpretive reading in the first chapter of *Edmund Spenser's The Faerie Queene: A Reading Guide* (Edinburgh: Edinburgh University Press, 2011), pp. 1–15. See also Donald Kimball Smith, *The Cartographic Imagination in Early Modern England: Rewriting the World in Marlowe, Spenser, Raleigh and Marvell* (Aldershot: Ashgate, 2008), p. 79 and pp. 85–94.
83 Mary Thomas Crane, 'Surface, Depth and the Spatial Imaginary: A Cognitive Reading of *The Political Unconscious*', *Representations*, 108.1 (2009), 76–97, p. 86. Crane's excellent article contains more insight than she acknowledges for a reading of *The Faerie Queene*.

backward glance towards the site of his near wreck still admits his grief at having left Duessa behind (I.vi.2), suggesting that he has still not learned from his experience.

Within *The Faerie Queene* as a whole, which contains gestures towards heights and depths while occupying in the main the labyrinthine vagaries of 'the middest' ('A Letter of the Authors', p. 716), the constant and latent threat of destruction is given shifting form by the Protean Archimago, whose verbal and visual image-making situates him as the poet's own 'dark double'.[84] To Archimago and his kin belong the allegorical 'Depths, Soundings, or ought els mistaken': the other dangers 'left out' (see *The Mariners Mirrour*, sig. ¶1ʳ). To be suspended *in medias res* is thus to be in process, and the Spenserian 'middest' consequently comes into being as a strange place: like the coastlines, wetlands, and islands that populate the readings of the second part of this study, it is a space of transition and confusion. In the images of coasts and waters framed by *The Mariners Mirrour*, uncharted space is a deliberate conceptual feature, and it is to such aesthetic and epistemological structures that readers of *The Faerie Queene* must also commit their attention: if they are to be challenged in the way that Spenser's letter to Ralegh suggests they will be, they cannot remain wholly within the comfort of the study like Cuningham's armchair travellers. Reading the selected mirror works and their paratexts together thus offers something of an object lesson: like Spenser's allegories, their spatial representations comment implicitly upon their methods. Cosmography may claim to be a totalising art, which aims at providing full rather than 'foolehappie ouersight', but navigation, one of its many branches, emphasises how provisional and fragmentary its artefacts can be: the mirror metaphor may offer the illusion of undistorted surface, but temporal concerns remain present within the submerged reflection. *The Faerie Queene*'s spaces could perhaps only be 'mapped' if the map created was sufficiently self-critical of its own processes: it would be an act of making, or poetry, in itself.[85] The blank spaces on charts, then, across which the mariner must navigate, are analogous to the hidden dangers, depths, and silences of Spenser's text. For readers of *The Faerie Queene* it is ultimately their own task to fill in the blank seas

---

84 Patrick Cheney and Lauren Silberman, 'Introduction', in *Worldmaking Spenser* (Lexington: University Press of Kentucky, 2000), pp. 1–6 (p. 2).

85 As Joseph D. Parry observes, 'the phenomenal world' of *The Faerie Queene* 'is always moving, shifting, reshaping itself according to the changing rhetorical demands of the narrative'. See 'Phaedria and Guyon: Travelling Alone in *The Faerie Queene*, Book II', *Spenser Studies*, 15 (2001), 53–77, p. 62.

and sites of 'endlesse worke' where Spenser admits defeat.[86] After all, it is they who have volunteered to be fashioned and whose discoveries can only ever be their own.

---

86 For Fletcher, for example, 'the forces of Spenserian narrative ... are cosmological'. See *The Prophetic Moment*, p. 304. For the challenges of textual rifts see Stephen B. Dobranski, *Readers and Authorship in Early Modern England* (Cambridge: Cambridge University Press, 2005), p. 9.

# 2

# Movement and measurement

For as directly to walke is good, and to goe astraye daungerous: so to be moved with affections to a good purpose is commendable, but to an yll ende and purpose altogether damnable.[1]

wee finde no open tract, or constant manuduction in this labyrinth; but are oft-times faine to wander in the America and untravelled parts of truth.[2]

As Thomas Browne observes in his preface to *Pseudodoxia Epidemica*, the obstructions of erroneous common knowledge cannot be traversed merely by corrective recollection: 'Would truth dispense, we could be content, with Plato, that knowledge were but remembrance'. Instead, he finds himself having to advocate a radical process of erasure, for 'to purchase a clear and warrantable body of truth, we must forget and part with much wee know'.[3] Browne likens the task at hand to the strenuous discovery of an unmapped continent, through which there is no hope of 'manuduction': a witty play on the idea that a rhetorical composition such as his should ordinarily consider how a reader's percipient mind is conducted through the text by the author's oversight, as if led by the hand.[4] Within the cognitive wasteland Browne identifies there is neither a recently ploughed field nor a fresh 'open tract' to cultivate: instead, the 'untravelled parts' of the uncharted continent function as a figure for authorial anxiety in spite of Browne's masterful manipulation of

---

1 Thomas Rogers, *The Anatomie of the Minde* (London, 1576), sig. B2$^{r-v}$.
2 Thomas Browne, *Pseudodoxia Epidemica* (1646) in *21st-Century Oxford Authors: Thomas Browne*, ed. Kevin Killeen (Oxford: Oxford University Press, 2014), pp. 85–506 (p. 90).
3 Ibid., p. 88.
4 See Mary Carruthers's discussion of *ductus* in *The Craft of Thought: Meditation, Rhetoric, and the Making of Images, 400–1200* (Cambridge: Cambridge University Press, 1998; repr. 2008), pp. 77–81 (p. 77).

metaphor.⁵ For Kevin Killeen, 'the defining and exemplary loss that characterises *Pseudodoxia*' comes into focus in the way that Browne combines the quality of postlapsarian knowledge with the nature of the curse put on Adam to work the ground after the Fall: 'The curse has thrown up its benighted landscape, its tangled place of thorns, which the learned author can merely stumble through, weeding the occasional tare'.⁶

Spenser's writing may not exhibit the same level of scepticism as Browne's mid-seventeenth-century collection of essays; however, Browne's interconnected images of exile, memory, epistemology, and painful labour participate in traditions of thinking spatially that also shape the earlier author's work. Making error legible by figuring an interaction between imagined spaces and moving bodies creates a discourse through which readers are invited to trace their own interpretative paths: the association of movement with ethical conditions and states of knowing thus becomes recognisable as a commonplace conceit.⁷ For Spenser, as for Plato before him, error and 'the space of recreative wandering' act as what Linda Gregerson has identified as 'the chief antidote to the seamless lie of rhetoric and the chief means of progress in truth-seeking and self-fashioning'.⁸ As in the proem to Book II of *The Faerie Queene*, the tracing of *terra incognita* offers a way of figuring the boundaries of the known, since 'of the world least part to vs is red' (II.pro.2). The association of a deserted landscape with conditions of unknowing, trial, and revelation, of course, is a familiar literary trope, epitomised by the frequent appearance of desert terrain as both symbol and geographical reality in the Old and New Testaments.⁹ For Spenser's purposes, the multitudinous spaces of testing present in *The Faerie Queene* expose the processes of his allegorical methods, showing their workings through

5 For the ancient 'comparison between the dressing of a field and writing' see Ernst Robert Curtius, *European Literature and the Latin Middle Ages*, trans. Willard R. Trask (London: Routledge and Kegan Paul, 1953), pp. 313–14. For Browne's rhetorical poise see Sharon Cadman Seelig, '"Speake, That I May See Thee": The Styles of Sir Thomas Browne', in *Sir Thomas Browne: The World Proposed*, ed. Reid Barbour and Claire Preston (Oxford: Oxford University Press, 2008), pp. 13–35 (p. 23).
6 Kevin Killeen, *Biblical Scholarship, Science and Politics in Early Modern England: Thomas Browne and the Thorny Place of Knowledge* (Aldershot: Ashgate, 2009), p. 8.
7 See John M. Steadman, *The Hill and the Labyrinth: Discourse and Certitude in Milton and His Near-Contemporaries* (Berkeley: University of California Press, 1984), pp. 1–16 and pp. 132–3.
8 Linda Gregerson, 'Protestant Erotics: Idolatry and Interpretation in Spenser's *Faerie Queene*', *ELH*, 58.1 (1991), 1–34, p. 16.
9 See Jacques Le Goff, 'The Wilderness in the Medieval West', in *The Medieval Imagination*, trans. Arthur Goldhammer (Chicago: University of Chicago Press, 1988; repr. 1992), pp. 47–59.

Movement and measurement 63

deliberate misdirection and mis-measurement.¹⁰ It is no coincidence, as Margaret W. Ferguson observes of the writing of St Augustine, that 'works which are thematically concerned with a loss of a "proper" place – in Augustine's case, the Heavenly City – should also be concerned with the problematic distinction between proper and figurative language'.¹¹ The nature of error is perversely generative and its progeny has the potential to carve out unexpected ways to travel.

This chapter is concerned with the representation of movement and measurement and explores the ways in which Spenser produces epistemological geographies in *The Faerie Queene*.¹² In several of the examples discussed, a percipient figure is seen to face a topographical limit or is halted by something that is beyond immediate resolution: an encounter that sometimes results in inertia and occasionally in unprecedented motion. For Spenser's knights, mobility is a qualified virtue and, as William A. Oram has observed, Spenser's poem returns 'insistently to the idea of paralysis in its various forms – stalemated battle, imprisonment, amazement, astonishment, encumbrance'.¹³ Of additional interest are figures who offer directional aid, some of whom offer their hands in truth and friendship and others whose purpose is not manuduction but betrayal. After all, the act of questing (from the Latin, *quaerere*), is one of seeking, not finding, and the figurative representation and negotiation of *terrae incognitae* serve as an object lesson in processes of 'becoming'.¹⁴ The chapter begins by introducing the relationship understood to exist between spatial form, movement, and the representation of cognition in

10 For Spenser as one of the period's 'extraordinary agnotologists' see Katherine Eggert, *Disknowledge: Literature, Alchemy, and the End of Humanism in Renaissance England* (Philadelphia: University of Pennsylvania Press, 2015), p. 6.
11 Margaret W. Ferguson, 'Saint Augustine's Region of Unlikeness: The Crossing of Exile and Language', in *Innovations of Antiquity*, ed. Ralph Hexter and Daniel Selden (London: Routledge, 1992), pp. 69–94 (p. 69). See also Kenneth Gross, *Spenserian Poetics: Idolatry, Iconoclasm, and Magic* (Ithaca: Cornell University Press, 1985), pp. 64–5 and pp. 68–9. For this problem in secular terms see Catherine Nicholson, *Uncommon Tongues: Eloquence and Eccentricity in the English Renaissance* (Philadelphia: University of Pennsylvania Press, 2014), pp. 1–18.
12 For how the poem invites contemplation of upper and lower limits and the overlap of temporal, political, and literary geographies see Wayne Erickson, *Mapping the Faerie Queene: Quest Structures and the World of the Poem* (New York: Garland Publishing, 1996), pp. 59–86.
13 William A. Oram, 'Spenserian Paralysis', *SEL*, 41.1 (2001), 49–70, p. 51.
14 See Catherine Bates, *Masculinity and the Hunt: Wyatt to Spenser* (Oxford: Oxford University Press, 2013). As she observes, 'other words that derived from the same root – inquire, inquiry, inquest, inquisition, query, question, request, require, and so forth' are 'all activities that have a more abstract, cerebral, and epistemological air than the strictly physical business of trawling sweatily through the undergrowth' (p. 270).

the early modern period, and uses this as a contextual frame for reading the self-consciously mobile allegories of Spenser's poetry.[15] The final sections of the chapter focus on Spenser's Knight of Temperance in order to consider Guyon's place in Book II as a figure, if an ultimately flawed one, of moral and spatial perspectival orientation in a contingent world. In making this argument, I build on the models of active reading already outlined and further explore the extent to which allegory is an implicitly spatial practice.

## Towards an epistemological geography

The burden carried by the allegorical traveller is a particularly cumbersome one. The kinetic energy of a travelling figure is frequently placed at the heart of allegorical narratives, where, with no place of steadfastness or measure of constant guidance, they play an organising role. Whether shaping narratives that imitate the labour of travail, or participating in the visionary mode associated with dream poetry, the traveller's movement allows for the introduction of new characters, landscapes, and situations.[16] Spatial orientation becomes a matter of existential condition underwritten by a transformative desire for discovery, certainty, and eventual stasis: a legacy of how the Bible repeatedly connects living in the world to a state of exile and the attainment of salvation to a journey ended.[17] As Edwards observes, the ethics of travel, and the writing filled with semi-truths and tall tales associated with it, had always occupied a questionable history: 'all travel', he writes, 'is a mark of the loss of ... happiness, a mark of discontent, and a restless search for what has been lost', referencing the Fall, the marking and wanderings of Cain, and the Exodus.[18] Within Spenser's imagination, the traditional movements

---

15 My approach to representations of mobility, embodiment, and the geographical imagination is informed by Tim Cresswell's work in *On the Move: Mobility in the Modern Western World* (New York: Routledge, 2006).
16 See Angus Fletcher, *Allegory: The Theory of a Symbolic Mode* (Ithaca: Cornell University Press, 1964), pp. 36–7 and John Erskine Hankins, *Source and Meaning in Spenser's Allegory: A Study of The Faerie Queene* (Oxford: Clarendon Press, 1971).
17 See Dee Dyas, *Pilgrimage in Medieval English Literature 700–1500* (Cambridge: D.S. Brewer, 2001), p. 13 and Marco Nievergelt, *Allegorical Quests from Deguileville to Spenser* (Cambridge: D.S. Brewer, 2012), p. 15. See also Jeffrey N. Peters, *Mapping Discord: Allegorical Cartography in Early Modern French Writing* (Newark: University of Delaware Press, 2004), pp. 190–1 and Gay Clifford, *The Transformations of Allegory* (London: Routledge and Kegan Paul, 1974), p. 11.
18 Philip Edwards, *Sea-Mark: The Metaphorical Voyage, Spenser to Milton* (Liverpool: Liverpool University Press, 1997), p. 5.

employed in representing the conflicts of the soul, or *psychomachia*, meet the temporal challenges of bodily travail.

In Desiderius Erasmus's *The Praise of Folly*, which appeared in an English translation by Thomas Chaloner in 1549, the personification of Folly is highly alert to the absurdity of the play between worldliness and wisdom, and to the nature of misleading yearnings that result only in vagrancy.[19] As she suggests, a compulsive restlessness accompanies the foolish, which only ever results in misguided speculation:

> This man loketh for a new worlde. That man compasseth some depe drifte in his head. Some one hath an especiall devocion to goe to Jerusalem, to Rome, or to sainct *James in Galice*, levyng his wife and children succourlesse in the meane while at home.[20]

The descriptive list of the will to search out new situations indiscriminately, to plot the realisation of illusory dreams, and to leave homelands behind in order to chase the false promises of pilgrimage, illustrates the slippages that occur between literal and epistemological travail. The pilgrim is criticised for leaving his home in search of something he will fail to find and the self-proclaimed wise man's 'knowlage and cunnyng' is dismissed as intemperate hubris; one should get one's home and one's mind in order, Folly seems to suggest, before venturing forth to confront the vanities of the wide world.

In one copy of Erasmus's work, an edition printed by Johannes Froben in Basel in 1515, an inked marginal illustration by Hans Holbein the Younger appears drawn around the printed marginal note that singles out 'Qui sacra visunt loca' or 'those who visit sacred places'. The pilgrim heads unquestioningly in the direction indicated by empty wayside shrine (see Figure 4).[21]

The travel indicated across the space of the page to the left exposes the pilgrim's spiritual lack to ridicule: this is a sinister journey that visually abjures the finding of the 'right way'.[22] Although Spenser's use of

19 See Richard Helgerson, 'The Folly of Maps and Modernity', in *Literature, Mapping and the Politics of Space in Early Modern Britain*, ed. Andrew Gordon and Bernhard Klein (Cambridge: Cambridge University Press, 2001), pp. 241–62. For the challenges of worldliness see Ayesha Ramachandran, *The Worldmakers: Global Imagining in Early Modern Europe* (Chicago: University of Chicago Press, 2015), pp. 1–21.
20 Desiderius Erasmus, *The Praise of Folie*, trans. Thomas Chaloner (London, 1549), sig. K3ᵛ.
21 See Erika Michael, *The Drawings by Hans Holbein the Younger for Erasmus' 'Praise of Folly'* (New York: Garland, 1985), p. 405.
22 See Erich Auerbach's observations concerning Sir Calogrenant's discovery of the 'right way' in Chrétien de Troyes's romance *Yvain*. In response to the knight's recollection that he 'turned off the main road to a path on the right, full of thorns and briars, leading

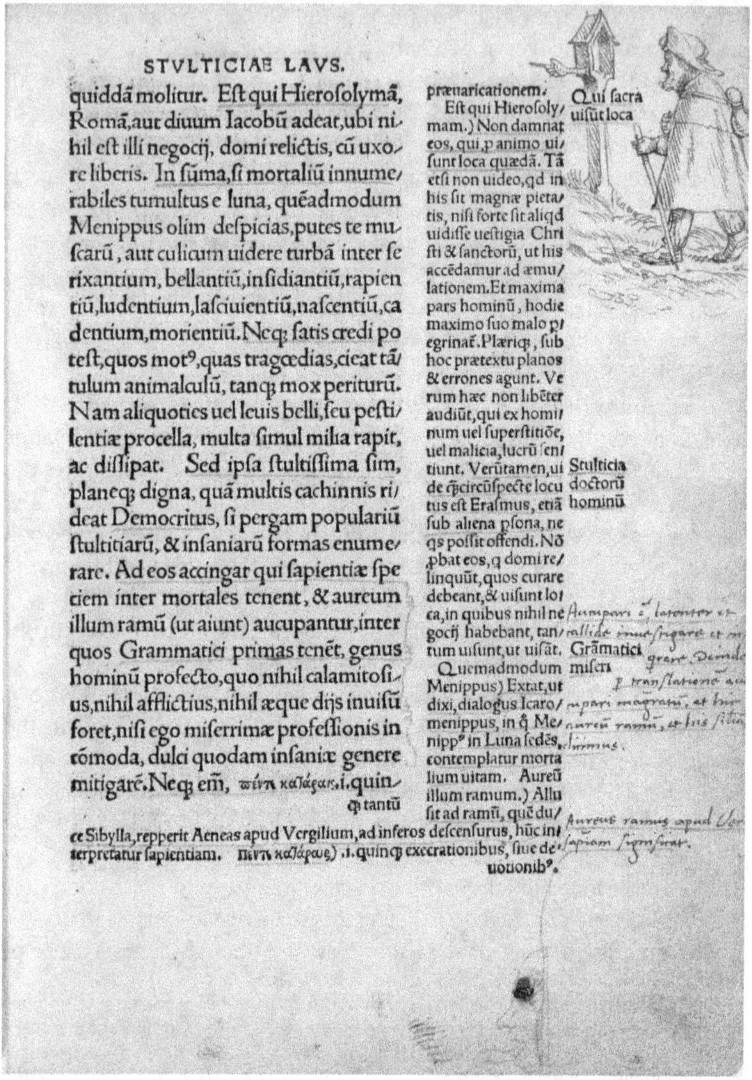

STVLTICIAE LAVS.

quiddā molitur. Est qui Hierosolymā, Romā, aut diuum Iacobū adeat, ubi nihil est illi negocij, domi relictis, cū uxore liberis. In sūma, si mortaliū innumerabiles tumultus e luna, quéadmodum Menippus olim despicias, putes te muscarū, aut culicum uidere turbā inter se rixantium, bellantiū, insidiantiū, rapientiū, ludentium, lasciuientiū, nascentiū, cadentium, morientiū. Neqɜ satis credi potest, quos mot⁹, quas tragœdias, cieat tātulum animalculū, tanqɜ mox periturū. Nam aliquoties uel leuis belli, seu pestilentiæ procella, multa simul milia rapit, ac dissipat. Sed ipsa stultissima sim, planeqɜ digna, quā multis cachinnis rideat Democritus, si pergam populariū stultitiarū, & insaniarū formas enumerare. Ad eos accingar qui sapientiæ speciem inter mortales tenent, & aureum illum ramū (ut aiunt) aucupantur, inter quos Grammatici primas tenēt, genus hominū profecto, quo nihil calamitosius, nihil afflictius, nihil æque dijs inuisū foret, nisi ego miserrimæ professionis in cōmoda, dulci quodam insaniæ genere mitigarē. Neqɜ eṁ, πάντα καθάρας. i. quinqɜ tantū

præuaricationem.
Est qui Hierosoly/
mam.) Non damnat
eos, qui, p animo ui/
sunt loca quædā. Tā
etsi non uideo, qd in
his sit magnæ pietatis, nisi forte sit aliqd
uidisse uestigia Christi & sanctorū, ut his
accēdamur ad æmu/
lationem. Et maxima
pars hominū, hodie
maximo suo malo p/
egrināt. Plæriqɜ, sub
hoc prætextu planos
& errones agunt. Verum hæc non libēter
audiūt, qui ex homi/
num uel superstitiōe,
uel malicia, lucrū sentiunt. Verūtamen, ui Stulticia
de qɜcircūspecte locu doctorū
tus est Erasmus, etiā hominū
sub aliena psona, ne
qs possit offendi. Nō
pbat eos, q domi re/
linquūt, quos curare
debeant, & uisunt loca, in quibus nihil ne
gocij habebant, tan/
tum uisunt, ut uisat. Grāmatici
Quemadmodum miseri
Menippus) Extat, ut
dixi, dialogus Icaro/
menippus, in q̄ Me
nipp⁹ in Luna sedēs,
contemplatur mortalium uitam. Aureū
illum ramum.) Allu
sit ad ramū, quē du/

Qui sacra
uisūt loca

ce Sibylla, repperit Aeneas apud Vergilium, ad inferos descensurus, hūc interpretatur sapientiam. πάντα καθάρως . i. quinqɜ execrationibus, siue deuotionib⁹.

*Figure 4* Hans Holbein the Younger. Inked illustration of a pilgrim from a single copy of Erasmus's *Moriae Encomium* (Basel, 1515), sig. M4ʳ. The volume was owned by the scholar and schoolmaster Oswald Myconius, who was a friend of Erasmus.

directional allegory is typically more subtle, the same critical charge that fuels Folly's mockery of travellers and Holbein's illuminating satire could also be levelled at the Redcrosse Knight at the beginning of the Legend of Holiness.[23] On his first meeting with Archimago, who appears in disguise as a hermit, Redcrosse is keen to hear tidings of 'straunge aduentures, which abroad did pas' (I.i.30). Like Erasmus's foolish traveller, he is one who 'compasseth some depe drifte' in his head; the road to adventure curls out pleasingly in front of him, networked by the ghosts of crossroads, labyrinths, and highways. His attempts to find the 'right way' are typified by errancy, and by what Patricia A. Parker describes as 'its associations – mental, geographical, and narrative – with varieties of "de-viation"', the straying from the way.[24]

Spenser's mobile allegories famously draw on classical ideas regarding the relationship between cognition and virtue, and the poet's interest in Platonism has been widely discussed, particularly in relation to the attitudes expressed in his poetry concerning the nature of love and beauty, appearance and being, cosmic order, and the soul.[25] The poet's allusions to Plato's *Republic*, *Timaeus*, and *Phaedrus*, for example, are well-documented;[26] however, in terms of the way that Spenser associates particular kinds of movement with both ethical development and the accrual of knowledge, the dialogues that feature the words or ventriloquised presence of the sophist Protagoras also seem present in his thought, in a manner almost wholly unattended by critics.[27] Both

---

to a thick forest', Auerbach notes that the description presents 'a strange indication of locality when, as in this case, it is used absolutely'. See 'The Knight with the Lion', in *The Complete Romances of Chrétien de Troyes*, trans. David Staines (Bloomington: Indiana University Press, 1993), pp. 257–338 (p. 259) and Auerbach, *Mimesis*, trans. Willard R. Trask (Garden City, NY: Doubleday, 1957), p. 112.

23 For the crossroads motif in classical philosophy and literature see S.K. Heninger, Jr., *Touches of Sweet Harmony* (San Marino: The Huntington Library, 1974), pp. 269–70 and p. 356.

24 Patricia A. Parker, *Inescapable Romance: Studies in the Poetics of a Mode* (Princeton: Princeton University Press, 1979), p. 7.

25 See Robert Ellrodt, *Neoplatonism in the Poetry of Spenser* (Geneva: E. Droz, 1960); Elizabeth Bieman, *Plato Baptized: Towards the Interpretation of Spenser's Mimetic Fictions* (Toronto: University of Toronto Press, 1988); Jon A. Quitslund, *Spenser's Supreme Fiction: Platonic Natural Philosophy and The Faerie Queene* (Toronto: University of Toronto Press, 2001); the special edition of *Spenser Studies*, 24 (2009); and Kenneth Borris, *Visionary Spenser and the Poetics of Early Modern Platonism* (Oxford: Oxford University Press, 2017).

26 See Jon A. Quitslund, 'Platonism', in *SEnc*, pp. 546–8.

27 Charles G. Osgood notes, however, how Spenser's Braggadochio personifies Plato's thoughts on cowardice in *Protagoras*. See 'Comments on the Moral Allegory of *The Faerie Queene*', *MLN*, 46.8 (1931), 502–7.

*Protagoras* and *Theaetetus* were translated from Greek into Latin by Marsilio Ficino in the 1460s and printed in his *Platonis Opera Omnia* of 1484, and both dialogues use the metaphorical language of space and embodied motion to discuss the nature of perception and cognition.[28] In *Theaetetus*, for example, Socrates's recollection that Protagoras was known for the puzzling maxim that 'Man is the measure of all things' is widely recognised as a tantalisingly provocative fragment of sophistry.[29] As Paula Blank summarises, 'Protagoras's *homo mensura* – the man measure – determines "truth" or "reality" according to the scope and scale of human cognizance and capacity'; yet, as discussed in *Theaetetus*, the nature of sense perception is relative and fallible, more attuned to the seeming of things rather than their being.[30] A more literal interpretation, as Witold Kula comments, concerns the formation of metrological concepts in response to the dimensions of the human body: first man used 'his foot, arm, finger, palm of his hand, outstretched arms, pace' to measure the world around him, and then developed 'units of measure derived from the conditions, objective, and outcomes of human labor'.[31] For the purposes of the readings that follow, it is particularly interesting that Socrates describes himself in *Theaetetus* as '*atopos* – as strange or, literally, placeless': a description that, as Paul Stern observes, compounds the dialogue's sense that 'the available knowledge of the soul, of the human things' is itself '*a-topos*'.[32]

When Spenser's Neoplatonic interests are put in dialogue with medieval rhetorical and allegorical traditions, the steps taken by Spenser's knights can be read as part of an orientating strategy, which is also related to the process of composition. For allegorists such as Guillaume de Deguileville and William Langland, whose dream vision *Piers Plowman* is structured by division into steps or 'passus', pilgrim figures measure

---

28 See James Hankins, *Plato in the Italian Renaissance*, Vol. 1 (Leiden: Brill, 1990), pp. 300–1. For a literary analysis of this pair of dialogues see Harry Berger, Jr., 'Facing Sophists: Socrates' Charismatic Bondage in *Protagoras*', *Representations*, 5 (1984), 66–91. Neither critic discusses Spenser in these terms.
29 Plato, *Theaetetus*, trans. M.J. Levett and Myles Burnyeat, in *Plato: Complete Works*, ed. John M. Cooper (Indianapolis: Hackett, 1997), pp. 157–234 (152a, p. 169).
30 Paula Blank, *Shakespeare and the Mismeasure of Renaissance Man* (Ithaca: Cornell University Press, 2006), p. 1.
31 Witold Kula, *Measures and Men*, trans. R. Szreter (Princeton: Princeton University Press, 2014), p. 24 and p. 5.
32 Paul Stern, *Knowledge and Politics in Plato's Theaetetus* (Cambridge: Cambridge University Press, 2008), p. 67. See *Theaetetus*, 149a, p. 166. See also Pierre Hadot, *What is Ancient Philopsophy?*, trans. Michael Chase (Cambridge, MA: Harvard University Press, 2004), p. 30.

space via lived experience, in opposition to the remote divine perspective offered by what we might associate with a katascopic view.[33] The potential for such a change in perspective can be thought of as a rhetorical move, as Mary Carruthers explains: a distinction made between *ductus*, which refers to 'the way that a composition guides a person to its various goals' and *skopos*, the destination or 'aerial view'.[34] 'The paths of man are directed by the Lord', suggests Psalm 37, 'for the Law of his God is in his heart, and his steppes shall not slide';[35] yet, Spenser's knights typically move in itinerant ways through 'saluage forrests, and in deserts wide,/ ... Withouten comfort, and withouten guide' (IV.vii.2). By emphasising the scarcity of divine guidance and overview, Spenser typically presents the orientation of his knights as a fraught and bodily process. To borrow Anne Whiston Spirn's perception of how landscape description is reliant upon anthropomorphic terms, the 'sense of up and down, forward and backward, left and right is determined by the form of the body that perceives them: by head and feet, face and back, by the distinction between one eye, one arm, one breast, one leg, and the other'.[36] In Spenser's allegory, instrumental bodies operate as measures of both physical and metaphysical progress, tracing connections between microcosm and macrocosm and creating the fiction of a measurable world.[37]

## Bodies and minds in motion

Archetypal images of orientational failure populate the first book of *The Faerie Queene* and narrative movement is halting in spite of Redcrosse's initial propulsive enthusiasm. The blind gatekeeper Ignaro, for example, whom Arthur encounters in Orgoglio's castle, may function primarily

33 Nievergelt, *Allegorical Quests*, p. 106.
34 Carruthers, *The Craft of Thought*, p. 78 and p. 79. Similar rhetorical moves frame Michel de Certeau's analysis of two distinct narrative techniques: the 'map' and the 'tour', or 'either *seeing* (the knowledge of an order of places) or *going* (spatializing actions)'. See *The Practice of Everyday Life*, trans. Steven Rendall (Berkeley: University of California Press, 1984), p. 119. A similar distinction is made by Bernhard Klein, who observes how the map presents a 'totality of spatial relations' and the itinerary explores space 'through movement and operative action'. See *Maps and the Writing of Space in Early Modern England and Ireland* (Basingstoke: Palgrave, 2001), p. 142. For the effect in romance see Parker, *Inescapable Romance*, p. 20.
35 *The Bible* (London, 1576), Psalm 37:23 and 31.
36 Anne Whiston Spirn, *The Language of Landscape* (New Haven: Yale University Press, 1998), p. 37.
37 See Catherine Gimelli Martin, 'Spenser's Neoplatonic Geography of the Passions: Mapping Allegory in the "Legend of Temperance", *Faerie Queene*, Book II', *Spenser Studies*, 24 (2009), 269–307, pp. 272–4.

as a caustic allegory for the blindness of the Catholic Church, but his defining retrograde motion also serves as a broader object lesson in the limiting ways of ignorance:

> At last with creeping crooked pace forth came
>   An old old man, with beard as white as snow,
>   That on a staffe his feeble steps did frame,
>   And guyde his wearie gate both too and fro;
>   For his eye sight him fayled long ygo,
>   And on his arme a bounch of keyes he bore,
>   The which vnused rust did ouergrow:
>   Those were the keyes of euery inner dore,
> But he could not them vse, but kept them still in store.
>
> But very vncouth sight was to behold,
>   How he did fashion his vntoward pace,
>   For as he forward mooud his footing old,
>   So backward still was turnd his wrincled face,
>   Vnlike to men, who euer as they trace,
>
> Both feet and face one way are wont to lead.
>   This was the aunciet keeper of that place,
>   And foster father of the Gyaunt dead;
>   His name *Ignaro* did his nature right aread. (I.viii.30–1)

As keeper of the keys to 'euery inner dore' (I.viii.30), his ruined status as a type of demi-Janus embodies only futility. Trapped by his own corruption he evokes both pathos, for he cannot use the keys he carries, and humour. His existence is 'vntoward': a playfully situated pun that is 'preposterous', or that puts 'behind for before'.[38] He can but answer Arthur's increasingly frustrated questions concerning what lies beyond him with the inevitably negative response that 'he could not tell' (I.viii.32). In an echo of the criticism directed towards the interpreters of the Old Testament in Luke's gospel, Ignaro has locked his own doors against him: 'for ye have taken away the keye of knowledge: ye entred not in your selves, and they that came in, ye forbade'.[39] Yet, a reader should not look

---

38 Patricia A. Parker explains that '*Preposterous* – from *posterus* (after or behind) and *prae* (in front or before) – connotes a reversal of "post" for "pre," behind for before, back for front, second for first, end or sequel for beginning'. See *Shakespeare from the Margins: Language, Culture, Context* (Chicago: University of Chicago Press, 1996), pp. 21–2.
39 *The Bible* (London, 1576), Luke 11:52, fol. 32ʳ. A.C. Hamilton observes that Ignaro's defining retrograde motion references Isaiah 44:25, namely God's declaration that he will 'turne the wise men backward, and make their knowledge foolishnes'. See *FQ*, note to I.viii.31 (p. 108).

too unkindly on the stumbling figure. For Arthur, who 'ghest his nature by his countenance' (I.viii.34), the lesson learned reverberates beyond its immediate location.

Spenser often brings the spaces of *The Faerie Queene* into being using the progress recorded by his protagonists' feet, creating the semblance of geographical processes though the interaction of body and world.[40] As shown in Chapter 1, Redcrosse follows ready-made but perilous paths, traced by footprints through the wandering wood: he follows what Robert Macfarlane in *The Old Ways* calls 'the habits of a landscape' and 'acts of consensual making'.[41] Such habits, of course, can be misleading, as the 'broad high way that led,/ All bare through peoples feet' to the ruinous House of Pride demonstrates (see I.iv.2). In a secular echo of St Augustine, Michel de Certeau's essay *Walking in the City* describes the act of moving on foot between places, having not yet arrived, as a way of reading and existing as if within a fallen world: 'To walk is to lack a place. It is the indefinite process of being absent and in search of a proper'.[42] For de Certeau, the appearance of footprints acts as a marker of both transience and permanence:

> They allow us to grasp only a relic set in the nowhen of a surface of projection. Itself visible, it has the effect of making invisible the operation that made it possible. These fixations constitute procedures for forgetting. The trace left behind is substituted for the practice. It exhibits the (voracious) property that the geographical system has of being able to transform action into legibility, but in doing so it causes a way of being in the world to be forgotten.[43]

The marks of past activity suggest quantifiable motion yet deny the possibility of fully recovering past actions: a loss that is concurrent with Spenser's refusal to provide his reader with a coherent overview of his fictional world. The drive to reconstitute presence, to search for 'a proper', and to give place and name to things that are '*a-topos*', runs throughout the 'nowhen' of *The Faerie Queene*. By omitting a wider 'geographical system', Spenser issues a challenge whereby any acts of reading must

---

40 In *Masculinity and the Hunt*, Bates contrasts Ignaro's motion with the 'orthopaedic exemplarity' of Guyon's 'forward' movement (see p. 274). Guyon, as Maureen Quilligan observes, is 'a curiously pedestrian knight'. See *Milton's Spenser: The Politics of Reading* (Ithaca: Cornell University Press, 1983), p. 61.
41 Robert Macfarlane, *The Old Ways: A Journey on Foot* (London: Penguin, 2012), p. 17.
42 De Certeau, *The Practice of Everyday Life*, p. 103. For St Augustine as the 'common progenitor of Spenserian romance and Lacan's … theory of signs and subjectivity' see Gregerson, 'Protestant Erotics', pp. 14–17.
43 De Certeau, *The Practice of Everyday Life*, p. 97.

occur without causing 'a way of being in the world to be forgotten'. As miniatures of Arthur's pressed grass, discussed below, such footprints offer material traces of the afterimage, not the action: a vision of a scattered self in transit, searching for a place of rest.[44] As commemorative sites, they prompt complex mental activity which involves both recollection and remaking.

The aesthetic choices of *The Faerie Queene* evidence Spenser's distrust of outward shows of religious fervour; however, in his images of traced paths, the poet incorporates elements of pilgrimage into his poem.[45] Spenser's Arthur seeks not the possession of empty relics but the living and tangible presence of glory, and to borrow Wes Williams's formulation,

> it is clear that the ideal Pilgrim is one who travels towards the visible trace of a now absent person, whether the bones of a saint or the marks of Christ's footsteps. The place is a sign at once of an absence ('He is not here', the angels said) and of presence ('This is where he was, and look, there's the mark', the guides say).[46]

The foot-worn paths initially followed by Redcrosse may eventually reveal their misdirective nature, but via encounters with multitudinous surrogates, anti-types, and warped refractions on the journey towards 'a proper', such anthropometric traces offer an allegory of the allegorical process itself. As in Walter Benjamin's evocative meditation on the aesthetics of baroque allegory, which values transience and fragmentary remains, 'allegories are, in the realm of thoughts, what ruins are in the realm of things'.[47] Allegory draws attention to negative space and to what has been lost in the process of figuration; for the belated reader, the material referent is grasped more readily than the abstract, but even this, which emerges from the allegorical landscape as a series of vestigial

---

44 For a reading of the paradigmatic works of St Augustine in such terms see Sandra Lee Dixon, *Augustine: The Scattered and Gathered Self* (St Louis, Missouri: Chalice Press, 1999).

45 See Nievergelt, *Allegorical Quests*, pp. 17–18 and Philip Edwards, *Pilgrimage and Literary Tradition* (Cambridge: Cambridge University Press, 2006). For changing attitudes towards sacred space and movement see Eamon Duffy, *The Stripping of the Altars: Traditional Religion in England, c. 1400–c. 1580* (New Haven: Yale University Press, 1992) and Alexandra Walsham, *The Reformation of the Landscape: Religion, Identity, and Memory in Early Modern Britain and Ireland* (Oxford: Oxford University Press, 2011).

46 Wes Williams, *Pilgrimage and Narrative in the French Renaissance: 'The Undiscovered Country'* (Oxford: Clarendon, 1998), p. 179.

47 Walter Benjamin, *The Origin of German Tragic Drama*, trans. John Osborne (London: NLB, 1977), p. 178.

marks eroded by time and tide, often loses its stable surfaces owing to the commotion of subsequent centuries.[48]

As Mary Carruthers explains, the '"art of memory" is actually the "art of recollection"', and the 'crucial task of recollection is *investigatio*, "tracking down," a word related to *vestigia*, "tracks" or "footprints"'.[49] This has implications for *The Faerie Queene*'s narrative plotting as well as for the manner in which the poem's movements inhabit and retrace the ways of earlier works. Catherine Bates observes how Spenser's poem is tracked throughout with 'cyphers, marks, and indicative signs', which suggests that the 'investigation' of such footprints is also connected to the formation of literary traditions: the 'whole business of writing and reading poetry thus comes to be figured as an endless chase'.[50] As Spenser would have learned from Geoffrey Chaucer, his beloved literary forebear in whose 'footing' he claims to follow (IV.ii.34), an author of allegory has much to manipulate when depicting specific kinds of let or hindrance, particularly when measuring the efficacy of his own chosen modes.[51] In Chaucer's *House of Fame*, for example, a dream vision deeply concerned with the reputation of poets and poetry, the ekphrastic episode that details the dreamer's experience within and without the Temple of Venus offers a fascinating forerunner for several of Spenser's techniques: the search for 'a proper' gives way to unending pursuit.[52]

After Chaucer's poet-dreamer falls asleep he finds himself in a temple dedicated to the goddess Venus: a strange but splendid place all 'ymad of glas', and which presents the story of Dido and Aeneas engraved within its walls.[53] By crossing the threshold of the temple the dreamer enters an earlier narrative world, which appears in the dream as a three-dimensional memory-theatre writ large.[54] As the dreamer voices the narrative aloud, the architectural frame encloses him within its logic; yet,

---

48 See Burlinson, *Allegory, Space and the Material World*, p. 15.
49 Mary Carruthers, *The Book of Memory: A Study of Memory in Medieval Culture* (Cambridge: Cambridge University Press, 1990; repr. 2008), p. 23.
50 Bates, *Masculinity and the Hunt*, p. 238 and p. 241.
51 See Carol A.N. Martin, 'Authority and the Defense of Fiction: Renaissance Poetics and Chaucer's *House of Fame*', in *Refiguring Chaucer in the Renaissance*, ed. Theresa M. Krier (Gainesville: University Press of Florida, 1998), pp. 40–65.
52 See T.S. Miller, 'Writing Dreams to Good: Reading as Writing and Writing as Reading in Chaucer's Dream Visions', *Style*, 45.3 (2011), 528–48.
53 Geoffrey Chaucer, *The House of Fame* in *The Riverside Chaucer*, pp. 347–73, line 120. All subsequent references are placed in the text.
54 For the importance of the 'architectural mnemonic' in medieval thought see Carruthers, *The Book of Memory*, pp. 71–9 and *The Craft of Thought*, pp. 16–21. See also Frances Yates, *The Art of Memory* (Chicago: University of Chicago Press, 1966).

once the tale has ended and its apparent moral has been learned, he is ejected into a wilderness, void of landmark and any living thing:

> 'A, Lord,' thoughte I, 'that madest us,
> Yet sawgh I never such noblesse
> Of ymages, ne such richesse,
> As I saugh graven in this chirche;
> But not wot I whoo did hem wirche,
> Ne where I am, ne in what contree.
> But now wol I goo out and see,
> Ryght at the wiket, yf y kan
> See owhere any stiryng man,
> That may me telle where I am.' (470-9)

When required to position himself outside the auspices of the temple's ordered narrative, the dreamer finds himself at a complete loss. With no knowledge of the work's maker or his present location, his desire to meet someone who will offer an orientating explanation is met instead with an expanse of desert: no cultivated, or 'eryd lond', this, but a trackless field of sand that opens up to his gaze like 'the desert of Lybye' (485, 488). Stranded thus, the dreamer expresses anxiety concerning the craftsman who framed the laborious 'wirche' out of which he has been ejected: another creator, counter to him 'that madest us'. When confronted by the abrupt transition, his concerns for his whereabouts are heightened, prompting a call for divine intercession: '"O Crist," thoughte I, "that art in blysse/ Fro fantome and illusion/ Me save!"' (492-4). The plea to be saved from 'fantome and illusion' reveals a conscious concern about the nature of the dream; yet, anticipating the endless quests of *The Faerie Queene*, Chaucer's poem is unfinished and its central protagonist is famously left unsatisfied. Its 'dynamic restlessness', as A.C. Spearing comments, 'is positively enhanced by incompleteness'.[55] The still-dreaming narrator may be temporarily rescued from the desert by a giant eagle, but at the poem's close he breaks off in mid-sentence, still chasing after an anonymous 'man of gret auctorite' (2158).

The dreamer's anxieties concerning the threatening proximity of illusion anticipate the false fantasies woven by Spenser's Archimago. For a Protestant poet concerned with the efficacy of images, 'fantome and illusion' are kept proximate in the allegorical verbal labyrinths by which

---

55 A.C. Spearing, *Medieval Dream-Poetry* (Cambridge: Cambridge University Press, 1976), p. 89.

the incautious can be misled.⁵⁶ Spenser chose not to make his sustained allegory a dream vision in its entirety but he was, as William Hazlitt writes, 'the poet of our waking dreams' and the memory of an unending oneiric chase haunts Spenser's poem, in which figures of authority are similarly difficult to find.⁵⁷ In the case of Arthur's dream of Gloriana, which occurs in the ninth canto of the first book of *The Faerie Queene*, the line between fitful wakefulness, guiding vision, and erotic fantasy is difficult to draw. The dream seems to be authoritative in that it appears to function for Arthur as enigmatic *somnium*, prophetic *visio*, and instructive *oraculum*;⁵⁸ yet, owing to its proximity to the false dreams or *insomnium* and *visum* crafted by Archimago to compromise Redcrosse, the recent memory of moral failure retains the taint of erotic apparition and illusory nightmare.⁵⁹ The vulnerability of the sleeper, whose mind is subject to ungoverned motion while the body is in stasis, becomes a vehicle for the poet to explore the ways in which the relationship between the rational soul and its attendant body can be compromised.⁶⁰ For all Arthur's promised magnificence, an ascent above the labyrinth is unforthcoming.

Arthur enters Spenser's narrative as someone who is himself '*a-topos*', in that the circumstances of his birth and ancestry are hidden from him as a 'thing without the compas of [his] witt' (I.ix.3). Yet, his recollection of the period preceding his slumbers offers a description of a world in which self and cosmos exist in collusion:

> For on a day prickt forth with iollitiee
> Of looser life, and heat of hardiment,
> Raunging the forest wide on courser free,
> The fields, the floods, the heauens with one consent
> Did seeme to laugh on me, and fauour mine intent. (I.ix.12)

Having previously been wearied 'with ... sports' (I.ix.13) rather than with the labour of questing, post-dream Arthur is tasked with reorienting his

---

56 See Gregerson, 'Protestant Erotics', pp. 11–12.
57 William Hazlitt, 'Lecture II: On Chaucer and Spenser', in *Lectures on the English Poets* (London: Taylor and Hessey, 1818), pp. 39–85 (p. 85).
58 See Spearing, *Medieval Dream-Poetry*, pp. 8–11 and pp. 73–89 and Maria Ruvoldt, *The Italian Renaissance Imagery of Inspiration* (Cambridge: Cambridge University Press, 2004), p. 15.
59 See Isabel G. MacCaffrey, *Spenser's Allegory: The Anatomy of Imagination* (Princeton: Princeton University Press, 1976), pp. 4–6. See also Parker, *Inescapable Romance*, pp. 83–6.
60 See Garrett Sullivan, Jr., *Sleep, Romance and Human Embodiment* (Cambridge: Cambridge University Press, 2012), pp. 29–46.

movements so that play becomes purposeful. Famously, when he awakes from his reverie, Gloriana is gone, 'her place deuoyd,/ And nought but pressed gras where she had lyen' (I.ix.15). In the impression made upon the 'verdant gras' (I.ix.13), her fugitive presence is given temporary spatial form in the afterimage, an absence as real as the 'unseen city' of Cleopolis: a version of de Certeau's 'proper' that occupies the *terra incognita* at the heart of Faery land.[61] In David Lee Miller's reading, Gloriana's utopian combination of 'desirability and ... terminal elusiveness' make her 'what we might call a topos of ectopia, or being-out-of-place, the radical of chivalric errancy'.[62] For Chaucer's dreamer, the nowhere of the desert expanse exceeds the character's ability to perceive its magnitude; for Spenser's Arthur, the vision of Gloriana creates a personal *terra incognita* that takes both external and internalised form in the allegory.[63]

Furthermore, the imprint made by Gloriana's body provides a measure of the strange interactions between the material world and its presence in Spenser's fabricated dreams and allegories. The existence of the 'pressed gras' and the way that Arthur weeps 'with watry eyen' to mark the place are achingly tangible; yet, these material traces serve only to delineate absence. Spenser's allegory frequently troubles the boundaries between cognition and materiality and the episode demonstrates what Kenneth Gross has described as a recurrent feature of Spenser's poem, whereby 'even small traces of allegorical expression' seem to force 'the world into new forms around them, hollowing out or animating spaces once solid'.[64] Gross's reading of allegory emphasises its possession of kinetic energy, whereby the new forms produced constantly combine mind, movement, and matter.[65]

61 Elizabeth J. Bellamy, *Translations of Power: Narcissism and the Unconscious in Epic History* (Ithaca: Cornell University Press, 1992), p. 50. See also Matthew Woodcock, *Fairy in The Faerie Queene: Renaissance Elf-Fashioning and Elizabethan Myth-Making* (Aldershot: Ashgate, 2004), pp. 88–102.
62 David Lee Miller, *The Poem's Two Bodies: The Poetics of the 1590 Faerie Queene* (Princeton: Princeton University Press, 1988), p. 139.
63 For the relationship between the 'seen and the unseen' as a point of religious doctrine see James A. Knapp, *Image Ethics in Shakespeare and Spenser* (New York: Palgrave Macmillan 2011), pp. 82–3.
64 Kenneth Gross, 'The Postures of Allegory', in *Edmund Spenser: Essays on Culture and Allegory*, ed. Jennifer Klein Morrison and Matthew Greenfield (Aldershot: Ashgate, 2000), pp. 167–79 (p. 167).
65 See Judith H. Anderson, *Reading the Allegorical Intertext: Chaucer, Spenser, Shakespeare, Milton* (New York: Fordham University Press, 2008), p. 5 and Christopher Burlinson, *Allegory, Space and the Material World in the Writings of Edmund Spenser* (Cambridge: D.S. Brewer, 2006), p. 15.

This combination of mental and material labour comes into focus in Spenser's representation of movement as both travel and *travail*. In *Theaetetus*, Socrates famously likens himself to a midwife, who helps his interlocutors to determine whether their thoughts and ideas have come to full term, or whether their mind 'is being delivered of a phantom, that is, an error, or a fertile truth'.[66] In Socrates's playful discussion, cognitive offspring often turn out to be mere 'wind-eggs', and as Stern observes, as 'an inducer of perplexity, Socrates causes those who previously had a way to lose it, to be placed in *aporia*. Such questioning and the resultant perplexity, Socrates admits, is painful: hence, the association with labor pains'.[67] In Spenser's allegory, the travails of cognition are similarly connected with space and embodied movement: ways are lost and motion is effortful.[68] Thoughts and dreams can be written in restless flesh and, for Arthur, the experience of meeting Gloriana changes him both physically and mentally, as if his muscle memory must become his guide. The narrator emphasises the ways in which Arthur's body reacts to what has been lost, accenting not the immaterial nature of thoughts and dreams, but their dependence on the body of the thinker:

> From that day forth I lou'd that face diuyne;
> From that day forth I cast in carefull mynd,
> To seeke her out with labor, and long tyne,
> And neuer vowd to rest, till her I fynd,
> Nyne monethes I seek in vain yet ni'll that vow unbynd. (I.ix.15)

To 'cast in carefull mynd' suggests a variety of actions owing to the manifold interpretive possibilities of the word 'cast'. If the most prevalent meaning, that of throwing, is taken, Arthur might be thought of as casting a fathoming line, or anchor, into his unconscious as if his mind is itself the space into which he must direct his search. Simultaneously, an outwards and physical journey is suggested by reading 'cast' as a means of reckoning or calculating actions, or even 'forecasting' what is to come: to 'cast' is 'to resolve in the mind, devise, contrive, purpose, plan'. Finally, the poet's use of the word 'cast' to describe Arthur's resolve suggests that his 'careful mynd' is subjected to a form-giving action, whereby

---

66 Plato, *Theaetetus*, 150c, p. 167.
67 Stern, *Knowledge and Politics in Plato's Theaetetus*, p. 67.
68 See Mary Thomas Crane's argument that a 'consequence of the embodied brain is the dependence of thought on kinaesthetic and spatial experiences of embodiment'. See 'Surface, Depth and the Spatial Imaginary: A Cognitive Reading of *The Political Unconscious*', *Representations*, 108.1 (2009), 76–97 (p. 79).

malleable substance takes on solid shape.⁶⁹ The prince's description of his memory, for example, recalls Socrates's description in *Theaetetus* of how the mind preserves images like soft wax retains the impression of a seal.⁷⁰ And later, when Spenser writes of Arthur as of one 'whose minde did trauell as with chylde' (IV.ix.17), we see Spenser make the same analogy between the condition of doubt, *aporia*, or unknowing, and the potential agony of travail. Within Spenser's poem, which continually blends categories of experience, Redcrosse's pricking is refashioned as Arthur's 'labour' and the image of voyaging is combined with the agony of childbirth: the product of 'nyne monethes' gestation.⁷¹

In the quest prompted by the vision, Gloriana's penumbral attendance is only glimpsed through veiled surrogates and antitypes: a series of impressions that concurs with Paul Piehler's observation that 'fundamentally the quest of the visionary is for a principle of authority, usually manifested as a *potentia*': *potentia* being a goddess or other personified authority situated in a specific locus, usually of sacred import.⁷² Although Spenser's Arthur may wake from his dream, it is the remembered sight of Gloriana's 'face diuyne' that propels his quest; as in *The House of Fame* before it, the expected didactic dialogue with the figure of authority does not occur. Chaucer's 'man of gret auctorite' is left unnamed and unidentified; however, as a result of her obscurity, Gloriana becomes fleetingly reminiscent of scriptural wisdom, searched for as if she is an elusive mistress, hid from every mortal gaze:

> The deepe sayeth she is not with me. The sea sayeth she is not with me. ... From whence then commeth wisdome? and where is the place of understandinge? She is hid from the eies of al men living, yea, and from the foules of the ayre. Destruction and death saye: we have heard tell of her with our eares. But God seeth her way, and knoweth her place. For hee beholdeth the endes of the worlde, and looketh upon all that is under heaven. When he weyed the windes, and measured the waters: when he sette the rayne in order, and gave the mightie flouds a law.⁷³

---

69 See 'cast, v.' *OED Online*. Oxford University Press, June 2018 (last accessed 26 July 2018). See 1.6a, VI.38 and 41, VII.42, IX.49.
70 See Carruthers, *The Book of Memory*, p. 21. See Plato, *Theaetetus*, 191c–e, p. 212.
71 For Arthur as the physical embodiment of the 'immaterial ideas that the poem itself is designed to achieve' see Elizabeth Spiller, *Science, Reading, and Renaissance Literature* (Cambridge: Cambridge University Press, 2004; repr. 2005), pp. 77–80.
72 Paul Piehler, *The Visionary Landscape: A Study in Medieval Allegory* (London: Edward Arnold, 1971), p. 20.
73 *The Bible in English* (London, 1568), Job 28:C–D, fol. 157ᵛ. For Gloriana as a sapiential figure see Jeffrey P. Fruen, 'The Faery Queen Unveiled? Five Glimpses of Gloriana', *Spenser Studies*, 11 (1994), 53–87.

As Job's words suggest, the wisdom of God, as measurer and ecological lawmaker, cannot be located: it is '*a-topos*'. The deep and the sea voice their lack of knowledge, and the alternative prospects offered by the surface of the land and by suspension in the sky offer no hold to gain a better perspective. The use of personification enables the fiction that Wisdom is something to be sought after, prompting a game of hide and seek written across the cosmos. Seen only by God, she is strangely hidden, not by the mysteries of the natural world but at their peripheries, and certainly beyond the compass of Job's failing, yet visionary, mind. Singing of herself in Ecclesiasticus, it is Wisdom alone who has 'gone round about the compasse of heaven' and who has 'walked in the botome of the depth'.[74] In the absence of Gloriana's presence, the landscape of Spenser's allegory takes on a similarly benighted cast and the task set is to navigate the epistemological geography provided. As an untested youth, Arthur may charge through fields, floods, and heavens that favour him 'with one consent', but the terms of his quest remake his perception of a world that he knows and that knows him.

### Walking in the world

In Plato's dialogue *Theaetetus*, while deliberating Protagoras's maxim, *homo mensura*, Socrates sets up a comparison between the way that physical exercise changes the state of the body and the way that the accrual of knowledge improves the condition of the soul:

> SOCRATES: And isn't it also true that bodily condition deteriorates with rest and idleness? While by exertion and motion it can be preserved for a long time?
> THEAETETUS: Yes.
> SOCRATES: And what about the condition of the soul? Isn't it by learning and study, which are motions, that the soul gains knowledge and is preserved and becomes a better thing? Whereas in a state of rest, that is, when it will not study or learn, it not only fails to acquire knowledge but forgets what it has already learned?[75]

To return to the eighth canto of the Legend of Holiness and the encounter with Ignaro, a reader of Spenser will recognise Redcrosse's fate while held captive by Orgoglio in this exchange. More so than for any other of Spenser's protagonists, Redcrosse's prowess is measured by his ability to preserve forward motion. His lowest point, both in terms of the poem's

74 *The Bible* (London, 1576), Ecclesiasticus 24:8, fol. 46ʳ.
75 Plato, *Theaetetus*, 153b–c, p. 170.

geography and the moral allegory, comes with his imprisonment in the unfathomed dungeon, where the effect of stasis on his person is catastrophic. For Arthur, who finally finds the door behind which Redcrosse has been held captive for thrice 'three Moones' (I.viii.38), full comprehension of the location is enough to make 'trembling horrour' run 'though euery ioynt' of his body (I.viii.39). The sight of the broken knight could even 'make a stony hart his hap to rew' (I.viii.41). With his 'eies deepe sunck in hollow pits', 'rawbone armes' that 'were clene consum'd', and brittle 'flesh shronk vp like withered flowres' (I.viii.41), Redcrosse's loss of cognitive function, or temporary inability to distinguish knowledge and virtue from folly and pride, is figured allegorically in terms of complete muscular waste. The emotional shock experienced by Arthur when he witnesses Redcrosse's state of living death suggests the power of the physical and emotional affect produced by proximity to a moment of extreme moral failure. In closing his soul to the acquisition of virtue, Redcrosse shares in the fleshly condition of Idleness, through whose 'lustlesse limbs …/ A shaking feuer raignd continually' and who functions as a figure of absolute directional ineptitude: 'the wayne was very euill ledd,/ When such an one had guiding of the way,/ That knew not, whether right he went, or else astray' (I.iv.19–20).

In Spenser's allegory the cautionary words of Socrates concerning the preservation of 'exertion and motion' function not in isolation but alongside important biblical passages. When entrapped by Errour in the first canto, Redcrosse is constricted by her 'huge traine' which 'All suddenly about his body wound,/ That hand or foot to stirr he stroue in vaine' (I.i.18). This force, which anticipates his later imprisonment and wasting, can be recognised in the threats described by Baldad the Suhite as the punishments of the wicked in the Book of Job:

> The steps of his strength shalbe restrayned, and his owne counsel shall cast hym downe.
> For he is taken in the net by his feete, and he walketh upon the snares.
> The grenne shall take him by the heele, and the theefe shall come upon him. …
> His strength shalbe famine: and destruction shalbe readie at his side.
> It shall devour the partes of his skinne, and the first borne of death shall devour his strength.[76]

The snares are also recognisable as the 'subtile engins', 'craftie stales', and 'priuy spyals' set for Redcrosse by Archimago, 'that conning

---

76 *The Bible* (London, 1576), Job 18:7–13, fol. 212r.

Architect of cancred guyle' (II.i.1,3,4); yet, most important, perhaps, is the suggestion that it is the wicked man's 'owne counsel' that 'shall cast hym downe'. When Redcrosse's path is finally righted, the climax of the journey is made in the company of Contemplation, a 'father graue,/ Whose staggering steps' his 'steady hand doth lead,/ And shewes the way, his sinfull soule to saue' (I.x.51). The image is of manuduction, uniting 'labors long, and sad delay' (I.x.52) with a reliance upon a figure of authority: an exodus likened to the 'dry-foot' passage of the Israelites through the 'blood-red billowes' of the Red Sea to Mount Sinai (I.x.53). From the summit, Redcrosse is granted the vision of the New Jerusalem, 'a goodly Citty' accessed by 'a litle path, that was both steepe and long' (I.x.55). It is only when the knight has achieved a measure of the world's horizon that he is granted a utopian vision: his 'stupefied gaze' is 'led to its visual limit'.[77] The brief perspective achieved by his elevated body only confirms that he must once again face the world and 'shortly back returne vnto this place,/ To walke this way in Pilgrims poore estate' (I.x.64).

The poem, of course, delights in repetition, inversion, and doubling. In Book II, the transfer of the allegorical traveller's burden from the Knight of Holiness to the Knight of Temperance happens via the temporary tracing of a shared path: kinetic energy is carried over from Redcrosse to his successor, who must walk 'with equall steps' (II.i.7).[78] When Guyon consults with Archimago in an attempt to gain knowledge of Redcrosse's whereabouts, the enchanter immediately sees an opportunity to turn the knights against each other: 'by what meanes may I his footing tract' (II.i.12), Guyon innocently enquires, simultaneously renewing the connection between movement and embodied measurement.[79] The threat of Archimago's tricks and devices, which for Redcrosse functioned as a fully externalised part of Book I's allegorical landscape, are for Guyon internalised as the failing of his 'owne council'. When Redcrosse and Guyon finally meet and recognise each other, the course they run appears far from perfected:

---

77 Louis Marin, 'Frontiers of Utopia: Past and Present', *Critical Inquiry*, 19 (1993), 397–420, p. 397.

78 See Tiffany Jo Werth, *The Fabulous Dark Cloister: Romance in England after the Reformation* (Baltimore: Johns Hopkins University Press, 2011), pp. 117–20.

79 As Syrithe Pugh observes, the vocabulary of Guyon's question echoes the narrator's evocation of 'cognitive deficiency' in the proem to Book II. See 'Acrasia and Bondage: Guyon's Perversion of the Ovidian Erotic in Book II of *The Faerie Queene*', in *Edmund Spenser: New and Renewed Directions*, ed. J.B. Lethbridge (Madison: Fairleigh Dickinson University Press, 2006), pp. 153–94 (p. 154).

> Ioy may you haue, and euerlasting fame,
>   Of late most hard atchieu'ment by you donne,
>   For which enrolled is your glorious name
>   In heauenly Regesters aboue the Sunne,
>   Where you a Saint with Saints your Seat haue wonne:
>   But wretched we, where ye haue left your marke,
>   Must now anew begin, like race to ronne;
>   God guide thee, *Guyon*, well to end thy warke,
> And to the wished hauen bring thy weary barke. (II.i.32)

Ending as it does, the stanza privileges the agony of travail; bodily suffering is transformed into maritime labour that anticipates the book's final canto. Guyon's 'warke' suggests a kind of pain that throbs and aches,[80] where his 'like' journey gains little from his predecessor's accomplishments: once again, the word 'like' bears testimony to previous success while serving to break ground for future iterative struggle, from the 'first adventure' to the many that 'like succeed it may' (I.i.27). The stanza imagines a fictional world of constant work, 'warke', and motion, where repose can only be found in another, canonised, existence.

Of all Spenser's knights, Guyon is held the most responsible for his actions, owing to the presence of the over-watching Palmer, who stands steadfast as a figure of moral and spatial guidance, and of lessons learned over a lifetime of travail. As Davis observes, there is something intrinsically 'compass-like' in the way that the character of the Palmer directs his charge using his staff following the friendly parting of Redcrosse and Guyon:[81]

> Then *Guyon* forward gan his voyage make,
>   With his blacke Palmer, that him guided still.
>   Still he him guided ouer dale and hill,
>   And with his steedy staffe did point his way:
>   His race with reason, and with words his will,
>   From fowle intemperance he ofte did stay,
> And suffred not in wrath his hasty steps to stray. (II.i.34)

The duplication of the word 'still' (found at the end of the fourth and at the beginning of the fifth lines of the stanza as a whole) qualifies the way that movement is described. Guyon's voyage paradoxically incorporates stasis, where the forces propelling him are held in

---

80 See 'wark | warch, n.1.', *OED Online*. Oxford University Press, December 2015 (last accessed 18 December 2015).
81 Nick Davis, *Stories of Chaos: Reason and its Displacement in Early Modern English Narrative* (Aldershot: Ashgate, 1999), p. 84.

perfect balance, equal and opposing. He moves and is yet unmoved: an image that modifies the earlier failure of Redcrosse and refashions inertia as steadfastness, as opposed to atrophy and failure. As Michael Schoenfeldt explains, Spenser's allegory unites classical ethics with Protestant belief and the exercise of human labour with the workmanship of God: embodied in the Palmer and Guyon respectively, 'temperance' manifests as 'literally a static virtue, a physiological and psychological *state*' and 'continence' as 'a perpetually active virtue ... demanding unending vigilance'.[82] Important, therefore, is Guyon's separation from his horse, an event that forces him to progress on foot, shaming as that is for a knight:

> So forth he far'd, as now befell, on foot,
>   Sith his good steed is lately from him gone;
>   Patience perforce; helplesse what may it boot
>   To frett for anger, or for griefe to mone?
>   His Palmer now shall foot no more alone ... (II.iii.3)

Temporarily, Guyon falls into step with the Palmer, who, as something of a professional traveller, seeks to hold his pupil-knight to account. To borrow an observation from a fifteenth-century educational treatise, someone 'who thinks that he need never render account of his studies will skip many things and will run through most things lightly and, as they say, superficially, with unwashed feet; he will not try to look into anything deeply, down to its essence'.[83] Guyon, it seems, must experience the exercise of patience and the agony of exertion: the result being a particular soreness of foot that eludes his fellow long-distance travellers.

In the encounter between Guyon, Sir Huddibras, and Sansloy, for example, Spenser offers a series of permeable epic similes that seek to analyse the exertions of the knight and his adversaries. The primary identification of Guyon as a traveller is moved through a range of correspondences that put the fluid nature of Spenser's 'moving metaphors' on display.[84] From the moment Sir Huddibras and Sansloy proceed to

---

82  Michael C. Schoenfeldt, *Bodies and Selves in Early Modern England: Physiology and Inwardness in Spenser, Shakespeare, Herbert, and Milton* (Cambridge: Cambridge University Press, 1999), p. 43.

83  Battista Guarino, 'A Program of Teaching and Learning', in *Humanist Educational Treatises*, ed. and trans. Craig W. Kallendorf (Cambridge, MA: Harvard University Press, 2002), pp. 260–309 (p. 293).

84  For Book II's variegated movements see Joseph D. Parry, 'Phaedria and Guyon: Travelling Alone in *The Faerie Queene*, Book II', *Spenser Studies*, 15 (2001), 53–77.

turn their attention towards 'that straunger knight' in a predatory way, it becomes clear that the battle ahead will not take anthropomorphically or topographically stable terms:

> As when a Beare and Tygre being met
> 　In cruell fight on lybicke Ocean wide,
> 　Espye a traueiler with feet surbet,
> 　Whom they in equall pray hope to diuide,
> They stint their strife, and him assayle on euerie side.
>
> But he, not like a weary traueilere,
> 　Their sharp assault right boldly did rebut,
> 　And suffred not their blowes to byte him nere,
> 　But with redoubled buffes them backe did put:
> 　Whose grieued mindes, which choler did englut,
> 　Against themselues turning their wrathfull spight,
> 　Gan with new rage their shieldes to hew and cut;
> 　But still when Guyon came to part their fight,
> With heauie load on him they freshly gan to smight.
>
> As a tall ship tossed in troublous seas,
> 　Whom raging windes threatning to make the pray
> 　Of the rough rockes, doe diuersly disease,
> 　Meetes two contrarie billowes by the way,
> 　That her on either side doe sore assay,
> 　And boast to swallow her in greedy graue;
> 　Shee scorning both their spights, does make wide way,
> 　And with her brest breaking the fomy waue,
> Does ride on both their backs, and faire her self doth saue.
>
> So boldly he him beares, and rusheth forth
> 　Betweene them both, by conduct of his blade. (II.ii.22–5)

Initially arriving on the scene as a peacemaker, Guyon only serves to unite the ire of the quarrelling knights against him. Yet, after mistakenly perceiving Guyon to be in a vulnerable exhausted state, like a traveller whose feet are 'surbet', or bruised from much walking,[85] Sir Huddibras and Sansloy soon discover that he is not 'like' his appearance. The stanzas mobilise a series of metamorphoses that exploit the initial figurative image of a deserted hostile space: the wrath of prowling adversaries transforms into cresting waves and when intemperate minds become self-destructive amidst a sea of choler, the ocean-like Libyan desert

---

85　See 'surbated, adj.' *OED Online*. Oxford University Press, June 2016 (last accessed 18 July 2016).

completes its transformation into the 'troublous' deep. In the narrator's description of Guyon's movements, the figure initially perceived as the 'surbet' traveller abandons land in favour of a maritime existence: as the metaphors shift, the foot-weary wayfarer becomes a tall ship, capable of surging forward and 'breaking the fomy waue' in spite of retaining the memory of the previous pedestrian travail. Via a striking blend of motion and continuity, the image of virtue as a kinaesthetic activity is constantly reframed in order to deepen the representation of a particular kind of allegorical environment and the shaping of the conflicts within.[86]

## All(egory) at sea

In their introduction to *Renaissance Go-Betweens*, Andreas Höfele and Werner von Koppenfels evoke three images taken from Theodor de Bry's *America*, which 'focus on the central figure of a man standing or sitting on the foredeck of a ship whose bow is pointed away from the observer towards a distant horizon'.[87] The editors describe the human figure in terms that could also be used to describe Spenser's Guyon:

> Although at the centre of the scene, he seems strangely aloof, decentred. Caught up in an in-between space, he does not fully belong to either of the worlds intersecting in the picture: not to the old world from which he has set out nor to the new one which he has not yet reached; not to the world of 'antique fable', but neither to that of incipient modern commerce represented by the ship, itself a perennial trope of 'in-betweenness'.[88]

In Spenser's poem, the straight and narrow path to salvation revealed to Redcrosse at the end of Book I is given a second set of identities by Guyon's voyaging as both the *via media* and the *vita activa*, bringing the abstract vision of holiness present in the previous book into collision with the demanding lived experience of both the reformed church

---

86 See James Nohrnberg, *The Analogy of The Faerie Queene* (Princeton: Princeton University Press, 1976), p. 300. The sequence also offers an example of what Gordon Teskey describes as '*kinestasis*, a moment of motion held still before us for contemplation'. See 'Notes on Reading *The Faerie Queene*: From Moment to Moment', in *Spenser in the Moment*, ed. Paul J. Hecht and J.B. Lethbridge (Madison: Fairleigh Dickinson University Press, 2015), pp. 217–34 (p. 227).
87 Andreas Höfele and Werner von Koppenfels, 'Introduction', in *Renaissance Go-Betweens: Cultural Exchange in Early Modern Europe* (Berlin: de Gruyter, 2005), p. 1. The figure represents Columbus but in Jan Van der Straet's original design the figure is 'identified as Amerigo Vespucci'.
88 Ibid., p. 3. For the ship as a heterotopian space see Michel Foucault, 'Of Other Spaces', trans. Jay Miskowiec, *Diacritics*, 16.1 (1986), 22–7, p. 27.

and broader worldly contingency.[89] Guyon's initial footsore labours are difficult to recognise as a continuance of the tempestuous 'pricking' that characterised the untested Redcrosse knight; it is as if he must feel at every stage the *travail* of his travels. Moving through a fictional space that at every moment threatens to overwhelm him with 'fantome and illusion', to recall the threat articulated in Chaucer's *House of Fame*, Guyon must once again learn to read the terrain, his loneliness a further aspect of Redcrosse's legacy.

As Book II progresses, the connection between movement and knowledge-making is reframed within a newly aqueous terrain, where the misleading traces and footprints constituting the itinerary for Redcrosse's adventure are subjected to erasure, washed away by the watery tenor of Guyon's voyaging. Travel no longer functions merely as a metaphor for finding the right path, as it did in Book I, but increasingly as a way of measuring via the art of navigation.[90] Several interpretations have been provided for Spenser's choice of name for his Knight of Temperance,[91] and at least one embedded pun relies on the etymology of 'guide'. The *Oxford English Dictionary*, for example, lists the now obsolete meanings of the verb 'to guy' as 'to conduct or lead on the way'; ... to control or direct (a person or his actions); to conduct or rule (oneself)'. Spatial guidance uses the same verbal expression as the government of oneself or a nation and Spenser's allegory holds both meanings in suspension. Used as a noun, 'guy' not only refers to a 'guide; a conductor or leader' but also to something used 'to secure or steady anything liable to shift its position or to be carried away'.[92]

The resonances are present in Spenser's depiction of Guyon as a mariner, sailing with his meagre crew of resolute Palmer and steadfast Ferryman to the Bower of Bliss: 'to guy', is also to fasten and secure a ship with ropes. In order to make landfall on the territories of the enchantress Acrasia, the knight must keep an 'euen course' (II.xii.3). Yet, throughout the journey, Spenser is keen to remind the reader about the deceptive power of appearances. As soon as Archimago identifies Guyon, he plots

---

89  See A.C. Hamilton, *FQ*, note to II.ii.14 (p. 174). See also Nievergelt, *Allegorical Quests*, p. 5.
90  See Elizabeth Mazzola, *The Pathology of the English Renaissance: Sacred Remains and Holy Ghosts* (Leiden: Brill, 1998), pp. 37–63.
91  See Susan Snyder, 'Guyon the Wrestler', *Renaissance News*, 14.4 (1961), 249–52 and Alastair Fowler, 'The River Guyon', *MLN*, 75.4 (1960), 289–92. Guyon's name also recalls that of the romance hero Guy of Warwick.
92  See 'guy, n.1.' and 'guy, v.1.' *OED Online*. Oxford University Press, December 2015 (last accessed 18 December 2015).

to lead the knight astray and 'Eftsoones vntwisting his deceiptfull clew,/ He gan to weaue a web of wicked guyle' (II.i.8). Here, Spenser's vocabulary draws on Chaucer's 'Legend of Ariadne': Theseus is given the famous 'clewe of twyn' in order that he may escape the labyrinth, and so that 'the same weye he may returne anon,/ Folwynge alwey the thred as he hath come'.[93] Archimago's 'guyle' is characteristic of Spenser's own dissembling poetics. The enchanter's guile is a mockery of the true thread: the steadfast 'guy' that is 'like to lead the labyrinth about' (I.i.11). Ariadne's 'clewe' of twine, like the threads of Penelope's weaving, thus find a further parallel in the guy-ropes that keep the enchanted boat of romance safely moored and the Circe-like temptations of Acrasia contained.[94]

As something of a figure of guidance himself, then, but with fewer roads to follow, Guyon becomes the anthropometric measure of orientation. Like the human figure used by the Italian polymath Leon Battista Alberti to explain the measure of proportion in a painting, his body serves as a perspectival instrument, providing a measure of scale and comparison:

> As man is the best known of all things to man, perhaps Protagoras, in saying that man is the scale and measure of all things, meant that accidents in all things are duly compared to and known by the accidents in man. All of which should persuade us that, however small you paint the objects in a painting, they will seem large or small according to the size of any man in the picture.[95]

Alberti appropriates Protagoras's maxim in order to suggest that the presence of a human figure in a painting not only draws the eye of the beholder but also provides a subjective impression of proportion and scale.[96] To draw an analogy between the image and the image's observer, and the travelling figure within the allegory and the reader, the viewer, 'in seeking to gauge another, assays himself'.[97]

Alberti's impression of the subjectivity of perception, where 'accidents in all things are duly compared to and known by the accidents in

---

93 Geoffrey Chaucer, 'The Legend of Ariadne', from *The Legend of Good Women* in *The Riverside Chaucer*, pp. 587–630, lines 2016–18.
94 See David Quint, *Epic and Empire: Politics and Generic Form from Virgil to Milton* (Princeton: Princeton University Press, 1993), p. 249.
95 Leon Battista Alberti, *On Painting and On Sculpture: The Latin Texts of De Pictura and De Statua*, trans. Cecil Grayson (London: Phaidon Press, 1972), p. 53.
96 See Charles Trinkaus, 'Protagoras in the Renaissance: An Exploration', in *Philosophy and Humanism: Renaissance Essays in Honour of Paul Oskar Kristeller*, ed. Edward P. Mahoney (Leiden: E.J. Brill, 1976), pp. 190–213.
97 Blank, *Shakespeare and the Mismeasure of Renaissance Man*, p. 22.

man', is of particular interest in light of the hindrances encountered by Guyon, whose 'mastery over the passions', as Hamilton explains, is often 'expressed as a victory over water'.[98] Such 'accidents' can be likened to what John Dee describes in his definition of the art of navigation as the 'naturall disturbances chauncyng' that send the mariner off course (*Mathematicall Praeface*, sig. D4$^v$). At the mercy of various sources of propulsion and impetus, Guyon can only draw on his own strength and resolve. He is himself the measure of progress, whereby his powers of perception and judgement serve figuratively as his 'card and compass':

> As Pilot well expert in perilous waue,
>   That to a stedfast starre his course hath bent,
> When foggy mistes, or cloudy tempests haue
>   The faithfull light of that faire lampe yblent,
>   And couer'd heauen with hideous dreriment,
> Vpon his card and compas firmes his eye,
>   The maysters of his long experiment,
> And to them does the steddy helme apply,
> Bidding his winged vessell fairely forward fly.
>
> So Guyon hauing lost his trustie guyde,
>   Late left beyond that *Ydle lake*, proceedes
> Yet on his way, of none accompanyde;
>   And euermore himselfe with comfort feedes,
>   Of his owne vertues, and praise-worthie deedes. (II.vii.1–2)

Guyon's reliance on 'his owne vertues' suggests that he must also know his limits: a type of self-knowledge born of experience. As Robert Norman explains in the dedicatory epistle to his translation of Cornelis Antoniszoon's *The Safegard of Sailers* (1584), the navigational treatise not only contains 'the gatherings of divers experimented men, necessarie to be knowne and observed in our common Navigation, as Tides, Depths, Soundings, Markes, and Sands' but also an intimation of that which 'by no Chart or Plat is expressed or knowne, but resteth only upon the relation of the experimented Traveller'.[99] When compared with the Palmer, Guyon has a long way to go before claiming the title of 'experimented Traveller'; yet, the 'maysters' of Guyon's own 'long experiment' offer a reflection on the efficacy of self-perception and self-knowledge

---

98 A.C. Hamilton, 'Our New Poet: Spenser, "Well of English Undefyled"', in *A Theatre for Spenserians*, ed. Judith M. Kennedy and James A. Reither (Manchester: Manchester University Press, 1973), pp. 101–23 (p. 106).
99 Cornelis Antoniszoon, *The Safegarde of Saylers, or Great Rutter* (London, 1584), sig. A3$^r$.

in process. There is something uncharacteristic in the way that Guyon's mariner-surrogate in the allegory 'firmes his eye'. For Greg Dening, the design of a mariner's instruments already speaks of a way of knowing the world that has its own agenda and space for play:

> The word *compass* and with it *encompass* is one of those words in the *Oxford English Dictionary* with a small discursive introduction puzzling at the word's origins. To 'measure,' 'walk in pace,' 'stride across' belong to the oldest meanings of *compass* and *encompass*. But surprisingly, so do 'contrivance,' 'artifice,' 'designing skill, 'stratagem.' So power is in *encompass*. Something of a Colossus astride the globe. There's trickster in the word, too. A touch of fraud and gullibility.[100]

The richness of these associations catches at the full mobilised capacity of Spenser's allegory to hold meanings in suspension, where Guyon's perceptual compass shares in the 'daedale' nature of Spenser's craft (see Chapter 1). 'To compass' might be to master but, as Dening observes, the action remains unperfected. It is a figure for self-direction and self-deception, guidance and guile, art and artifice.

In Book II's discourse of allegorical navigations and measurings, the mariner's 'card and compass' are cognate with the Palmer's metaphorical set square, used to explain the capacity of temperance to mediate between extremes of passion: for 'temperaunce (said he) with golden squire/ Betwixt them both can measure out a meane' (II.i.58).[101] Within this context of instrumentally guided labour, the association between temperance and proportion reaches its climax in the composition of the Castle of Alma: an edifice that attracts the narrator's praise owing to the 'goodly order, and great workmans skill' (II.ix.33) that has gone into its construction, which is 'proportioned equally' (II.ix.22), 'with comely compasse, and compacture strong' (II.ix.24). When describing the position of the castle's highest point, Guyon and Arthur are shown to follow Alma up ten vertebral steps to a head-like turret, from which all things below can be surveyed:

> The Turrets frame most admirable was,
> Like highest heauen compassed around,

---

100 Greg Dening, 'Deep Times, Deep Spaces', in *Sea Changes: Historicizing the Ocean*, ed. Bernhard Klein and Gesa Mackenthun (New York: Routledge, 2004), pp. 13–35 (p. 17). See also Joanne Woolway, 'Spenser and the Culture of Place', Guest Lecture: University of Oslo, 17 April 1996. Archived by *EMLS* at http://extra.shu.ac.uk/emls/iemls/conf/texts/woolway.html (last accessed 2 June 2016).
101 See Piotr Sadowski, 'Spenser's "Golden Squire" and "Golden Meane": Numbers and Proportions in Book II of *The Faerie Queene*', *Spenser Studies*, 14 (2000), 107–31.

> And lifted high aboue this earthly masse,
> Which it suruewd, as hils doen lower ground; ... (II.ix.45)

Spenser imagines a landscape contoured by height and depth: natural vantage points overlook or survey the lower ground. Situated as it is, the Castle of Alma appears to belong as an organic part of this hierarchical ecology, and as a body standing tall in a landscape, poised on a coastal periphery between earth and water, it organises the attribution of meaning and form to space:[102] an image of Alberti's perspectival human figure writ large. The vantage point recalls Redcrosse's heightened perception while elevated on the Mount of Contemplation; yet, as a temperate body, the Castle of Alma occupies a position between fixity and flux. As both living body and anchored edifice, its architectural structure holds the exercise of mathematical precision and the 'compacture' of chaotic matter in constant tension.[103]

The metaphorical appearance of the architect's set-square, along with both geometric and magnetic compasses, implies that aspects of Spenser's allegories invite comparison with the methodological application of technical knowledge associated with the art of building. The translation of Redcrosse's wandering into Guyon's reactive immersion suggests that Spenser's handling of virtue shifts as an epistemological category. Holiness as an abstraction is redefined; in Book II, the actions of temperance are seen to manifest in the midst of contingent situations, in response to what Davis has called the 'continuing onslaught of unschedulable phenomena'.[104] For Redcrosse, who travels with truth as a guide, holiness ought to be an *episteme*, whereas for Guyon, who moves through a world whose allegorical core is structured by skilled and embodied practice, the temperate response belongs to the arts of *technai*.[105]

The labours of the master builder and master mariner, evoked by Spenser's instrumental pairing of square and compass, are thus also cognate as emblems of 'craft mastery' and applied skill: what seem like literary metaphors in Spenser's poetry often draw on historically and materially vital emblems and vocabularies used by particular trades and

---

102 Donald Kimball Smith notes that the coastal position 'helps to give the landscape of the poem an implicitly cartographic shape'. See *The Cartographic Imagination in Early Modern England* (Aldershot: Ashgate, 2008), p. 99.
103 See Rayna Kalas, *Frame, Glass, Verse: The Technology of Poetic Invention in the English Renaissance* (Ithaca: Cornell University Press, 2007), pp. 95–105.
104 Davis, *Stories of Chaos*, p. 92.
105 For the distinction between these ways of knowing see Pamela H. Smith, *The Body of the Artisan: Art and Experience in the Scientific Revolution* (Chicago: University of Chicago Press, 2004), pp. 17–18.

practices.[106] In the prologue to his translation of Pierre Garcie's pilot book, *The Rutter of the Sea* (1560), for example, Robert Copland's explanation of the relationship between 'reason, speculacyon, and practyse' moves the reader away from his immediate concern with the fluidity of the unpredictable sea towards an image of balance and endurance:

> Every man that entendeth to buyld be it habytacyon, fortresse or other edifice on lande or water, behovethe to have suche worekemen that can cast the plat and know the substaunce and the grounde for the foundacion: and that can saflye, and dyrectlye frame, and rayse the hole worke. For whoso hathe not the veray scyence of Arsmetryke, and geometry to ayme and measure the platte and conjecture of the hyght, drede and lenght, and to fortifye it with Pryncypalles, gistes, beames, tenauntes, morteses, countrebrases, and not knowing the nombre in every piece duely framed is in doute and peryll to lese all the frame.[107]

In coming to rest on an image of the art of building, Copland emphasises the importance of the 'foundation' and the 'frame': material images that pertain to cognitive and reactive processes.[108] A builder must have the right 'tooles therto belonging, as rule squyre, cumpas, lyne, prychel, tryangle' in the same way that a mariner must have 'suche necessary instrumentes as behoveth to the industry of his practyse, as the carde, compasse, rutter dyal and other whiche by speculate practyse sheweth the place' (sig. A3$^v$). As Copland continues, the analogy between skilfully crafted structures and the art of navigation turns into a metaphor for different ways of knowing, serving to illustrate the disparity between the theoretical and the practical:

> ... by reason a man that never was builder by speculacion may rease and edify, but nothing like that entired practise. In lyke maner I conjecte that in the feate and course of Navigacyon or sealyng a man may presume and take upon him by his speculacyon to conducte a vessell, as a blynde man in a desolate wyldernes doth walk tyl he be lost. (sig. A3$^v$)

Without lived experience and practice, Copland argues, the would-be mariner is as helpless as a man wandering impaired and alone in a desert. The analogy is a familiar one, which recalls both the unmapped sands of

---

106 For the 'master builder' as a figure for inventive authority see Carruthers, *The Craft of Thought*, pp. 16–24.
107 Robert Copland, 'The Prologue of Robart Copland the Translatour of this Sayde Rutter', in Pierre Garcie, *The Rutter of the Sea* (London, 1560), sig. A3$^v$. Subsequent references are placed in the text.
108 See Kalas, *Frame, Glass, Verse*, p. 54.

Chaucer's dreamer and the untravelled parts of Browne's America: as such, it anticipates the final stages of Guyon's voyage.

On his way to Acrasia's island, Guyon opens to his mind to the prospect of release from his 'troublous toyle' and the poem is temporarily flooded with Siren song. Spenser's mermaids sing of the spirit of the place, of safe harbours, and of welcoming shores:

> So now to *Guyon*, as he passed by,
>   Their pleasaunt tunes they sweetly thus applyde;
>   O thou fayre sonne of gentle Faery,
>   That art in mightie armes most magnifyde
>   Aboue all knights, that euer batteill tryde,
>   O turne thy rudder hetherward a while:
>   Here may thy storme-bett vessell safely ryde;
>   This is the Port of rest from troublous toyle,
> The worldes sweet In, from paine and wearisome turmoyle.
>
> With that the rolling sea resounding soft,
>   In his big base them fitly answered,
>   And on the rocke the waues breaking aloft,
>   A solemne Meane vnto them measured,
>   The whiles sweet *Zephyrus* lowd whisteled
>   His treble, a straunge kinde of harmony;
>   Which *Guyons* senses softly tickeled,
>   That he the boteman bad row easily,
> And let him heare some part of their rare melody. (II.xii.32–3)

Siren voices merge and blend with the wind and waves in a seductive four-part harmony. The top notes of Zephyrus complete a chord which slows Guyon's senses; like Odysseus he opens his ears to temptation, to hear the promises of a sentient seascape that temporarily resonates with his own intemperate desires. Unlike the polyvocal world that appears in the Book of Job, the world navigated by Guyon *en route* to the Bower of Bliss sings only of falsehoods and empty promises. The 'worldes sweet In' of which the Sirens sing is not where wisdom can be found, nor is it the place of understanding; instead, it relies on the power of artifice to misguide and betray all who pass by. Spenser's allegory of temperance incorporates within it allegories of making and counter-creation: the tempering and what Rayna Kalas terms the 'poiesis of allegory itself'.[109]

Towards the end of *Protagoras*, Socrates poses a series of hypotheses

---

[109] Ibid., p. 102. See also Colleen Ruth Rosenfeld, *Indecorous Thinking: Figures of Speech in Early Modern Poetics* (New York: Fordham University Press, 2018), pp. 40–7.

concerning the ability of the individual to measure, to gauge, and to act with art and knowledge. 'Measurement', he supposes, 'is the study of relative excess and deficiency and equality', and

> While the power of appearance often makes us wander all over the place in confusion, often changing our minds about the same things and regretting our actions and choices with respect to things large and small, the art of measurement in contrast, would make the appearances lose their power by showing us the truth, would give us peace of mind firmly rooted in the truth and would save our life.[110]

In Spenser's poem, moral lessons happen most often in the midst of wandering and confusion. Socrates may posit that 'no one goes willingly toward the bad or what he believes to be bad; neither is it in human nature, so it seems, to want to go toward what one believes to be bad instead of to the good';[111] yet, in Spenser's allegory, the distinction between false harbours, dark doubles, and abstract virtue is difficult to gauge. For, following the earlier sensory overload, Guyon and his fellow travellers pass into a scene of sensual deprivation, where the path is once again occluded:

> But him the Palmer from that vanity,
>   With temperate aduice discounselled,
>   That they it past, and shortly gan descry
>   The land, to which their course they leueled;
>   When suddeinly a grosse fog ouer spred
>   With his dull vapour all that desert has,
>   And heauens chearefull face enueloped,
>   That all things one, and one as nothing was,
> And this great Vniuerse seemd one confused mas.
>
> Thereat they greatly were dismayd, ne wist
>   How to direct theyr way in darkenes wide,
>   But feard to wander in that wastefull mist,
>   For tombling into mischiefe vnespide.
>   Worse is the daunger hidden, then descride. (II.xii.34–5)

Spenser's use of the word 'descry' to describe the action of sighting land counters the dreamlike seascape with a fleeting sense of empirical certainty; to 'descry' is 'to discover by observation' and 'to distinguish (one thing) from another', suggesting that the approaching coast offers a fleeting chance of cognitive *terra firma*, or a safe harbour at the end

---

110 Plato, *Protagoras*, trans. Stanley Lombardo and Karen Bell, in *Plato: Complete Works*, pp. 746–90 (357b and 356d–e, pp. 785–6).
111 Ibid., 358d, p. 787.

of a 'leueled' course. Yet, the repetition of the word in a new context in the following stanza modifies hope with caution. After all, that which is 'descride' often carries with it more than the suggestion of mere description. A 'daunger ... descride' is that which is revealed 'with a sense of injurious revelation': a secret which has been disclosed or betrayed.[112]

In the final stanzas of Book II, Acrasia's silent beauty, which collaborates with the siren song shaping her enchanting insular environment, creates a test that few would want to pass. Unlike her classical ancestor, Spenser's enchantress conveys no directions for an onward journey; she cannot warn Guyon against herself, nor that which he carries within him.[113] In Homer's *Odyssey*, it is during Odysseus's encounter with Circe that the endlessness of wandering and the possibility of return and arrival are brought into focus.[114] For as Circe promises:

> ... I will set you a course and chart each seamark,
> so neither on sea nor land will some new trap
> ensnare you in trouble, make you suffer more.
>
> ... But once your crew has rowed you past the Sirens
> a choice of routes is yours. I cannot advise you
> which to take, or lead you through it all –
> you must decide for yourself –
> but I can tell you the ways of either course.[115]

In the final canto of Book II it is as if Spenser evokes and swiftly erases the memory of Homer's demi-goddess in order to emphasise the extent to which his own enchantress can only hold dominion over false harbours and dead ends; in his overgoing of Ariosto he also erases the residual aspect of Circe that functions as a figure of guidance and leaves only the play of misleading shadows and afterimages in her place. When Guyon eventually arrives at the Bower of Bliss he has already passed Spenser's equivalent of Scylla and Charybdis – 'the *Gulfe of Greedinesse*', the 'mightie *Magnes* stone', and '*the Rock of* vile *Reproach*' (II.xii.3,8) –

---

112 See 'descry, v.1.' *OED Online*. Oxford University Press, December 2015 (last accessed 18 December 2015).
113 Merritt Y. Hughes also demonstrates that Spenser's reception of the Circe figure is via many subsequent imitations, rather than coming directly from Homer's poem. See 'Spenser's Acrasia and the Circe of the Renaissance', *Journal of the History of Ideas*, 4 (1943), 381–99.
114 See Silvia Montiglio, *Wandering in Ancient Greek Culture* (Chicago: University of Chicago Press, 2005), pp. 56–61.
115 Homer, *The Odyssey*, trans. Robert Fagles (London: Penguin, 2006), XII, lines 28–30 and 61–5.

and so in Spenser's belated revision of Homer's narrative, the provision of sailing directions is redundant. As an 'experimented Traueller', the Palmer already understands that seamarks known by such names cannot be used in navigation. Their names undo themselves as they are uttered.

One of the most striking features of the canto's final stanzas is Guyon's own silence. Following the song of the Sirens, his own mouth appears to be stopped. The lack of reported or implied speech assumes that Guyon offers no word of either consent or dissent to the Palmer's counsel, presenting an image of unspoken obedience. The narrator reports that he 'hearkned' the Palmer's urgent orders (II.xii.38), but in the exchanges with the bower's inhabitants Guyon typically repays hospitality with violence, not dialogue. His eyes, sometimes 'gazing' and sometimes 'wandring' (II.xii.69), are left to widen at sights that would tempt even the most temperate of men, and when the destruction of the bower occurs, it is as if Guyon and the Palmer capture Acrasia and her lover Verdant in wordless coordinated agreement:

> The noble Elfe, and carefull Palmer drew
>   So nigh them, minding nought, but lustfull game,
>   That suddein forth they on them rusht, and threw
>   A subtile net, which only for that same
>   The skilfull Palmer formally did frame.
>   So held them vnder fast, the whiles the rest
>   Fled all away for feare of fowler shame.
>   The faire Enchauntresse, so vnwares opprest,
> Tryde all her arts, and all her sleights, thence out to wrest.
>
> And eke her louer stroue: but all in vaine;
>   For that same net so cunningly was wound,
>   That neither guile, nor force might it distraine.
>   They tooke them both, and both them strongly bound
>   In captiue bandes, which there they readie found:
>   But her in chaines of adamant he tyde;
>   For nothing else might keepe her safe and sound;
>   But *Verdant* (so he hight) he soone vntyde,
> And counsell sage in steed thereof to him applyde.
>
> But all those pleasant bowres and Pallace braue,
>   *Guyon* broke downe, with rigour pittilesse;
>   Ne ought their goodly workmanship might saue
>   Them from the tempest of his wrathfulnesse,
>   But that their blisse he turn'd to balefulnesse:
>   Their groues he feld, their gardins did deface,

> Their arbers spoyle, their Cabinets suppresse,
> heir banket houses burne, their buildings race,
> And of the fayrest late, now made the fowlest place. (II.xii.81–3)

By the final lines of stanza 82, the tightly united actions of the Palmer and Guyon are once again unbound. The 'he' who binds Acrasia but offers 'counsell sage' to Verdant is unnamed; yet, as the maker of the 'subtile net', these labours more fittingly belong to the Palmer alone. His selective mercy offers a contrast to Guyon's 'rigour pittilesse' in the subsequent, even simultaneous, action described in the following stanza. An impression lingers that Guyon's 'card and compass' are perhaps not always reliable when it comes to the recollection and making of the right way.[116] Any sea card is only as truthful as its owner in an allegorical space and, as Sir Philip Sidney notes in his meditation on the fugitive presence of 'the mistress-knowledge', even 'the mathematician might draw forth a straight line with a crooked heart'.[117]

---

116 See Stephen Greenblatt, *Renaissance Self-Fashioning from More to Shakespeare* (Chicago: University of Chicago Press, 1980), p. 177.
117 Sir Philip Sidney, *The Defence of Poesy*, in *The Oxford Authors: Sir Philip Sidney*, ed. Katherine Duncan-Jones (Oxford: Oxford University Press, 1989; repr. 1992), pp. 212–50 (p. 219). As Carruthers observes, 'such mental *rationes* are constructing instruments, only as good as the craft of their user'. See *The Craft of Thought*, p. 34.

# 3

# Feyned no where acts

A Poynt or a Prycke, is named of Geometricians that small and unsensible shape, whiche hath in it no partes, that is to say: nother length, breadth nor depth.¹

The utopian representation always takes the figure, the form, of a map. In the complex unity of its ensemble, ... it gives a location to all journeys, all itineraries, all voyages and their paths: all are potentially present because they are all there, but implicitly it negates them all. The eye that sees it is an abstract eye, since it has no viewpoint: its place is everywhere and nowhere.²

In the first stanza of Spenser's *Faerie Queene* a figure named only as a 'Gentle Knight' appears, 'pricking on the plaine' (I.i.1). In one sense, this fair unknown rides out into a neutral space that contains no milestone or landmark, and in which no stories have yet been fashioned; yet, in another, the author's choice of vocabulary recalls Geoffrey Chaucer's parody of the romance mode, the *Tale of Sir Thopas*. As Spenser's 'knight prickant' rides into an expanse that is alive with the expectation of adventure, the poet embarks on a parallel journey of paper and ink.³ The wilful movement creates chivalric space, resonant with narrative potential.⁴

1 Robert Recorde, *The Pathway to Knowledge* (London, 1551), sig. A1ʳ.
2 Louis Marin, 'Frontiers of Utopia: Past and Present', *Critical Inquiry*, 19 (1993), 397–420, p. 413.
3 For the 'Chaucerian intertext' see Judith H. Anderson, *Reading the Allegorical Intertext: Chaucer, Spenser, Shakespeare, Milton* (New York: Fordham University Press, 2008), pp. 54–60 (p. 54). See also Chris Butler, '"Pricking" and Ambiguity at the Start of *The Faerie Queene*', *Notes and Queries*, 55.2 (2008), 159–61.
4 See William F. Woods, *Chaucerian Spaces: Spatial Poetics in Chaucer's Opening Tales* (Albany: State University of New York Press, 2008), p. 21. See also Mikhail M. Bakhtin, 'Forms of Time and of the Chronotope in the Novel', in *The Dialogic Imagination*, ed. Michael Holquist, trans. Caryl Emerson and Michael Holquist (Austin: University of Texas Press, 1981; repr. 2002), pp. 84–258 (see 'adventure-time', 'encounter', and 'the road' in particular).

And the word 'pricking', which can refer to the 'small printe of penne, pencyle, or other instrumente, whiche is not moved, nor drawen from his fyrst touche',[5] and to the act of spurring a horse, where the 'sharpe pricking spurre' encourages the mount 'to bee quicke in his course', offers the only measure of the distance travelled.[6] The embedded conceit, which associates movement with work done, expresses both the curious sense of motion so crucial to Spenser's work, and the creative, shaping, and threateningly discontinuous, act of writing. The progression of the inked words across the page is a travail: an itinerary created by the author for the reader to follow.[7] The pricking motion catches at the paradox that this is both a beginning and a part of a pattern that has been traced before: it is both the propulsive marker of a space of infinite extension and a vestigial mark that can claim 'no partes', or region, of its own.[8]

## The spaces of romance

This chapter considers the ways in which writers of romance think spatially, and draw consciously on a self-referential, idealised, and enduring literary geography.[9] The spaces of romance typically transform the representation of the regional into something or *'somewhere else'* entirely;[10] yet, of all the genres under discussion in this study, it is romance that gets closest to illuminating the geographer J.K. Wright's impression that 'the most fascinating *terrae incognitae* of all are those that lie within the minds and hearts of men'.[11] In previous chapters, I have examined Spenser's participation in an epistemological tradition of representing intellectual and ethical challenges in spatial terms, wherein labyrinthine

---

5 Recorde, *The Pathway to Knowledge*, sig. A1ʳ.
6 Diego Ortúñez de Calahorra, *The Third Part of the First Booke, of the Mirrour of Knighthood*, trans. R.P. (London, 1586), sig. Bb1ᵛ.
7 See Elizabeth Heale, 'Travailing Abroad: The Poet as Adventurer', in *Travels and Translations in the Sixteenth Century*, ed. Mike Pincombe (Aldershot: Ashgate, 2004), pp. 3–18.
8 Indeed, as Philip Edwards writes, 'No map, Elizabethan or modern, could conceivably convey these wanderings, which range far and wide and yet remain within a confine so limited that every traveller can meet every other'. See *Sea-Mark: The Metaphorical Voyage, Spenser to Milton* (Liverpool: Liverpool University Press, 1997), p. 27.
9 See Robert Rouse, 'Walking (between) the Lines: Romance as Itinerary / Map', in *Medieval Romance, Medieval Contexts*, ed. Rhiannon Purdie and Michael Cichon (Cambridge: D.S. Brewer, 2011), pp. 135–48.
10 See Helen Cooper, *The English Romance in Time: Transforming Motifs from Geoffrey of Monmouth to the Death of Shakespeare* (Oxford: Oxford University Press, 2004), p. 71.
11 John K. Wright, 'Terrae Incognitae: The Place of the Imagination in Geography', *Annals of the Association of American Geographers*, 37.1 (1947), 1–15, p. 15.

desert, wooded, and watery terrain provide realms in which to delineate cognition as movement. Here, I build on my analysis of these rhetorical practices to investigate what happens when conditions of unknowing are given shape in narrative fiction. The entangled roots of the forests of romance suggest the longevity of particular literary *topoi* as well as the capacity of romance landscaping to act metafictionally. Once interlaced narrative patterns and digressions are recognised in their intertwined entirety and symmetry, as Eugène Vinaver observes, the reader is invited to appreciate the capacity of romance to enact a 'conquest of space' wherein 'everything we see or read about is part of a wider canvas, of a work still unwritten, or a design still unfulfilled'.[12] For readers of Spenser's 'endlesse work', of course, the 'conquest of space' shapes not only how Spenser appropriates the interlaced structure of continental romance, most notably in the middle books of his poem, but also the colonial and political agendas in which his sprawling fictions are complicit.

Written in the vernacular, or romance, languages, romance can be considered to be 'the major secular genre from the time of Chrétien de Troyes (c. 1180) to Chaucer (d. 1400) and beyond', and although terminologies vary from critic to critic, from genre, mode, tradition, strategy, and motif to 'meme', it is usually agreed that the permutations of romance are historically and culturally determined.[13] Medieval romance was reprinted from manuscript copies, disseminated, and alluded to by major authors well into the seventeenth century, providing evidence that the reading of native romance was a popular pastime for Spenser and his contemporaries.[14] As Barbara Fuchs observes, it was during the Renaissance that romance entered 'into a rich conversation with its classical and medieval antecedents' and was 'extensively refashioned into a range of new possibilities'.[15] For my purposes here,

---

12 Eugène Vinaver, *The Rise of Romance* (Oxford: Clarendon Press, 1971), p. 81. As Maureen Quilligan observes, *The Faerie Queene*, as if 'growing like dense foliage over its own analysing anatomy, ... exists in a spatial dimension of forest and clearing; book and canto divisions of the linear sequence seem like mere signposts until there is leisure for a synchronic criticism'. See *Milton's Spenser: The Politics of Reading* (Ithaca: Cornell University Press, 1983), p. 44.
13 John E. Stevens, *Medieval Romance: Themes and Approaches* (London: Hutchinson, 1973), p. 15.
14 Cooper uses the term 'meme' to describe how romance 'behaves like a gene in its ability to replicate faithfully and abundantly, but also on occasion to adapt, mutate, and therefore survive in different forms and cultures'. See *The English Romance in Time*, p. 3. See her appendix for evidence, pp. 409–29.
15 Barbara Fuchs, *Romance* (New York: Routledge, 2004), p. 66.

these 'new possibilities' are framed in ways that are associated with the responsibilities of imaginative literature as it responds to a spatially hybrid moment, in which older cosmographical and devotional ways of thinking about space and movement were revised by intellectual engagements with the burgeoning literature of travel, exploration, and conquest.[16] In order to place Spenser's poem within a tradition of encounters between romance and space, I interrupt my readings of *The Faerie Queene* with three brief case studies of works that demonstrate the vagrancies of romance emplotment: namely, *Sir Gawain and the Green Knight*, which Spenser could not have known but whose author synthesises techniques used by more widely disseminated writers; *The Hystorye of Olyver of Castylle*, which resonates with *The Faerie Queene* on the level of both plot and character; and the *Tale of Sir Thopas*, on which Spenser draws directly.

In imitation of its medieval sources, the topography of *The Faerie Queene* is shaped by heightened topographical tropes; its bowers and wastes retain the imperfect memory of having been ordered by an understanding of the doctrine of universal symbolism.[17] Such spaces are populated by questing knights in search of idealised virtues: vestigial reminders of the romance mode's historical preoccupation with the attainment of a perfectible world, which runs parallel to the capacity of romance to convey that which is intended to endure.[18] Subject to continual renewal, the recovery of traditional themes corresponds to the quest, or 'exile and return' narrative movements of the texts themselves.[19] The trope of 'exile and return', of course, can be recognised in Spenser's self-fashioning of his own authorial identity. It offers a response to both literary tradition and personal circumstance and gives shape to his sense of what is required to reconcile the roles of poet and planter, where what consti-

---

16 See John G. Demaray, *Cosmos and Epic Representation* (Pittsburgh: Duquesne University Press, 1991), p. 5. For the poem's 'volatile romance cosmology' see Elizabeth Mazzola, *The Pathology of the English Renaissance: Sacred Remains and Holy Ghosts* (Leiden: Brill, 1998), p. 39.
17 See Rosalie Vermette, 'Terrae Incantatae: The Symbolic Geography of Twelfth-Century Arthurian Romance', in *Geography and Literature: A Meeting of the Disciplines*, ed. William E. Mallory and Paul Simpson-Housley (Syracuse: Syracuse University Press, 1987), pp. 145–60.
18 See Stevens, *Medieval Romance*, p. 277. See also Carol Fewster, *Traditionality and Genre in Middle English Romance* (Cambridge: D.S. Brewer, 1987).
19 See Rosalind Field, 'The King Over the Water: Exile-and-Return Revisited', in *Cultural Encounters in the Romance of Medieval England*, ed. Corinne Saunders (Cambridge: D.S. Brewer, 2005), pp. 41–53 and Terry Comito, 'Exile and Return in the Greek Romances', *Arion*, 2.1 (1975), 58–80.

tutes home is difficult to define.[20] The question raised by Geraldine Heng concerning whether '*geography* and *place*' can be 'a subject of romance, along with human actors engaged in love, quest, and marvelous adventure', thus remains an important one for this study, drawing attention as it does to both the complexity of spatial forms in the representation of cultural fantasy and the role of the spatial in what Heng describes as romance's distinctive '*structure of desire*'.[21] As she explains, the development of imaginative literature has always depended on the technologies and horizons of the culture it reflects, where the driving impulse of medieval romance, she argues, is 'the discovery (and the making) of a safe harbor out of dangerous waters, in order that a *safe* language of cultural discussion accrues'.[22] As the legacy of Spenser's medieval predecessors, to whom he simultaneously looks back and in whose footsteps he follows, this impulse persists throughout *The Faerie Queene*, from the poem's veiling of historical figures to its plotting of terrestrial hopes and challenges.

It has long been recognised that Spenser's travails are sustained by those of his romance-making forebears and Chaucer in particular, as if, as he explicitly mentions in Book IV's continuation of the *Squire's Tale*, such 'labours lost may thus reuiue' (IV.ii.34);[23] yet, for all its resilience, the romance mode also suffered a decline in favour during the early modern period owing to the ways in which it came to be perceived as a morally and artistically inferior type of literature. During the mid-eighteenth century, Bishop Richard Hurd was to reflect in his *Letters on Chivalry and Romance* (1762), with reference to Spenser, on how 'at length the magic of the old romances was perfectly dissolved'.[24] In advocating the marvels of Spenser's use of 'expiring' forms, Hurd writes of how the demise of this dissolving genre was temporarily stayed by allegories

---

20 See Donald Cheney, 'Colin Clout's Homecoming: The Imaginative Travels of Edmund Spenser', *Connotations*, 7.2 (1997–1998), 146–58.
21 Geraldine Heng, *Empire of Magic: Medieval Romance and the Politics of Cultural Fantasy* (New York: Columbia University Press, 2003), p. 1 and p. 3.
22 Ibid., p. 3. When put in such terms, Spenser's epistemological games participate in what Katherine Eggert terms 'disknowledge': 'a deliberate means by which a culture can manage epistemological risk'. See *Disknowledge: Literature, Alchemy, and the End of Humanism in Renaissance England* (Philadelphia: University of Pennsylvania Press, 2015), p. 8.
23 See Rachel Stenner, Tamsin Badcoe, and Gareth Griffith, eds, *Rereading Chaucer and Spenser: Dan Geffrey with the New Poete* (Manchester: Manchester University Press, 2019).
24 Bishop Richard Hurd, *Hurd's Letters on Chivalry and Romance*, ed. Edith J. Morley (London: Henry Frowde, 1911), p. 153.

under whose guise it 'walked the world a while'.[25] In response to the perceived vulnerability of romance to intellectual criticism, Andrew King convincingly argues that Spenser actively defied contemporary slights on the genre, as if the 'native romances, lately suffering from the censure of Elizabethan moralists and literary wits, are suddenly in Spenser's text remembered as legitimately conceived'.[26] Nostalgia offers a stark challenge to the present. In the readings presented here, romance can be seen to interweave geographical representation with formal literary principles, allowing for drift and unexpected progress. When combined, such strategies function for Spenser as a way of remobilising romance as a legitimate site of sixteenth-century knowledge-making and offer ways of thinking about how romance seeks not only to idealise and recreate, but also to order and understand.[27]

## Conquests of space

The proem to Book II of *The Faerie Queene* is frequently evoked by critics as both a defence of imaginative literature and a commentary on the poetics of early modern epistemology.[28] The stanzas confront the lacunae created by a constant exchange of textual 'discoveries', each replacing the authority and novelty of the last, and question the status of provisional knowledge when confronting a rapidly expanding world.[29] For Spenser, who does careful work to position his 'faery lond' in the realm of thought experiment, or utopian hypothesis, the slower motion of the imagined eye-witness is superseded by the potentially rapid travel of the speculative reader, who is challenged to participate freely in his ludic geosophical exchange:

25 Ibid., p. 154.
26 Andrew King, *The Faerie Queene and Middle English Romance: The Matter of Just Memory* (Oxford: Clarendon, 2000), p. 212.
27 See Vinaver, *The Rise of Romance*, p. 32.
28 See Syrithe Pugh, 'Acrasia and Bondage: Guyon's Perversion of the Ovidian Erotic in Book II of *The Faerie Queene*', in *Edmund Spenser: New and Renewed Directions*, ed. J.B. Lethbridge (Madison: Fairleigh Dickinson University Press, 2006), pp. 153–94 and Lauren Silberman, *Transforming Desire: Erotic Knowledge in Books III and IV of The Faerie Queene* (Berkeley: University of California Press, 1995), pp. 21–2.
29 See Robert Appelbaum, 'Anti-Geography', *EMLS*, 4.2 (1998), 12.1–17. See also Ayesha Ramachandran, *The Worldmakers: Global Imagining in Early Modern Europe* (Chicago: University of Chicago Press, 2015), pp. 126–8 and Daniel Viktus, 'The New Globalism: Transcultural Commerce, Global Systems Theory, and Spenser's Mammon', in *A Companion to the Global Renaissance: English Literature and Culture in the Era of Expansion*, ed. Jyotsna Singh (Chichester: Wiley-Blackwell, 2009), pp. 31–49 (p. 37 in particular).

> But let that man with better sence aduize,
> That of the world least part to vs is red:
> And daily how through hardy enterprize,
> Many great Regions are discouered,
> Which to late age were neuer mentioned.
> Who euer heard of th'Indian *Peru*?
> Or who in venturous vessell measured
> The *Amazons* huge riuer now found trew?
> Or fruitfullest *Virginia* who did euer vew?
>
> Yet all these were when no man did them know,
> Yet haue from wisest ages hidden beene
> And later times thinges more vnknowne shall show.
> Why then should witlesse man so much misweene
> That nothing is but that which he hath seene?
> What if within the Moones fayre shining spheare,
> What if in euery other starre vnseene
> Of other worldes he happily should heare?
> He wonder would much more: yet such to some appeare.
>
> Of faery lond yet if he more inquyre,
> By certein signes here sett in sondrie place
> He may it fynd; ne let him then admyre
> But yield his sence to bee too blunt and bace
> That n'ote without an hound fine footing trace. (2.Pro.2-4)

As an epitome of the making of an epistemological geography and a commentary on the travel accounts of his contemporaries, the stanzas prepare *terrae incognitae* for inscription: an idea of a world or worlds that can be re-ordered, re-imagined, and re-written while remaining within, or at least only just beyond, the bounds of known Creation.[30] In a now classic discussion of the romance mode, Northrop Frye argues that romance fills the space between myth and realism, transcending a particular historical moment: as a 'secular scripture', it contains 'the outlines of an imaginative universe' and claims worldmaking tendencies for the art of fiction.[31] Here, Spenser's imagination moves across different kinds of proposed sensual encounter with new terrain – hearing about Peru,

---

30 See S.K. Heninger, Jr., 'Poem as Literary Microcosm', in *Touches of Sweet Harmony: Pythagorean Cosmology and Renaissance Poetics* (San Marino: Huntington Library, 1974), pp. 364–97. For a 'heterotopian' reading see Anne Fogarty, 'Narrative Strategy in *The Faerie Queene*, Book VI' in *Edmund Spenser*, ed. Andrew Hadfield (London: Longman, 1996), pp. 196–210 (pp. 198–9).
31 Northrop Frye, *The Secular Scripture: A Study of the Structure of Romance* (Cambridge, MA: Harvard University Press, 1976), p. 15.

navigating the Amazon, and witnessing Virginia – before speculating on the existence of further possible worlds within a celestial region increasingly conceived as being mobile and expansive.[32]

The 'certein signes ... sett in sondrie place' are no landmarks in any real sense but the movements of the poem.[33] The poet positions the reader at a particular kind of 'here' and demands a self-aware engagement with the nature of situated knowledge, as if 'faery lond' is itself a kind of commonplace by which a reader can gauge the probability of the poet's fictions.[34] For Thomas Wilson, writing of how to recognise rhetorical commonplaces in *The Arte of Logique* (1551), for example,

> A place is the restyng corner of an argument, or els a marke whiche giveth warnyng to our memory what we maie speake probablie, either in the one parte, or the other, upon all causes that fall in question. Those that be good hare finders will sone finde the hare by her fourme. For when they se the grounde beaten flatte round about, and faire to the sight: thei have a narow gesse by al likelihod that the hare was there a litle before. Likewyse the hontesman in huntyng the foxe, wil sone espie when he seeth a hole, whether it be a foxe borough, or not. So he that will take profite in this parte of logique, must be like a hunter, and learne by labour to knowe the boroughes. For these places be nothyng els but covertes or boroughes, wherein if any one searche diligentlie, he maie fynde game at pleasure.[35]

Wilson, like Spenser after him, imagines a reader who can read traces in the figurative landscape, interpreting not only plainly visible pressed grass but also the covert and hidden spaces where an object of the hunt might seek shelter. The rhetorically self-conscious stanzas of Book II's proem may thus appropriate the discourse of contemporary scientific writing, for they share an investigative interest in empirical proving, as the 'fine footing' of Spenser's scent-hound suggests;[36] however, as in

---

32 See, for example, the material added by Thomas Digges to the work done by his father in Leonard Digges, *A Prognostication Everlastinge of Right Good Effecte* (London, 1576).
33 See Michael Murrin, 'The Rhetoric of Fairyland', in *The Rhetoric of Renaissance Poetry From Wyatt to Milton*, ed. Thomas O. Sloan and Raymond B. Waddington (Berkeley: University of California Press, 1974), pp. 73–95.
34 My thinking about commonplaces here and throughout is indebted to Catherine Nicholson's discussion of 'plausibility and place' in '*Othello* and the Geography of Persuasion', *ELR*, 40.1 (2010), 56–87.
35 Thomas Wilson, *The Rule of Reason, Conteinyng the Arte of Logique* (London, 1551), sig. Jv$^v$.
36 See Catherine Bates, *Masculinity and the Hunt: Wyatt to Spenser* (Oxford: Oxford University Press, 2013), pp. 238–9. Bates writes with reference to Carlo Ginzburg, *Clues, Myths, and the Historical Method*, trans. John and Anne C. Tedeschi (Baltimore: Johns Hopkins University Press, 1989), pp. 102–5.

Wilson's promise of locating coveted intellectual pleasure, they also leave the reader with an image of uncertain proximity. The proem shares with contemporary debates a concern for how to gauge the limits of authority across spatial and temporal distance, where narratives constructed by both travellers and poets, it seems, are subject to epistemological vagrancy.

Andrew Bennett describes one of the defining categories of literature as the capacity to play epistemological games: literature is 'the place where ignorance can be entertained, explored, enacted' and which can 'unlike many forms of philosophy, accommodate, for example, self-contradiction, permanent perplexity, aporia'.[37] Spenser's *Faerie Queene*, the proem to the second book suggests, takes form within a debatable space: as a 'fayre mirrhour' for Elizabeth's 'owne realmes' (II.pro.4), it occludes as much as it reveals, awaiting a final moment of recognition in which the poet's vision aligns with that of creation.[38] In the meanwhile it is *ou topos*, where this, for Spenser, is the 'design still unfulfilled': a condition that enables Spenser to conceive of *The Faerie Queene* as an 'epistemological romance', to use David Lee Miller's somewhat tautologous term, which is as interested in novelty and nostalgia, as it is in recognition.[39] The workings of Spenser's romance, then, are positioned as microcosmic, rather than heterotopian: they are of, and in, the world, rather than outside it.[40] And indeed, the romance mode is particularly well-positioned to deal with states of worldly aporia and uncertainty. For Patricia A. Parker its 'organizing principle ... simultaneously quests for and postpones a particular end, objective, or object'.[41] Her definition is inherently spatial, suggesting that romance offers a way of charting the spaces between self and other, the known and unknown, the recognised

---

37 Andrew Bennett, *Ignorance: Literature and Agnoiology* (Manchester: Manchester University Press, 2009), p. 22.
38 For the theological implications of witnessing see James A. Knapp, *Image Ethics in Shakespeare and Spenser* (New York: Palgrave Macmillan 2011), pp. 75–80.
39 David Lee Miller uses the term to suggest 'a consolidation of knowledge with masculine desire' in *The Poem's Two Bodies: The Poetics of the 1590 Faerie Queene* (Princeton: Princeton University Press, 1988), pp. 92–8 (p. 95). See also Terence Cave, *Recognitions: A Study in Poetics* (Oxford: Clarendon Press, 1988).
40 M.H. Abrams argues that Sir Philip Sidney's *Defence* holds this distinction 'in suspension'. See *The Mirror and the Lamp: Romantic Theory and the Critical Tradition* (Oxford: Oxford University Press, 1953; repr. 1976), p. 274. See also Wayne Erickson, *Mapping the Faerie Queene: Quest Structures and the World of the Poem* (New York: Garland Publishing, 1996), pp. 30–3 and pp. 60–4.
41 Patricia A. Parker, *Inescapable Romance: Studies in the Poetics of a Mode* (Princeton: Princeton University Press, 1979), p. 4.

and unfamiliar. Spenser's 'signes' thus participate in a process that demands a willing suspension of disbelief in the capacity of empirical thought to know and decide all.[42]

As Spenser playfully acknowledges, authors of fiction are free to exploit the territories left uncharted by their more cautious friends: men who, although they may travel to the edges of the known world, are ultimately subject to time, tide, and the threat of a less than credulous reception.[43] In an alchemical treatise written by Joseph Duchesne, and translated into English by John Hester in 1591, for example, a letter addressing the book's readers contains the following defence, which privileges personal experience over abstract learning. The book's author, in order to persuade his readers of the work's validity, purposefully reaches for a far-fetched image and, like Spenser, resorts to a geographical analogy:

> *Experientia stultorum gubernatrix*, is with some held as a Proverbe autenticke: but in mine opinion (freendlie Reader) they are most fooles that want it. For without it howsoever otherwise well read, a man can say no more in Artes then the great Travailer (who in some fewe daies, having coasted the worlde in a Card-makers shop) can discourse directlie eyther of this or that, but must be faine if fault be found, to confesse his owne ignoraunce, and blame the Maps falsenes; yet as wee have with us a custome, when we heare things incredible spoken from a far, to say, it is better beleeving it, then going thether to disprove it.[44]

The proverbial commonplace to which the author disparagingly refers holds that 'experience is the governor of fools'; and so, in contrast to the man who is content with hearsay (whereby foresight might be more typically thought of as the teacher of wise men), he promises to trace his own 'perilous passage' to its end. The effect of the analogy, which criticises the credulous position of armchair travellers who delightedly coast 'the worlde in a Card-makers shop', anticipates Spenser's proem by identifying a phenomenon that results from an epistemological discrepancy: the

---

42 For the precedent set by Plato in giving '*muthoi* ... an irreplaceable structural role in the exposition of philosophy' see Nick Davis, *Stories of Chaos: Reason and its Displacement in Early Modern English Narrative* (Aldershot: Ashgate, 1999), p. vii. See also David Galbraith, *Architectonics of Imitation in Spenser, Daniel and Drayton* (Toronto: University of Toronto Press, 2000), pp. 14–17.

43 For the anxiety of men such as Walter Ralegh, who 'were haunted by the fear that their tales of other lands would be treated as fictions' see Thomas Betteridge, 'Introduction', in *Borders and Travellers in Early Modern Europe* (Aldershot: Ashgate, 2007), pp. 1–14 (p. 7).

44 Joseph Duchesne, *A Breefe Aunswere of Josephus Quercetanus Armeniacus, Doctor of Phisick, to the Exposition of Jacobus Aubertus Vindonis*, trans. John Hester (London, 1591), sig. A3$^r$.

active witnessing of other lands is pitched against the handling of textual counterparts and reports some space away.⁴⁵

Sir Thomas More, of course, exploited such lacunae in the fashioning of his own imagined society, Utopia, which memorably functions as both good place (*eu-topos*) and no place (*ou-topos*): its location, famously difficult to find unless a member of the island state, is accessed via channels 'known only' to the initiated, and even then skilled Utopian pilots 'could scarcely enter without jeopardy, but that their way is directed and ruled by certain landmarks standing on the shore'. As More's narrator Hythloday continues, serving to subvert any readerly desire to situate and chart further, such seamarks can be manipulated, and by 'turning, translating, and removing these marks into other places they may destroy their enemies' navies'.⁴⁶ More's dialogic ironies, which draw on Socratic models of knowledge as '*a-topos*', are themselves notoriously difficult to navigate; like Spenser's shifting 'certein signes', the 'turning, translating' seamarks of the Utopians bear testimony to the capacity of literary language and rhetorical figuration not only to help ideas travel but also to achieve obfuscating and dilatory ends.⁴⁷ Spenser's Book II proem, which shares in More's distancing games, thus appears to stage what happens when the playful and ironic set of the serio-ludic humanist mind bears down on the local textures of a romance worldscape suspended 'bitwixe ernest and game'.⁴⁸

---

45 See Matthew Woodcock, *Fairy in The Faerie Queene: Renaissance Elf-Fashioning and Elizabethan Myth-Making* (Aldershot: Ashgate, 2004), pp. 68–72. For other travel texts to which Spenser might be alluding see Shannon Miller, *Invested with Meaning: The Raleigh Circle in the New World* (Philadelphia: University of Pennsylvania Press, 1998), p. 36 and Lorna Hutson, 'Chivalry for Merchants; or, Knights of Temperance in the Realms of Gold', *JMEMS*, 26.1 (1996), 29–59, p. 30. As Evelyn Mullally observes, 'distance in space ... lends enchantment'. See *The Artist at Work: Narrative Technique in Chrétien de Troyes* (Philadelphia: American Philosophical Society, 1988), p. 174.
46 Sir Thomas More, *Utopia*, trans. Ralph Robinson (1551), in *Three Early Modern Utopias*, ed. Susan Bruce (Oxford: Oxford University Press, 1999; repr. 2008), pp. 1–148 (pp. 49–50).
47 For Spenser's self-conscious manipulation of poetic figures see the chapters on Spenser in Susanne Lindgren Wofford, *The Choice of Achilles: The Ideology of Figure in the Epic* (Stanford: Stanford University Press, 1992).
48 Geoffrey Chaucer, *The Merchant's Tale*, in *The Riverside Chaucer*, pp. 153–68, line 1594. For a theory of the relationship between irony and allegory see Paul de Man, 'The Rhetoric of Temporality', in *Interpretation: Theory and Practice*, ed. Charles S. Singleton (Baltimore: Johns Hopkins University Press, 1969), pp. 173–209 (esp. pp. 191–209).

### Forests of romance

In the final complete book of *The Faerie Queene*, the forest encountered by Calepine and the foundling emerges from the psychomachia of the earlier parts of the poem as a strangely unvariegated space.[49] More than a projection of the knight's existential state, the setting is an alienating wilderness that is apparently indifferent to the knight's presence; where the 'wandring wood' of Book I had combined the ordered pageant of the epic tree catalogue with the chaos of Redcrosse's confusion and an adversary to overcome, this place appears as an obstacle to be countered on equal footing with the problem of what to do with the mewling babe. There are no enchanting figures of either guidance or treachery present and the knight is left to his own powers of endurance to break out of its environs. It is only after the brutal slaying of the bear that Calepine, unhorsed and unarmed, realises he has become lost:

> So hauing all his bands againe vptyde,
>   He with him thought back to returne againe:
>   But when he lookt about on euery syde,
>   To weet which way were best to entertaine,
>   To bring him to the place, where he would faine,
>   He could no path not tract of foot descry,
>   Ne by inquirie learne, nor ghesse by ayme.
>   For nought but woods and forests farre and nye,
> That all about did close the compasse of his eye.
>
> Much was he then encombred, ne could tell
>   Which way to take: now West he went a while,
>   Then North; then neither, but as fortune fell.
>   So vp and downe he wandred many a mile,
>   With wearie trauell and vncertaine toile,
>   Yet nought the nearer to his iourneys end;
>   And euermore his louely litle spoile
>   Crying for food, did greatly him offend.
> So all that day in wandring vainely he did spend.
>
> At last about the setting of the Sunne,
>   Himselfe out of the forest he did wynd,
>   And by good fortune the plaine champion wonne
>   Where looking all about, where he mote fynd
>   Some place of succour to content his mynd, ... (VI.iv.24–6)

---

49 Michael F.N. Dixon notes the 'fairytale' qualities of the story of Calepine and the foundling. See 'Bruin, Matilde', in *SEnc*, pp. 117–18.

With no defining features to orientate the knight, and no landmarks offered by which to navigate, the homogeneity of the forest serves to 'close the compass of his eye'. This imposed orientational blindness recalls how Guyon had been likened by the narrator to a mariner imperilled amidst a star-occluding tempest. Then, the knight-seafarer relied on 'his owne virtues' (II.vii.2), as if turning to a shipman's card and compass, but here the apparent thinness of the allegory raises the question of whether this wood may just be a wood in which Calepine is physically lost.

In Book I's 'wandring wood', there had been an implied true path to follow: the straight and narrow path invisible to Redcrosse in his untested state, which he spends the duration of his adventures learning to identify in a fallen world. Here, by contrast, Calepine's pathless wood seems to present little more than a holding position, as if the actions of the knight have little moral consequence: he just needs to find a way out of danger for both himself and the child before nightfall. The lesson perhaps suggests the importance of stoic resilience, of finding virtue 'not in outward shows, but inward thoughts defyned' (VI.pro.5). To represent this, the setting functions less like inscape and more like landscape: a believable organic threat that evades definitive allegorical exegesis. In addition, the explicit use of named cardinal compass points by the narrator after he has shut down his protagonist's navigational ability is particularly interesting. In one sense, Calepine perpetuates the westerly motion previously begun by Britomart and Artegall, demonstrating the emergent trend in the second half of *The Faerie Queene* to associate the landscapes of Faery land with the unmapped spaces of Ireland.[50] Yet, in another, Calepine's compulsive movement west, then north, 'then neither', then 'vp and downe', seems a particularly sadistic compression of the narrator's deployment of unlocated, and uninterpretable, romance travail.[51]

In *Mimesis*, Erich Auerbach argued that the function of romance geography is to provide a frame within which quests can occur; the world of 'knightly proving' he describes is a pre-determined and unsurprising space that contains nothing that 'is not either accessory or preparatory

---

50 Travelling west and then north takes Calepine, a more tired and lonely figure than Calidore, towards the lands of Sir Bruin, which lie, according to A.C. Hamilton, 'outside the English Pale and in the rebellious Tyrone county'. See *FQ*, notes to VI.vi.25, 29 (pp. 629–30). Although Christopher Burlinson does not mention Calepine's wood specifically, it provides a good example of what he calls Spenser's 'fluctuating material attention'. See 'The Spenserian Wood', in *Allegory, Space and the Material World in the Writings of Edmund Spenser* (Cambridge: D.S. Brewer, 2006), pp. 167–94 (p. 169).
51 For Arthur as a compulsive quester see Wofford, *The Choice of Achilles*, p. 259.

to an adventure'.⁵² Auerbach emphasises narrative determinism, for within such limits a questing figure could never be lost. Yet, for readers of Spenser's *Faerie Queene*, the through-roads never seem quite so certain. The space of 'knightly proving' in Spenser's poem is complicated by a continually evolving understanding of how the poem creates meaning, apparently resulting in forms of literary fashioning far in excess of the merely 'accessory or preparatory': in constantly testing the limits of his fiction Spenser engages with the metafictional capacities of the romance mode as if in a dialogue with his predecessors. For example, although there is no evidence to suggest that Spenser knew of the late fourteenth-century alliterative Arthurian romance *Sir Gawain and the Green Knight*,⁵³ this work offers an important demonstration of how romance blends chivalric space with an extraordinary engagement with a regional landscape. It is useful to consider its archetypal, and idiosyncratic, terrain in order to cast Spenser's allegorical romance into relief. In moving between a central court – the place of men, society and culture – and the wild periphery of a heightened wilderness, *Gawain*'s environments are characterised by the intersection of the marvellous with the quotidian: specific isolated features interrupt the everyday textures of the natural world by taking on aspects of the sacred or numinous.⁵⁴ Pre-empting the later literary conditions and techniques that shape Calepine's uneasy quest, the contours of Gawain's journey introduce resistant geographical forms that intensify and estrange what is at stake in negotiating a world of 'knightly proving'.

Following a grisly Christmas game played out at the court of Camelot, Sir Gawain is tasked with finding the Green Chapel on the morning of New Year's Day in order to face his challenger, the Green Knight, a year on from their first encounter. The undirected quest takes him though an unsympathetic landscape and the *Gawain*-poet emphasises the vulnerability, isolation, and disorientation of his protagonist. Prayer to God emerges as Gawain's only hope of preservation and comfort:

---

52 Erich Auerbach, *Mimesis: The Representation of Reality in Western Literature*, trans. Willard R. Trask (Garden City, NY: Doubleday, 1957), p. 119.
53 For the provenance of the single surviving manuscript source see A.S.G. Edwards, 'The Manuscript: British Library MS Cotton Nero A.x', in *A Companion to the Gawain-Poet*, ed. Derek Brewer and Jonathan Gibson (Cambridge: D.S. Brewer, 1997), 197–219.
54 See Ad Putter, 'The Landscape of Courtly Romance', in *Sir Gawain and the Green Knight and French Arthurian Romance* (Oxford: Clarendon Press, 1995; repr. 2001), pp. 10–50. As Jacques Le Goff writes, the diverse loci of the marvellous include 'natural sites' such as mountains, rocks, fountains, trees and islands, and 'sites of human action' such as 'cities, castles, towers, and tombs'. See *The Medieval Imagination*, trans. Arthur Goldhammer (Chicago: University of Chicago Press, 1985; repr. 1992), pp. 27–44 (p. 36).

> Now ridez þis renk þur3 þe ryalme of Logres,
> Sir Gauan, on Godez halue, þa3 hym no gomen þo3t.
> Oft leudlez alone he lengez on ny3tez
> Þer he fonde no3t hym byfore þe fare þat he lyked.
> Hade he no fere bot his fole bi frythez and dounez,
> Ne no gome bot God bi gate wyth to karp,
> Til þat he ne3ed ful neghe into þe Norþe Walez.
> Alle þe iles of Anglesay on lyft half he haldez,
> And farez ouer þe fordez by þe forlondez,
> Ouer at þe Holy Hede, til he hade eft bonk
> In þe wyldrenesse of Wyrale; wonde þer bot lyte
> Þat auþer God oþer gome wyth goud hert louied.[55]

In spite of the specificity with which place-names are used within the work, the challenge initially issued by the Green Knight does not specify a route. Instead, he insists that if Gawain has faith in his ability to find the Green Chapel, he will not fail in his quest to find it: 'þe kny3t of þe grene chapel men knowen me mony;/ Forþi me for to fynde if þou fraystez, faylez þou neuer' (454–5). If Gawain is to find the place, which is familiar to many, he must endeavour to learn of its location by trial and testing ('fraisten', v.). The self-directed labour shapes the poem's psychological intensity; however, if this is a world of 'knightly proving', then Gawain's progress through his temporary suspension between the court and his strange destination is directly proportional to the exercise of his faith, rather than to the physical distance he travels. He may travel north, passing Anglesey, Holyhead, and the Wirral, but the only bearing this has on his experience, as with Calepine's 'wearie trauell and vncertaine toile' (*FQ*, VI.iv.25), is to sustain it. For Gawain, eventual arrival at the Green Chapel is expected, even dreaded; yet, constancy and faith are curious kinds of spatial logic indeed. In the wilderness the place of trial is only recognised after arrival, where deferred recognition results in tautology: the end of the quest occurs when the quest is ended.[56] Gawain can only return to the court once he can recognise that he has been found wanting, and when the challenges of navigating the wilderness and fulfilling his festive promise are revealed as cover for the trial of his continence and fealty.

---

55 *Sir Gawain and the Green Knight*, ed. J.R.R. Tolkien and E.V. Gordon, 2nd edn revised by Norman Davis (Oxford: Clarendon Press, 1967), lines 691–702. Subsequent references are placed in the text.

56 See Kenneth Gross, *Spenserian Poetics: Idolatry, Iconoclasm, and Magic* (Ithaca: Cornell University Press, 1985), p. 156.

In spite of the concealed quality of the ordeal, the emergence of earnest topographical description in the *Gawain* poet's work produces, in R.V.W. Eliot's words, a 'dual mode of description', which responds to the poet's interest in the relationship between 'the imaginative world of Arthurian romance' and 'the real world of fallible human beings': a blend of categories that also sustains Spenser's work.[57] Gawain's travails may participate in romance games of 'exile and return', but the hostility of the material world ensures that the hope of arrival, let alone return, is fragile:

> Nade he ben duȝty and dryȝe, and Dryȝtyn had serued,
> Douteles he hade ben ded and dreped ful ofte.
> For werre wrathed hym not so much þat wynter nas wors,
> When þe colde cler water fro þe cloudez schadde,
> And fres er hit falle myȝt to þe fale erþe;
> Ner slayn wyth þe slete he sleped in his yrnes
> Mo nyȝtez þen innoghe in naked rokkez,
> Þer as claterande fro þe crest þe colde borne rennez,
> And henged heȝe ouer his hede in hard iisse-ikkles.
> Þus in peryl and payne and plytes ful harde
> Bi contray cayrez þis knyȝt, tyl Krystmasse euen,
>     al one; ... (724–35)

As Gawain progresses on his solitary quest, the frozen desert wilderness threatens to exceed its bounds. It encroaches on the space inhabited by the body of the beleaguered knight, who attempts to find brief respite by sleeping fitfully in his armour. At the turn of the year, civility and wilderness belong to permeable rather than oppositional categories, organised only by the interpretive perception of Gawain.[58] The following morning, as he passes through a place of 'hore okez', 'hasel', and 'raged mosse' (743–5), he prays for 'sum herber' (755) at which he might hear mass. It is out of the blend of his devotions with the marsh and mire of the shifting forest ground that a vision of shelter condenses: a transition that produces a complex vision of the knight's place in the ecology through which he moves.

Bertilak of Hautdesert, who extends hospitality to Gawain at Christmas, conveys the warmth, bravery, and civility of a cultured man; however, his

---

57 R.W.V. Elliot, *The Gawain Country* (Ilkley: University of Leeds, 1984), p. 41. Elliot's study of Middle English topographical words locates the green chapel as 'Lud-church' in Staffordshire (p. 44).
58 For the use of the gaze in organising space in the poem see Sarah Stanbury, *Seeing the Gawain Poet: Description and the Act of Perception* (Philadelphia: University of Pennsylvania Press, 1991), pp. 106–8.

name betrays an affinity with the wildness of the high-desert, or great forest, over which he is lord. The perspectival shift finally required to recognise him as the Green Knight Gawain seeks thus feels apposite. As Jacques Le Goff notes, the 'forest-desert' is a prominent feature of medieval imaginative literature but 'neither the forest nor the desert was wholly wild or isolated. Both were places on the extreme fringes of society, where men could venture and meet other men'.[59] This observation has implications for the narratives of Spenser's Legend of Courtesy, which inherits and extends this romance tradition via Spenser's fiction-making technique of drawing on the experiences of the New English in Ireland.[60] Le Goff's categorisation of the forest as liminal, rather than alien, is significant. It is a realm that can be reshaped by labouring hands from chaotic wilderness into rural idyll: a process that can also happen in reverse. Within the forest, the encounter between cultivation, or courtesy, and the contemplation of its loss, offers a space in which protagonists are threatened with their undoing. Gawain returns to Arthur's court a sadder and lonelier figure, who has ultimately failed a test he did not fully comprehend. Equally for Spenser's protagonists, for whom the space of 'knightly proving' is complicated by the multiplicity of centres and peripheries networking *The Faerie Queene*'s interwoven narratives, the place of apparent trial is rarely the place where its consequences are most deeply felt.

Calepine, like most of Spenser's protagonists, thus finds himself in a strange place because, unknown to him, he is navigating not only the spaces of his narrator's creation but also the spatial legacies of previous romance writers. The long-lived romance forest, as Corinne J. Saunders has shown, is fertile with symbolism, the roots of which run deep in the literary imagination from the wildernesses of the Bible to the green-worlds of Spenser and Shakespeare. As she observes, the 'landscape of quest, adventure and discovery is countered by the geographical and climatic reality of the British landscape', which produces 'a sense of a region ... poised midway between *ernest* and game'.[61] As well as being

---

59 Le Goff, *The Medieval Imagination*, pp. 55–6.
60 See Julia Reinhard Lupton, 'Mapping Mutability: or, Spenser's Irish Plot', in *Representing Ireland: Literature and the Origins of Conflict, 1534–1660*, ed. Brendan Bradshaw, Andrew Hadfield, and Willy Maley (Cambridge: Cambridge University Press, 1993), pp. 93–115. For the importance of English forests to the Legend of Courtesy see Elizabeth M. Weixel, 'Squires of the Wood: The Decline of the Aristocratic Forest in Book VI of *The Faerie Queene*', *Spenser Studies*, 25 (2010), 187–213.
61 Corinne J. Saunders, *The Forest of Medieval Romance: Avernus, Broceliande, Arden* (Cambridge: D.S. Brewer, 1993), p. 155.

a site of economic and cultural importance, the forest acts as a locus of malleable chaos,[62] the meta-fictional qualities of which can be used to plot processes of transformation that remain coupled to the workings of the mind's imaginative capacity, combining acts of making with processes of discovery.[63] For the purposes of this study, Saunders's observations concerning the British landscape can also be extended to Ireland, whose reflection in romance traditionally wavers between 'Otherworld Island' and geopolitical reality. The representation of Ireland in medieval romance is frequently coupled with a colonial agenda, even though, as Elizabeth Rambo observes, spatial specificity is often compromised by hyperbole, where 'the actual location' often 'seems irrelevant when, as in the *Alliterative Morte Arthure*, Ireland is included with lands such as Africa and Austria … in order to magnify Arthur's conquest'.[64] Spenser's own mythmaking typically ties English interests in the incorporation of Ireland under English rule to a focus on the proving of the young Prince Arthur.[65] And as John Gillingham explains, King Arthur's involvement in Ireland was firmly entrenched in English chronicle history: 'Geoffrey of Monmouth, writing in the late 1130s, took it for granted that the Irish were an uncivilised people. And it was Geoffrey, of course, who invented the story that King Arthur had conquered Ireland – the story with which Hakluyt began his *Principal Navigations*'.[66]

Hakluyt's image of Arthur as king and conqueror, who 'in the second yeere of his raigne … subdued all partes of Ireland' before sailing on to further northern conquests,[67] is echoed and even exceeded by Spenser when he reminds his readers in *A View* that 'it appeareth by good record yet extant, that King Arthur, and before him Gurgunt, had all that iland under their alleagiance and subjection' (p. 52). When Spenser refers to

62 Both Paul Piehler and Saunders mention Aristotle's cosmological 'conjunction of *nous* and *hyle*, where *hyle* denotes the chaos antecedent to the operation of Form, but literally means "forest"'. See Piehler, *The Visionary Landscape: A Study in Medieval Allegory* (London: Edward Arnold, 1971), p. 75.
63 See Kenneth Gross, 'Green Thoughts in a Green Shade', *Spenser Studies*, 24 (2009), 355–71.
64 Elizabeth L. Rambo, *Colonial Ireland in Medieval English Literature* (Selinsgrove: Susquehanna University Press, 1994), p. 48.
65 See Willy Maley, *Salvaging Spenser: Colonisation, Culture and Identity* (Basingstoke: Macmillan, 1997), pp. 100–4 and Richard A. McCabe, *Spenser's Monstrous Regiment: Elizabethan Ireland and the Poetics of Difference* (Oxford: Oxford University Press, 2002), pp. 13–23.
66 John Gillingham, 'The English Invasion of Ireland', in *Representing Ireland*, pp. 24–42 (p. 28).
67 Richard Hakluyt, *The Principall Navigations, Voiages and Discoveries of the English Nation* (London, 1589), sig. Aa1$^r$ (p. 243).

the subject matter of *The Faerie Queene*, as 'furthest from the daunger of envy, and suspition of present time' ('A Letter of the Authors', p. 715), then, the claim belies his acute awareness that the Arthurian frame had a currency independent of his fiction-making and which framed the attempted re-conquest of Ireland as recuperation.[68] Spenser, of course, was not the first to 'romance' Ireland in this way and Thomas Herron has recently observed that he may have drawn on the Irish settings and some of the plot details of the mid-fifteenth-century prose romance *The Hystorye of Olyver of Castylle* as source materials for *The Faerie Queene*, in addition to works such as *Bevis of Hampton* and *Guy of Warwick*.[69] As a work invested in the idealisation of colonial projects, the *Hystorye* tells the story of two young men, identical in virtues and physical appearance, who leave their native lands for northern Europe's hostile shores. Olyver of Castylle, whose self-imposed exile eventually leads to capture and imprisonment, and Arthur of Algarbe, who searches for his beloved friend, operate as surrogates: a motif that anticipates Spenser's drawing of the relationship between his own surrogate knights, Prince Arthur and Artegall, as well as the events of Book I, when Arthur rescues Redcrosse.

Based on a French text by Philippe Camus, the English translation by Henry Watson appears in a richly illustrated edition printed in 1518 by Wynkyn de Worde.[70] The Arthur of *Olyver of Castylle* is an Iberian monarch; yet, through a series of episodes concerned with diplomatic negation and ceremonial performance, the romance repeatedly returns to the relationship between Ireland and England.[71] When the English

68 See Andrew Hadfield and Willy Maley, 'Introduction: Irish Representations and English Alternatives', in *Representing Ireland*, pp. 1–23 (p. 6). See also David A. Summers, *Spenser's Arthur: The British Arthurian Tradition and The Faerie Queene* (Lanham: University Press of America, 1997), p. vii and Andrew Escobedo, *Nationalism and Historical Loss in Renaissance England* (Ithaca: Cornell University Press, 2004), pp. 45–80. For romance's investment in geopolitical conquest see Jennifer R. Goodman, *Chivalry and Exploration 1298–1630* (Woodbridge: Boydell Press, 1998), pp. 1–24 and pp. 45–77 and King, *The Faerie Queene and Middle English Romance*, pp. 198–206.

69 See Thomas Herron, 'Irish Romance: Spenser's Prince Arthur and the *Hystorye of Olyuer of Castile* (c. 1518)', *Notes and Queries*, 51.3 (2004), 254–6. Cooper and King also note the importance of *Bevis of Hampton* and *Guy of Warwick* as sources for Books I and II of *The Faerie Queene*.

70 Gail Orgelfinger speculates that there may have been an earlier English edition, printed to commemorate the union of 'the English prince Arthur and Spanish princess Catherine in 1501'. See 'Introduction', in *The Hystorye of Olyuer of Castylle* (New York: Garland Publishing, 1988), pp. ix–xxxvi (p. xv).

71 See Elizabeth Williams, 'England, Ireland and Iberia in *Olyver of Castylle*: The View from Burgundy', in *Boundaries in Medieval Romance*, ed. Neil Cartlidge (Cambridge: D.S. Brewer, 2008), pp. 93–102. Williams provides a summary of the plot and the motifs employed as well as a manuscript history.

invade Ireland with Olyver's help, for example, the 'Irysshmen' fight chivalrously during the brutal siege and are presented as worthy foes within the romance's idealising terms: they 'solde theyr lyves ryghte derely' and when faced with the threat that 'they sholde lese theyr countree/ ... theyr courage doubled' and they 'dyde as well as they myght'.[72] The seven defeated Irish kings brought to England as prisoners of war are notably present at both the marriage of Helayne and Olyver and the subsequent tournament, where two of them are killed in the tilts. Their eventual return to their own country, after paying homage by 'offrynge them alwaye at the kynges pleasure/ and Olyvers/ for god had gyven hym suche grace that every body loved hym' (sig. L5ᵛ), suggests that a diplomatic alliance has been formed in spite of bloodshed. The geopolitical complexity is increased in the second part of the romance when Olyver becomes separated from a hunt and subsequently abducted by the vengeful son of one of the Irish kings. This functions as a cue for Olyver's best friend Arthur to make 'an enterpryse for to fynde his felowe' (sig. L8ᵛ), having been notified of his friend's imperilled state by an instrument of divination: a magic mirror of romance that functions in similar ways to those of Chaucer's *Squire's Tale* and Spenser's Legend of Chastity. This glass, 'ful of clere water', changes colour after it detects the occurrence of the 'evyll adventure or empesshement' (sig. C1ᵛ–C2ʳ): 'that is ... the water was troubled and gretely obscure. In suche wyse that it was almoost lyke ynke' (sig. M1ʳ). The romance thus contains an example of one of the earliest forms of scrying found in literature, where the use of swirling water as a method of divination is known as *cyclicomancy*.[73]

*Olyver of Castylle* miniaturises conventional romance tropes by suggesting that the peripheral insularity of England and Ireland can stand in for the troubling exoticism of more distant lands;[74] however, the descriptions provided offer little sense of the territories involved having a connected relationship in space. Arthur's rescue attempt produces an itinerary that moves across Western Europe, which he undertakes without immediate knowledge of his friend's whereabouts:

---

72 *The Hystorye of Olyver of Castylle and of the fayre Helayne*, trans. Henry Watson (London, 1518), sig. K1ʳ. Subsequent references are placed in the text.
73 See Benjamin Goldberg, *The Mirror and Man* (Charlottesville: University of Virginia Press, 1985), pp. 8–9.
74 See Herron, 'Irish Romance', p. 256. Williams argues that the narrative's movements are orientated using 'an apparently factual European map' and describes Camus as an 'armchair-topographer'. See 'England, Ireland and Iberia in *Olyver of Castylle*', p. 94 and p. 99.

In suche maner as ye have herde departed the valyaunt and gentyll Arthur from his countree. And began for to serche tydynges of his felowe/ as he that hadde wyll never for to reste tyll that he had herde tydynges of hym. The fyrste countree that he arryved in was Portyngale/ in the whiche he founde nothynge that was pleasaunt unto hym. After he sought the remenaunt of Spayne/ and came in to that of Fraunce/ and wente so moche on one syde and other that he came to Calys/ where as he founde men that wente in to Englande/ and therfore he mounted on the see for to go theder. Ye maye well thynke that he was longe in serchynge the countrees that ye have herde above. In this meane whyle Olyver his felowe was alwaye in pryson/ with brede and water and often bette as he that had never hope to departe thens. And desyred nothynge but the dethe. (sig. M2$^r$)

The author invites mental collaboration in Arthur's restless but perfunctory travails, as if pre-empting the imaginative urge to fill in narrative lacunae. Yet, when Arthur sets sail, his linear progress is briefly suspended, as if the watery limits of the English Channel create an in-between space for the object of the quest to reassert his plight; as a place of mediation, or 'meane' space, the channel allows the author to contemplate what is happening elsewhere, in the 'meane whyle'. The abrupt narrative shift in time and space creates a rapid telescoping effect that contrasts Arthur's mobility with his friend's enforced confinement; Olyver's suffering is thus kept ever-present, and proximate, to Arthur's relative spatial freedom.

With the intimation of Olyver's desire for death then held in suspension, the description of Arthur's approach to Ireland blends credible detail with traditional romance motifs of seafaring and shipwreck.[75] After encountering a contrary wind, Arthur is blown off course into unfamiliar seas that initially surpass the knowledge and expertise of his ship's crew:

> As Arthur was on the see for to go in to Englande/ there happened a wynde contrary to aryse on the see/ and drove them in to the marches that the maryners knewe not atte that presente tyme. But whan that they had longe beholden and sene it/ they apperceyved that it was one of the countrees and realmes of Irlande/ the ferdest from that of Englande. Whan Arthur herde saye that it was one of the realme of Irlande/ he prayed them that they wolde set hym a lande for as hym semyd/ as sone myght he here tydynges

---

[75] For the work done by sea travel in romance see Cooper, 'Providence and the Sea', in *The English Romance in Time*, pp. 106–36 and David Quint, *Epic and Empire: Politics and Generic Form from Virgil to Milton* (Princeton: Princeton University Press, 1993), pp. 248–67.

of that whiche he soughte/ as in another countree/ so as he dyde by the wyll of god even so as ye shall here. Whan Arthur was on grounde/ he wente on fote in praynge our lorde for to adresse hym on his waye. He was well the space of two monethes in that countree. And whan he wolde have ony thynge he muste make some sygne/ or elles they coude not understande hym. He hadde neyther hors nor mule for to ryde on/ wherfore he wente on fote/ and soo longe he wente that on a daye he founde hymselfe in a thycke forest/ in the whiche dyvers wylde beestes dydde remayne. (sig. M2$^{r-v}$)

The narrative stages a gradual process of recognition, fashioning a view of Ireland from the hearsay of fifteenth-century geographical knowledge; the arrival of the mariners in the 'realmes of Irlande/ the ferdest from ... Englande' offers a deliberate attempt to obfuscate a sense of place.[76] Subject to drift, Arthur's passage towards a coastline that exists on epistemological margins ultimately provides him with entrance into the forest cover of romance territory: a familiar trope used to represent the unfamiliar.[77]

Having made landfall, Arthur is hampered by his foot-sore isolation and an inability to speak the language of the place, his only comfort being 'whan he thoughte upon saynt Johan Baptyst that lyved by rotes' (sig. M3$^v$). Like Spenser's Guyon, and Calepine, who follows in Guyon's pedestrian footsteps, he is an isolated figure: as a knight without a horse, he must feel the labour of his travails. After a fight with a lion and a shrieking 'mervaylous beest' (sig. M3$^v$), Arthur is rescued by a man dressed in white garments, who addresses him by name and salves his wounds with magic ointment.[78] Arthur's surprise at being recognised as a king prompts him to ask his saviour whether he is 'a thynge of the other worlde' (sig. N1$^r$), marking the place in which he wanders, or at least his perception of it, as somewhere that suddenly slips between the earthly and the marvellous.[79] Yet, as the narrative draws towards its conclusion, Arthur's travails depart the forest of romance for more familiar shores. In one notable Anglicisation of the French text, Henry Watson translates

---

76 For the trade routes between Spain and Ireland and the accuracy of medieval and early modern navigational charts see Timothy O'Neill, *Merchants and Mariners in Medieval Ireland* (Dublin: Irish Academic Press, 1987).
77 See David J. Baker, 'Charting Uncertainty in Renaissance Ireland', in *Representing Ireland*, pp. 76–92.
78 Herron proposes that this beast may be a predecessor of Spenser's Blatant Beast who appears in Book V of *The Faerie Queene*. See 'Irish Romance', p. 255.
79 For the relationship between Ireland and the Otherworld see Rambo, *Colonial Ireland in Medieval English Literature*, pp. 48–64 and pp. 121–4.

the obscurely named 'vausse montier', of Arthur's eventual landfall in England as 'Brystowe', where he is immediately misrecognised as his best friend, or 'knowen for Olyver' (sig. N2ʳ).[80] Owing to the inclusion of the English port city as a seamark, Watson's imposition suddenly relocates Arthur's passage back within navigable channels. From an Iberian court to Ireland, via both salt and forest wilderness, and to Bristol and London and back again, the twinned voyages of Olyver and Arthur prove that in romance, a reader can never be quite sure of the rules governing the writing of space.

## Making, drifting, plotting

In situating his poem within a corpus of 'Arthurian' romances, which multiply the resonances of person, place, and name, Spenser devised a protective strategy for the exploration of delicate content, even if the claims to archaic fancy were themselves a further fiction. Gabriel Harvey's description of his friend's allegorical romance as evidence of '*Hob-goblin runne away with the Garland from Apollo*', for example, suggests how the deliberate vagrancies of Spenser's chosen modes left him vulnerable to intellectual criticism.[81] For many readers, deliberate archaism was associated with inertia, belatedness, and stagnation, and though Harvey's cautionary words concerning the threat of Hobgoblin may be primarily playful, they also imply a particular kind of appropriation.[82] The interlacing of Apollonian reason and poetry in the laureate object of theft implies a combination of metamorphosis and authority; however, the figure of the hobgoblin is not Apollo's opposite, for he rather belongs to a different order of myth. As a character of mischievous transport, ever running in Harvey's formulation, and a shape-shifter according to early modern folktale, he figures a route to alternative modes of poetic making.[83]

Romance, of course, received satirical treatment well before the attacks of Spenser's immediate contemporaries.[84] Chaucer's brief travesty of the

---

80 See Orgelfinger, ed., *The Hystorye of Olyuer of Castylle*, p. xx and p. 239, n. 157.
81 Gabriel Harvey, *Three Proper, and Wittie, Familiar Letters* (London, 1580), sig. F1ᵛ.
82 Conversely, for a reading of Spenser's productive archaism, see Lucy Munro, *Archaic Style in English Literature, 1590–1674* (Cambridge: Cambridge University Press, 2013), pp. 1–31.
83 See Jenny C. Mann, *Outlaw Rhetoric: Figuring Vernacular Eloquence in Shakespeare's England* (Ithaca: Cornell University Press, 2012), p. 129.
84 As Saunders comments, Chaucer's *Tale of Sir Thopas* used 'the epithet "fair forest" … to exemplify the foolish doggerel of metrical romance'. See *The Forest of Medieval Romance*, p. 155.

romance mode, the *Tale of Sir Thopas*, which is recounted by a fictionalised version of the author himself in *The Canterbury Tales*, has long been acknowledged as one of Spenser's immediate sources for *The Faerie Queene*.[85] The famously interrupted narrative includes an exemplary romance landscape, charged by the 'prikynge' motion of the titular knight, who is sick with 'love-longynge'.[86] As Sir Thopas impulsively 'priketh north and est' he encounters a scene of spiced vegetative splendour, where 'lycorys and the cetewale' grow alongside 'clowe-gylofre' and 'notemuge' (757, 761–3), and skies filled with the songs of exotic and predatory birds (766–71). The scene is both indeterminate in its idealised impossibility and over-determined in its accumulation of cliché.[87] The knight's horse sweats with exertion, his sides bloodied as if nearly flogged to death, and so Sir Thopas briefly lies down to rest; while asleep he dreams of an 'elf-queene' who shall his 'lemman be' (788). Events are even further compressed when the remounted Sir Thopas departs for and arrives at 'the contree of Fairye' within the space of a stanza, having determined to lay eyes on his love, who exists as little more than a figuration of his own desire:

> Into his sadel he clamb anon,
> And priketh over stile and stoon
>    An elf-queene for t'espye,
> Til he so longe hath riden and goon
> That he foond, in a pryve woon,
>    The contree of Fairye
>         So wilde;
> For in that contree was ther noon
> That to him durste ride or goon,
>    Neither wyf ne childe;
>
> Til that ther cam a greet geaunt,
> His name was sire Olifaunt,
>    A perilous man of dede.
> He seyde, 'Child, by Termagaunt,
> But if thou prike out of myn haunt,
>    Anon I sle thy steede
>         With mace.
> Heere is the queene of Fayerye,
> With harpe and pipe and symphonye,
>    Dwellynge in this place.' (797–816)

85 See King, *The Faerie Queene and Middle English Romance*, pp. 9–11.
86 Geoffrey Chaucer, *The Tale of Sir Thopas* in *The Riverside Chaucer*, pp. 212–17, lines 772 and 775. Subsequent references are placed in the text.
87 See Woodcock, *Fairy in* The Faerie Queene, pp. 90–4.

The eruption of the giant out of the unpopulated landscape compresses the threat of violence with the confirmation that Sir Thopas has found the right place; yet, as in Spenser's poem, the encounter with the fairy mistress does not occur, and the location of the meeting between Sir Thopas and Sir Oliphaunt becomes instead a site of knowing parody.[88] Because this episode is framed within the collection of tales as a whole, the rapidly disoriented reader remains with one foot firmly planted in Chaucer's world of pilgrims, merchants, and religious folk, rendering the reported encounter all the more ludicrous.[89] And with a call made by the host for the end of such nonsense, the everyday pleasures of travelling companions exchanging tales on their journey recalls the reader to the quotidian almost immediately.

The spaces of Sir Thopas's tale are interesting nonetheless. The wild 'contree of Fairye', for example, is located in 'a pryve woon', or place characterised by its privacy or secrecy, and thus suggests no geographical location but an epistemological one. Sir Thopas may make a discovery, but the effect is uncanny owing to the familiarity of the literary device. His knowledge may be his own, allowing him to prick out a route that cannot be followed, but the sudden encounter burlesques the ways in which the romance mode is capable of changing the rules governing the navigation of place on a whim. Passing from one order of nature into another across an invisible and unexplained limit, Sir Thopas easily exchanges the everyday for the marvellous. The fluctuating value placed on this fragile transition, as Chaucer's parody demonstrates, can be exploited for comic effect, making Spenser's rewriting of the narrative as a lengthy Arthurian quest all the more extraordinary.[90]

The *Tale of Sir Thopas* also anticipates later satirical responses to romance, which proliferated in the sixteenth century. The pamphleteer Thomas Nashe, for example, showily comments on his reading of Spenser's longest work towards the end of *Pierce Pennilesse his Supplication to the Devil* (1592) and presents his own reader with a sonnet that criticises Spenser both as a peddler of romance and as an author remiss in thanking his patrons appropriately. Nashe's own

---

88 See Angela Jane Weisl, 'The Absent Woman: Generic Stasis in the *Tale of Sir Thopas*', in *Conquering the Reign of Femeny: Gender and Genre in Chaucer's Romance* (Cambridge: D.S. Brewer, 1995), pp. 70–84.

89 See Ad Putter, *An Introduction to The Gawain Poet* (London: Longman, 1996), pp. 45–8.

90 See J.A. Burrow, '"Sir Thopas": An Agony in Three Fits', *RES*, 22 (1971), 54–8, p. 57. See also Lee Patterson, '"What Man Artow?" Authorial Self-Definition in *The Tale of Sir Thopas* and *The Tale of Melibee*', *Studies in the Age of Chaucer*, 11 (1989), 117–75, p. 124.

desired patron, Ferdinando Stanley, Lord Strange, is absent from *The Faerie Queene*'s unusually placed sequence of dedicatory sonnets, and so Nashe, via his thinly veiled authorial persona, Pierce Pennilesse, offers a mock rectification of the omission:

> Perusing yesternight with idle eyes,
>     The Fairy Singers stately tuned verse:
> And viewing after Chap-mens wonted guise,
>     What strange contents the title did rehearse.
> I streight leapt over to the latter end,
>     Where like the queint Comaedians of our time,
> That when their Play is doone do fal to ryme,
>     I found short lines, to sundry Nobles pend.
> Whom he as speciall Mirrours singled fourth,
>     To be the Patrons of his Poetry;
> I read them all, and reuerenc't their worth,
>     Yet wondred he left out thy memory.
> But therefore gest I he supprest thy name,
> Because few words might not comprise thy fame.[91]

As an author who always appears sensitive to the spatial qualities of printed books and to their material and typographic forms, Nashe depicts Pierce bounding over the main matter of Spenser's work after glancing at its title page in order to suggest an assumed familiarity with the production and distribution of vernacular romance: the leap is a mocking and 'vigorously kinetic' action that denies Spenser's lengthy poem its ambition to carve out epic space.[92] Nashe's use of the phrase 'idle eyes' in the description of Pierce's reading practices, which sounds suspiciously like 'idolise' when read aloud, also makes no case for author worship; it suggests instead a satirical association of fairy song, no matter how 'stately', with the capacity of romance to dull the critical judgement of both author and reader.[93] In the syntactical games Nashe plays, Spenser's habit of loading the ends of lines with favoured rhymes is subject to careful aping; the sonnet's delightful paradox is that it cannot help but betray its author as one of the period's most

---

91 Thomas Nashe, *Pierce Pennilesse his Supplication to the Devil* (London, 1592), sig. I4ᵛ.
92 See Judith Owens, *Enabling Engagements: Edmund Spenser and the Poetics of Patronage* (Montreal: McGill-Queen's University Press, 2002), p. 93.
93 For reading and romance in the early modern period see Lori Humphrey Newcomb, *Reading Popular Romance in Early Modern England* (New York: Columbia University Press, 2002); Stephen B. Dobranski, *Readers and Authorship in Early Modern England* (Cambridge: Cambridge University Press, 2005); and Jeff Dolven, *Scenes of Instruction in Renaissance Romance* (Chicago: University of Chicago Press, 2007).

keen-eyed and keen-eared readers, in spite of Pierce's protestations to the contrary.

Nashe's pointed comments concerning the follies of sixteenth-century literary culture are scattered liberally amongst his aberrant writings. In his earlier prose work *The Anatomy of Absurdity* (1589), for example, he addresses the value of particular kinds of imaginative literature, targeting those that are likely to lead the reader astray from their moral and devotional convictions.[94] The idealised subjects of romance are, admittedly, a far cry from the urban and the grotesque: tales of which Nashe would produce later in his career. As he writes, detailing the absurdities of marketing such a belated generic choice:

> What els I pray you doe these bable bookemungers endevor, but to repair the ruinous wals of Venus Court, to restore to the worlde, that forgotten Legendary licence of lying, to imitate afresh the fantastical dreames of those exiled Abbie-lubbers, from whose idle pens proceeded those worne out impressions of the feyned no where acts of Arthur of the rounde table, Arthur of litle Brittaine, Sir Tristram, Hewon of Burdeaux, The Squire of low degree, The four sons of Aymon, with infinite others.[95]

By calling on the names of several romances, Nashe identifies them as well-known and pervasive features of sixteenth-century literary culture. His catalogue recalls similarly critical passages from earlier works such as Edward Dering's *A Brief and Necessary Instruction* (1572), which bewails the contamination of the book trade with the products of 'dronken imaginations', and Roger Ascham's *The Scholemaster* (1570), which anxiously associates romance's perceived focus on unedifying subjects with the threat of an overflow of Papistry and related Italianate seductions.[96] In Nashe's opinion, the 'fantastical dreames' of romance carry little currency in an increasingly nightmarish age because they stray from the rigors of history into the realm of superstition, offering only 'worne out impressions of … feyned no where acts'. If Nashe claims that their futile aim is to rebuild the walls of the court of Venus, he must have perceived it to be a secular place in his lifetime, standing in a state of ruin. In turn, the association of romance with the cloistered and the clerical evokes the

---

94 For discussion of this anxiety see Tiffany Jo Werth, *The Fabulous Dark Cloister: Romance in England after the Reformation* (Baltimore: Johns Hopkins University Press, 2011), p. 26 in particular.

95 Thomas Nashe, *The Anatomy of Absurdity* (London, 1589), sig. A2$^r$. Subsequent references are placed in the text.

96 Edward Dering, *A Brief and Necessary Instruction* (London, 1572), sig. A2$^r$. On the impulse to index offending texts see Werth, *The Fabulous Dark Cloister*, pp. 7–14.

literal ruination of the abbeys that had served as sites of manuscript production, and which occupied a problematic site of origin and authority after the Reformation.[97]

Nashe's dismissive description of romances as 'feyned no where acts' is particularly interesting. The chosen terms are compromised by the self-evident fashion in which the titles of printed romances are frequently tied to geographical referents, which commemorate not only people but also places. In part, Nashe's reaction is charged by the fundamental spatial dislocation implied by the movement of knowledge production away from the Catholic Church; as Thomas A. Prendergast observes, Nashe's comment makes the problem of 'mistaking poets for historians' explicit.[98] For Protestant writers, forging new models for humanistic history, disassociated from the 'fantastical dreames of those exiled Abbie-lubbers', was of prime importance; however, more importantly for my purposes here, the additional problem that Nashe addresses concerns the related complication of mistaking writers of imaginative literature for geographers. It seems, albeit unintentionally, that Nashe identifies a complicating tension present in the status of a 'feyned no where act', in which fictional and geographical referents compete for an audience's investment. In an attempt to formulate a corrective, Nashe provides a gloss of what he believes imaginative literature should think itself capable of:

> I account of Poetrie as a more hidden and divine kinde of Philosophy, enwrapped in blind Fables and dark Stories, wherein the principles of more excellent Arts and morral precepts of manners, illustrated with divers examples of other Kingdomes and countries, are contained. (sig. C1$^r$)

Although Nashe's words seem to resonate with Spenser's own description of *The Faerie Queene*, whose matter appears as a 'darke conceit' or 'clowdily enwrapped in Allegoricall deuices' ('A Letter of the Authors', p. 714 and p. 716), Nashe also emphasises the interest that transparent 'examples of other Kingdomes and countries' hold for a reader. These regions are not feigned 'nowheres' but models of diplomatic, cultural, and intellectual humanist exchange. His words indicate a new value put upon the realism of place in fiction and on the use of geographi-

---

97 See Helen Cooper, 'Romance after 1400', in *The Cambridge History of Medieval English Literature*, ed. David Wallace (Cambridge: Cambridge University Press, 2002), pp. 690–719.
98 Thomas A. Prendergast, *Poetical Dust: Poets' Corner and the Making of Britain* (Philadelphia: University of Pennsylvania Press, 2015), p. 49.

cal description to educate a reader; accurate knowledge of such things is thus presented as a political manoeuvre, of service to the commonwealth as a whole.[99] It was perhaps even within his own fictions, such as *The Unfortunate Traveller*, that he attempted a fuller criticism of the romance mode, outlining the first inklings of the dark dystopian shadow cast by the mobile and idealising fictions of the pre-Reformation age. Yet, even in works such as this, Nashe's ambivalence is adept at figuring the wide gulf between textual encounter and lived experience. In the words of *The Unfortunate Traveller*'s exiled English earl, himself the most unfortunate of itinerants: 'So let others tell you straunge accidents, treasons, poysonings, close packings in Fraunce, Spaine and Italy: it is no harme for you to heare of them, but come not neere them'.[100]

The words of Nashe's earl participate in the same debate outlined at the beginning of this chapter concerning the relationship between witnessing and hearsay: as in Spenser's second proem, a generative space of in-betweenness invites self-conscious reflection on the negotiation of *aporia* and action. What this comes down to, perhaps, is a question of plotting: as seen above, from Calepine's searching movements west, then north, 'then neither', (VI.iv.25) to Gawain's toponymic route towards something far wilder, and from Arthur of Algarbe's European odyssey to Sir Thopas's pricking 'north and est' and 'over stile and stoon' into overdetermined absurdity, narrative movement often relies on the conjunction of space and defined meaning, which then gives way to something far stranger. Lorna Hutson, for example, suggests that acts of emplotment are fundamentally 'concerned with establishing conviction as the condition of undertaking a successful action': an observation which has serious implications for the ways in which causality appears to function in imaginative writing.[101] As she observes, 'For humanists, discourses in which the plot solution emerged from the order of telling were superior to discourses such as chivalric romance in which solutions were reached through the lapse, rather than the ordering, of narrative time':[102] a sentiment with which Nashe, in spite of his own notoriously vagrant plotting, might in principle be thought to agree.

Indeed, cognitive connections between narrative and spatial plotting

---

99 See Goodman, *Chivalry and Exploration*, pp. 45–77.
100 Thomas Nashe, *The Unfortunate Traveller. Or, The Life of Jacke Wilton* (London, 1594), sig. L4ʳ.
101 Lorna Hutson, 'Fortunate Travellers: Reading for the Plot in Sixteenth-Century England', *Representations*, 41 (1993), 83–103, p. 88.
102 Ibid., p. 86.

have long been recognised by critics of late sixteenth- and early seventeenth-century literature, where the uses to which words such as 'plat', 'plot', 'groundplot', and 'complot' are put seem particularly resonant owing to their ability to connect geometrical ways of knowing to human action.[103] In his translated complaint 'Virgil's Gnat', for example, Spenser invokes the action of plotting while playing with scale and orientation. He describes an aged shepherd in the act of designing and digging a tomb for the gnat who saved his life, and whom he subsequently, and inadvertently, killed:

> By that same Riuer lurking vnder greene,
> Eftsoones he gins to fashion forth a place,
> And squaring it in compasse well beseene,
> There plotteth out a tombe by measured space:
> His yron headed spade tho making cleene,
> To dig vp sods out of the flowrie grasse,
> His worke he shortly to good purpose brought,
> Like as he had conceiu'd it in his thought. (649–56)

The movements of the stanza connect deliberate spatial measurement with imagination, intention, and finally, physical labour and satisfaction; the removal of multiple sods suggests that the shepherd's plotting is directly proportional to his gratitude, rather than to the gnat's meagre dimensions in death. Far less playfully, in *A Brief Note of Ireland*, a short prose work not un-controversially attributed to Spenser, the word 'plott' is used, again in both its spatial and projective senses, to connect the poor oversight and government of the Munster plantation with an initial inaccurate survey: 'some think that the first plott by which the late vndertakers of your maiestes Landes here in Mounster were planted was not well instituted nor grounded vpon sound aduisement and knowledg of the Countrie'.[104] Importantly, in their discussion of 'plot' as a geodetic term that takes in an understanding of both land and strategy, Martin Brückner and Kristen Poole take account of the discussions of error and inaccuracy that proliferate within early modern surveying manuals,

---

103 See Henry S. Turner, *The English Renaissance Stage: Geometry, Poetics and the Practical Spatial Arts 1580–1630* (Oxford: Oxford University Press, 2006; repr. 2010), pp. 21–5. See 'plot, n.' *OED Online*. Oxford University Press, June 2018 (last accessed 8 August 2018).

104 *A Brief Note of Ireland*, in *The Works of Edmund Spenser: A Variorum Edition, X: The Prose Works*, ed. Rudolf Gottfried (Baltimore: Johns Hopkins University Press, 1949), pp. 235–45 (p. 239). See John Breen, '"Imaginatiue Groundplot": *A View of the Present State of Ireland*', *Spenser Studies*, 12 (1998), 151–68 and Ciaran Brady, 'A Brief Note of Ireland', in *SEnc*, pp. 111–12.

observing that 'while the plat emerges as an early modern icon of organizational system, it also becomes a glaring manifestation of the fissures and erosion inherent to that system'.[105] To plot is thus to wrestle with the matter that muddies the work of abstraction and hypothesis.

It is now commonplace to speak of the 'plot' of a novel, but the use of the word within literary contexts was only just emerging in the late sixteenth century.[106] In Sir Philip Sidney's *Defence of Poesy*, for example, the poet-critic suggests that readers of fiction should use 'the narration' not as an end in itself 'but as an imaginative ground-plot of a profitable invention',[107] as if prospecting for a defined course of action that could take inspiring reading as its foundation: the term thus retains its connection to land and earth as its primary significance. And in the *Art of English Poesy*, George Puttenham famously advises the maker, or poet, to first 'devise his plat or subject' before thinking about metre, language, and style. For Puttenham, the use of the word 'plat' connects poetry to the skilled design-work of artisanal labour, whereby he that 'useth his metrical proportions ..., is like the carpenter or joiner', he that 'reports of another man's doings, ... is as the painter or carver that work by imitation', and he that 'speaks figuratively, or argues subtly ... doth as the cunning gardener that, using nature as a coadjutor, furthers her conclusions and many times makes her effects more absolute and strange'. It is interesting that Puttenham then undoes these analogies in order to make the distinction that the work of poetry 'rests only in device', or in the mind, as if the poet-artisan is 'as nature herself'.[108]

In its barest sense, then, the language of plotting does not sit easily alongside the world of 'knightly proving', nor even the subject of epic, even though, as Jonathan Lamb observes, 'an epic navigation proceeds to an outcome that is already foretold ..., and therefore ineluctable, immune to individual initiative and lacking in suspense'.[109] It only takes on resonance when the threat of error and the need for skilled labour is

---

105 Martin Brückner and Kristen Poole, 'The Plot Thickens: Surveying Manuals, Drama, and the Materiality of Narrative Form in Early Modern England', *ELH*, 69 (2002), 617–48, p. 642.
106 See Peter Turchi, *Maps of the Imagination: The Writer as Cartographer* (Texas: Trinity University Press, 2004), p. 188.
107 Sir Philip Sidney, *The Defence of Poesy*, in *The Oxford Authors: Sir Philip Sidney*, ed. Katherine Duncan-Jones (Oxford: Oxford University Press, 1989; repr. 1992), pp. 212–50 (p. 235).
108 George Puttenham, *The Art of English Poesy: A Critical Edition*, ed. Frank Whigham and Wayne A. Rebhorn (Ithaca: Cornell University Press, 2007), pp. 385–6.
109 Jonathan Lamb, *Preserving the Self in the South Seas, 1680–1840* (Chicago: University of Chicago Press, 2001), p. 54.

recognised as being as present as it is in the surveying manuals of early modern England, which ward against 'untrue waies of measuring, as also sundry true rules ... falsely applied'.[110] For the authors of the blended modes and vagrant genres of the Renaissance, it is similarly rare to find protagonists who travel anywhere 'by the shortest good way, by the aptest direction, and in the shortest time' (see Dee, *Mathematicall Praeface*, sig. D4$^v$), and this contributes to the sense that there is something immediately, and inexhaustibly, still at stake in how narrative meaning is made. Predetermined endings make for dull storytelling and, as Spenser's work and that of his predecessors demonstrates, the romance mode offers space for innovation, experiment, and desire; it moulds a 'naïve, drifting, erring reader' who is ready to be both challenged and delighted in equal measure.[111]

To return again to Book II, then, this time to a moment in the final canto, Spenser's chosen vocabulary holds determinacy and its opposites in suspension, suggesting that Guyon's waylaid progress exists in full collusion with the challenges issued by a world at sea:

> Said then the Boteman, Palmer stere aright,
>   And keepe an euen course; for yonder way
>   We needes must pas (God doe vs well acquight,) ... (II.xii.3)

The Palmer's intimation that this particular way must 'needes' be passed suggests a steadfast, charted purpose: a cause for wry humour if the destination is 'the figurative heart of romance' itself.[112] Perceived necessity may be Guyon's saviour and his means of piloting through the watery labyrinth; yet, his masculine judgement is challenged by sensual and erotic delights, which he requires the Palmer's help to resist.[113] When he reaches the island of Acrasia, Guyon finds his gaze is drawn by the sporting of semi-clad maidens who 'to him becknd, to approach more neare' (II.xii.68):

> Of which when gazing him the Palmer saw,
>   He much rebukt those wandring eyes of his,
>   And counseld well, him forward thence did draw.
>   Now are they come nigh to the *Bowre of blis*

---

110 Edward Worsop, *A Discoverie of Sundrie Errours and Faults Daily Committed by Landemeaters* (London, 1582), sig. A2$^r$. See Martin Brückner and Kristen Poole, 'The Plot Thickens', p. 620.
111 See Julian Yates, *Error, Misuse, Failure: Object Lessons from the English Renaissance* (Minneapolis: University of Minnesota Press, 2003), p. xx.
112 Werth, *The Fabulous Dark Cloister*, p. 128.
113 Cooper, *The English Romance in Time*, pp. 107–8.

> Of her fond fauorites so nam'd amis:
> When thus the Palmer, Now Sir, well auise;
> For here the end of all our traueill is:
> Here wonnes *Acrasia*, whom we must surprise,
> Els she will slip away, and all our drift despise. (II.xii.69)

Guyon's partial visual possession of an alternative prize is pitched against preventing Acrasia from slipping away, epitomising a drive of the poem as a whole. The Palmer's apparent foreknowledge of the promised 'end of all our traueill' is anticipatory and, for a moment, Acrasia takes on the shadow of the Queene of Faeries herself, whose penumbral attendance is repeatedly glimpsed in the poem in this way, through veiled surrogates and antitypes.

In the final couplet, the Palmer evaluates the precarious condition of Guyon's quest and in the reported dialogue, the use of the word 'drift' to describe the purpose of the voyage seems particularly ambivalent, offering an apparent comment on the crew's resolve. During the early modern period, the word 'drift' was typically used to convey a deliberate action: 'a scheme, plot, design, device' or 'the act of driving; propulsion, impulse, impetus' – meanings now considered by the *Oxford English Dictionary* to be obsolete. The emerging, and now fully current, definition conveys what is in practical terms the exact opposite: 'the deviation of a ship from its course in consequence of currents', where 'to drift' is also 'to put off', to 'delay' and to 'defer'.[114] As Philip Edwards comments in his study of the metaphor of voyaging in early modern literature, 'it is the definition of a voyage that it has a motivation, an end in view. … Drifting is the negation of voyaging'.[115] The ambivalence of the term is further revealed by the variety of characters with which it is associated: 'to drift' in the world of Spenser's fiction is certainly not to lack agency. In Book I, for example, the action is used to describe Archimago's temporary triumph over Una, who has been cast off course by his machinations:

> But subtill *Archimago* when his guests
>   He saw diuided into double parts,
>   And *Vna* wandring in woods and forrests,
>   Th'end of his drift, he praisd his diuelish arts,
>   That had such might ouer true meaning harts … (I.ii.9)

---

114 See 'drift, n.' and 'drift, v.' *OED Online*. Oxford University Press, December 2015 (last accessed 8 January 2016).
115 Philip Edwards, *Sea-Mark*, p. 3.

To 'plot' in *The Faerie Queene*, it seems, is thus to drift. In Spenser's poem, the erotic temptations of the chase delay, yet conspire with, the progress of the onward journey and for the Palmer, a confident sense of directed, intentional 'drift' is diverted by the implicit contradictions of his expression: an undoing that is simultaneously a mark of progress. As a reader, we experience the divergence that Monika Fludernick recognises within narrative fiction as the irreconcilable 'interplay between the characters' plotting on the level of the fictional world and the narrative's overall counter-plotting'.[116] In Spenser's case, the poem's verbal texture comments on the ways in which uncertainty, drift, and the pleasures of the detour inhabit and cultivate the poem's romance world, even when the allegorical subject matter demands the recognition of an alternate and more rational path.

The unstable qualities of the Palmer's 'drift' draw Guyon's quest into uncertain waters. Through his sounding of the virtue of temperance, Spenser confronts the way that an allegorical desire for linearity is tempered by the shifting drifts of the romance mode; for Spenser, this duality is held in tension by Guyon's experience of the temperamental space of the sea and his ability to read its dangers. Guyon's waters are unmeasured, and the way in which they change shape throughout Book II has drawn frequent commentary, suggesting that Spenser had, in the words of David Read, an 'instinctive understanding that travel by water is characterized (at least in sixteenth-century terms) by both physical and epistemological fluidity'.[117] The reader is immersed in a landscape of the marvellous, in which a river can become a 'deepe ford' (II.vi.4), an 'inland sea' can be called the 'Idle Lake' (II.vi.10), a 'wide strond' can be crossed in a rowboat (II.vi.19), and fresh and salt water can flow through shared channels. The 'Idle Lake' itself is viscous, 'slow and sluggish' (II.vi.46), allowing nothing to sink through standing waters that are heavy with the residue of literary ancestors and the threat of cognitive atrophy.[118] Spenser's manipulation of the forms and boundaries given to liquid, together with the likening of Guyon to a pilot engaged in 'long experiment' (II.vii.1), reveal a constant process of trial and tempering.[119] For Elizabeth Spiller, the metafictional commentary contained within

---

116 Monika Fludernik, *Towards a 'Natural' Narratology* (London: Routledge, 1996), p. 16.
117 David Read, *Temperate Conquests: Spenser and the Spanish New World* (Detroit: Wayne State University Press, 2000), p. 50.
118 See Brenda M. Hosington, 'Idle Lake', in *SEnc*, p. 387.
119 For the narrator's role in this process of 'unfolding' see Jerome S. Dees, 'The Narrator of *The Faerie Queene*: Patterns of Response', *Texas Studies in Literature and Language*, 12.4 (1971), 537–68, p. 538.

*The Faerie Queene* means that each quest 'involves not so much an act of discovery (the knowing by finding of traditional romance) but rather the act of putting ideas into physical form (knowing through making)'.[120] The discovery of the shifting limits of the temperate self are recorded by the drifts and traces of words and water throughout Guyon's voyage: acts of 'making' and 'discovery' are thus seen not as oppositional but as allied undertakings.

As we have already seen, Spenser demands an active reader, who travails, toils, and seeks to bridge interpretive *terrae incognitae*. A far cry from the indolent reader of romance literature feared by Ascham and satirised by Nashe, the reader of Spenserian romance is constantly challenged by the author's self-conscious use of drifting, self-dissolving modes. In effect, his poetry constantly recalls and reforms that which Ascham found so disturbing:

> In our forefathers tyme, whan Papistrie, as a standyng poole, covered and overflowed all England, fewe bookes were read in our tong, savyng certaine bookes of Chevalrie, as they sayd, for pastime and pleasure, which, as some say, were made in Monasteries, by idle Monkes, or wanton Chanons: as one for example, Morte Arthure: the whole pleasure of which booke standeth in two speciall poyntes, in open manslaughter, and bold bawdrye.[121]

Ascham's own prose employs the same figurative language of literary and epistemological geography that Spenser appropriates in order to turn romance into allegory;[122] in ways that recall the approach to spatial images outlined in Chapter 2, Ascham's 'standing pool', like Spenser's 'Idle Lake', speaks of indolent waters, where the defined borders of intellectual *terra firma* remain under threat of erosion from a loss of progressive Protestant values.[123] As Thomas Rogers explains in *The Anatomie of the Mind* (1576), like 'that water which is always standing, and never runneth, must needes bee noysome and infectious: so that man, which is never moved in mind, can never be eyther good to himselfe, or profitable to others'.[124] From this perspective, it is perhaps even Ascham himself

---

120 Elizabeth Spiller, *Science, Reading, and Renaissance Literature: The Art of Making Knowledge, 1580–1670* (Cambridge: Cambridge University Press, 2004; repr. 2005), p. 73.
121 Roger Ascham, *The Scholemaster* (London, 1570), sig. I3$^r$.
122 See Linda Bradley Salamon, 'The Imagery of Roger Ascham', *Texas Studies in Literature and Language*, 15.1 (1973), 5–23, pp. 14–15.
123 See Werth, *The Fabulous Dark Cloister*, pp. 120–3. For 'the cognitive difficulties Guyon experiences in Phaedria's world' see Joseph D. Parry, 'Phaedria and Guyon: Travelling Alone in *The Faerie Queene*, Book II', *Spenser Studies*, 15 (2001), 53–77, pp. 58–9.
124 Thomas Rogers, *The Anatomie of the Minde* (London, 1576), sig. B3$^r$.

who provides the most apt figuring of the reader-as-traveller. Writing of Homer's Ulysses, he describes a man who is 'ware in all places' and who travails with the grace and wisdom of Pallas Athena, 'alwayes at his elbow'.[125]

For Ascham, the culture of romance may have carried the risk of stagnation and submergence; however, for Spenser, the site of wandering becomes one of remaking and recuperation. The well-worn ideals and extraordinary spatial strategies of romance offered conditions that could not only act as a prompt for revealing cultural instabilities but also confront them as a central and preoccupying theme. The struggle to be at least complicit in the discourse of error anticipates the subtle metaphorical connections between travel, encounter, and authorship identified by Peter Turchi in *Maps of the Imagination* as the foremost challenge to all writers of imaginative literature:

> In our own eyes, we are off the map. The excitement of potential discovery is accompanied by anxiety, despair, caution, perhaps, perhaps boldness, and, always, the risk of failure. Failure can take the form of our becoming hopelessly lost, or pointlessly lost, or not finding what we came for.[126]

The conceptual connections made by Turchi provide a way of approaching Spenser's writing as the work of a poet whose life coincided with the efforts of men who made it their business to re-fashion the known world and its representations. For Turchi, the uncharted terrain marked by the author, and the void between the author and reader, is crossed merely by the written word. For Spenser, this is where the work is done. In its images of discovery and colonised land, then, Book II's proem and the subsequent voyages it pre-empts connects Guyon's drift with Artegall's trials and those of his surrogates, such as the unfortunate Calepine: after all, Acrasia and Irena occupy similar positions as errant women, their movements subject to masculine desire. The threat of failure remains a constant travelling companion where becoming hopelessly lost is the peril most feared: to look ahead to Britomart's travails in Book III of *The Faerie Queene*, then, '*Be bolde, be bolde, ... Be not too bold*' (III.xi.54).

---

125 Roger Ascham, *The Scholemaster*, sig. H4ʳ. For Ascham's travails in rhetoric and pedagogy see Catherine Nicholson, *Uncommon Tongues: Eloquence and Eccentricity in the English Renaissance* (Philadelphia: University of Pennsylvania Press, 2014), pp. 19–44.
126 Turchi, *Maps of the Imagination*, p. 13.

# 4

# Compassing desire: cosmography and chorography

This is how space begins, with words only, signs traced on the blank page. To describe space: to name it, to trace it, like those portolano-makers who saturated the coastlines with the names of harbours, the names of capes, the names of inlets, until in the end the land was only separated from the sea by a continuous ribbon of text.[1]

Our perceptions ... are Janus-faced, and move back and forth along the littoral of consciousness, endlessly, tidally negotiating the back and forth between inner and outer worlds.[2]

The likeness drawn by Perec moves between the contours of a material world and their manifestation as something imagined, described, and represented. The process he defines, a conjunction of conceptual activity and literary expression, follows the inscription of names as they anchor coastal curves and anticipate the addition of connective compass lines. As Peter Whitfield writes, marvelling at the intellectual advances required to transform the *periploi* of the Greeks, which listed the names of ports and the relative distances between them, into the fully formed portolan charts of the Middle Ages: 'the transition from a list of names and bearings to an accurate map is an enormous one, requiring not only a high degree of geometric and drafting skill, but also an imaginative leap to create a graphic form for which there was no parallel'.[3] For Perec, the making of the portolan retains the figurative associations of the imaginative

---

1 Georges Perec, *Species of Spaces* in *Species of Spaces and Other Pieces*, ed. and trans. John Sturrock (London: Penguin, 1997; repr. 1999), pp. 1–96 (p. 13).
2 Paul Carter, 'Dark with Excess of Bright: Mapping the Coastlines of Knowledge', in *Mappings*, ed. Denis Cosgrove (London: Reaktion, 1999), pp. 125–47 (p. 134).
3 Peter Whitfield, *The Charting of the Oceans: Ten Centuries of Maritime Maps* (London: The British Library, 1996), p. 17. See also Richard W. Unger, *Ships on Maps: Pictures of Power in Renaissance Europe* (Basingstoke: Palgrave Macmillan, 2010), pp. 37–61.

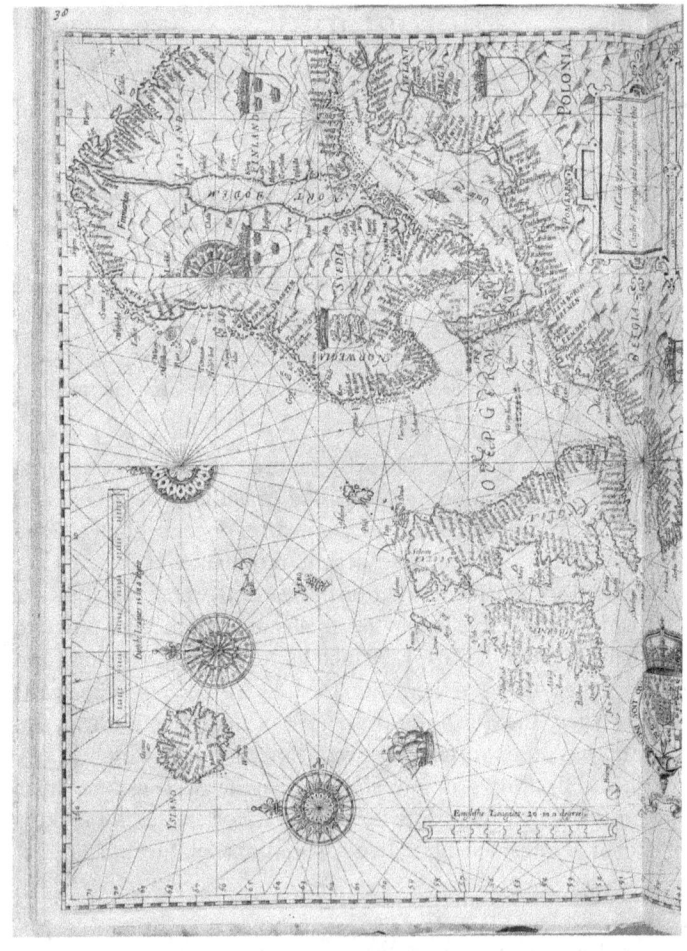

*Figure 5* Lucas Janzoon Waghenaer. Northern Europe from 'A Generall Carde, and Description of the Sea Coastes of Europe', in *The Mariners Mirrour*, trans. Anthony Ashley (London, 1588).

leap involved in its creation: scattered port cities become safe harbours through the incantation of names, as demonstrated by the charts created to illustrate Waghenaer's *Mariners Mirrour* (see Figure 5).

The marking of limits creates charged boundaries while terrestrial interiors and coastal waters are left in blank; after all, these are subject to different kinds of cartographical practices. A textual frontier emerges that hints at the capacity of the literary, specifically the act of naming, to give form, shape, and meaning to space. As a knowledge-making act, it confers a certain kind of permanence, even if this is only temporary illusion.

### 'By sea, by land, where so they may be mett'

This chapter focuses on two moments from Book III of *The Faerie Queene*, namely Britomart's first glimpse of Artegall in Merlin's glass, and then her journey, prompted by Glauce, to seek out the maker of her vision. Both instances think about the tracing of limits and, in the case of the second example, a way of approaching coastal space, which Elizabeth Jane Bellamy has described as the possible site of 'a numinous poetics' in Spenser's poem.[4] Spenser's Knight of Chastity is famously good at crossing thresholds and the origins of her quest are located using both the contours of regional Welsh geography and an unusual interest in the names of places.[5] In order to sound Glauce's meaning when she avows to her charge that she will try 'by wrong or right/ To compas [her] desire, and find that loued knight' (III.ii.46), I connect Spenser's regional descriptions to other forms of writing space, which allow the scale of his poetic project to unfold. Prompted by a vision beheld in Merlin's perspective and prospective glass, Britomart's search for an 'vnknowne Paramoure,/ From the worlds end' (III.iii.3) is undertaken 'Withouten compasse, or withouten card,/ Far fro [her] natiue soyle' (III.ii.7). Running in parallel to her quest, Venus searches for her errant son, and Florimell flees pursued by a series of unwanted admirers: narrative elements that have led previous critics to focus on how the central books of *The Faerie Queene* are shaped by desire.[6] As a virginal

---

4 Elizabeth Jane Bellamy, *Dire Straits: The Perils of Writing the Early Modern English Coastline from Leland to Milton* (Toronto: University of Toronto Press, 2013), p. 10.
5 As Linda Gregerson observes, 'Chastity in *The Faerie Queene* is considerably more complex than, is even opposed to, mere self-containment'. See *The Reformation of the Subject: Spenser, Milton, and the English Protestant Epic* (Cambridge: Cambridge University Press, 1995), p. 26.
6 See Jonathan Goldberg, *Endlesse Worke: Spenser and the Structures of Discourse*

lady-knight and virgin territory, Britomart is assailed and emblematically wounded by a beloved, who is himself an invader: a reminder that chivalric romance relies on the exercise of intrinsically martial pursuits and that Christian epic is informed by the pursuit of love.[7] As we discover, the man Britomart seeks is Artegall, half-brother of Prince Arthur, and this charges Spenser's use of romance motifs with an epic trajectory. The prophecy made by Merlin in the third canto of Book III reveals that the eventual union will establish a line of kings, whose progeny will include the Tudor dynasty.[8]

In order to synthesise the ideas presented so far with a renewed focus on the nature of geopolitical peripheries, I build on my earlier readings of William Cuningham, Lucas Waghenaer, and John Dee: the speculations of these spatial makers, I suggest, cast Spenser's movements between the global and the local, and the macrocosm and microcosm, into relief. In her transformation from royal daughter to knight errant, for example, Britomart exchanges the static speculations of gazing upon her father's 'looking glasse' (III.ii.18) for 'aduentures hard' (III.ii.7), an alteration that exchanges the armchair travail associated with cosmography for the wayfaring craft of the navigator. By fusing different orders of spatial representation, namely the cosmographical, which mediates the relationship between self and world, and the chorographical, which concerns itself with the writing of landscapes charged with prior and still-unfolding narratives, Spenser blends the emblems of allegory and the vagrancies of romance with the speculative ambitions of epic.[9] As a mirror for Spenser's play of genders, nations, and motives, Britomart appears, as

  (Baltimore: Johns Hopkins University Press, 1981) and Lauren Silberman, *Transforming Desire: Erotic Knowledge in Books III and IV of The Faerie Queene* (Berkeley: University of California Press, 1995).
7 See Jennifer R. Goodman, *Chivalry and Exploration 1298–1630* (Woodbridge: Boydell Press, 1998) and Mary B. Campbell, *The Witness and the Other World: Exotic European Travel Writing, 400–1600* (Ithaca: Cornell University Press, 1988), pp. 211–54. For the idea that love is 'empire's most basic element' see Andrew Fichter, *Poets Historical: Dynastic Epic in the Renaissance* (New Haven: Yale University Press, 1982), p. 157 and p. 161.
8 See Gregerson, *The Reformation of the Subject*, pp. 6–20 and pp. 36–47. See also Andrew Escobedo, *Nationalism and Historical Loss in Renaissance England* (Ithaca: Cornell University Press, 2004), p. 47.
9 For Spenser's use of Britomart as a figure who transitions between genres, from epyllion and prophecy, romance and epic, see Colin Burrow, *Epic Romance: Homer to Milton* (Oxford: Clarendon, 1993), pp. 100–46. For the relationship between Spenser's choices of genre and Britain as a geopolitical and temporal construct see Wayne Erickson, *Mapping the Faerie Queene: Quest Structures and the World of the Poem* (New York: Garland Publishing, 1996), pp. 87–117. See also See Bart van Es, *Spenser's Forms of History* (Oxford: Oxford University Press, 2002), pp. 49–77.

Andrew Fichter provocatively argues, to contain 'in the lesser world of her self all the conflicts she sees in the larger world in which she moves'.[10]

The scales and perspectives at work in the crafting of Merlin's dwelling also evoke the techniques of cosmography and chorography, and it seems no coincidence that Spenser locates his magician-prophet using the textual traces of a port – Maridunum – that once stood as the most westward city of Roman Britain. For, as Paul Carter observes, coastal forms offer a spatial figure for the processes involved in the acquisition of knowledge: in his words, a coast 'cannot strictly speaking be bounded and possessed; it can provide the ground of knowledge – the suitable place to make astronomical observations; it can provide the limit of knowledge, the horizon as concrete edge'.[11] Even the syntax used by Britomart in her description of her search for 'perilles and aduentures hard,/ By sea, by land, where so they may be mett' (III.ii.7), suggests that the place of convergence, where land and sea act upon each other, and where inner and outer worlds collide, is the place where the knight errant might meet her fate.

## Cosmography: romance and the perspective glass

In order to situate Britomart's quest alongside the travails of her predecessors, the first canto of Book III begins with a summary of the progress made by Arthur and Guyon following the delivery of the captive enchantress Acrasia to the court of the Faerie Queene:

> Long so they traueiled through wastefull wayes,
>   Where daungers dwelt, and perils most did wonne,
> To hunt for glorie and renowmed prayse;
> Full many Countreyes they did ouerronne,
> From the vprising to the setting Sunne,
> And many hard aduentures did atchieue;
> Of all the which they honour euer wonne,
> Seeking the weake oppressed to relieue,
> And to recouer right for such, as wrong did grieue. (III.i.3)

Having spent his own book trying to find the middle ground, the Guyon of Book III traverses easterly and westerly extremities safe in the company of the 'famous Briton Prince' (III.i.1), their collaboration providing an example of the interlace structure of romance and the 'conquest of space'

---

10 Fichter, *Poets Historical*, p. 161.
11 Carter, 'Dark with Excess of Bright: Mapping the Coastlines of Knowledge', p. 131.

it holds in potential.[12] The spatial conquest suggested by their long and difficult travails, which 'Full many Countreyes ... did ouerronne,/ From the vprising to the setting Sunne' moves between romance commonplace and geopolitical fantasy, where to 'ouerronne' suggests swift, but hard-won, comprehension and mastery, even if the quest itself is described as recuperative. Pre-empting Britomart's own speculative quest, their wide-ranging movements sound the limits of the known world, both new and old: the formulaic phrasing may empty their efforts of geographical precision, but it claims an ambition and reach that is global in scope. Echoing Una's wandering pursuit of Redcrosse in Book I, an inadvertent circumnavigation 'from one to other *Ynd*' (I.vi.2), the cosmographical hyperbole blends geopolitical investment with rhetorical artifice.[13]

For readers of *The Faerie Queene*, Spenser's geography is rhetorical in the sense that it is not just descriptive, but persuasive. When readers encounter the artifice of his fictions, they also encounter the technical work done by poetry in combination with other disciplinary modes; as Roland Greene notes, for example, as 'a habit of thought as well as a dis-cipline, geography is conditioned by figures: a writing about landscape rather than the landscape itself'.[14] This suggests conscious design that complicates the process of representation and its employment of generic, structural, and figurative patterns.[15] Historically, literary critics have been highly attentive to spatial patterns in Spenser's work, providing readings of the poem's allegorical landscaping,[16] as well as more complex analyses of space and symbolism. Angus Fletcher's sense that *The Faerie Queene* is structured by a 'dialectic of the temple and the labyrinth', identifies spatial emblems that diagram 'the emergence of vision'.[17] The temple may be a city or a garden, just as the labyrinth finds parallels in the path-

---

12 Eugène Vinaver, *The Rise of Romance* (Oxford: Clarendon Press, 1971), p. 81.
13 See Michael Murrin, 'The Rhetoric of Fairyland', in *The Rhetoric of Renaissance Poetry From Wyatt to Milton*, ed. Thomas O. Sloan and Raymond B. Waddington (Berkeley: University of California Press, 1974), pp. 73–95.
14 Roland Greene, 'The "Scriene" and the Channel: England and Spain in Book V of *The Faerie Queene*', *JMEMS*, 39.1 (2009), 43–64, p. 43.
15 See Jonathan M. Smith, 'Geographical Rhetoric: Modes and Tropes of Appeal', *Annals of the Association of American Geographers*, 86.1 (1996), 1–20.
16 See John Erskine Hankins, *Source and Meaning in Spenser's Allegory: A Study of The Faerie Queene* (Oxford: Clarendon Press, 1971), pp. 55–98.
17 Angus Fletcher, *The Prophetic Moment: An Essay on Spenser* (Chicago: University of Chicago Press, 1971), pp. 45–6. Fletcher adopts his terms from Mircea Eliade, *The Sacred and the Profane: The Nature of Religion*, trans. Willard R. Trask (New York: Harper, 1957; repr. 1959), p. 21 and p. 23.

*Compassing desire: cosmography and chorography* 139

less forest, desert wilderness, and teeming sea.[18] And for Bellamy, who incorporates Fletcher's terminology into her reading of dynastic epic, *The Faerie Queene*'s 'indeterminate topography of thresholds ... suspends the subject, the questing "libido," on the verge – but only on the verge – of identity and selfhood'.[19] Most recently, Roland Greene's analysis of the *palus*, the 'man-made boundary', and the *via*, 'or way' in Book V, has offered a geopolitical refinement of Michel de Certeau's interest in the narrative figuration of 'delimitation' using the figures of 'the *frontier* and the *bridge*'.[20] Implicit within each schematic binary is the sense that the poem's spaces stage the acquisition of knowledge of both world and self: evidence that Spenser's poem is cosmographical in method.[21]

Merlin's cave, which Spenser locates in Wales, and towards which this chapter moves, is a strange place. It is not a temple, a labyrinth, a barrier, or a way; for, although it shares aspects of all these narrative figures, it inhabits a different and more fully composite order of spatial representation.[22] At the centre of the blend of knowledge-making practices stands Merlin himself, a familiar presence from both native and continental romance, who provides an anchoring figure not only for the writing of myth and poetry but also for what Stephen Knight describes as 'Renaissance technical skill'.[23] Although Spenser's geographies are decidedly 'anti-cartographic', to use Bernhard Klein's term, an unusual level of spatial detail accrues around Britomart's encounter with Merlin at the port city of Maridunum, holding together multiple perspectives that draw on different ways of imagining space.[24] Christopher Highley

18 See Philip W. Porter and Fred E. Lukermann, 'The Geography of Utopia', in *Geographies of the Mind: Essays in Historical Geosophy*, ed. David Lowenthal and Martyn J. Bowden (New York: Oxford University Press, 1976), pp. 197–223 (p. 199).
19 Elizabeth J. Bellamy, *Translations of Power: Narcissism and the Unconscious in Epic History* (Ithaca: Cornell University Press, 1992), p. 28.
20 Greene, 'The "Scriene" and the Channel', p. 45. See also Michel De Certeau, *The Practice of Everyday Life*, trans. Steven Rendall (Berkeley: University of California Press, 1984), p. 123.
21 See Fletcher, *The Prophetic Moment*, p. 304.
22 As Mary Villeponteaux observes, the cave in Ariosto's *Orlando Furioso*, on which Britomart's encounter with Merlin is modelled, is 'like a temple, supported by alabaster pillars and with an altar placed in the middle'. See 'Displacing Feminine Authority in *The Faerie Queene*', *SEL*, 35.1 (1995), 53–67, p. 62.
23 Stephen Knight, *Merlin: Knowledge and Power Through the Ages* (Ithaca: Cornell University Press, 2009), p. 105. See also Gareth Griffith, 'Merlin', in *Heroes and Anti-Heroes in Medieval Romance*, ed. Neil Cartlidge (Cambridge: D.S. Brewer, 2012), pp. 99–114.
24 See Bernhard Klein, *Maps and the Writing of Space in Early Modern England and Ireland* (Basingstoke: Palgrave, 2001), p. 74.

associates the figure of Merlin with 'Spenser's claims about the status of the artist and his creations' but also, owing to his peripheral geopolitical location, with Spenser's experiences of Gaelic Ireland.[25] For my purposes, Merlin, as might be thought fitting for a legendary figure of enchantment, appears to have feet placed in several overlapping worlds. His located presence connects spatial control with the art of prophecy.

Although Britomart travels 'Withouten compasse, or withouten card' (III.ii.7), her book constantly engages with how the relationship between space and self can be imagined. The romance mode may demonstrate a tendency to court ambiguity and to idealise through the cultivation of distance, but, as Neil Cartlidge has observed, romance is 'notorious for its indifference to limits – its apparent readiness to breach the rules both of literary decorum and of literary realism'.[26] Book III opens with Britomart already in what are to her 'straunge' lands, and in the false explanation of her purpose given to the Redcrosse Knight, she identifies herself as a stranger in Faery land, having left the place of her birth far behind. Her voyage may be made without navigational aids, but like Guyon, whose course comes into focus through the private knowings of his allegorical 'sea-card', she is guided by prior inward vision: a far more powerful device than those possessed by an ordinary traveller. Although she begins in ways reminiscent of Spenser's other wandering heroines, her errant progress accrues agency following the realisation that her movements have already been foretold. Importantly, when Spenser writes of the moment, and means, of Britomart's vision of Artegall, he also writes of its location. Within the inset narrative that traces the visionary encounter, Britomart is careful to conceal her secret knowledge and lovesick state. While Redcrosse tells her tales of Artegall's deeds she feigns ignorance of the savage knight:

> Yet him in euerie part before she knew,
>   How euer list her now her knowledge fayne,
>   Sith him whylome in *Brytayne* she did vew,
>   To her reuealed in a mirrhour playne,
>   Whereof did grow her first engraffed payne;
>   Whose root and stalke so bitter yet did taste,
>   That but the fruit more sweetnes did contayne,

---

25 Christopher Highley, *Shakespeare, Spenser and the Crisis in Ireland* (Cambridge: Cambridge University Press, 1997), p. 15–16. As Highley argues, the Merlin Spenser would have read about in Geoffrey of Monmouth's *Historia Regum Britanniae* is 'actually shown assisting in the oppression of the Irish'. See pp. 19–20.
26 Neil Cartlidge, 'Introduction', in *Boundaries in Medieval Romance*, ed. Neil Cartlidge (Cambridge: D.S. Brewer, 2008), pp. 1–11 (p. 1).

> Her wretched dayes in dolour she mote wast,
> And yield the pray of loue to lothsome death at last.
>
> By straunge occasion she did him behold,
> And much more straungely gan to loue his sight,
> As it in bookes hath written beene of old.
> In *Deheubarth* than now South-wales is hight,
> What time king *Ryence* raign'd, and dealed right,
> The great Magitien *Merlin* had deuiz'd,
> By his deepe science, and hell-dreaded might,
> A looking glasse, right wondrously aguiz'd,
> Whose virtues through the wyde worlde soone were solemniz'd.
>
> It vertue had, to shew in perfect sight,
> What euer thing was in the world contaynd,
> Betwixt the lowest earth and heuens hight,
> So that it to the looker appertaynd;
> What euer foe had wrought, or frend had faynd,
> Therein discouered was, ne ought mote pas,
> Ne ought in secret from the same remaynd;
> For thy it round and hollow shaped was,
> Like to the world it selfe, and seemd a world of glas. (III.ii.17–19)

Merlin's glass, as described here, is a strange kind of perspectival instrument: its reflective surfaces blend apparent objectivity with self-interest.[27] Its ability to elevate the capacity of human vision to achieve speculative fantasies not only recalls the spatial caprices of earlier fictions, such as the magic mirrors of romance, but also reflects emergent ways of making knowledge in the late sixteenth century, including the period's fascination for maps and globes. Although its material construction is very different from the 'lytell glasse' kept by Arthur in *Olyuer of Castylle*, it performs a similar narrative function in that it allows its beholder insight into events happening elsewhere. An instrument of wish-fulfilment, its powers of scrutiny effect acts of measuring and judging in both spatial and moral senses.

The mirror's predecessor can be found in Geoffrey Chaucer's incomplete *Squire's Tale*.[28] The narrator of *The Faerie Queene* laments how the fragmentary nature of Chaucer's unfinished labour 'robd the world of threasure endlesse deare' (IV.ii.33), and as if in order to rectify this

---

27 See Gregerson, *The Reformation of the Subject*, pp. 9–20.
28 See Craig A. Berry, '"Sundrie Doubts": Vulnerable Understanding and Dubious Origins in Spenser's Continuation of the Squire's Tale', in *Refiguring Chaucer in the Renaissance*, ed. Theresa M. Krier (Gainesville: University Press of Florida, 1998), pp. 106–27.

situation, its characters and incidents are recovered in various places in Spenser's poem.[29] As Helen Cooper observes, Chaucer 'assembles a fine collection of magic objects in the *Squire's Tale*, and then stops short, as if, having once gathered all these marvels together for display, he was not really interested in developing a plot from them'.[30] One of these abandoned objects is a magic mirror, the glass of which is already double edged; it shows the beholder 'openly who is youre freend or foo', and reveals both political treachery and betrayal in love, 'so openly that ther shal no thyng hyde'.[31] In Chaucer's tale, one of the most captivating aspects of the mirror's description concerns its technical construction; it hovers on the cusp of possibility, and the narrator hypothesises that it could be the work of 'composiciouns/ Of anglis and of slye reflexiouns' (229–30). As its onlookers speculate, the mirror is kin to the optical devices crafted by 'Alocen, and Vitulon,/ And Aristotle' (232–3), all of whom have written of 'queynte mirours and of perspectives' (234) and thus provide an authoritative means by which to delineate a tentative, yet permeable, boundary between technology and magic.[32]

In *The Faerie Queene*, Spenser's allusions to technology, though pervasive, are more diffuse. Merlin's glass is a 'wonderous worke' (III.ii.20), whose round hollowness suggests capacious internal space, but whose transparency suggests an object that is to be looked through in the manner of a perspective frame: its shifting form invites a consideration of spatial representations and relationships.[33] For Kenneth Borris, who focuses on its imitative capacity, Merlin's mirror participates in 'a self-reflexive allegory of poetics' that finds its dark reflection in the creation of the False Florimell: if Merlin's mirror 'presents Britomart with a sign inducing pursuit of its genuine signified, the bad enchantress creates an

---

29 See Patrick Cheney, 'Spenser's Completion of *The Squire's Tale*: Love, Magic and Heroic Action in the Legend of Cambell and Triamond', *Journal of Medieval and Renaissance Studies*, 15 (1985), 135–55. See also Goldberg, *Endlesse Worke*, pp. 31–72 in particular.
30 Helen Cooper, *The English Romance in Time: Transforming Motifs from Geoffrey of Monmouth to the Death of Shakespeare* (Oxford: Oxford University Press, 2004), p. 138.
31 Geoffrey Chaucer, 'The Squire's Tale' in *The Riverside Chaucer*, pp. 169–177, lines 136 and 141. All subsequent references are placed in the text.
32 Arab philosopher and mathematician Ibn al-Haytham (d. c. 1040) and the thirteenth-century Polish scientist and theologian Erazmus Ciolek Witelo. See Joyce Tally Lionarons, 'Magic, Machines, and Deception: Technology in the *Canterbury Tales*', *The Chaucer Review*, 27.4 (1993), 377–86, p. 379. For medieval optical theory see Suzanne Conklin Akbari, *Seeing Through the Veil: Optical Theory and Medieval Allegory* (Toronto: University of Toronto Press, 2004).
33 For the paradoxes of mirrors see Henri Lefebvre, *The Production of Space*, trans. Donald Nicholson-Smith (Oxford: Blackwell, 1991), p. 186.

illusion of glamour that deceives perception in order to conceal its total disjunction from what it purports to be'.[34] The distinction Borris makes, of course, can also be seen at work in the writing of early modern cosmography, which characteristically drew attention to the limitations of its capacity to figure forth ideal forms as part of its methodology (see Chapter 1). Like the translucent tower inhabited by the Egyptian king's lover Phao, which Spenser describes as analogous in material construction and impregnability, Merlin's 'glassy globe' (III.ii.21) allows the seer privileged visual access without self-exposure. As Patrick Cheney importantly observes, however, noting how the image also reveals the danger of brittle promises, 'the simile forecasts what would happen to Britomart if she were to misunderstand her vision: like Phao, she would become imprisoned in her own glass world of imaginative desire'.[35]

When initially mentioned in the first canto of Book III, the composite mirror is connected to Venus. As the instrument of a goddess, it prompts Britomart to pursue a 'straunge aduenture': 'To seeke her louer (loue far sought alas,)/ Whose image shee had seene in *Venus* looking glas' (III.i.8). The venal associations of the epithet suggest that the visions provided by Merlin's mirror are shaped by an erotic agenda. The iconography of Venus's mirror was traditionally associated with vanity, narcissism, and lasciviousness; however, in its capacity to refract interpretive attempts, it also holds together as many ways of making knowledge as correspond to the many aspects of the goddess herself.[36] Narcissistic desire may be sterile, but when directed under the auspices of *Venus Genetrix*, the aspect of the goddess that animates Spenser's Garden of Adonis, love is intrinsically generative:

> Therefore the antique wisards well inuented,
> That *Venus* of the fomy sea was bred;
> For that the seas by her are most augmented.
> Witnesse th'exceeding fry, which there are fed,
> And wondrous sholes, which may of none be red. (IV.xii.2)

---

34 Kenneth Borris, 'Platonism and Spenser's Poetic: Idealized Imitation, Merlin's Mirror, and the Florimells', *Spenser Studies*, 24 (2009), 209–68, p. 210 and p. 246.
35 Patrick Cheney, '"Secret Powre Unseene": Good Magic in Spenser's Legend of Britomart', *Studies in Philology*, 85.1 (1988), 1–28, p. 18. See also Mary Villeponteaux, 'Displacing Feminine Authority', pp. 60–2; and Silberman, *Transforming Desire*, pp. 22–4.
36 See Liana De Girolami Cheney, 'Giorgio Vasari's *The Toilet of Venus*: Neoplatonic Notion of Female Beauty', in *Neoplatonism and Western Aesthetics*, ed. Aphrodite Alexandrakis and Nicholas J. Moutafakis (Albany: State University of New York Press, 2002), pp. 99–112 (p. 108). See also Cathy Santore, 'The Tools of Venus', *Renaissance Studies*, 11.3 (1997), 179–207.

The mirror trope also performed a wide variety of roles within Neoplatonic discourse in order to represent the motion between sensual perception and the realm of ideas.[37] In 'Sonnet XLV' of Spenser's *Amoretti*, for example, the interactions between the lover and the beloved involve imagined reflective reciprocity, where the lover's heart is like a mirror, 'clearer then christall', for the subject of their desires:

> Leaue lady in your glasse of christall clene,
>   Your goodly selfe for euermore to vew:
>   and in my selfe, my inward selfe I meane,
>   most liuely lyke behold your semblant trew.
> Within my hart, though hardly it can shew
>   thing so diuine to vew of earthly eye:
>   the fayre Idea of your celestiall hew,
>   and euery part remains immortally: ...

In Spenser's sonnet, the poet asks his lady to forsake external, worldly appearances in order to participate in his inward contemplation of her perfection; within such terms, Venus's mirror shows not mutable surfaces but the 'fayre Idea' and the 'inward selfe' that lies beyond them.

John Demaray has observed that although Merlin's globe is indebted to 'magical glasses in Ptolemaic and literary mythology; ... the seer's glass most closely resembles, with certain distinctions, the "glasses" of sixteenth century cosmographers'.[38] Indeed, the mirror conceit is current across genres and a similar sleight of hand can be identified in the writing of world and waters by Spenser's contemporaries. A a similar process, for example, which plays the mutable world off against a repository of ideal forms, is at work in the poem prefacing the English edition of *The Mariners Mirrour*. In this poem, introduced in Chapter 1, the representational modes of Lucas Waghenaer's sea atlas are compared to the imitative capacities of the mirror of Venus:

> Moreover unlesse that peradventure a Searcher of East-seas,
> Or Northern passage, should want any thing that he searcheth:
> Thou shewst each Region farr of, what sort it ariseth.

---

37 Herbert Grabes, *The Mutable Glass: Mirror-Imagery in Titles and Texts of the Middle Ages and English Renaissance*, trans. Gordon Collier (Cambridge: Cambridge University Press, 1973; repr. 1982), p. 78.
38 John G. Demaray, *Cosmos and Epic Representation: Dante, Spenser, Milton and the Transformation of Renaissance Heroic Poetry* (Pittsburgh: Duquesne University Press, 1991), p. 111.

Nor *Venus* in Mirrour could view her selfe any cleerer,
Then *Tethys* in this Glasse may well discerne her apeeraunce. (sig. ¶3ʳ, 16–20)

The mirror is evoked as a didactic and exemplary instrument that has the capacity to augment perception by imitating divine vision; it is Waghenaer's book, rather than '*Venus* looking glas', that is praised as the tool by which the sea goddess Tethys is made visible. The laudatory poem thus imagines the book as a repository of ideal forms, over-going divine reflection; in so doing, its rhetoric transgresses the cautious claims of Waghenaer and Anthony Ashley, the work's English translator, who both seek to emphasise how 'things to come, and uncerteine, can by no meanes possible, bee perfectly described' (sig. ¶2ʳ). Waghenaer's own refusal to promote his manual as a work of prophecy casts Spenser's characterisation of Merlin as a prophetic maker into relief: the flickering forms shown in the magus's mirror are of an order no other cosmographer could reasonably dare to articulate.

Instead, Merlin's globe appears to literalise the figurative language used by cosmographical texts to sound the range of their ambitions and aims; within a poem such as Spenser's, this kind of mirror work can take on mirror form. The envoi on the title page of *The Cosmographical Glasse*, for example, promises Cuningham's readers a visionary experience gained via the labour of parsing the relationship between macrocosm and the microcosm:

> In this Glasse if you will beholde
>     The Sterry Skie, and th'earth so wide,
>     The Seas also, with windes so colde,
>         Yea and thy selfe all these to guide:
>     What this Type meane first learne a right,
>         So shall the gayne thy travaill quight.

For Cuningham's readers, the cosmographer's glass is meant to act as a means of mediating between self and world. The beholder is invited to act simultaneously as subject, guide, and perspectival frame, and to participate in an active mode of making knowledge. In his depiction of Merlin's globe, then, Spenser appears to translate the 'cosmographical glasses' of ink and paper charts and tables into a unifying piece of technology that reflects both the heart's desire and the desire to monitor the borders of one's realms: the mirror shows, after all, whatever 'to the looker appertayned' (III.ii.19). For Britomart, learning to read 'a right' requires an understanding of this design, gained by interrogating the craftsman responsible for the glass, and whose prophecy thus acts as a form of paratext for the object embedded within the poem.

The glass suggestively unites the magic mirrors of medieval romance with early modern military technologies: a further reminder that acts of questing manifest in Spenser's central books as something 'ambiguously martial and erotic'.[39] This aspect of Merlin's glass also focuses the ways in which maps were often figuratively described in the early modern period as mirrors. In *The Cosmographical Glasse*, for example, Cuningham observes how the practical application of cosmography is martial in inflection: as he notes in his preface to the work, Alexander had 'so many victories' and was 'so great a Conqueror' because he was 'accustomed to have the Mappe and Carte of the Country, by his Cosmographers set out, with which he would warre' (sig. A4$^r$). Famously, as Abraham Ortelius also explains in the letter to the reader prefacing his atlas, *Theatrum Orbis Terrarum*, geography is 'not without just cause called *The eye of History*': the perusal of the contained maps can be likened to having 'as it were certain glasses before our eyes', after which 'whatsoever we shall read ... will the longer be kept in memory, and make the deeper impression in us'.[40] For more recent theorists of cartography, such as J.B. Harley, maps work to mobilise the representation of power as it exists in a constant state of flux, thus serving to reflect the shaping capacity of personal and political desire. Highly critical of the map-mirror metaphor, whereby representational qualities are too readily aligned with mimetic transparency, Harley draws attention to the distorting capacity of subjective agendas.[41] Although of value to the modern reader, Harley's corrective would perhaps have been self-evident to early modern map lovers, owing to their ever-tested understanding of mirror images and imitative modes.

Merlin's mirror, because it appears in a poem and not in an atlas, thus functions not only as something magical but also as something, to use P.D.A. Harvey's term, 'mapminded':[42] an impression further evoked by the similarity of the ocular globe to an eye.[43] With its heightened

---

39 Harry Berger, Jr., *Revisionary Play: Studies in the Spenserian Dynamics* (Berkeley: University of California Press, 1990), p. 98.
40 Abraham Ortelius, 'To the Courteous Reader', in *Theatrum Orbis Terrarum*, trans. William Bedwell (London, 1606[08]).
41 See J.B. Harley, *The New Nature of Maps: Essays in the History of Cartography*, ed. Paul Laxton (Baltimore: Johns Hopkins University Press, 2001), p. 35.
42 P.D.A. Harvey, *Maps in Tudor England* (London: Public Record Office and the British Library, 1993), p. 15.
43 See Denis Cosgrove, *Apollo's Eye: A Cartographic Genealogy of the Earth in the Western Imagination* (Baltimore: Johns Hopkins University Press, 2001), p. 118.

characteristics, Merlin's glass transcends any representational medium available to the typical early modern cosmographer or cartographer; instead, it appears to interrogate the way that both cosmography and cartography work as imitative activities. Sometimes a mirror, sometimes a sphere, sometimes two dimensional, and sometimes three, Merlin's glass appears as the fantasy of a map, or terraqueous globe, which can move and adjust to the eye of its beholder. In its ability to combine map, mirror, and oracle, it realises the fantasy of a divine viewpoint through a rhetorical and highly performative process: a process of displacement that Frank Lestringant identifies in early modern cosmographical practices as 'spatial hyperbole', wherein 'the closeted world of chorography' is allowed to reach 'that imaginary point' where 'the eye of the cosmographer ideally coincided with that of the Creator'.[44] It ultimately functions as a representation of a series of representational modes.[45]

Like the contents of the atlas of Ortelius, the image in Merlin's glass 'will … make the deeper impression', as Britomart discovers. The mirror plots desire in both personal and geopolitical terms, displaying a body that is both desired and politic.[46] The use of the word 'impression' in the English edition of Ortelius's atlas invites a reading in which the matter of his *Theatrum* is imagined to act upon the mind of the reader, and in Spenser's poem, via a vision that seeks fulfilment in another rather than in the self, embodied passion is translated into movement. There are a variety of desires at work here, not least one which is predominantly concerned with territory and the location of allies. As Lesel Dawson argues, Britomart is changed by her perspectival encounter: her 'amorous affection is Platonic, not narcissistic, rendering the image that Britomart sees a revelatory vision rather than a solipsistic illusion' and thus transforming 'what initially appears to be an illicit, disorderly passion, into something ennobling and heroic'.[47] Artegall appears in the mirror not only because

---

44 Frank Lestringant, *Mapping the Renaissance World: The Geographical Imagination in the Age of Discovery*, trans. David Fausett (Cambridge: Polity, 1994), p. 5.
45 The glass could thus be said to render in allegory Fredric Jameson's 'innerworldly object' of romance worldmaking. As he writes, expanding upon Northrop Frye's work in *The Secular Scripture*, 'romance is that form in which the *world-ness* of *world* reveals itself', where '*world* in the technical sense of the transcendental horizon of … experience becomes precisely visible as something like an innerworldly object in its own right'. See 'Magical Narratives: Romance as Genre', *NLH*, 7.1 (1975), 135–63, p. 142.
46 See Kenneth Gross, *Spenserian Poetics: Idolatry, Iconoclasm, and Magic* (Ithaca: Cornell University Press, 1985), pp. 145–52. For a psychoanalytic reading see Bellamy, *Translations of Power*, p. 207.
47 Lesel Dawson, *Lovesickness and Gender in Early Modern English Literature* (Oxford: Oxford University Press, 2008), p. 128. See also pp. 12–45.

he is Britomart's future beloved but also because he is an armed invader and military presence; as Spenser reveals, he is a savage knight, destined for Ireland and terrible in the arms of Achilles, *'which Arthogall did win'* (III.ii.25). After all, like the work done by Alexander's cosmographers to visualise territory:

> Such was the glassy globe that *Merlin* made,
>   And gaue vnto king *Ryence* for his gard,
> That neuer foes his kingdome might inuade,
>   But he it knew at home before he hard
> Tydings thereof, and so them still debar'd.
>   It was a famous Present for a Prince,
>   And worthy worke of infinite reward,
> That treasons could bewray, and foes conuince;
> Happy this Realme, had it remayned euer since. (III.ii.21)

A realm that can be visualised to its limits is one that can be defended. As a tool of prognostication, the information shown by Merlin's globe is also temporal, a reminder that maps often plot time as well as space.[48] Sixteenth-century maps, as John Gillies has noted, conspicuously include future hopes, plotting a '*semiosis* of desire' that seeks the traversal of new territories that only time can bring.[49]

Cosmography, as comprised of the connected arts of geography, chorography, navigation, and astrology, links the writing of space to prognostication: an exercise of practical use to navigators and agriculturalists, as well as being suggestive of a '*situated* rationality' that allows, as David N. Livingstone explains, a 'geographical involvement with the numinous'.[50] In *The Faerie Queene*, Britomart's challenges are played out in the spaces in between different ways of knowing and representing the shape and form of the world. She has no map because she is travelling in a poem which slips between representational modes and textual traditions, and in which allegory and magic can, in Cheney's words, 'work ... to unite physical and spiritual reality, earth and heaven, human desire and divine will, moral action and metaphysical truth'.[51] In this vein, and owing to its perspective and prospective qualities,

---

[48] See Naomi Reed Klein, *Maps of Medieval Thought: The Hereford Paradigm* (Woodbridge: Boydell Press, 2001).

[49] John Gillies, *Shakespeare and the Geography of Difference* (Cambridge: Cambridge University Press, 1994), p. 62.

[50] David N. Livingstone, *The Geographical Tradition* (Oxford: Blackwell, 1993), p. 28 and p. 350. See also John Rennie Short, *Making Space: Revisioning the World, 1475–1600* (New York: Syracuse University Press, 2004), pp. 59–67.

[51] Cheney, 'Good Magic in Spenser's Legend of Britomart', p. 12.

Merlin's glass can also be thought of as a literary emblem that is allied to the imperialist interests of Spenser's contemporaries such as John Dee, who has been cited as a contemporary model for Spenser's Merlin, the instrument's maker.[52] When writing of the development of geography as an academic discipline, Lesley B. Cormack comments that as a self-titled 'perfect Cosmographer', Dee was responsible for 'the clearest articulation of imperial thinking' during this period:[53] a way of reading Dee's career that has been fully evidenced by William H. Sherman's study of Dee's activities as a court intellectual, engaged political advisor, and intelligencer.[54] While working in these capacities, Dee developed an interest in material objects that could be used to manipulate and enhance a viewer's perception of space, as his writings on other areas of applied geometry, maritime history, and geography also demonstrate.[55] In his *Mathematicall Praeface* (1570), for example, which was written as a way of introducing the English reader to Euclid's *Elements* while also offering a survey of the applications of mathematics, Dee ends his description of geography with a reflection on the fascination derived from its object-driven culture of spatial representation, offering a tactile, almost fetishised, appreciation of cosmographical artefacts. His description of how men 'liketh, loveth, getteth and useth, Mappes, Chartes, and Geographical Globes', speaks of an insatiable desire to possess and handle, which can be seen mediated in literary terms in Spenser's allegories, as well as in the later work of the poet and preacher John Donne (sig. a4$^r$).

Dee also includes a discussion of '*Catoptrike*' geometry in his *Mathematicall Praeface*, which involves the branch of optics concerned with reflection. He provides readers with tantalising hints concerning his own handling and knowledge of 'perspective Glasses' and predicts that their use in 'our posterity will prove more skillfull and expert, and to greater purposes, then in these dayes, can (almost) be credited to be possible' (sig. b1$^{r-v}$). Dee's interest in mirrors has long been associated

52 See Frances A. Yates, 'Spenser's Neoplatonism and the Occult Philosophy: John Dee and *The Faerie Queene*', in *The Occult Philosophy in the Elizabethan Age* (London: Routledge, 1979), pp. 95–108 (pp. 106–7). See also Peter J. French, *John Dee: The World of an Elizabethan Magus* (London: Routledge and Kegan Paul, 1972), pp. 126–59.
53 Lesley B. Cormack, *Charting an Empire: Geography at the English Universities, 1580–1620* (Chicago: University of Chicago Press, 1997), p. 1.
54 See William H. Sherman, *John Dee: The Politics of Reading and Writing in the English Renaissance* (Amherst: University of Massachusetts Press, 1995).
55 For an appraisal of Dee's activities and the critical reception of his life and work see *John Dee: Interdisciplinary Studies in English Renaissance Thought*, ed. Stephen Clucas (Dordrecht: Springer, 2006).

with scrying and *catoptromantia*, the art of using mirrors in divination; however, his interest in catoptrics and perspective glasses also extended to the practical and scientific applications of the properties and behaviours of light.[56] With reference to entries from Dee's private diary, Richard Deacon has observed that Spenser may have crafted the Britomart-Merlin episode in imitation of the visit made by Elizabeth I to Dee in March 1575, which gave Dee the opportunity to demonstrate the properties of one of his experimental glasses. As Deacon explains, Dee 'was one of the first to suggest that mirrors could be used for signalling' and 'not only predicted the invention of the telescope, but urged that perspective glasses should be installed in every one of Her Majesty's ships'.[57] A later insight into the development and efficacy of such glasses is given by William Bourne in his *Inventions and Devices* (1590), when he describes the setup of telescopic lenses:

> it is possible for to place a glasse in a chamber or a parler in a house, for to see any thing abroade in the fields, or if that it be neere unto any haven or river where as shippes or boates doo passe too and fro, that they may see in the glasse within the house, the things that are abroade, as playnely as if that they should goe abroad .... And by this meanes you may convey the beame or shadow of any thyng by glasses made of due proportion from one place unto an other, untill that you have brought it unto what place you doe desire at your pleasure.[58]

My purpose here in juxtaposing Spenser's allegories with Dee's experiments, and Bourne's devices, is not to suggest that Dee's mystical leanings should acquire any additional emphasis from their later association with the poet's Merlin, but that the implications of Spenser's images can be enhanced by an understanding of what a cosmographer and his glass (or glasses), both material and metaphorical, could claim to accomplish in service of the commonwealth.[59] The representation of Merlin's globe

---

56 See György E. Szönyi, 'Paracelsus, Scrying and the *Lingua Adamica*: Contexts for John Dee's Angel Magic', in *John Dee: Interdisciplinary Studies in English Renaissance Thought*, pp. 207–29.
57 Richard Deacon, *John Dee: Scientist, Geographer, Astrologer and Secret Agent to Elizabeth I* (London: Frederick Muller, 1968), p. 81. Elizabeth's visit to Mortlake is also discussed by Howard Dobin, *Merlin's Disciples: Prophecy, Poetry, and Power in Renaissance England* (Stanford: Stanford University Press, 1990), p. 5. See also James Orchard Halliwell, ed., *The Private Diary of Dr. John Dee and the Catalogue of His Library of Manuscripts* (London: Camden Society, 1842), p. 10.
58 William Bourne, *Inventions or Devises* (London, 1590), sig. N2$^v$–N3$^r$.
59 See Sherman, *John Dee*, pp. 143–6. See also Jess Edwards, *Writing, Geometry and Space in Seventeenth Century England and America: Circles in the Sand* (London: Routledge, 2006), pp. 34–7.

as an object fashioned to exist in the mind somewhere between the arts of *techne* and those of prophetic *catoptromancy*, is thus given precedent in the work of an Elizabethan polymath whose expansionist designs for Elizabethan England were tied to civic pragmatism and national forms of mythmaking.[60]

## Chorography: the global and the local

Following the visionary encounter, Britomart's quest to seek out the maker of the perspectival instrument takes her on a journey with a potential trajectory that is played out globally, sending the maid, or at least her imagination, to the opposite ends of the earth. First, a different kind of enchantment is shown to fail, where Britomart's nurse and erstwhile squire Glauce exhausts the scope of her own homely magic:

> Full many wayes within her troubled mind,
>     Old *Glauce* cast, to cure this Ladies griefe:
>     Full many waies she sought, but none could find,
>     Nor herbes, nor charmes, nor counsel that is chiefe,
>     And choisest med'cine for sick harts reliefe:
>     For thy great care she tooke, and greater feare,
>     Least that it should her turne to fowle repriefe,
>     And sore reproch, when so her father deare
> Should of his dearest daughters hard misfortune heare.
>
> At last she her auisde, that he, which made
>     That mirrhour, wherein the sicke Damosell
>     So straungely vewed her straunge louers shade,
>     To weet, the learned *Merlin*, well could tell,
>     Vnder what coast of heauen the man did dwell,
>     And by what means his loue might best be wrought:
>     For though beyond the *Africk Ismael*,
>     Or th'Indian *Peru* he were, she thought
> Him forth through infinite endeuour to haue sought.
>
> Forthwith them selues disguising both in straunge
>     And base atyre, that none might them bewray,
>     To *Maridunum*, that is now by chaunge
>     Of name *Cayr-Merdin* cald, they tooke their way:
>     There the wise *Merlin* whylome wont (they say)

---

60 See Sherman, *John Dee*, p. 150 and Charlotte Artese, 'King Arthur in America: Making Space in History for *The Faerie Queene* and John Dee's *Brytanici Imperii Limites*', *JMEMS*, 33.1 (2003), 125–41.

> To make his wonne, low vnderneath the ground,
> In a deepe delue, farre from the vew of day,
> That of no liuing wight he mote be found,
> When so he counseld with his sprights encompast round.
>
> And if thou euer happen that same way
> To traueill, go to see that dreadfull place:
> It is an hideous hollow caue (they say)
> Vnder a rocke that lyes a litle space
> From the swift *Barry*, tombling downe apace,
> Emongst the woody hilles of *Dyneuowre*:
> But dare thou not, I charge, in any cace,
> To enter into that same balefull Bowre,
> For feare the cruell Feendes should thee vnwares deuowre. (III.iii.5–8)

The geographical intimacy of Britomart's birthplace in Wales, a peripheral but comfortably European setting, is juxtaposed with a brief invocation of the continents of Africa and Asia-America: the nomenclature of 'th'Indian *Peru*' slips between the old world and the new, retaining the memory of Columbus's belief that he could reach the East by sailing west.[61] Spenser's Faery land, as Michael Murrin argues, is 'in India and … America': a paradox made imaginatively possible by the flattening distensions that occur in cartography.[62] The spatial elision of east and west, as David Wallace notes in *Premodern Places*, also 'haunted Hakluyt':[63] an intimation of the 'narrative contradictions' latent in the construction of a European imperial gaze.[64] For Spenser, it creates a crucial paradox that could reconcile the geographical speculations of medieval romance, in which the East evoked the image of another world, with those of his present audience, for whom westward exploration invited the contemplation of uncharted space.[65]

---

61 See Valerie I.J. Flint, *The Imaginative Landscape of Christopher Columbus* (Princeton: Princeton University Press, 1992).

62 Murrin, 'The Rhetoric of Fairyland', p. 79. The suggestion that Spenser had America in mind when he writes of Faery is evidenced by the medicinal herb likened to 'diuine *Tobacco*' (III.v.32) gathered by Belphoebe to heal Timias's wounds. See Jeffrey Knapp, *An Empire Nowhere: England, America, and Literature from Utopia to The Tempest* (Berkeley: University of California Press, 1992), pp. 134–74. The personification of Fansy in the House of Busirane is described as having feathered garments like those worn by 'sunburnt *Indians*' (III.xii.8).

63 David Wallace, *Premodern Places: Calais to Surinam, Chaucer to Aphra Behn* (Oxford: Blackwell, 2004; repr. 2006), p. 193.

64 See Elizabeth J. Bellamy 'Spenser's Faeryland and "The Curious Genealogy of India"', in *Worldmaking Spenser: Explorations in the Early Modern Age*, ed. Patrick Cheney and Lauren Silberman (Lexington: University Press of Kentucky, 2000), pp. 177–92 (p. 186).

65 See Cooper, *The English Romance in Time*, p. 72 and p. 75.

For all the gestures towards cartographic prediction, however, most striking is the figure used to probe the whereabouts of Artegall's location. If the first stage of Britomart's quest is to contextualise her vision of Artegall using Merlin's help, the next is to ascertain 'Vnder what coast of heauen the man did dwell' (III.iii.6). Spenser describes this limit by combining a figure from terrestrial geography with an otherworldly location: owing to the way that the word 'coast' can suggest both an edge and a cardinal compass direction, Spenser's choice of phrase suggests both a means of determining direction and a frontier of exploratory knowledge, if not a destination in itself.[66] When writing of the knowledge and experience required during naval warfare, for example, John Sadler's translation of *The Foure Bookes of Flavius Vegetius Renatus* (1572) employs the technical application of the phrase in a discussion of gauging wind direction:

> Whosoever caryeth an armye with his Navye, ought to foreknow the signes of stormes and whirlewindes. ... Therefore he that wilbe skilfull in saylinge, ought first to consider the nomber, and also the names of wyndes. Olde warriours perswaded themselves that according to the situation of the foure coastes of Heaven, that onlye foure principall windes did usuallye blowe from every part therof, but a latter tyme founde oute twelve windes by experience.[67]

As the author's promotion of the benefits of weather-forecasting suggests, there is an element of prognostication involved in the art of successful seafaring: advice that also has implications for Spenser's poetics.[68] In service of the latter, the phrase was also used by Thomas Phaer in his translation of the first book of Virgil's *Aeneid*, when Venus, disguised as an armed nymph of Diana, appears to her shipwrecked son: 'What lond is this?', Aeneas asks, 'What coast of heaven be we come under here?'[69] As critics have long since recognised, this encounter prefigures

---

66 See 'coast, n.' *OED Online*. Oxford University Press, June 2013 (last accessed 16 August 2013).
67 Flavius Vegetius Renatus, *The Foure Bookes of Flavius Vegetius Renatus*, trans. John Sadler (London, 1572), fol. 62ᵛ–63ʳ.
68 See van Es, *Spenser's Forms of History*, pp. 164–96. See also S.K. Heninger, *A Handbook of Renaissance Meteorology* (Durham, NC: Duke University Press, 1960).
69 See *The Whole .xii. Bookes of the AEneidos of Virgill*, trans. Thomas Phaer (London, 1573), sig. B1ʳ. The Latin reads, 'quo sub caelo tandem, quibus orbis in oris iactemur, doceas; ignari hominumque locorumque erramus, vento huc vastis et fluctibus acti', which, in a modern English translation, is a request to be told 'beneath what sky, on what coasts of the world, we are cast; knowing nothing of countries or peoples we wander driven hither by wind and huge billows'. See Virgil, *Eclogues; Georgics; Aeneid I–VI*, trans. H. Rushton Fairclough; revised by G.P. Goold (Cambridge, MA: Harvard University Press, 1916; repr. 2006), pp. 284–5.

the meeting of Artegall and Britomart and is also parodied in the meeting of Belphoebe with Trompart and Braggadocchio (II.iii.21–31).[70] To imagine a coast of heaven is to imagine something both mutable and eternal, material and divine: something contoured and, paradoxically, without physical place.[71] It offers a figure for order and arrival without needing to posit either a centre or its absence.

In spite of their evocatively cosmographical and even utopian qualities, then, the stanzas also mark one of the few places in the poem where the poet produces a sustained geographical description through the accrual of discrete, if discontinuous, place-names. From the expansive range of Britomart's imagination, the location of Merlin's cave is unusually particular, marked by an incantation of names, which despite being subject to change over time, ground the action in Wales. Bart van Es remarks on the unusual nature of this passage, commenting that 'nowhere else in *The Faerie Queene* does Spenser address the world of sixteenth-century England in this way. The Merlin of whom we first hear is presented not as a character in the romance plot, but as a legend, whose tale emerges in response to a geographical feature'.[72] On the whole, van Es's comments concerning the 'chorographic element ... latent within all romances' are highly productive; however, they are also telling of the slippage that occurs around borders.[73] Spenser does not truly address 'the world of sixteenth-century England' even here. As the place-names indicate, it is of Wales as a separate geopolitical kingdom, and not of England, that Spenser writes.[74] Even then, it is of a magician's haunt, a place of retreat and darkness, and a liminal, subterranean site. Merlin's fortified cave, a 'balefull Bowre' surrounded by 'cruell Feendes' (III.iii.8), expresses Spenser's ambivalence concerning retreats, despite its peculiar status as a defended site of vision: for Highley, the cave even offers a model of an alternative court, 'the locus of real power in the realm',[75] and for Bellamy it maps 'nothing less than the center of Tudor England as a

---

70 See Philip R. Hardie, *The Last Trojan Hero: A Cultural History of Virgil's Aeneid* (London: I.B. Taurus, 2014), pp. 60–2.
71 The English translation of Jean Calvin's exploration of the paradoxes of Christ's ascension are also expressed in such terms: 'Shall we then (will some man saye) assigne to Christe some certaine coast of heaven?' See *The Institution of Christian Religion*, trans. Thomas Norton (London, 1561), sig. R2$^r$.
72 van Es, *Spenser's Forms of History*, p. 55. See also pp. 164–71.
73 Ibid., p. 52.
74 Fichter obscures Wales in a similar way, referring to the origin of Britomart's journey as the 'England of King Ryence'. See *Poets Historical*, p. 168.
75 Highley, *Shakespeare, Spenser and the Crisis in Ireland*, p. 16.

Trojan *renovatio*'.⁷⁶ We think we know where we are, only to find that we are somewhere else entirely.

Spenser's inclusion of chorographical material ties the making of knowledge to regional geography and draws attention, as Bart van Es notes, to the non-linear quality of Spenserian movement, which 'allows Spenser to parcel up the narrative of Britain's past with a very similar freedom to that used by Camden'.⁷⁷ The use of the word 'parcel' is interesting and suggestive of discontinuity, concurrent with Dee's definition of chorography in the *Mathematicall Praeface*. Here, Dee describes chorography as a mathematical rather than a narrative art – 'an underling, and a twig, of Geographie' – which takes as its focus 'a small portion or circuite of ground, with the contentes: not regarding what commensuration it hath to the whole, or any parcell without it, contained. ... Yea and sometimes, of things under ground, geveth some peculier marke: or warning' (sig. b1ʳ). His definition becomes a meditation on fragmentation, apportioning, and the relationship between surface and depth, as if chorography can address that which is amassed within the memory of a particular allocation of soil and bring it back into consciousness.⁷⁸ Dee may be thinking in material terms, but his words capture the way that the scattered monuments and place-names of chorographical writing offer brief orientating flashes of the effect of time on place. To move back once again into the modes of romance, as signs of 'of sundry way' (II. xi.35), they produce an effect that Andrew King calls 'the topos of things "still there"', where the appearance of a name or a 'vestigial object may be likened to a memory of the earlier narrative world'.⁷⁹ As King's work demonstrates, the ground shared by chorography and romance allowed poets and antiquarians such as John Leland to write of the numinous contours of England, 'as if the landscape were a mirror in which the nation's history and character might be viewed'.⁸⁰ Such writing engages in the preservation of cultural memory, where 'to write', as we have seen, is 'to try meticulously to retain something, to cause something to survive'.⁸¹

In *Britannia*, William Camden explains in the section on

---

76 Bellamy, *Dire Straits*, p. 54.
77 van Es, *Spenser's Forms of History*, p. 52.
78 See Philip Schwyzer, *Archaeologies of English Renaissance Literature* (Oxford: Oxford University Press, 2007).
79 Andrew King, *The Faerie Queene and Middle English Romance: The Matter of Just Memory* (Oxford: Clarendon Press, 2000), p. 77.
80 Ibid., p. 163.
81 Perec, *Species of Spaces*, p. 92.

'Caer-mardhin-shire' that 'this South-Wales has been call'd Deheubarth; i.e. the Southern Part'. His glosses explain the change of place-names mentioned by Spenser, noting that '*Caer-mardhin*' was known by the 'Britains' as '*Kaer-Vyrdhin*, Ptolemy *Maridunum*, and Antoninus *Muridunum*',[82] and we can trace the two latter terms as variations of 'Moridunum': a name that is derived from *mori-* 'sea' and *–dunum*, 'fort'.[83] Berger notes the way that the place-name 'draws our attention to the bond between ocean and war':[84] an intimation of Britomart's future role in wars to come, until she exchanges the battlefield for motherhood, as prophesised by Merlin (III.iii.27–9).[85] As William Camden explains, Carmarthen is

> the chief town of the Country, pleasantly seated for Meadows and Woods, and a place of venerable Antiquity; fortified neatly (saith Giraldus) with brick-walls partly yet standing, on the noble river of Towy: navigable with ships of small burden; tho' the mouth of it be now almost stopp'd with a bed of Sand.

Camden ties the meanings of place-names to local landmarks, such as Dinevor castle, the 'Royal Seat of the Princes of South-Wales' and legends, including those of Merlin, or 'Merdhin Emrys (for so our Writers call him)'. Camden's note that this prophetic figure 'flourish'd An. 480' acts as a reminder of Spenser's untimely inclusion of antiquarian monuments and serves to emphasise the deliberate past-ness of the meeting of sixth-century Britomart and Merlin.[86] Within this context, Camden's observation that the once-navigable harbour has been silted up is particularly striking; in a world where 'many havens are decayed, and many are altered', to recall Waghenaer's admonition (*The Mariners Mirrour*, sig. ¶2ʳ), its impermanence distinguishes it from the 'coast of heauen' sought by Britomart, whose triumphs belong to a long gone age. A 'bed of Sand', accrued over time, hints at the worldly material fluctuations underlying Spenser's allegory, in which hydrographic forms retain the memory of inevitable change, and which for Camden provide the residual material traces of a once legendary landscape.

---

82 William Camden, *Camden's Britannia* (London, 1695). All quotations from Camden are from sig. Qq2ʳ⁻ᵛ.

83 See Hywel Wyn Owen and Richard Morgan, *Dictionary of the Place-Names of Wales* (Llandysul: Gomer, 2007), p. 71.

84 Berger, *Revisionary Play*, p. 102. As he observes, Book III's fractured 'elemental landscapes ... are not only places in Faerie but also *topoi* of the collective cultural imagination' (p. 92).

85 See Erickson, *Mapping the Faerie Queene*, pp. 99–106 and p. 122.

86 See van Es, *Spenser's Forms of History*, pp. 52–8.

According to Camden himself, the legends of Merlin are shadowed by superstition and heresy and are fit only for the misguided entertainment of the unlearned; he names only one judicious authority, 'H. Lhwyd', who is reported to have recorded that Merlin 'was a man of extraordinary learning and prudence for the time he liv'd in'. As Humphrey Llwyd writes in *The Breviary of Britayne* (1573), Merlin was known for 'his passyng skill in the *Mathematicals*, and wonderful knowledge in al other kinde of learnyng'.[87] Noting the similarity of Merlin's name to the name of the place in which he was supposedly born, Llwyd makes the city his namesake; yet, as a purveyor of insular fantasies, Camden's Merlin is recalled by Spenser's character only in the loose association of person, location, and myth:

> Here our Merlin, the British Tages, was born: for as Tages was reported to have been the son of a Genius, and to have taught the Tuscans Southsaying; so our Merlin, who was said to have been the son of an Incubus, devised Prophecies, or rather mere Phantastical Dreams, for our Britains. Insomuch, that in this Island he has the reputation of an eminent Prophet, amongst the ignorant common people.[88]

As Robert Allott's gatherings on the subject 'Of Prophecies, Visions, &c.' in *Wits Theater of the Little World* (1599) record, the story of the birth of Tages tells of a child prophet, who 'sprung up from the ground', surprising a mortal man who was 'ploughing in the field'.[89] The Etruscan soothsayer, like Spenser's Merlin, emerges in relation to a particular kind of place, suggesting that his legend has what Nancy Thomson de Grummond describes as the 'characteristics of a "charter" myth, since it provides a paradigm for the acquisition and usage of divine revelation, valid in both religious and political contexts': for, once encountered, Tages taught the art of prognostication to the Etruscans, specifically Tarchon, the 'founder-hero' of the city Tarquinia.[90] In Spenser's case, 'Maridunum', or '*Cayr-Merdin*', the birthplace of Merlin, is situated at a martial and coastal periphery beyond which, Spenser perhaps suggests, Faery land may be found. By writing in detail up to this geographical cusp he marks the ancient city as a threshold between a legend-haunted

---

87 Humfrey Lhwyd, *The Breviary of Britayne*, trans. Thomas Twyne (London, 1573), fol. 79ʳ.
88 Camden, *Camden's Britannia*, sig. Qq2ʳ.
89 Robert Allott, *Wits Theatre of the Little World* (London, 1599), fol. 159ᵛ.
90 Nancy Thomson de Grummond, *Etruscan Myth, Sacred History, and Legend* (Philadelphia: University of Pennsylvania Museum of Archaeology and Anthropology, 2006), pp. 23–7 (p. 24 and p. 23).

known world and an otherworld into which the ordinary traveller cannot and should not pass. In so doing, he prepares the way for Britomart to hear her own charter myth, or myth of origins, in which Merlin speaks of wars and cities, islands and wastes, waves and monuments, before breaking off overcome by the vision.

At the place of prophecy, Britomart finds herself where the land and sea 'may be mett', and where 'perilles and aduentures hard' may be found (III.ii.7). When Britomart and Glauce eventually arrive at Merlin's cave, they observe him to be at work on binding magic.[91] Standing on his threshold looking in, they initially fear the place at which they have arrived:

> They here ariuing, staid a while without,
>   Ne durst aduenture rashly in to wend,
>   But of their first intent gan make new dout
>   For dread of daunger, which it might portend:
>   Vntill the hardy Mayd (with loue to frend)
>   First entering, the dreadfull Mage there fownd
>   Deepe busied bout worke of wondrous end,
>   And writing straunge characters in the grownd,
> With which the stubborne feendes he to his seruice bownd. (III.iii.14)

The reader is granted another glimpse of Merlin's art, which takes the form of limning enchantments on the earth, as if wresting 'from the void as it grows ... a trace, a mark or a few signs'.[92] At once maker and cosmographer, Sidney's *vates*, Spenser's Merlin grants both vision and access to new territories to be explored and charted. His mirror may realise the fantasy of a divine viewpoint within the poem; however, his real skill is his ability to write the world anew and to transform its aspects through language:

> For he by wordes could call out of the sky
>   Both Sunne and Moone, and make them him obay:
>   The Land to sea, and sea to maineland dry,
>   And darksom night he eke could turne to day: ... (III.iii.12)

Tellingly, Spenser's Merlin, like Cuningham before him, does not attempt through writing to move the earth, which remains a steadfast point amidst the motion of the heavens. Instead, from his dark, cavelike residence, the spatial negative of the luminous crystal sphere, he can command the

---

91 See Susanne Lindgren Wofford, 'Gendering Allegory: Spenser's Bold Reader and the Emergence of Character in *The Faerie Queene* III', *Criticism*, 30.1 (1988), 1–22.
92 Perec, *Species of Spaces*, p. 92.

celestial spheres and govern the motion of the tides: turning one thing into its opposite, he occupies the point of balance between making and unmaking.[93] Merlin may be an artificer, but his labour is distinguished by Spenser from the making of illusion.

Wholly aligning himself with neither Merlin nor Archimago, then, Spenser is sceptical of his art. Sometimes poet and cosmographer, reflecting on the relationship between self and world, and sometimes chorographer and antiquarian, searching for monuments and landmarks, he writes and rewrites geographies; as such, the implied connection between the touch of the poet's hand and the compass of the human gaze participates in what Tom Conley has figured as the 'errant' or 'haptic eye' of the sixteenth century, which 'becomes a point of reference for poets and artists who look closely at their territory, who discern its size and scale; who carefully draw the lines defining the nooks, edges, and crannies and relief of its surface; who follow the roads and rivers cutting and winding through it; and … who touch the lairs and recesses inspiring the fantasies that mark what they see'.[94] The placement of a 'glassy globe' within Spenser's poem, shaped by the author's hands as both writer of romance and colonial administrator, mobilises many of the metaphorical associations found in the figurative prose and paratexts of his 'mapminded' contemporaries. Placed as a prospective instrument at the borders of South Wales, and showing what it does, a savage knight destined for trials in the west, the glass offers an emblem of geopolitical desire, catching at what A. Kent Hieatt has described as 'the will-o'-the-wisp of Elizabethan imperium'.[95]

Refashioning the 'lying wonders' of romance, in ways pertaining to colonial schemes, offers a further measure of Spenser's awareness of the mutability of territory: the urge to name and to charter is countered by the apparent distance, in both time and space, of stasis. Merlin may begin to imagine and articulate the state of Spenser's sixteenth-century present and what lies to the west of Wales, 'But yet the end is not' (III.iii.50). The arrival of Britomart at Maridunum, the port city beyond which lies the sea, an 'other world', and what Spenser would call elsewhere the 'saluage

---

93 Fichter aligns Merlin's powers with those of Fidelia, associated with 'Christian miracle' in Book I. See *Poets Historical*, pp. 172–3.
94 Tom Conley, *An Errant Eye: Poetry and Topography in Early Modern France* (Minneapolis: University of Minnesota Press, 2011), p. 2.
95 See A. Kent Hieatt, 'Room of One's Own for Decisions: Chaucer and *The Faerie Queene*', in *Refiguring Chaucer in the Renaissance*, pp. 147–64 (p. 148). See also Bruce McLeod, *The Geography of Empire in English Literature, 1580–1745* (Cambridge: Cambridge University Press, 1999; repr. 2009), p. 64.

soyl' of Ireland, focuses a particular aspect of Spenser's poetic vision.[96] The reader is shown something that appears to juxtapose the spaces and topographies of imagined worlds with the problematic desires and views of late sixteenth-century colonialism. The romance mode, as it engages with the writing of geography during the early modern period, it seems, is not concerned with the representation of 'feyned no where acts' at all, to recall Thomas Nashe's dismissive indictment, but with the expression of desire as it plays out across territory. As a mythopoetic contribution to the *speculum principis* tradition, which presents strategies of memory and anticipation, praise and blame, Britomart's inaugural episodes anticipate the poem's increasingly freighted engagement with questions of imaginative capacity and control.

---

96 See the dedicatory sonnet following the *FQ*, 'To the right Honourable the Earle of Ormond and Ossory'.

# PART II

Environments

# 5

# Seamarks and coastal waters

The one essential quality of the imagination is that it moves – in wide sweeps, in pinched steps, out to sea, down into the interior. The imagination is polytheistic and polygamous; its groundspring is multiplicity, not singularity. Trying to press a single meaning on its imagery is like asking a river to hold still. ... Image invites image, which suggests mirrors and the ceaseless, duplicitous interplay of one thing and its reflection.[1]

Then first I pray you begin with the division of the water, expounding such names as they take of ther place.[2]

The dialogue portion of *The Cosmographical Glasse* suggests that the acquisition of practical spatial knowledge is impossible without the play of an engaged imagination: an indication, perhaps, that Cuningham's treatise was most successful as a work of rhetoric, capable of restructuring the image of the cosmos as it existed in the mind.[3] For example, when writing of hydrography, the practical art of representing the liquid aspect of the natural world, Cuningham initiates the discussion by employing a display of *copia*. The pupil Spoudaeus articulates his desire for knowledge of navigational matters using a metaphorical blend that obeys few rules of decorum:

> There is nothing under the Globe of the mone conteined, whiche unto man, beast and everye living wite, semeth more tedious, more ickesome, and long then time, when as they once fele the wante of that they moste desire. Whiche sayinge to be true (althoughe manye do confesse) yet I above all other muste of force affirme, remembringe your promesse, touchinge

---

1 Barbara Hurd, *Stirring the Mud: On Swamps, Bogs, and Human Imagination* (Boston, MA: Beacon Press, 2001), pp. 36–7.
2 William Cuningham, *The Cosmographical Glasse* (London, 1559), sig. N6$^r$.
3 For the methods and aesthetics of Renaissance cosmography see S.K. Heninger, Jr., *The Cosmographical Glass: Renaissance Diagrams of the Universe* (San Marino: Huntington Library Press, 1977; repr. 2004).

th'Arte of Navigation. For sence your departure, the greadye Greyhounde (I assure you) never more desired his pray, nor the thirstye harte, the flowynge fountaine, or the languishinge sicke paciente, the recovery of his health: then my minde wanting her fode and Nutrimente, thoughte longe, wished, and thirsted, after youre presence and companye. (sig. N5$^v$)

The absence of instruction is described using the language of lovesickness, whereby Spoudaeus's perception that he has been neglected incites a sublunary erotic charge. When relieved by the reappearance of his tutor, the eager pupil drinks in information concerning the shapes and names, and the ebb and flow, of waters: 'Fretum, Lacus, Stagnum, Palus, Fluvius', he recites, in hope of receiving definitions from Philonicus in return. Though conscious of the need to explain the relationship of the parts to the whole, his teacher and friend stops short after listing the qualities of distant waters, as if suddenly remembering the limits of the printed word: 'There are also the English, Germaine, Spanishe and other seas, of whiche I neade to make no mention, no more then of the notable rivers, as the Themes, the Rhine, Confluence, Neccarus, Danubie, Tyber, Nilus. etc. Because they are manifest unto suche as travell in any of them' (sig. N6$^v$). For a work that aims at encyclopaedic coverage it is a strange omission, which gestures awkwardly to the inability of Cuningham's work to replace experience. The names and narratives bound in his narrow printed pages can do little to compass the wide waters themselves. Philonicus's justification for the occlusion, made because such waters 'are manifest' to those that confront them, is a jolt to the steady progress of the armchair traveller: a gesture towards the idea that a reader should already be in possession of the ability to discern the familiar from the unfamiliar, the known from the unpossessed, and the literary from the physical encounter.

Part of the pleasure derived from reading Cuningham's dialogue is found in the declarations of friendship made by its interlocutors; expressions of interpersonal curiosity, familiarity, and affection draw the reader into a social and intellectual exchange that happily coexists with fluctuating descriptions of the material world outside the study. In this chapter, which focuses on moments from Books III and IV of *The Faerie Queene*, similar formal and figurative modes can be seen at work, where the names and forms of multitudinous waters provide constantly changing structures for Spenser's analysis of human interaction. Historically, Spenser's rivers have been singled out by critics owing to their provision of a network of correspondences that acts as a 'poetic signature': an engagement with literary tradition that uses, as W.H. Herendeen observes, 'patterns in nature ... to frame social myth'.[4] Figures of the coastline or strand are similarly loaded with this mythopoeic work, and it is with these spaces of solubility and dissolution that this chapter continues to engage.

In Spenser's hands, images of coastlines suggest naturally fluctuating limits where form and matter exist in constant inconstancy, posing an interpretive and mimetic challenge also faced by the writers of hydrographical works. As discussed previously, the paratexts of *The Mariners Mirrour* (1588) actively emphasise the fluid correspondence of Waghenaer's representations to an embodied encounter with shifting strands and salt water, where 'sandy coastes and shoares ... have not alwaies their being in one self place' (sig. ¶2ʳ). As a responsible hydrographer, he alerts his readers to the mutability of the natural world and the dangers of both authorial and readerly apathy. Furthermore, although a sonnet and a sea atlas share little common ground in terms of genre, a similar impulse to acknowledge the ways in which the action of water can undo the author's labour can be found in 'Sonnet LXXV' of Spenser's *Amoretti* (1595). The poet imagines the tideline as a writing surface; yet, this place, located by 'sea, by land, where so they may be mett' (*FQ*, III. ii.7), is resistant to the hand of the artificer:

> One day I wrote her name vpon the strand,
>   but came the waues and washed it away:
>   agayne I wrote it with a second hand,
>   but came the tyde, and made my paynes his pray.
> Vayne man, sayd she, that doest in vaine assay,
>   a mortall thing so to immortalize,
>   for I my selue shall lyke to this decay,
>   and eek my name bee wyped out lykewize.
> Not so (quod I), let baser things deuize
>   to dy in dust, but you shall liue by fame:
>   my verse your vertues rare shall eternize,
>   and in the heuens wryte your glorious name.

---

4 W.H. Herendeen, 'Rivers', in *SEnc*, pp. 608–9 (p. 608). See also Bart van Es, *Spenser's Forms of History* (Oxford: Oxford University Press, 2002), pp. 58–64; Andrew McRae, 'Fluvial Nation: Rivers, Mobility and Poetry in Early Modern England', *ELR*, 38.3 (2008), 506–34; and Joan Fitzpatrick, 'Marrying Waterways: Politicizing and Gendering the Landscape', in *Archipelagic Identities: Literature and Identity in the Atlantic Archipelago, 1550–1800*, ed. Philip Schwyzer and Simon Mealor (Aldershot: Ashgate, 2004), pp. 81–91. For a summary of the critical positions prompted by the river pageant see Rachel E. Hile, 'The Limitations of Concord in the Thames-Medway Marriage Canto of *The Faerie Queene*', *Studies in Philology*, 108.1 (2011), 70–85 (pp. 72–4).

> Where whenas death shall all the world subdew,
> our loue shall liue, and later life renew.

As if performing another instance of 'writing straunge characters in the grownd' (III.iii.14), the lover-poet fathoms a process more fragile than the incantatory labours of Merlin in *The Faerie Queene*. With no enchantments to aid his travail, his recurrent attempts to trace the name of his beloved in wet sand is defeated by the saltwater motion, which parallels the beloved's evasion of her lover's will.[5]

Writing the coastline, it seems, invites the contemplation of a space in which practical solutions are sought for longstanding philosophical problems concerning form, being, and representation. As Margaret W. Ferguson observes, writing in response to the moment in Plato's *Cratylus* when Socrates attacks the followers of Heraclitus, 'Socrates argues that if words "name" only things which are in constant flux, such words – unlike words which imitate unchanging ideas – cannot give any certain knowledge since their referent is literally nonexistent as an object of epistemology'.[6] Within the compressed form of Spenser's sonnet, which admits imagined dialogue and allows for the play of counter-arguments, the beloved articulates her awareness of her own mortality: she resists the poet's attempts to know her and his endeavours to hold her still, her voice refiguring the image he creates and her changeable being eluding his poetry of praise. In his attempted handling of material body and inscribed name, and the confrontation with erasure and decay that results, the poet encounters an impasse; although the vocal mortal woman who plays the part of the beloved has been identified as Elizabeth Boyle, she remains anonymous within the sonnet, as unknowable as the ways of the waves.[7] With reference to previous readings of the poem, Steve Mentz's observation that the 'strand occupies the same mixed brown materiality as the decayed corpse' can be pitched against Elizabeth Jane Bellamy's perception that the poet's focus, via his improvised resolution to make impossible alteration to the unchanging heavens, moves 'from a mutable, tide-scoured coastline to a celestial

---

5 See William C. Johnson, *Spenser's Amoretti: Analogies of Love* (Lewisburg: Bucknell University Press, 1990) and Emilien Mohsen, *Time and the Calendar in Edmund Spenser's Poetical Works* (Paris: Publibook, 2005).

6 Margaret W. Ferguson 'Saint Augustine's Region of Unlikeness: The Crossing of Exile and Language', in *Innovations of Antiquity*, ed. Ralph Hexter and Daniel Selden (London: Routledge, 1992), pp. 69–94 (p. 80).

7 See Fred Blick, 'Spenser's *Amoretti* and Elizabeth Boyle: Her Names Immortalized', *Spenser Studies*, 23 (2008), 309–15.

home'.[8] As discussed below, the combination of mortality and sublimation suggested by the tidal movement also informs Spenser's myth of dynastic succession and his representations of the monarch who shares his beloved's name.

With their full awareness of the distorting capacity of the imitative arts, then, Spenser's poems are not unique: like the hydrographic practices of the sixteenth century, they wrestle with the problem of binding something intrinsically mutable. As Francis Bacon would later explain in *De Augmentis* (1623): 'For like as a man's disposition is never well known or proved till he be crossed, nor Proteus ever changed shapes till he was straitened and held fast; so nature exhibits herself more clearly under the trials and vexations of art than when left to herself'.[9] *The Faerie Queene*, of course, is notoriously full of shape shifters, and in the poem's middle books they take the form of Cupid, the agent of desire, who 'wandred in the world in straunge aray,/ Disguiz'd in thousand shapes, that none might him bewray' (III.vi.11) and Proteus himself, who 'To dreadfull shapes ... did him selfe transforme,/ ... Raging within the waues' (III. viii.41). As characters who also embody formal principles, the pair figure the play of desire and the potential for transformation that operates at the cusp of order and chaos.

By offering reflections on how the terraqueous imaginary of Spenser's poem is shared by other writers in the period, namely John Dee and Walter Ralegh, this chapter identifies a collective interest in the tidal poetics of the coastline: a hydrographic feature that prompts intellectual and aesthetic responses to the challenges of temporality and contingency.[10] In the first instance, I read extracts from Book III of *The Faerie Queene* alongside Dee's *General and Rare Memorials Pertayning to the Perfect Arte of Navigation* (1577). In this text, Dee's interests in issues of speculation and possession project past English coastlines to those of England's immediate insular neighbour Ireland and beyond. This chapter

---

8 Steve Mentz, 'Brown', in *Prismatic Ecology: Ecotheory Beyond Green*, ed. Jeffrey Jerome Cohen (Minneapolis: University of Minnesota Press, 2013), pp. 193–212 (p. 197) and Elizabeth Jane Bellamy, *Dire Straits: The Perils of Writing the Early Modern English Coastline from Leland to Milton* (Toronto: University of Toronto Press, 2013), p. 68.

9 Francis Bacon, *De Augmentis*, in *The Philosophical Works of Francis Bacon* (Routledge Revivals), ed. John M. Robertson (Oxford: Routledge, 1905; repr. 2011), p. 429. See also Kenneth Gross, *Spenserian Poetics: Idolatry, Iconoclasm, and Magic* (Ithaca: Cornell University Press, 1985), pp. 23–4 and A. Bartlett Giamatti, *Exile and Change in Renaissance Literature* (New Haven: Yale University Press, 1984), p. 150.

10 For Shakespeare's interest in tidal metaphors and phenomena see Dan Brayton, *Shakespeare's Ocean: An Ecocritical Exploration* (Charlottesville: University of Virginia Press, 2012), pp. 86–106.

considers the ways in which the littoral imagery used by both Spenser and Dee reflects back Elizabeth's image 'in mirrours more then one' (III. pro.5), offering a glimpse of the ground shared by their imperial projecting. As Charlotte Artese explains, both Spenser and Dee exploited the ill-defined thresholds between fiction and history, *fabula* and *historia*, in order to 'create the spaces in which their works can exist': a strategy evidenced by Dee's attempt to persuade Elizabeth that King Arthur had indeed 'trafficked in the New World'.[11]

Engagement with Dee's works of hydrography and navigation is then used to frame the poetic investment shared by Spenser and Ralegh in the processes governing the tideline; the environments inhabited by Spenser's friends and lovers in Book IV of *The Faerie Queene* find an elegiac mirror image in Ralegh's vision of sterile 'brinish sand' (24) in his fragmentary poem, the '21th: and last booke of the Ocean to Scinthia'.[12] If the work of the two poets is read as part of an ongoing dialogue, used in part to fashion a response to Elizabeth I, Ralegh's speaker can be seen to inhabit the same tidal imaginary as Spenser, but admits none of the temperate renewal that shapes his fellow poet's mythmaking.[13] When read together, the work of all three writers participates in what Louis Montrose has called the 'Elizabethan political imaginary', and the contrast between Dee's performance of counsel and Ralegh's of personal despair, extends and enriches an understanding of the terms of the spatial imaginary of Spenser's middle books and the place of Elizabeth I in Spenser's allegory.[14] *The Faerie Queene* often overwrites the mutable surfaces of the natural world with personal and national myth; however,

11 Charlotte Artese, 'King Arthur in America: Making Space in History for *The Faerie Queene* and John Dee's *Brytanici Imperii Limites*', *JMEMS*, 33.1 (2003), 125–41, p. 126 and p. 127. See also David A. Summers, *Spenser's Arthur: The British Arthurian Tradition and The Faerie Queene* (Lanham: University Press of America, 1997), pp. 125–30. For investment in King Arthur's northern conquests see E.G.R. Taylor, 'A Letter Dated 1577 from Mercator to John Dee', *Imago Mundi*, 13.1 (1956), 56–68.
12 Walter Ralegh, 'The 21th and last booke of the Ocean to Scinthia', in *The Poems of Sir Walter Ralegh: A Historical Edition*, ed. Michael Rudick (Tempe: Arizona Center for Medieval and Renaissance Studies, 1999), pp. 48–66. All line references are placed in the text.
13 For a historicised approach to this dialogue see Jerome S. Dees, 'Colin Clout and the Shepherd of the Ocean', *Spenser Studies*, 15 (2001), 185–95, pp. 186–7 and pp. 190–1 in particular. See also essays by William A. Oram (pp. 165–74) and Wayne Erickson (pp. 175–84) in this volume of *Spenser Studies*.
14 Louis Montrose, 'Spenser and the Elizabethan Political Imaginary', *ELH*, 69.4 (2002), 907–46. For Elizabeth I as the inspiration, subject, and audience of the dialogic poetics crafted by Spenser and Ralegh see Michael Rudick, 'Three Views on Ralegh and Spenser: A Comment', *Spenser Studies*, 15 (2001), 197–203.

hydrographical features, as the writings of Dee and Ralegh also demonstrate, are often resistant to an author's will and serve instead as conduits for ambivalence.

The Protean subject of hydrography holds together reflections on aesthetic representation, political and personal ambition, and the use of a specialist vocabulary that readily lends itself to poetic expression. Dee, for example, writing in his *Mathematicall Praeface*, captures the challenges posed by the element of water when he attempts to set the limits of the hydrographer's art:

> Hydrographie, delivereth to our knowledge, on Globe or in Plaine, the perfect Analogicall description of the Ocean Sea coastes, through the whole world or in the chiefe and principall partes thereof: with the iles and chiefe particular places of daungers, conteyned within the boundes, and Sea coastes described: as, of Quicksandes, Bankes, Pittes, Rockes, Races, Countertides, Whorlepooles. etc. This, dealeth with the Element of the water chiefly: as *Geographie* did principally take the Element of the Earthes description (with his appertenances) to taske. And besides thys, *Hydrographie*, requireth a particular Register of certaine Landmarkes (where they may be had) from the sea, well hable to be skried, in what point of the Seacumpase they appeare .... And in all Coastes, what Mone, maketh full Sea: and what way, the Tides and Ebbes, come and go, the *Hydrographer* ought to recorde. The Soundinges likewise: and the Chanels wayes: their number, and depthes ordinarily, at ebbe and flud. (sig. a4$^{r-v}$)

Dee writes of needing to know about surfaces and depths, and about boundaries and their transgression: of being able to measure waning and excess, and to gauge the place where liquid becomes solid, and safety, danger. Although his description belongs to an ostensibly objective work of prose, the language used, which speaks of ever-altering fullness and loss, readily lends itself to figurative depictions of the vicissitudes of fortune. The mind of the visionary courtier and mathematician handles a vocabulary that is generative, not reductive, characterised by multiplicity, movement, and a mode of definition by division that negates singularity.

As Dee writes, the hydrographical method relies on producing 'the perfect Analogicall description' of things in constant flux: a labour that also carries the suggestion, to borrow Hurd's words, of 'the ceaseless, duplicitous interplay of one thing and its reflection'.[15] Used to clarify meaning and intent through correspondence or similarity, analogy

---

15 Hurd, *Stirring the Mud*, p. 37.

facilitates the writing of a world in miniature.¹⁶ When defining the arts of geography, chorography, and hydrography, for example, Dee claims that these practices name the processes by which world and water 'may be described and designed, in comensurations Analogicall to Nature and veritie' (sig. a4ʳ). As defined by a contemporary of Dee's, the rhetorical figure of analogy looks for 'aptnes, proportion and a certeine convenience of the signe to the thing signified so that this maye be seene in that as in a loking-glasse'.¹⁷ The work done by the perspective, or prospective, glass, it seems, provides its own analogy for the analogical process: a move that reveals the work's reuse of the title page associated with Cuningham's *Cosmographical Glasse* as a meaningful choice.¹⁸ Analogy, as a rhetorical figure that looks for 'correlation, harmony and agreement', can also be thought of as a thematic and formal feature of Spenser's Legend of Friendship as it develops out of, and enriches, the legends which precede it.¹⁹ As Goldberg has observed, the concept of friendship 'is not simply a term that names an analogical universe but the very word for the structure of discourse with its possibilities of substitution, exchange and union, one word in place of another, one story in place of another'.²⁰ In the interlaced narratives of Books III and IV, there is a new determination to name, catalogue, and contain matter within form, through the conventions of both romance and epic, and their affinities with natural philosophy.

Spenser's sea, as Gordon Braden observes, relies on the poet's shaping hand, and 'would be simply undifferentiated water if it were not for the names that have flowed into it'.²¹ In the following readings, the writing of literary hydrography reveals not an objective conjunction of world and water but a reflection of the mind at work: a mind that delights in names and etymologies.²² Among the catalogue of the fifty *Nereides* that

16 See Katherine Park, 'Bacon's "Enchanted Glass"', *Isis*, 75.2 (1984), 290–302, p. 294.
17 Heinrich Bullinger, *Fiftie Godlie and Learned Sermons*, trans. H.I. (London, 1577), sig. Ooool ʳ.
18 See Lesley B. Cormack, 'Britannia Rules the Waves? Images of Empire in Elizabethan England', *EMLS*, 4.2 (1998), 10.1–20 (18).
19 'analogy, n.' *OED Online*. Oxford University Press, September 2015 (last accessed 2 November 2015).
20 Jonathan Goldberg, *Endlesse Worke: Spenser and the Structures of Discourse* (Baltimore: Johns Hopkins University Press, 1981), pp. 27–8.
21 Gordon Braden, 'Riverrun: An Epic Catalogue in *The Faerie Queene*', *ELR*, 5.1 (1975), 25–48, p. 37.
22 See Goldberg, *Endlesse Worke*, pp. 68–72 and Richard Helgerson, *Forms of Nationhood: The Elizabethan Writing of England* (Chicago: The University of Chicago Press, 1992), p. 142.

Spenser borrows from Hesiod, for example, there is 'she that hight of many heastes *Polynome*' (IV.xi.50), a daughter of the ocean who embodies the paradox of trying to possess that which exists in constant flux. The word 'hest', though etymologically related to the action of calling by name, also suggests a promise, purpose, or command: a reminder that the saturation of littoral spaces with names may separate the land from the sea but that this occurs in a way that illustrates the temporality of verbal description when it seeks to gauge the changing material surfaces of the natural world.[23] When Hurd describes the imaginative charge of an encounter with the liquid landscapes of the bayous of Southern Louisiana in *Stirring the Mud*, then, as quoted in the epigraph to this chapter, her chosen words also suggest ways of catching at what is at stake in the hydrographic *discordia concors* of *The Faerie Queene*'s middle books. The poet may imagine a space in which the bonds of Proteus can be temporarily tightened before being released; yet, unlike the grip of Peleus, his hold on the *genius loci*, like that of Dee and Ralegh, is temporary.

## Complaint and supplication: Spenser's Britomart and Dee's Brytanica

In Spenser's allegory of chastity, the open sea, embodied and inhabited by figures such as Marinell and Proteus, replaces the inland waters of Guyon's adventures, providing an impression, as Gordon Braden observes, that 'characters in *The Faerie Queene* are forever arriving at the shore'.[24] Spenser's allegories in Book II contain geographies woven from the drifts of the erotic and the alluring; yet, Guyon's destruction of the insular Bower of Bliss only seems to diffuse its intensity, and subsequent books retain the memory of the threat posed by any 'spatious playne,/ Mantled with greene' that 'it selfe did spredden wyde' (III.i.20).[25] Once created, the spaces of poetry are difficult to raze from the mind.[26]

---

23 'hest, n.' *OED Online*. Oxford University Press, September 2015 (last accessed 2 November 2015).
24 Gordon Braden, 'Riverrun', p. 39. See also Bellamy, *Dire Straits*, pp. 46–87.
25 It is beyond the scope of this chapter to address Spenser's Garden of Adonis, but for excellent readings see Kenneth Gross, 'Green Thoughts in a Green Shade', *Spenser Studies*, 24 (2009), 355–71; Gross, *Spenserian Poetics*, pp. 181–209; and Berger, 'Spenser's Garden of Adonis', in *Revisionary Play*, pp. 131–53.
26 G. Wilson Knight observes the Bower of Bliss-like character of the whole poem in 'The Spenserian Fluidity', in *Elizabethan Poetry: Modern Essays in Criticism*, ed. Paul J. Alpers (Oxford: Oxford University Press, 1967), pp. 329–44 (pp. 339–40).

Book III famously mirrors its verdant gardens with coastal places and the accompanying threat of sterile salinity. In Daniel M. Murtaugh's reading, the shifting spaces of the garden and the sea are oppositional spaces of creative invention: one luxuriant and fertile, and the other, for the purposes of Book III at least, initially treacherous and forbidding.[27] Like many Spenserian spaces, the shores, seas, and gardens of Britomart's terraqueous world cannot be perceived as stable allegorical loci; they do not hold consistent forms but instead exist in the play of generation and destruction. Embodied by the characters of Marinell and Florimell, the 'creatures of sea and of meadows, wave and flower', whose paired nature underlines the narrative's cosmic scope and interest in *concordia*, the spaces of the central books speak of the capacity for growth, development, and change.[28] The oppositional ecologies find temporary resolution, of course, in Marinell and Florimell's union at the Castle of the Strond in Book V, where the antagonisms of ocean waves and fertile land are reconciled, and where empty imitations are dissolved, like the false Florimell, into nothing.[29]

As discussed in Chapter 4, Britomart's arrival at a coastal city recognisable from the real world, '*Maridunum*, that is now by chaunge/ Of name *Cayr-Merdin* cald' (III.iii.7), pre-empts another, less certain journey. By giving her position relative to the shifting foundations and barriers of coastal space, Spenser confers shape to a literary subject on the cusp of transformation: as in Humphrey Tonkin's description of Spenser's Garden of Adonis, distinctions between physical and metaphysical space fluctuate freely, and the coastline figures states 'at the borderline between being and becoming, stasis and action'.[30] In the fourth canto of Book III, Britomart approaches a further coastline and her progress prompts the making of a complaint that merges movement with articulation, for 'to

---

27 See Daniel M. Murtaugh, 'The Garden and the Sea: The Topography of *The Faerie Queene*, III', *ELH*, 40.3 (1973), 325–38.
28 Kathleen Williams, 'Venus and Diana: Some Uses of Myth in *The Faerie Queene*', *ELH*, 28.2 (1961), 101–20, p. 118.
29 For two very divergent readings of Marinell and Florimell see Philip Edwards, *Sea-Mark: The Metaphorical Voyage, Spenser to Milton* (Liverpool: Liverpool University Press, 1997), pp. 33–6 and Thomas P. Roche, Jr., *The Kindly Flame: A Study of the Third and Fourth Books of Spenser's Faerie Queene* (Princeton: Princeton University Press, 1964), pp. 150–94. For Marinell's role in the allegory see Bellamy, *Dire Straits*, pp. 55–65.
30 Humphrey Tonkin, 'Spenser's Garden of Adonis and Britomart's Quest', *PMLA*, 88.3 (1973), 408–17, p. 410. See also Margaret Anne Doody, 'Marshes, Shores and Muddy Margins', in *The True Story of the Novel* (New Brunswick: Rutgers University Press, 1996), pp. 319–36.

the seacoast at length she her addrest' (III.iv.6). Although she may not physically set sail, her heart and imagination project beyond the coastal limits; after writing of how she sits 'downe vpon the rocky shore', the narrator explains how 'hauing vewd a while the surges hore,/ That gainst the craggy clifts did loudly rore' (III.iv.7) she extends the reach of her complaint into the space beyond the shoreline. Operating across the place where the 'raging surquedry' and 'deuouring couertize' of the waves is 'affronted' by the 'fast earth' (III.iv.7), her language blends the displacements and self-divisions implicit in the conventions of Petrarchan poetry with the tempestuous winds and intemperate seas familiar from the Psalms and sermon literature.[31] She figures herself as a 'feeble barke', tossed far from a safe harbour:

> Huge sea of sorrow, and tempestuous griefe,
>   Wherein my feeble barke is tossed long,
>   Far from the hoped hauen of reliefe,
>   Why doe thy cruel billowes beat so strong,
>   And thy moyst mountaines each on others throng,
>   Threatning to swallow vp my fearefull lyfe?
>   O doe thy cruell wrath and spightfull wrong
>   At length allay, and stint thy stormy stryfe,
> Which in thy troubled bowels raignes, and rageth ryfe.
>
> For els my feeble vessell crazd, and crackt
>   Through thy strong buffets and outrageous blowes,
>   Cannot endure, but needes it must be wrackt
>   On the rough rocks, or on the sandy shallowes,
>   The whiles that loue it steres, and fortune rowes;
>   Loue my lewd Pilott hath a restless minde
>   And fortune Boteswaine no assuraunce knowes,
>   But saile withouten starres, gainst tyde and winde:
> How can they other doe, sith both are bold and blinde? (III.iv.8–9)

Her complaint, which is also an invocation and prayer, recalls the devotional petitions of early modern seafarers in its fusing of spiritual and existential turmoil with the awareness of physical threat.[32] With her

---

31 For the complex doublings of 'inner and outer experience' see Susanne Lindgren Wofford, 'Britomart's Petrarchan Lament: Allegory and Narrative in *The Faerie Queene* III, iv', *Comparative Literature*, 39.1 (1987), 28–57. See also Lynn Enterline, *The Rhetoric of the Body from Ovid to Shakespeare* (Cambridge: Cambridge University Press, 2000), p. 23 and Judith H. Anderson, *Reading the Allegorical Intertext: Chaucer, Spenser, Shakespeare, Milton* (New York: Fordham, 2008), pp. 69–78.

32 See, for example, Anthony Anderson, 'A Forme of Prayer for Sea Men', in *A Godly Sermon* (London, 1575).

body on shore but her mind at sea, Britomart's inhabitation of two distinct spaces suggests the threat of being cruelly 'wrackt' on unsounded rocks or shallows: she becomes a spectator of her own condition.[33] The dominant lingering image is of self-division: like the littoral spaces of Waghenaer's atlas she does not have her subjective being 'in one self place' (sig. ¶2ʳ).

The subsequent address to Aeolus characterises her as one who seeks strategically 'to foreknow the signes of stormes and whirlewindes',[34] where in Spenser's allegory the threatened tempest evokes the movement and government of the passions.[35] Importantly, there is the potential for triumph present in the oath sworn to Neptune, which replaces the despairing tonal quality of the complaint with fortitude:

> Thou God of windes, that raignest in the seas,
>   That raignest also in the Continent,
>   At last blow vp some gentle gale of ease,
>   The which may bring my ship, ere it be rent,
>   Vnto the gladsome port of her intent:
>   Then when I shall my selfe in safety see,
>   A table for eternall moniment
>   Of thy great grace, and my great ieopardee,
> Great *Neptune*, I auow to hallow vnto thee. (III.iv.10)

The fusion of tenor and vehicle in Britomart's proximity to water achieves a moment of clarity and self-actualisation, which turns on the word 'then' in the sixth line of the stanza;[36] after this, present grief becomes the foundation of imagined conquest, of both self and space. Right rule nonetheless retains a capacity for tempestuousness; even when continence should be expected from the land, or 'continent' itself, Spenser's wordplay

---

33 See Hans Blumenberg, *Shipwreck with Spectator: Paradigm of a Metaphor for Existence*, trans. Steven Rendall (Cambridge, MA: MIT Press, 1997), p. 59. As Steve Mentz notes, 'looking at a shipwreck from the safety of shore, as in the famous image from the Roman poet Lucretius, provides a philosophical perspective that uses wet events to create dry wisdom'. See *Shipwreck Modernity: Ecologies of Globalization, 1550–1719* (Minneapolis: University of Minnesota Press, 2015), p. 11.
34 Flavius Vegetius Renatus, *The Foure Bookes of Flavius Vegetius Renatus*, trans. John Sadler (London, 1572), fol. 62ᵛ.
35 See Gail Kern Paster, 'Becoming the Landscape: The Ecology of the Passions in the Legend of Temperance', in *Environment and Embodiment in Early Modern England*, ed. Mary Floyd-Wilson and Garrett A. Sullivan, Jr. (Basingstoke: Palgrave Macmillan, 2007), pp. 137–52 (p. 138). See also her *Humouring the Body: Emotions and the Shakespearean Stage* (Chicago: University of Chicago Press, 2004), pp. 1–24.
36 See Isabel G. MacCaffrey, *Spenser's Allegory: The Anatomy of Imagination* (Princeton: Princeton University Press, 1976), p. 292.

reminds the reader of the threat of untempered passion.[37] Spenser may write of dissolving monuments elsewhere, but here the 'moniment' promised by Britomart speaks of prospective hard-won victory in spite of 'ieopardee' at sea. Owing to the early modern use of the word 'table' to mean both a writing surface and a float used after shipwreck, and the word 'moniment' to mean both commemorative structure and written document, visualising the promised record of Britomart's travails issues the reader with an imaginative challenge: the ambiguity of the perspectival object evoked encompasses statue, chart, and book.[38] For one who travels without the instrumental means of orientation typically hard won by experiment, the moment salvages meaning from the threat of dissolution.

Although short-lived, a visionary quality is retained in the way that Britomart's resolution, supplemented by Glauce's counsel, condenses out of the microclimate of her personal elementary environment:

> As when a foggy mist hath ouercast
>   The face of heauen, and the cleare ayre engroste,
>   The world in darkenes dwels, till that at last
>   The watry Southwinde from the seabord coste
>   Vpblowing, doth disperse the vapour lo'ste,
>   And poures it selfe forth in a stormy showre;
>   So the fayre *Britomart* hauing disclo'ste
>   Her clowdy care into a wrathfull stowre,
> The mist of griefe dissolu'd, did into vengeance powre. (III.iv.13)

An understanding of Glauce's gaze can be enhanced by Alfred K. Siewers's glossing of 'the Irish color term *glas*', from which her name takes inspiration, as 'the colour of a southwest wind, from the quadrant of Ireland oriented by tradition towards the Otherworld and by geography toward the ocean'.[39] As Glauce watches Britomart, intent and will are imagined as precipitation, capable of changing state and density in

---

37 See Margaret Christian, '"Waves of Weary Wretchedness": Florimell and the Sea', *Spenser Studies*, 14 (2000), 133–61, p. 143.
38 See 'table, n.' *OED Online*. Oxford University Press, September 2015 (last accessed 2 November 2015), and 'monument, n.' *OED Online*. Oxford University Press, September 2015 (last accessed 2 November 2015). Andrew Escobedo glosses '"monument" (stemming from *monēre*, "to remind")' in *Nationalism and Historical Loss in Renaissance England* (Ithaca: Cornell University Press, 2004), p. 48. For the move from 'confused poetic analogy toward … religious vow' see Jerome S. Dees, 'The Ship Conceit in *The Faerie Queene*: "Conspicuous Allusion" and Poetic Structure', *Studies in Philology*, 72 (1975), 208–25, p. 219.
39 Alfred K. Siewers, *Strange Beauty: Ecocritical Approaches to Early Medieval Landscape* (Basingstoke: Palgrave Macmillan, 2009), p. 103.

order to alter atmospheric conditions at the point where heavens, land, and water meet. It is from this visionary blend of self and environment that Britomart summons the requisite strength to fell 'proud *Marinell* vpon the pretious shore' (III.iv.17) and enter his dominion: a 'strond … bestrowed all with rich aray/ Of pearles and pretious stones of great assay'. Unburdened by the temptations of hoarded wealth, Britomart's reaction is contempt: she 'despised all; for all was in her powre' (III. iv.18).[40] By condensing an image of conquest, of both self and perceived territory, the stanzas seem to turn a motif associated with fragmentation into one of self-realisation.

The triumphant tableau, in which Britomart's agency is divided and consciously positioned both at sea and on shore, is playfully reminiscent of the image displayed on the title page of John Dee's *General and Rare Memorials Pertayning to the Perfect Arte of Navigation* (1577), in which the kneeling figure of 'Brytanica' looks out to sea at a ship on which Queen Elizabeth sits in state (see Figure 6). The scroll held by the supplicant woman bears an inscription in Greek letters, petitioning the monarch for 'a fully-equipped expeditionary force'.[41] Although it cannot be argued that Spenser knew Dee's treatise directly, for Dee's intended audience was deliberately restricted,[42] the mythmaking of both authors shares a similar spatial imaginary, and is complicit in what Montrose describes as the 'collective repertoire of representational forms and figures – mythological, rhetorical, narrative, iconic – in which the beliefs and practices of Tudor political culture were pervasively articulated'.[43] Dee's striking images, it seems, are mirrored by Spenser's later fictions.

Dee's anonymously published treatise, which participates in the literature of counsel, begins with 'An Advertisement to the Reader'. Here, the author defends himself, 'one extraordinary Studious Ientleman', from slanderous untruths and accusations: namely, that 'the Foresaid

---

40 For this moment as a channelling of Elizabeth and 'her imperial power' see Susanne Lindgren Wofford, *The Choice of Achilles: The Ideology of Figure in the Epic* (Stanford: Stanford University Press, 1992), p. 283.
41 Margery Corbett and Ronald Lightbown, *The Comely Frontispiece: The Emblematic Title-Page in England 1550–1660* (London: Routledge and Kegan Paul, 1979), p. 50 (and for a full description see pp. 48–56).
42 For Dee's hoarding of a substantial quantity of the volume's print run in his library see Robert Baldwin, 'John Dee's Interest in the Application of Nautical Science, Mathematics and Law to English Naval Affairs', in *John Dee: Interdisciplinary Studies in English Renaissance Thought*, ed. Stephen Clucas (Dordrecht: Springer, 2006), pp. 97–130 (p. 118).
43 Montrose, 'Spenser and the Elizabethan Political Imaginary', p. 907.

Seamarks and coastal waters 177

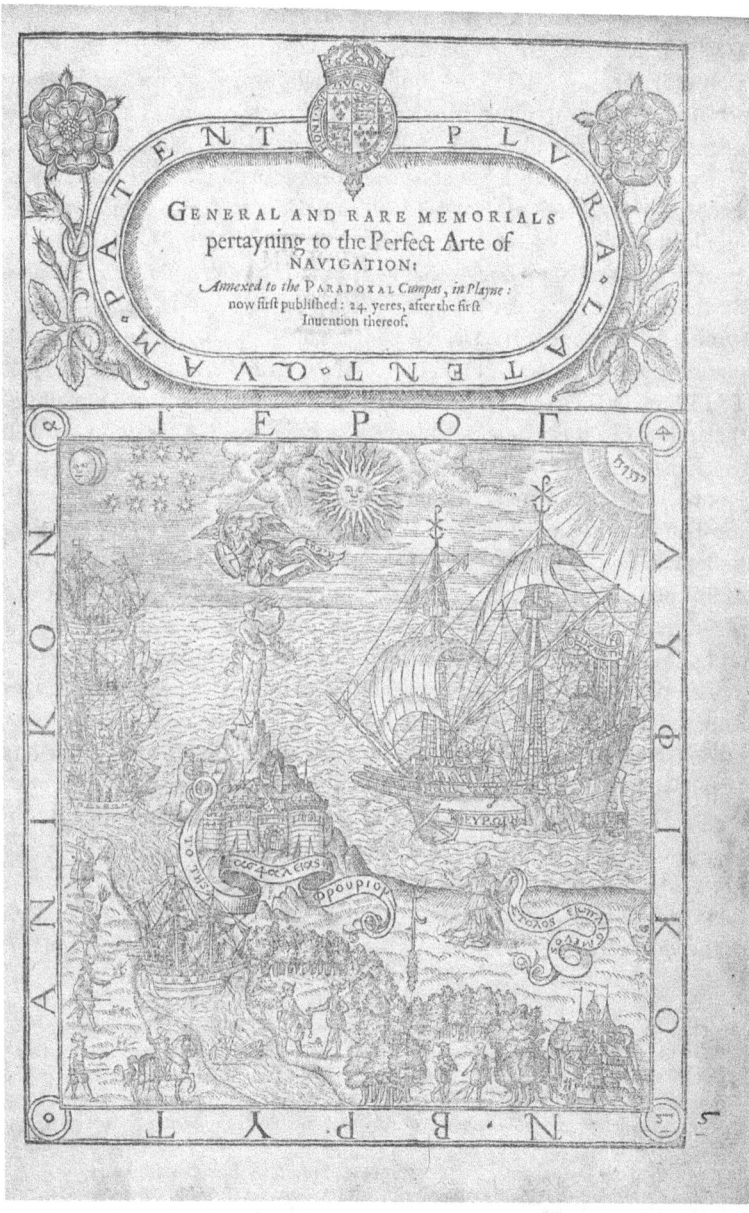

*Figure 6* John Dee. Title page from *General and Rare Memorials Pertayning to the Perfect Arte of Navigation* (London, 1577).

Ientleman, is, or was' accused, not only of being a 'Conjurer, or Caller of Divels: but, ... The Great Conjurer: &so (as some would say,) The Arche Conjurer, of this whole kingdom'.⁴⁴ By elliptically addressing his own reputation as an architect of occult and illusory promises and simultaneously defending the virtue and legitimacy of the mathematical arts, Dee gradually paves the way for presenting a sustained argument for the establishment of a 'Pety-Navy-Royall': a flexible tool that would provide, in addition to coastal and economic protection, 'the onely Maister Key, wherewith to open all Locks, that kepe out, or hinder, this Incomparable Brytish Impire' (sig. A4ᵛ). Written to promote imperial aspirations to sympathetic listeners, the treatise continually looks to the author's future plans: when writing of 'THE BRYTISH QUEENE ELIZABETH, HER TABLES GUBERNAUTIK' that would follow, for example, he imagines that pilots 'all the whole world over, yea, among the Heathen, as well as Christen: what language so ever they speake, that have to deale with Hydrography, or Dangerous and long voyages by Sea: even they, will, most thankfully, and for ever, sing and extoll her marveilous Princely Benefit herein' (sig. ε*3ʳ). He imagines these 'tables gubernautic' as a monument, which will bear witness throughout the world to Elizabeth's magnificence. The word 'gubernautic', which speaks of both government and pilotage, finds full visualisation in the image of Elizabeth on the previous work's title page, where Elizabeth is imagined as the navigator of an imperial Ship of State, beside which the bull Europa swims.⁴⁵

As David N. Livingstone writes, the title-page image 'displays various hermetic symbols urging the queen to expand her overseas dominions', and in Lesley B. Cormack's more sustained discussion of the image, the *momento mori* disappearing into the right margin together with the inverted ear of wheat can be read as an 'ominous warning' to readers if they 'ignore Dee's perspicacious proposal'.⁴⁶ As Dee explains in the text of the work itself:

---

44 John Dee, *General and Rare Memorials Pertayning to the Perfect Arte of Navigation* (London, 1577), sig. Δ3ᵛ. Subsequent references are placed in the text. For the text's agenda see William Sherman, *John Dee: The Politics of Reading and Writing in the English Renaissance* (Amherst: University of Massachusetts Press, 1995), pp. 152–62.
45 See 'gubernator, n.' *OED Online*. Oxford University Press, June 2018 (last accessed 30 July 2018).
46 See David N. Livingstone, *The Geographical Tradition: Episodes in the History of a Contested Enterprise* (Oxford: Blackwell, 1993), p. 78 and Lesley B. Cormack, *Charting an Empire: Geography at the English Universities, 1580–1620* (Chicago: University of Chicago Press, 1997), pp. 2–4. Bellamy reads the image's 'visual allegory of Elizabethan coastlines as a witness to the nation's rising maritime power'. See *Dire Straits*, p. 27.

Why should not we HOPE, that, RES-PUBL. BRYTANICA, on her knees, very Humbly, and ernestly Soliciting the most Excellent Royall Majesty, of our ELIZABETH (Sitting at the HELM of this Imperiall Monarchy: or, rather, at the Helm of the IMPERIALL SHIP, of the most parte of Christendome: if so, it be her Graces Pleasure) shall obteyn (or Perfect Policie, may perswade her Highnes,) that, which is the Pyth, or Intent of RES-PUBL. BRYTANICA, Her Supplication? (sig. G3$^r$)

The author's textual gloss to the highly rhetorical image suggests that Elizabeth must respond responsibly to the hopes and desires of her country, which has taken on flesh and voice in order to express the 'pith' of her intent. As in Spenser's poem, which explicitly advertises the poet's use of the political and mystical fiction of the King's Two Bodies, Dee's use of 'Brytanica' as a medium for his message appears to present the argument to Elizabeth I using an aspect of the monarch herself: the composition thus suggests the symbolic body of the royal estate seeking the ear of the body natural.[47] In addition, the landscape, which situates 'Brytanica' rather than being embodied by her, is itself similarly symbolic, presenting a microcosm or 'faire mirrhour' in which the queen may behold her face, her 'owne realmes', and even her own 'great auncestry' as an insular monarch, to borrow Spenser's explanation of his own fictions (II.Pro.4). In its combination of seascape and landscape, which includes a castle situated on a coastline, a forest, and open fields in which knights are meeting, the image could serve as an illustration for an epic allegorical romance rather than as a title page for a political and practical work. In its careful balance of land, sea, river-mouth, and heavens, it shows a mobile and connected world, animated and enhanced by human and divine agency. The position of the ship in the lower left-hand corner indicates a navigable waterway, and the castle, built like that of Book II's Alma, 'on a rocke adioyning to the seas' provides additional strength and 'skilfull frame' to what is already a natural fortification (II.ii.12). For the reader, the river provides an entrance point into the image, inviting them to navigate the limits of the country and move out towards the horizon.

In another provocative manipulation of sight-lines within the image, the reciprocal gaze of Elizabeth and 'Brytanica' is mediated by the presence of Occasion, whose self-displayed forelock is angled towards the monarch's grasp. As Dee explains, the opportunity to hand is part of a recuperative process: one which, rather than newly establishing an

---

47 See Ernst H. Kantorowicz, *The King's Two Bodies: A Study in Mediaeval Political Theology* (Princeton: Princeton University Press, 1957).

empire, will recover one that has been lost. In the accompanying prose, the reader is also invited to reach out with the author:

> But, yet, ... there is a Little lock of LADY OCCASION, Flickring in the Ayre, by our hands, to catch hold on: wherby, we may, yet ones more (before, all, be utterly past, and for ever) discretely, and valiantly recover, and enjoy, if not all our Ancient and due Appertenances, to this Imperiall Brytish Monarchy, Yet, at the least, some such Notable Portion therof. (sig. G3$^v$–G4$^r$)

The treatise, which ultimately combines propaganda with mythmaking, argues that the proportional augmentation of 'Sea forces' could engender 'Fame, Renowm, Estimation, and Love, or Feare, of this Brytish Microcosmus, all the whole and Great world over' (sig. B1$^v$). Lady Occasion embodies the promise of speculation, holding opportunities to be both loved and feared *in potentia*. Her streaming hair may be almost tangible but the prose that follows engages in constant qualification; if 'not all' appurtenances can be recovered, then 'some' at least could be retrieved. Dee tentatively promotes national advancement to his monarch under the banner of recuperation, and as Frances A. Yates explains, the 'tale of the lands and seas to which she can lay claim is based both on the dominions mythically reported to have been held by the British King Arthur and on those over which the Saxon King Edgar ruled'.[48] In King Edgar, Andrew Escobedo notes, Dee identified an English ruler who sustained a naval force: an example from 'the past to motivate the English in the present'.[49] However, although Dee may promote the establishment of a 'Navy-Royall' as a key 'to open all Locks', suggesting new discoveries, the overall impression given by his treatise is conservative, belated, and inward-looking.[50]

The difference in scale between 'this Brytish Microcosmus' and 'all the whole and Great world' suggests an insular fragility that shapes the way that the work promotes the idea of establishing confines and boundaries that would protect the British maritime economy, to 'the skyrts and Purlewes (as it were) of our Brytish, naturall, and appropriat Sea Limits' (sig. B3$^r$). Natural contours shape a national agenda dictated by geographical necessity, and for Dee, the consequences of easy maritime transaction include the threat of exposure to unnamed and unknown assailants:

---

48 Frances A. Yates, *Astraea: The Imperial Theme in the Sixteenth Century* (London: Routledge and Kegan Paul, 1975), p. 48.
49 Escobedo, *Nationalism and Historical Loss*, pp. 58–66.
50 See David Armitage, 'The Elizabethan Idea of Empire', *TRHS*, 14 (2004), 269–77.

And, of these sorte of people they be, which (other whiles) by collour and pretence of comming about their feat of fishing, doo subtilly and secretly use Sowndings, and Serchings, of our Channells, Deeps, Showles, Banks, or Bars, along the Sea Coasts, and in our Haven Mowthes allso, and up in our Creeks, sometymes in our Bayes, and sometimes in our Roads, etc. Taking good Marks, for avoiding of the dangers: And allso trying good Landings. And (so, making perfect Chartes of all our Coasts, rownd about England, and Ireland) are become (allmost) perfecter in them, then the most parte of our Maisters, Loadmen, or Pylots, are: to the dubble danger of mischief in tymes of War: And, allso to no little hazard of the State Royall: Yf (maliciously bent), they should purpose to land any puissant Army, in tyme to come. (sig. A4ʳ)

Dee describes his imagined insular empire as vulnerable to a multitude of different searchings and penetrations, as if every coastal feature is open to the gaze, movement, and hydrographical expertise of intruders who are covertly '(allmost) perfecter' in their knowledge than native authorities. A cognate threat is later given literary voice in Thomas Middleton's seventeenth-century allegorical drama *A Game at Chess* via the character of the Black Knight, a shadowing of Count Gondomar, the Spanish Ambassador, who extravagantly boasts of both his skill as an intelligencer and the speculative might of Catholic Spain:

>             No fortification,
> Haven, creek, landing-place 'bout the White coast
> But I got draught and platform, learned the depth
> Of all their channels, knowledge of all sands,
> Shelves, rocks, and rivers for invasion properist;
> A catalogue of all the navy royal,
> The burden of each ship, the brassy murderers,
> The number of the men, to what cape bound;
> Again, for the discovery of the islands,
> Never a shire but the state better known
> To me than to her breast inhabitants ...[51]

Within Middleton's shallowly shadowed fiction of contemporary events, the Black Knight offers an articulate survey of all that Dee outlines as an insular nation's vulnerabilities; a reminder, as Spenser's *A View of the Present State of Ireland* also demonstrates, that unrestricted vision and

---

51 Thomas Middleton, *A Game at Chess* in *Women Beware Women and Other Plays*, ed. Richard Dutton (Oxford: Oxford University Press, 1999; repr. 2009), pp. 237–316 (IV. ii.59–70).

movement is coveted as an indication of sovereignty, particularly where port-cities and harbours are concerned.[52]

In his intimation of the skill needed to take 'good Marks' and make 'perfect Chartes', Dee gestures towards the difficulty of writing the strand authoritatively, and his list of abstract hydrographic features – 'our Channells, Deeps, Showles, Banks, or Bars' – anticipates a list of proper names later in the treatise: a moment that articulates a deeply felt need for the mastery granted by recent intelligence. When writing of the fertile fishing grounds located off the Irish coast, he assumes ownership with each place-name he articulates:

> Yet, Surely, I think it necessary, to leave to our Posterity, some Remembrance of the places, where, our rich Fishings els, are, about Ireland: As at Kilsale, Cork, Carlingford, Saltesses, Dungarwen: Yowghall, Waterford, La foy, The Band, Calibeg. etc. And all, chiefly enjoyed, as securely and freely, from us, by Strangers, as if they were within their own Kings peculiar Sea Limits: Nay, rather, as if those Coasts, Seas, and Bayes (etc.) were of their private and severall purchases: To our unspeakable los, discredit, and discomfort: And to no small danger (farder) in these perillous tymes, of most subtle Trecheries, and fickle fidelity. (sig. C4$^v$)

In this instance, the litany of named harbours has an implied totemic effect, where the act of naming in itself appears to offer a meagre kind of protection against the perceived treachery of England's rivals in the maritime economy.[53] Furthermore, the perceived threat of improper identification implied by the catalogue is accompanied by a sense that there is something intrinsically treacherous in the form and matter of 'coasts, seas, and bayes'; only the most skilled of pilots can claim mastery over them, an ideal betrayed by Dee's own vagrant syntax and interchangeable use of tenses. Dee might term the threatened loss of revenue 'unspeakable', but here it is given voice in a highly specific lamentation of the ways in which the fishing grounds are enjoyed by 'strangers', from which Dee unselfconsciously excludes the appropriations made by the English

---

[52] See William J. Smyth, *Map Making, Landscapes and Memory: A Geography of Colonial and Early Modern Ireland, c. 1530–1750* (Cork: Cork University Press, 2006), p. 25 and pp. 33–5.

[53] As Patricia Palmer observes, the listing of place-names is a generic feature of colonial writing: 'at some point, almost all the Elizabethan works reel off toponymic incantations as mantras of possession'. See *Language and Conquest in Early Modern Ireland: English Renaissance Literature and Elizabethan Imperial Expansion* (Cambridge: Cambridge University Press, 2001), p. 184. See also Gerry Smyth, 'Mapping/naming', in *Space and the Irish Cultural Imagination* (Basingstoke: Palgrave, 2001), pp. 40–56.

themselves.⁵⁴ In the accompanying prognostication of Spanish attempts to land an Armada on English shores, Dee's fears of a seaborne 'puissant Army' suggest how his optimism elsewhere is countered by well-founded anxieties, particularly concerning how 'Spaine, nor any other Cuntry' should 'have such liberty, for Invasion, ... to annoy the blessed State of our Tranquillitie' (sig. A2ᵛ).

A similar desire to realise an auspicious imperial agenda distinct from Iberian success can be seen in *The Faerie Queene*, and is refracted in Merlin's prophecy that maritime prowess will result in Protestant union during the reign of the 'royall virgin', Elizabeth:

> Thenceforth eternall vnion shall be made
> Betweene the nations different afore,
> And sacred Peace shall louingly persuade
> The warlike minds, to learne her goodly lore,
> And ciuile armes to exercise no more:
> Then shall a royall virgin raine, which shall
> Stretch her white rod ouer the *Belgicke* shore,
> And the great Castle smite so sore with all,
> That it shall make him shake, and shortly learne to fall. (III.iii.49)

Spenser here, like Dee had before him, imagines a united 'Brytish Ilandish Monarchy' ready to support the Netherlands and to protect itself against the interests of Philip II, King of Castile (see sig. B2ᵛ). For the purposes of Spenser's poem, the other 'royall virgin' Britomart can body forth generative desire for union *in potentia*; as Louis Montrose reminds us, she functions as a 'fictional progenetrix for Queen Elizabeth herself'.⁵⁵ And like Merlin's glass, which is similarly manifold, the lady-knight's existence within a poem and not within a work of propaganda allows her to take on the pith and future desires of the royal body politic while retaining the tempers and body natural of a chaste woman in love.

Dee and Spenser draw on similar symbolic imaginaries and represent future political union by blending physical and mystical terms. Dee, for example, imagines the success of his promoted enterprise as a marriage and the fruits of the labour as children: the use of a conjugal analogy that relies on finding metaphors of generation and procreation familiar in political contexts, and which, of course, also shapes Spenser's Legends

---

54 For the obfuscating tendency of imperial propaganda see Cormack, 'Britannia Rules the Waves?' (4).
55 Montrose, 'Spenser and the Elizabethan Political Imaginary', p. 935.

of Chastity and Friendship.[56] And, like Spenser's poem, his ambitious propositions ultimately look to Elizabeth's presence for approval:

> Well (Sayd he) my Hope is, that under our good Soverayn Elizabeth (ere long, if it be her pleasure) the AEquity of this Case, will, or may, be maryed, with the Security of the whole State of this Impire: And that they two, will bring furth COMMON [1.] WEALTH, INVINCIBLE [2.] STRENGTH, AND IMMORTALL TRIUMPHANT [3.] FAME: Three most lawfull Brytish Childern, and long wished for, of the true, Brytish, and Christian Druides, they being also, Politicall Philosophers, and not Sophisticate. (sig. C4$^r$)

This is no hasty plot, Dee emphasises, but an act of recuperation that has been foretold: the epic qualities of his ambitions are tempered by the conservative modes of romance, wherein the labours of spatial and spiritual travail, with an eye ever on the coastline, result in self-becoming and self-realisation. As we have seen, the reciprocal gaze of the female figures on the work's title page, 'Brytanica' and Elizabeth I, meets across the strand; as well as directing the monarch's gaze to the borders and shape of her realm, Dee's framing fiction anticipates Spenser's promise to Elizabeth, that she would 'in mirrours more then one her selfe to see' (III.pro.5). As in Spenser's fiction, fragmentation, or a splitting of aspects of the self, is ultimately intended to engender unity, which can then be seen and appreciated for its component parts, here named as commonwealth, invincible strength, and triumphant fame. The aim, once again, is of reuniting component parts within a sense of self-identity: the aspiration of attaining 'being in one self place' (*The Mariners Mirrour*, sig. ¶2$^r$). For Dee, as for Spenser, this is something to be dreamt of only at the monarch's pleasure: a reminder of the fragility of any attempt to make myths without collaboration and consent.[57]

## Time and tide

In *The Faerie Queene*, which delights in the presentation of divided, refracted selves, the meeting of the land and sea is embodied in the eventual nuptial union of Marinell and Florimell, which happens in Book V, the Book of Justice; however, as Florimell's initial travails indicate, the sea is often resistant to land-based agencies, a fictive resonance

---

56 See Melissa E. Sanchez, *Erotic Subjects: The Sexuality of Politics in Early Modern English Literature* (Oxford: Oxford University Press, 2011), p. 11.
57 See Glyn Parry, 'John Dee and the Elizabethan British Empire in its European Context', *The Historical Journal*, 49.3 (2006), 643–75, p. 665 and p. 670 in particular.

that appears to record the failure of Elizabeth I's maritime prospecting in spite of Dee's best efforts and advocacy.[58] In the seventh and eighth cantos of Book III, Spenser writes of Florimell's plight after arriving in desperation at the shore; having outrun her pursuers, she is 'taught the carefull Mariner to play' and 'compleld to chaunge/ The land for sea, at random there to raunge' (III.viii.20). As another reflection of Elizabeth I's maritime concerns, Florimell's adventures at sea in a 'shallop' allude to a precarious transition of agency (III.vii.27). For a fragile creature of terrestrial perfection, the translation from 'floting strand' and 'roaring shore' (III.vii.27) to open water from which 'no more we can the maynland see' (III.viii.24) enacts a shift into an alien element: a moment which blends the adventures of romance with modes of the *speculum principis* tradition. The image offers a further example of what Bellamy describes as the mapping of the queen's realm in Spenser's poem as innately 'peripheral – not an increasingly metropolitan center but antiquity's *ultima Britannia*': as she argues, 'the queen was, at least implicitly, induced to ... picture herself as shadowed by the cultural threat of being stranded on antiquity's edges of the earth'.[59] For Florimell, the threat is cultural and gendered; during her escape, the aging boat-fellow's attempt to rape her is an allegorical suggestion that the relative rationality of firm ground has been relinquished for the unrestrained passions of the waters. Unfortunately for Florimell, the fisherman's 'cock-bote' (III.viii.24) is built of the same libidinous frame as that of Book II's Phaedria. Although they are slow to awaken, the drowsy pilot's desires are misdirected, and the character expects possession without labour or legitimacy: a dynamic that also complicates Spenser's handling of Florimell's later isolation in captivity and the episode's shadowing of Elizabeth's vulnerable position as a female insular monarch.[60]

In the stanzas that follow Florimell's first experience of seafaring, the narrator emphasises the way in which the waters are empty of knights;

---

58 For extended studies on the relationship between imperial prospecting, failure, and fiction-making see Mary C. Fuller, *Voyages in Print: English Travel to America, 1576–1624* (Cambridge: Cambridge University Press, 1995) and Jeffrey Knapp, *An Empire Nowhere: England, America, and Literature from Utopia to the Tempest* (Berkeley: University of California Press, 1992).
59 Bellamy, *Dire Straits*, p. 52 and p. 54. See also p. 87.
60 In an uncomfortable mirroring that reflects England's own conscious sense of its vulnerable harbours, the miniature ships that appear to sail under Elizabeth's skirts in the Ditchley Portrait are, as Rhonda Lemke Sanford observes, suggestive of 'military invasion or commercial enterprise', rape or prostitution, and perhaps ought to be 'read as unacceptable transactions with a chaste queen'. See *Maps and Memory in Early Modern England: A Sense of Place* (New York: Palgrave, 2002), pp. 29–38 (p. 34 in particular).

it is a place where no fleet or 'Pety-Navy-Royall' has dominion. Without protection, Florimell is forced to look elsewhere for help:

> O ye braue knights, that boast this Ladies loue,
> Where be ye now, when she is nigh defild
> Of filthy wretch? well may she you reproue
> Of falsehood or of slouth, when most it may behoue.
>
> But if that thou, Sir *Satyran*, didst weete,
>   Or thou, Sir *Peridure*, her sory state,
>   How soone would yee assemble many a fleete,
> To fetch from sea, that ye at land lost late;
>   Towres, citties, kingdomes ye would ruinate,
>   In your auengement and dispiteous rage,
>   Ne ought your burning fury mote abate;
> But if Sir *Calidore* could it presage,
> No liuing creature could his cruelty asswage.
>
> But sith that none of all her knights is nye,
>   See how the heauens of voluntary grace,
>   And soueraine fauour towards chastity,
>   Doe succor send to her distressed cace:
>   So much high God doth innocence embrace.
>   It fortuned, whilest thus she stifly stroue,
>   And the wide sea importuned long space
>   With shrilling shriekes, *Proteus* abroad did roue,
> Along the fomy waues driuing his finny droue. (III.viii.27–9)

In the absence of mortal agents, Florimell is forced to rely on the sea itself for succour, finding herself in the arms, and finally the submerged prison, of Proteus. Like the archetypal sea of romance, he acts as both agent of providence and devouring tyrant, giving and taking indiscriminately.[61] It is only through the intervention of Neptune, 'the seas sole Soueraine' and temporary embodiment of maritime legal bureaucracy, that Florimell, as 'waift' and 'thrall', is returned from her watery exile to dry, or at least drier, land more than a whole book later (IV.xii.30–2).[62] The forms of romance, with their rhythmic interest exile and return, sep-

---

61 See Sebastian I. Sobecki, *The Sea and Medieval English Literature* (Cambridge: D.S. Brewer, 2008), pp. 56–71 and Helen Cooper, *The English Romance in Time: Transforming Motifs from Geoffrey of Monmouth to the Death of Shakespeare* (Oxford: Oxford University Press, 2004), pp. 106–36.
62 For Spenser's use of the language of maritime law see Andrew Zurcher, *Spenser's Legal Language: Law and Poetry in Early Modern England* (Cambridge: Cambridge University Press, 2012), p. 106.

aration and confluence, are thus written in the tidal eddies of the poem's hydrographies, which trouble the otherwise brittle surface of the *speculum principis* towards which Spenser works.[63]

In the final stanzas of the sixth and seventh cantos of the Legend of Friendship the presence of a striking verbal repetition suggests that Book IV was conceived as a tidal book, in which social bonds are refracted through the motions of the sea.[64] At the end of canto six, Britomart and Scudamour are left searching for Amoret, waiting to hear 'tydings ... of her estate' (IV.vi.47); the ebb and flow of water becomes the medium of the message. Conscious that the full story would potentially exceed its bounds, the narrator professes to stay its progress 'Vntill another tyde, that (he) it finish may' (IV.vi.47). In the formal echo found in the subsequent canto, Timias is met but not recognised by Arthur in a state where nothing can 'ease or mitigate his paine, .../ Till time for him should remedy prouide': a resolution that is deferred 'vntill another tide' (IV.vii.47). He is found repeatedly engraving the name of his beloved Belphoebe, Amoret's sister, into the bark of trees, where this action only seems to indicate the process of his own self-erasure, unmaking him, as a man that 'out of all mens knowledge ... was worne at last' (IV.vii.41). His writerly labours also mark him out as a poet; yet, as for the speaker of the *Amoretti* who makes marks in wet sand, the writing of a name indicates only the presence of hope and the material mutability of the natural world, not the reality of possession.[65] The recurrent tidal motif thus interrupts poetic labour, and encounters and reunions are left unresolved: it is not until Book VI that Arthur and Timias are reunited. Here, the imagery once again returns to its watery tenor, with weeping and with Arthur's searching questions, as if Timias has been lost at sea:

> Tell me what worlds despight, or heauens yre
> Hath you thus long away from me bereft?
> Where haue ye all this while bin wandring, where bene weft? (VI.v.23)

---

63 As Rosalind Field observes of the exile-and-return trope of medieval romance, 'once the pattern is familiar it reappears on the political scene every time the rulers of England look over their shoulders at the challenger landing on the shore'. See 'The King Over the Water: Exile-and-Return Revisited', in *Cultural Encounters in the Romance of Medieval England*, ed. Corinne Saunders (Cambridge: D.S. Brewer, 2005), pp. 41–53 (p. 53). For the play of praise and blame see Colin Burrow, *Epic Romance: Homer to Milton* (Oxford: Clarendon, 1993), p. 102 and p. 119.

64 Although her reading focuses on events in Book III, Wofford anticipates this argument, observing how 'places like the rich strand and other metaphorical tidewaters figure the ground of action of the poem itself'. See 'Britomart's Petrarchan Lament', p. 55.

65 See Goldberg, *Endlesse Worke*, p. 51.

Spenser's Timias, of course, has been frequently identified as a representation of Walter Ralegh, and the work of the two poets is famously interconnected: as members of the same 'sheapherds cumpanye' (29) they inhabit shared literary and imaginative worlds, which inform the roles they play as authors and the genres of poetry they write.[66]

Spenser's allegorical interest in tidal movement is established early on in Book IV. In the conflict between Paridel and Scudamour, tidal similes capture the fury and pressure of waters meeting in a narrow channel, creating the impression of intimate encounter and strained divergence:

> As when two billowes in the Irish sowndes,
>     Forcibly driuen with contrarie tydes
>     Do meete together, each abacke rebowndes
>     With roaring rage; and dashing on all sides,
>     That filleth all the sea with fome, diuydes
>     The doubtfull current into diuers wayes: ... (IV.i.42)

The sheer weight of tidal water expresses the force of elemental discord, producing a momentary scene of strife that contains within it a vast destructive fury that exists only to rebound on itself. In a tidal repetition, the enmity recurs in the subsequent canto, where each knight is likened to a frail vessel now standing fast against both the waters and each other:

> As when two warlike Brigandines at sea,
>     With murderous weapons arm'd to cruell fight,
>     Doe meete together on the watry lea ... (IV.ii.16)

Furthermore, during the battle of Triamond and Cambel, the tides produced at the mouth of the Shannon, the longest river system in Ireland, are used to map a metaphor of enduring and cyclical brutality:[67]

> Like as the tide that comes fro th'Ocean mayne,
>     Flowes vp the Shenan with contrarie forse,
>     And ouerruling him in his owne rayne,
>     Driues backe the current of his kindly course,
>     And makes it seeme to haue some other sourse:
>     But when the floud is spent, then backe againe
>     His borrowed waters forst to redisbourse,
>     He sends the sea his owne with double gaine,
> And tribute eke withall, as to his Soueraine. (IV.iii.27)

---

66 James P. Bednarz, 'The Collaborator as Thief: Ralegh's (Re)Vision of *The Faerie Queene*', *ELH*, 63.2 (1996), 279–307.
67 See Syrithe Pugh, *Spenser and Ovid* (Aldershot: Ashgate, 2005), pp. 206–7.

Serving as an antagonistic prologue to the marriage of the Thames and the Medway at the hall of Proteus, the stanza introduces what Klein identifies as a latent pun 'on the semantic overlap of tribute and tributary – feudal gesture and hydrographic label', whereby the interchange of sovereignty and submission are figured as intrinsic attributes of the natural world.[68] Chivalric glory is underwritten by futile violence begetting violence, and haemorrhaging occurs unheeded, soaking the ground with 'vitall flood' (IV.iii.28). At one moment the knights themselves are the river, exhibiting the force of 'borrowed waters' (IV.iii.27); yet, at another, their bodies serve as the space on which a savage river network is mapped, for 'all the while the disentrayled blood/ Adowne their sides like litle riuers stremed' (IV.iii.28). That which was once held in unity in metaphor becomes many within the fluctuations of the allegory; impermeable bodies become both open and vulnerable to the dissolute landscape in which they fight.

In order to offer a counterpoint to such images, and to act as a reminder to the reader that she carries the weight of Guyon's prior quest with her, Britomart's appearances in Book IV are often figured as a restoration, or a tempering of elemental strife. Where the Knight of Temperance faced the constant threat of archetypal worldly contingency, the Knight of Chastity moves through a lusher and more variegated cosmos. Her actions in the narrative revive both the poet's labour and that of her fellow Knights of Maidenhead, 'Like as in sommers day when raging heat/ Doth burne the earth, and boyled riuers drie' when falls 'a sudden shoure of raine,/ That all the wretched world recomforteth againe' (IV.iv.47). In her temperate presence, 'trauellers tormented ... with paine' are relieved, and when she finally comes face to face with Artegall, the moment is little short of revelation. After initial conflict, Britomart recognises Artegall to be 'the same which in her fathers hall/ Long since in that enchaunted glasse she saw' (IV.vi.26). When he strikes her helmet so that the 'ventayle' is sheared away to reveal 'her angels face' (IV.vi.19), Artegall is stunned by the disclosure of his opponent's beauty, which the reader temporarily sees through his eyes. The narrator describes her hair falling loose in waves, which appears:

> Like to a golden border ...,
> Framed in goldsmithes forge with cunning hand:
> Yet goldsmithes cunning could not vnderstand
> To frame such subtile wire, so shinie cleare.

---

68 Bernhard Klein, *Maps and the Writing of Space in Early Modern England and Ireland* (Basingstoke: Palgrave, 2001), p. 163. See also Goldberg, *Endlesse Worke*, pp. 136–7.

> For it did glister like the golden sand,
> The which *Pactolus* with his waters shere,
> Throwes forth vpon the riuage round about him nere. (IV.vi.20)

The hand of an artificer remains implicit in the likeness drawn, where the lingering impression of the substance of the goldsmith's craft evokes an image of luminous matter yoked to a mythical rendering of the natural world. Furthermore, the 'cunning hand' of the craftsman is retained in the figuring of Pactolus, the river in Asia in which Midas was said to have washed away his curse.[69] In the same way that Britomart had no appetite for the worldly lucre of Marinell's shore, so here she is associated with the erasure of worldly concerns. The image of gold-laden waters being thrown upon the 'rivage' uses an archaic word that figures the shoreline and both the act and place of making landfall;[70] in the myth, the banks of the Pactolus glitter with golden sand, a transformation that retains the memory of cathartic release. The littoral figure shapes the imagined geography of the fiction, which in turn shapes our perception of the heroine herself, seen as she is through Artegall's trembling gaze: she herself becomes the thing of value. Like Britomart in her earlier incarnations, Artegall stands at an unexpected threshold and 'of his wonder made religion' (IV.vi.22), as if Britomart herself was the 'coast of heauen', figuratively speaking, all along. In a humorous extension of the simile, Britomart dissembles her emotional reaction to hearing Artegall named by attempting to make herself unfathomable, 'Thinking to hide the depth by troubling of the flood' (IV.vi.29): a demonstration of the subtlety with which Spenser creates disturbances in the surfaces of his images.

The encounter is witnessed by Glauce's ocean-grey gaze: a reorientation of perspective that supersedes the literary echo of Virgil's *Aeneid* via a gesture towards the circumstances of Spenser's present:

> And you Sir *Artegall*, the saluage knight,
> Henceforth may not disdaine, that womans hand
> Hath conquered you anew in second fight:
> For whylome they haue conquerd sea and land,
> And heauen it selfe, that nought may them withstand. ... (IV.vi.31)

Through the use of the word 'whylome', Spenser invites the contemplation of temporal ambiguity; by associating female regiment with

---

69 See Dionysius Periegetes, *The Surveye of the World*, trans. Thomas Twyne (London, 1572), sig. D7ʳ.
70 'rivage, n.' *OED Online*. Oxford University Press, September 2015 (last accessed 2 November 2015).

all-encompassing conquest, Glauce's meaning is potentially both recuperative and prospective.[71] The moment is charged with the same untimely quality as Dee's imperial imaginings, wherein descriptions of historic 'discoveries', which looked to the past for imperial predecessors, are re-orientated as prophecy: a source of temporal prospecting, as William H. Sherman argues, that manifests in Dee's own writerly struggle 'with the appropriate *tense* of the imperial outlook'.[72] In Spenser's poem, the triumphant action of a woman's hand suggests a cosmological tribute to Elizabeth I: a flicker of an imperialist imagination that, as Philippa Berry has argued, recalls Giordano Bruno's vision of Elizabeth in *Cena de la ceneri* (1584), which imagines Elizabeth in terms that emphasise her spatial reach:

> If her earthly territory were a true reflection of the width and grandeur of her spirit this great Amphitrite would bring far horizons within her girdle and enlarge the circumference of her dominion to include not only Britain and Ireland but some new world, as vast as the universal frame, where her all-powerful hand should have full scope to raise a united monarchy.[73]

The characterisation of Elizabeth-as-ocean is striking, in that the etymology of the name Amphitrite suggests, to cite Abraham Fraunce's gloss, not only 'the water it selfe, governed by Neptune' but the act 'of compassing, envyroning, or turning about, as the sea embraceth and incloseth the earth'.[74] From the global to the local, the sea moves in currents and eddies. In her guise as Amphitrite, Elizabeth's conquering embrace is imagined as sufficient to encompass not only her own shores, but those of Ireland and beyond: her possession so total that it admits neither envy nor avarice, as if all were within her power.

---

71 See 'whilom, adv. (and adj.) and conj.' *OED Online*. Oxford University Press, March 2016 (last accessed 6 April 2016). For Spenser's use of the word 'whylome' in *FQ*, VII.vi.38 see Linda Gregerson, 'Telling Time: Temporality in *The Faerie Queene*', Hugh MacClean Memorial Lecture, International Spenser Society, 7 January 2012, *Spenser Review*, 42.7, p. 3.

72 Sherman, *John Dee*, p. 151. See also van Es, *Spenser's Forms of History*, p. 149 and p. 200; Escobedo, *Nationalism and Historical Loss*, pp. 57–69; and Andrew Fichter, *Poets Historical: Dynastic Epic in the Renaissance* (New Haven: Yale University Press, 1982), p. 1.

73 Quoted by Frances A. Yates in *Giordano Bruno and the Hermetic Tradition* (London: Routledge, 2002), p. 317. See Philippa Berry, *Of Chastity and Power: Elizabethan Literature and the Unmarried Queen* (London: Routledge, 1989), p. 76.

74 Abraham Fraunce, *The Third Part of the Countesse of Pembrokes Yuychurch* (London, 1592), sig. F3$^r$.

### Spenser, Ralegh, and the space of the tideline

As the above allegorical and thematic patterns demonstrate, Spenser conceived of Book IV as being highly invested in the place of the tideline, the place between 'sea and land,/ And heauen it selfe', as a space of encounter; in a tidal book, social bonds are as changeable but enduring as the sea itself. To speak of 'another tyde' (IV.vi.47, IV.vii.47), as we have seen, is to speak of another opportunity or occasion, and of events modifying those which have gone before. Spenser's tidal imagery gains further resonances if read alongside the poetry of Timias's historical counterpart, Sir Walter Ralegh.[75] As another refracted image of Elizabeth I, Timias's beloved Belphoebe activates another of the promises made by Spenser to Ralegh, namely that he would write of the monarch's two persons, following Ralegh's own conceit: 'the one of a most royall Queene or Empresse, the other of a most vertuous and beautifull Lady, this latter part in some places I doe expresse in Belphoebe, fashioning her name according to your owne excellent conceipt of Cynthia' ('A Letter of the Authors', p. 716). By drawing an analogy with the virgin goddess of the moon, the association speaks predominantly of chastity; however, as most sixteenth-century hydrographical works treating the motion of the tides tell their readers:

> Great accompt ought Pilottes and Mariners to have of the Tydes, to take Port, enter uppon Barres, passe by Flattes, and finally, for al maner of Navigations. For beyng ignoraunt heere of, great hurt and inconvenience myght chaunce unto them .... And the better to understand the increasyng and decreasyng of the Ocean Sea, it shall be convenient to knowe the cause thereof, wherunto we say, that the Moone is the cause of ebbyng and flowyng, or rysing and falling, increase or decrease of the Sea: not onely by her lyght, but also by her secrete or hyd propertie.[76]

As with Dee's description of the hydrographer's art, an ostensibly objective register can be seen to share its vocabulary with allegories of fortune. In the hands of a poet, the 'secrete or hyd propertie' possessed by the feminised and luminous lunar body provides an apt metaphor for the pull of desire. It is also, of course, the foundational metaphor on which Ralegh's own fragmentary poem, the '21th: and last booke of the Ocean

---

75 For Spenser's movement between historical and moral allegory see J.B. Lethbridge, 'Raleigh in Books III and IV of *The Faerie Queene*: The Primacy of Moral Allegory', *Studia Neophilologica*, 64 (1992), 55–66.
76 Martín Cortés, *The Arte of Navigation*, trans. Richard Eden (London, 1589), fol. 48[r–v].

to Scinthia' relies. As Spenser would write in his depiction of Ralegh in 'Colin Clouts Come Home Againe' (1595), 'His song was all a lamentable lay ... Of *Cynthia* the Ladie of the sea,/ Which from her presence faultlesse him debard' (see lines 164–7).

The shift in recent criticism towards the idea that Ralegh's poem, and wider writings, are vitally invested in the connections between form, metaphor, and the movement of water is exemplified by many of the essays published in *Literary and Visual Ralegh*, edited by Christopher Armitage.[77] In a masterful essay, James Nohrnberg writes of the way in which the 'mutable element of water, from which came Sir Wa'ter's nickname at court, ruefully appears in all of its forms and variety within his poem, pouring down, welling up, drying out, going vaporously away'.[78] Elizabeth, who is shadowed by Ralegh as a 'lunar goddess', has become in the poem 'one particular mortal's natural disaster':[79] a reading that associates Ralegh's speaker with the poet's own weathering of Elizabeth's displeasure.[80] The fragmentary verses participate in the play of landscape and seascape, suggesting that Spenser and Ralegh, like Spenser and Dee, shared a similar spatial imaginary at the time of composition, even if this may have occurred decades apart.[81] For Thomas Herron, who recognises the presence of Ralegh's practical and imaginative colonial investments in Ireland and the New World in the poem, the work is one 'of errant ocean-born desire'.[82]

The natural world appears in Ralegh's 'Ocean to Scinthia' as an

---

[77] Michael Booth, for example, identifies the habitual spatial metaphors of Spenser's fellow poet and planter and analyses Ralegh's ability to separate dense metaphorical blends 'into separate mental spaces'. See '"Moving on the Waters": Metaphor and Mental Space in Ralegh's *History of the World*', in *Literary and Visual Ralegh*, ed. Christopher M. Armitage (Manchester: Manchester University Press, 2013), pp. 200–16 (p. 207). For older critical perspectives that downplay water in the poem see Marion Campbell, 'Inscribing Imperfection: Sir Walter Ralegh and the Elizabethan Court', *ELR*, 20.2 (1990), 233–53 and Joyce Horner, 'The Large Landscape: A Study of Certain Images in Ralegh', *Essays in Criticism*, 5.3 (1955), 197–213.

[78] James Nohrnberg, 'Raleigh in Ruins, Raleigh on the Rocks', in *Literary and Visual Ralegh*, pp. 31–88 (p. 36).

[79] Ibid., p. 35.

[80] For Spenser's handling of Ralegh's fall from favour see A. Leigh DeNeef, 'Timias', in *SEnc*, pp. 690–1.

[81] See Katherine Duncan-Jones, 'The Date of Raleigh's "21th: And Last Booke of the Ocean to Scinthia"', *RES*, 21 (1970), 143–58, p. 158.

[82] Thomas Herron, 'Love's "Emperye": Raleigh's "Ocean to Scinthia," Spenser's "Colin Clouts Come Home Againe" and *The Faerie Queene* IV.vii in Colonial Context', in *Literary and Visual Ralegh*, pp. 100–39 (p. 126). For Ralegh's role as Timias in *The Faerie Queene* see Herron, *Spenser's Irish Work: Poetry, Plantation and Colonial Reformation* (Aldershot: Ashgate, 2007), pp. 185–224.

intemperate place, susceptible to apocalyptic drought: there is no Britomart figure present to relieve the speaker from his travails. He is left instead with 'the broken monuments' of his 'great desires' (14). His speaker contemplates a sterile landscape, as if reviewing the commonplaces of pastoral after an ecological catastrophe, seeking and failing to find 'faire floures amidd the brinish sand' (24).[83] Glancing back to the readings with which this chapter opened, the threat embodied by Proteus in *The Faerie Queene*, as Daniel M. Murtaugh observes, is related to the 'preservation of form in the shifting sands of matter: that, for Spenser as for Shakespeare in the Sonnets, is the true end of love. Its opposite, the shifting of forms in the same substratum of matter, is illusion and perversion. It negates the process of life while pretending to offer love'.[84] For Ralegh's speaker, the threat of fickle Eros is allied with that of Proteus: he is left behind and 'Lost in the mudd of thos hygh flowinge streames/ which through more fayrer feilds ther courses bend' (17–18). In the 'constant shifting from a world of dust to a world of mud and raging waters', identified by Stephen Greenblatt, both form and matter present a world out of kilter in which the imaginative capacity of the poet has failed.[85] There is no opportunity for a marriage of rivers here, for there are 'no pleasinge streames fast to the ocean wendinge' (33). In the author's 'misers hands' (22), all that was once fertile has turned to arid ground. Famously, Ralegh writes of past glories, inspired perhaps by his own travails at sea, but these are always tempered by an accompanying sense of exile, from both self and home:

> To seeke new worlds, for golde, for prayse, for glory,
> to try desire, to try love severed farr
> when I was gonn shee sent her memory
> more stronge then weare tenthowsand shipps of warr
> to call me back ...
> So my forsaken hart, my withered minde
> widdow of all the joyes it once possest
> my hopes cleane out of sight with forced wind
> to kyngdomes strange, to lands farr of addrest.
> Alone, forsaken, frindless onn the shore
> with many wounds, with deaths cold pangs inebrased
> writes in the dust as onn that could no more

83 Philip Edwards compares Ralegh's poem to T.S. Eliot's *The Waste Land*. See *Sir Walter Ralegh* (London: Longmans, Green, and Co., 1953), p. 110.
84 Murtaugh, 'The Garden and the Sea', p. 334.
85 Stephen Greenblatt, *Sir Walter Ralegh: The Renaissance Man and His Roles* (New Haven: Yale University Press, 1973), p. 87.

whom love, and tyme, and fortune, had defaced,
of things so great, so longe, so manefolde
with meanes so weake, the sowle yeven then departing
the weale, the wo, the passages of olde
and worlds of thoughts discribde by onn last sythinge. (61–5, 85–96)

The act of writing is imagined as occurring on the shore, where sand has turned to dust as if the sea no longer rushes in: this tide has gone out, never to return. Unlike in 'Sonnet LXXV' of Spenser's *Amoretti*, the beloved does not deign to engage in dialogue, as if Ralegh's speaker has decided he must belong to the 'baser things' dismissed by Spenser's lover-poet, fated rather to 'dy in dust' than 'liue by fame' (9–10). For Ralegh, the beloved's ability 'to master distance' (113), and to send a projection of herself to the other side of the world, reframes romance motifs with psychological realism; there is little need for a magic glass when the assaults of memory are freighted with searing clarity.

As the sole survivor of an unnamed wreck, Ralegh's speaker does not specify the content of his writerly labours, only that his 'world of thoughts' surpasses his ravaged body's ability to record them. Wrecked on the shore, the stranded speaker, a mariner-poet no longer, embodies a motif that has also passed through the hands of other authors. For Shakespeare, who fashions his own coastal poetics in Sonnet 60, the movement of the tide is both a birth and a death; the gathering waters mark out the passage of time and 'Nativity, once in the main of light,/ Crawls to maturity' (5–6).[86] Shakespeare's luminous main echoes 'the shores of light (*in luminis oras*)' of the fifth book of Lucretius's *De Rerum Natura*, which likens the advent of life to the casting up of a new born babe upon a seashore, as if wrecked, where they begin to wail in agony. As Hans Blumenberg observes, the image suggests that 'not only the course of life and its end are seen through the shipwreck metaphor, but even its beginning'.[87] Ralegh's speaker, it seems, exists out of time, and the exact moment of the implied wreck is occluded; favour turns to anguish and purpose to desolation, the point of no return lost to failing memory.

In Ralegh's verse, moisture only returns with the speaker's grief, producing a deluge that submerges his hopes and drowns his mind. The potential for renewal and ecological balance, as embodied by Spenser's Britomart, is directly denied here; instead, the fall of rain 'uppon the

---

86 William Shakespeare, 'Sonnet 60', in *Shakespeare's Sonnets*, ed. Katherine Duncan-Jones (London: Arden Shakespeare, 2010).
87 Blumenberg, *Shipwreck with Spectator*, p. 28. See Lucretius, *De Rerum Natura*, trans. W.H.D. Rouse (London: William Heinemann, 1924; repr. 1943), V.222–7.

parched grounde' is 'by heat up dried/ no coolinge moysture is percevde att all' (238-9). Careful artifices and performances do little to alter the course of nature, for

> in love thos things that weare no more may be
> for fancy seildume ends wher it begunn.
> And as a streame by stronge hand bounded in
> from natures course wher it did sumetyme runn
> by some small rent or loose part douth beginn
> to finde escape ... (219-24)

Even the 'stronge hand' is incapable of creating lasting structures and mastering available resources. Limited thus, the speaker's complaint models an observation made by Rod Giblett, prompted by Luce Irigaray's characterisation of female desire as something non-linear and unpolarised: the 'fluidity of women's desire', he writes, 'threatens to undermine the shores, banks, dykes, of phallic men's objects, private property, things, just as the sea and the swamp threaten to absorb "developments" built between them'.[88] In Ralegh's poem, the speaker's sense of his own devalued worth, an acute sense of lost favour engendering disappointment, is translated into images of failed projects; the 'stronge hand', like Spenser's 'second hand', is judged incapable of creating lasting forms. Water changes its movements, and

> Thos streames seeme standinge puddells which before,
> Wee saw our bewties in, so weare the[y] cleere
> Bellphebes course is now observde no more ...
> that faire resemblance weareth out of date
> our Ocean seas are but tempestius waves
> and all things bass that blessed wear of late ... (269-74)

In these famous lines, the poet writes as if the potential for poetry residing in the natural world has retreated with the beloved.[89] Freshwater no longer moves but remains still and stagnant, and the sea is just the sea, made hostile to any attempt to animate it with a numinous poetics. All 'secrete or hyd' properties have vanished, turning the poem into a lament for a lost symbolic order.[90] Ralegh may write of how 'Shee gave, shee

---

88 Rod Giblett, *Postmodern Wetlands: Culture, History, Ecology* (Edinburgh: Edinburgh University Press, 1996), p. 89.
89 Anna Beer, for example, reads these lines as critical of Spenser's fiction-making. See '"Bellphebes Course is Now Observde No More": Ralegh, Spenser and the Literary Politics of the Cynthia Holograph', *Literary and Visual Ralegh*, pp. 140-65 (pp. 153-5).
90 Robert E. Stillman describes Ralegh's poem as incorporating 'an elaborate game of "fort-da"'. See '"Words Cannot Knytt": Language and Desire in Ralegh's *The Ocean to Cynthia*', *SEL*, 27.1 (1987), 35-51, p. 42.

tooke, shee wounded, she appeased' (56) and later of how 'Shee is gonn, Shee is lost, shee is found, shee is ever faire' (493); yet, in the absence of the moon and her capacity to charge and govern water with a rhythmic ebb and flow, it is difficult to see what is eventually returned to the speaker. All is either tempest or void: chaotic movement or deathly stasis.

In later stanzas, the speaker seems to come to terms with the emptiness of his endeavour, finding in his own grief only the failure of his creative capacity, as if trying to locate water in the desert: 'to seeke for moysture in th'arabien sande/ is butt a losse of labor, and of rest' (478–9). The desert still harbours the memory of a lost, moving body of water: a mountainous place,

> agaynst whose bancks, the trobled ocean bett
> and weare the markes to finde thy hoped port
> into a soyle farr of them sealves remove
> onn Sestus shore Leanders late resorte
> Hero hath left no lampe to guyde her love (484–8)

The shore becomes a place of lateness: of death in Leander's case and belatedness in the case of the speaker. It is an inverted mirror-image of the tideline as a space of encounter. Here the shoreline conspires against the speaker's will, whereby seamarks once visible to the erstwhile mariner have developed a hostile agency of their own in order to recede from view, turning something once contoured and individuated into an undifferentiated figure. Without the presence of seamarks, 'well hable to be skried', the mariner could be anywhere, unable to recognise a once distinct coastal profile (see *Mathematicall Praeface*, sig. a4$^v$). After all, as William Bourne writes in *The Regiment for the Sea* (1574), noting the vulnerability of any ship's pilot to contingent events, and his need to reorient himself following a tempest, 'it is verye meete and necessarye to knowe any place, when that hee dothe see it'.[91] For Ralegh's speaker, this is no longer an option: loss is measured in terms of self-eroding land and seascapes, which are abruptly reframed by the poet's allusion to a literary geography that gained further currency in the hands of other authors.[92] 'Sestus shore' once provided a safe harbour but, for both Leander and Ralegh's speaker, now only figures the site of betrayal, belatedness, and what Anna Beer describes as 'the dark side of *otium*': a state that stages the displacement of 'Spenserian

---

91 William Bourne, *A Regiment for the Sea* (London, 1574), sig. B2$^v$.
92 See Christopher Marlowe, *Hero and Leander* (London, 1598) and Thomas Nashe, *Nashes Lenten Stuffe* (London, 1599).

desirous imaginings ... by true cognitive understanding'.[93] Indeed, as Bourne explains, reflecting on the need for the coastal pilot to be a skilled draughtsman:

> and what greater inconvenience may there growe by any meanes, than there may by mistaking of a place? For it were twentie times better to be throughly persuaded that he knoweth it not, than to thinke he doth knowe it not being that place. For whereas he doth thinke to prevent the dangers, he may willingly runne upon the dangers not known of him.[94]

In its absence of literary seamarks and the predictable tidal currents that connote a familiar shore, Ralegh's poem looks towards death, not-knowing, and the annihilation of the individual: 'all is desolvde, our labors cume to nought' (235). As he would write in *The History of the World*, the movement of time ensures only one certainty: 'For this tyde of mans life, after it once turneth and declineth, ever runneth with a perpetuall Ebbe and falling Streame, but never floweth againe'.[95] For an author whose identity as a poet was fashioned by himself and others in relation to water, the contemplated turning of this final tide suggests that there could be no subsequent movement that could 'great *Cynthiaes* sore displeasure breake,/ And moue to take him to her grace againe' (see 'Colin Clouts Come Home Againe', 174–5). Within such a romance, an exile can have no hope of return.

Ralegh's fascination with coastal figures throws Spenser's handling of elemental discord into sharp relief and, by contrast, reveals the extraordinary optimism of *The Faerie Queene*'s central books. The two poets seem to share an imagined coastal geography, rewriting the same images and metaphors in order to sound the depths of worldly contingency. In Book IV's continued interest in cosmic strife, the displeasure of '*Dan AEolus*' can through 'all foure parts of heauen ... rage full sore,/ And tosse the deepes, and teare the firmament' (IV.ix.23), and conflict return like tidal water, carrying barks on 'contrary courses' (IV.ix.26). Even 'raine, and haile, and sleet' may fall, first 'from one coast' then to the other, 'from side to side till all the world it weet' (IV.ix.33). And yet, in spite of this, the river pageant with which the book ends suggests that the world already contains within itself the capacity to self-regulate, recalling Bernard of

---

93 Beer, 'Ralegh, Spenser and the Literary Politics of the Cynthia Holograph', p. 143 and p. 164. Duncan-Jones argues that Leander is drowning not because Hero is negligent but perhaps because she is already dead. See 'The Date of Raleigh's "21th: And Last Booke of the Ocean to Scinthia"', pp. 150–1.
94 Bourne, *A Regiment for the Sea*, sig. D1ᵛ.
95 Walter Ralegh, *The History of the World* (London, 1614 [i.e. 1617]), Chap. 2, S. 5, p. 31.

Clairvaux's likening of the sea-as-source to Christ as the source and endpoint of all virtue and wisdom:

> If all waters seek incessantly to return to the sea, making their way thither sometimes by hidden and subterranean channels, so that they may go forth from it again in continual and untiring circuit, becoming visible once more to man and available to his service, why are not those spiritual streams rendered back constantly and without reserve to their legitimate source, that they may not cease to water the fields of our hearts? Let the rivers of divers graces return from whence they came, that they may flow forth anew. Let the heavenly shower rise again to its heavenly source, that it may be poured anew and still more plentifully on the earth.[96]

The analogy drawn between hydrological and spiritual renewal offers a glimpse of the regenerative capacity that is held in potential by Britomart as well as a vision of the divine in the world, which moves towards concord.[97]

Spenser's river pageant also provides a model for human interaction. Owing to Ralegh's secular focus on a single speaker, his poem lacks the visionary and multitudinous quality of Spenser's epic work; yet, the minds of these two poets seem to meet and diverge at the imagined space where waters ebb and flow. Unlike the errant watercourses and parched muddy rivulets of Ralegh's poem,[98] the participants in *The Faerie Queene*'s '*epithalamia fluviorum*' do not wholly resist the poet's shaping hand, even when Spenser's admonitory inclusion of un-mastered rivers such as the Orinoco and the Amazon, and his silence concerning the rivers of Ireland, suggests that their waters elude the nation's grasp.[99] When the work of both poets is read alongside Dee's hydrographic definitions and concerns, as undertaken above, it is even more striking that Elizabeth's motto, *semper eadem*, or 'always the same', appears even on the very maritime charts that elsewhere celebrate their susceptibility to change (see Figure 7).

As Cynthia, Amphitrite, and the Ladie of the Sea, the imagined reach of the monarch's embrace was perhaps insufficient to span an empire, but

---

96 Bernard of Clairvaux, 'Sermon XIII', in *Life and Works of Saint Bernard, Abbot of Clairvaux*, ed. John Mabillon, ed. and trans. Samuel J. Eales, Vol. IV (London: John Hodges, 1896), pp. 67–73 (p. 67). See Yi-Fu Tuan, *The Hydrologic Cycle and the Wisdom of God: A Theme in Geoteleology* (Toronto: University of Toronto Press, 1968), pp. 42–3.
97 Braden observes that the pageant offers a vision of 'political order not as a purposed human construct, but as a simile on the flow of the cosmos'. See 'Riverrun', p. 47.
98 For the relationship to Spenser's Bregog see Dees, 'Colin Clout and the Shepherd of the Ocean', p. 195.
99 See van Es, *Spenser's Forms of History*, pp. 60–4. See *FQ*, IV.xi.21–2, 40–4.

*Figure 7* Lucas Janzoon Waghenaer. Southern Europe from 'A Generall Carde, and Description of the Sea Coastes of Europe', in *The Mariners Mirrour*, trans. Anthony Ashley (London, 1588). In a notable addition to the map of Europe included in the English edition of this work, the royal coat of arms floats in possessive proximity to the 'Mare Hispanicum' or Bay of Biscay.

her influence was enough to shape the paper waters that proliferated in its absence: all three authors concern themselves with her changeability as well as her capacity for stillness and even paralysis.[100] All three writers also share a concern with memory; yet, the movement of water resists the monumental even as it generates matter for retention. In the following chapter, I consider the implications of terraqueous spaces when tidal order is threatened by muddied indistinction: a loss of conserving definition that confronts the aesthetic challenges of generative formlessness.

---

100 For Elizabeth and Proteus as *dei absconditi* see Goldberg, *Endlesse Worke*, p. 144. Dan Brayton observes a similar phenomenon in the tidal poetics of Shakespeare: 'we witness a poetic meditation on the historical and the natural that we might call an ecopoetical cosmology – a *poesis* that attempts to fathom the deep connections between the environmental forces and the political structures that rule the individual and the social body'. See *Shakespeare's Ocean*, p. 106.

# 6

# Wetlands and Spenser's 'personal curvature'

It is unlikely that any amount of utilitarian objectivizing will ever wholly dispel the symbolic resonance that arises from that strange tension between shaping line and unshaped space, between bounded and boundless.[1]

I ask you: Is it not time to slash Janus's face?[2]

In his translation of Sonnet 26 from *Les Antiquitez de Rome*, Spenser invokes the technical language of spatial representation only to dismiss it, in order to gauge the success of an empire that once stretched its influence to the limits of the known world. At the height of its powers, Rome defied measurement by applied geometry and instrumental means because it was the world entire:

> Who list the Romane greatnes forth to figure,
> Him needeth not to seeke for vsage right
> Of line, or lead, or rule, or squaire, to measure
> Her length, her breadth, her deepnes, or her hight,
>    But him behooues to vew in compasse round
> All that the Ocean graspes in his long armes;
> Be it where the yerely starre doth scortch the ground,
> Or where colde *Boreas* blowes his bitter stormes.
>    *Rome* was th'whole world, and al the world was *Rome*,
> And if things nam'd their names doo equalize,
> When land and sea ye name, then name ye *Rome*;
> And naming *Rome* ye land and sea comprize:
>    For th'auncient Plot of *Rome* displayed plaine,
>    The map of all the wide world doth containe.

---

1 Theodore Roszak, *Where the Wasteland Ends: Politics and Transcendence in Postindustrial Society* (Berkeley: Celestial Arts, 1989), p. 407.
2 Dagmar Reichert, 'On Boundaries', *Environment and Planning D: Society and Space*, 10.1 (1992), 87–98, p. 87.

Spenser makes few changes to Joachim du Bellay's poem. In the third line, he substitutes 'rule' for the third instrument in the catalogue, which originally lists 'la ligne et au plomb, au compass, à l'équerre', perhaps so that he can use 'in compasse round' in the fifth line instead of du Bellay's 'd'une egale rondeur', which implies the more literal drawing of a perfect circle. In the penultimate line, Spenser substitutes du Bellay's image of how 'le monde on peult sur Rome compasser' ('we can measure the world by measuring Rome') in favour of expanding the final line to emphasise how a 'plot', or city map of Rome, can 'containe', rather than 'compass' du Bellay's 'carte du monde': the 'map of the world'.[3] The differences allow Spenser to introduce du Bellay's final sense of 'compassing' Rome earlier in the sonnet, privileging the act of perceiving an idea in its entirety over the use of the compass as a draughtsman's instrument.

The remainder of the sonnet surveys a world that is given margins only by the embrace of the ocean, unmeasured by lead and line, and the extremities suggested by the warmth of Sirius and the chill of the north wind: elements that used elsewhere would retain a capacity for orientation associated with nautical charts. Land and sea are described as distinct elements that, once united under the name of empire, participate in an ordered cosmos. As a homogenous self-contained world, the sonnet obscures the geopolitical manoeuvres that determine the activities of colonialism. The world-ocean in this vision is the only hard limit: a boundary that does not permeate or dilute that which is held within its grasp. In its image of undifferentiated but privileged space, the poem's small frame holds together the dream of a city that can be both empire and cosmos; yet, for Spenser, it is rare to find an uncomplicated embrace in the movement of water. Only within the sequence as a whole does the sonnet figure a unity that has been lost to ruin: a reframing that anticipates Spenser's later writings in which images of conquest and expansion typically emerge from something already compromised.[4]

In Book V of *The Faerie Queene*, which is widely regarded by critics as the most geopolitically charged of Spenser's legends, the poet explicitly addresses the relationships between space, possession, measurement, and judgement, which have long been lying latent in the allegorical

---

[3] Joachim du Bellay, *Les Antiquitez de Rome*, in *The Regrets, with, The Antiquities of Rome, Three Latin Elegies, and The Defense and Enrichment of the French Language*, ed. and trans. Richard Helgerson (Philadelphia: University of Pennsylvania Press, 2006), pp. 272–3.
[4] See David Galbraith, *Architectonics of Imitation in Spenser, Daniel, and Drayton* (Toronto: University of Toronto Press, 2000), pp. 29–74.

terrain.⁵ In the Legend of Justice, earlier lessons concerning perspective and measurement give shape to increasingly divergent narratives of gain and loss, approximating the geopolitical negotiations of Ireland (Irena/ Malengin), Spain (Geryoneo), the Low Countries (Belge), and England (Mercilla), whose empire extends fantastically 'From th'vtmost brinke of the *Americke* shore,/ Vnto the margent of the *Molucas*' (V.x.3). A further figure for Elizabeth I, Mercilla is praised abroad by 'Nations farre' (V.x.3); yet, Elizabethan dreams of imperialism bear little comparison with the activities of the Roman Empire at its height.⁶ Instead, the description of Mercilla's reach as stretching from one 'brinke' to another 'margent' provides a literary example of David Armitage's perception that Elizabethan rhetoric seemed to think of England as an 'inside-out empire' or 'a shrunken insular core, detached both from continental Europe and from the surrounding Atlantic archipelago'.⁷

This chapter focuses on the writing of England's westward gaze towards Ireland, a country which, as William J. Smyth observes, appeared in sixteenth-century reports as 'a fractured landscape, full of internal borders and multiple forms of administration'.⁸ The impression of fractured distance can be found in Spenser's poetry, where Britomart's decision not to wait for Artegall's return near the end of Book V, for example, emerges out of a sense of disorientation that, within the terms of the allegory, bodily turns the direction of her gaze from the east. Restless, but forced to find a place of respite, she makes a temporary pause and her gaze becomes mediated by a window; it is out of this framed space that the iron man Talus eventually appears, bearing news that his lord has been captured by the emasculating 'Tyrannesse' Radigund (V.vi.11). The window itself is strangely disembodied, appearing without a surrounding structure like a fetishised oculus:

> One day, when as she long had sought for ease

---

5   For a review of critical attitudes see Willy Maley, '"To Weet to Work Irenaes Franchisement": Ireland in *The Faerie Queene*', *IUR*, 26.2 (1996), 303–19. See also Clare Carroll, 'The Construction of Gender and the Cultural and Political Other in *The Faerie Queene* 5 and *A View of the Present State of Ireland*: The Critics, The Context, and The Case of Radigund', *Criticism*, 32.2 (1990), 163–92.
6   See Bruce McLeod, *The Geography of Empire in English Literature, 1580–1745* (Cambridge: Cambridge University Press, 1999; repr. 2009), pp. 32–75 (p. 62).
7   David Armitage, 'The Elizabethan Idea of Empire', *TRHS*, 14 (2004), 269–77, p. 270.
8   William J. Smyth, *Map Making, Landscapes and Memory: A Geography of Colonial and Early Modern Ireland, c. 1530–1750* (Cork: Cork University Press, 2006), p. 42. See also Richard A. McCabe, 'Translated States: Spenser and Linguistic Colonialism', in *Edmund Spenser: Essays on Culture and Allegory*, ed. Jennifer Klein Morrison and Matthew Greenfield (Aldershot: Ashgate, 2000), pp. 67–88 (p. 68).

> In euery place, and euery place thought best,
> Yet found no place, that could her liking please,
> She to a window came, that opened West,
> Towards which coast her loue his way addrest.
> There looking forth, shee in her heart did find
> Many vaine fancies, working her vnrest;
> And sent her winged thoughts, more swift then wind,
> To beare vnto her loue the message of her mind. (V.vi.7)

The westward gaze aligns the poem's allegory with Spenser's political and administrative interests. The memory of Artegall's progress calls to mind a receding figure last seen heading towards a liquid horizon and Britomart's 'winged thoughts' suggest the force with which the imagination can be projected, as if anxious attention alone can bridge the distance between the thinker and the object of desire. The telescopic eroticism of the view channels hopes of possession into solipsistic image-making: the empty landscape stimulates the play of fancy and vanity, tainted by the suggestion of futility.

A perspective aligned with Britomart's gaze can be used to frame the attitudes of Spenser and his westward-gazing contemporaries, whose textual surveys, descriptions, and views mediate between 'vaine fancies' and a desire to meet the expectations of their readers.[9] This chapter, by focusing on moments from the second half of *The Faerie Queene*, Spenser's *A View of the Present State of Ireland*, and a selection of complementary prose writings, explores the commonplaces of accounts written by physical and imaginative sojourners in Ireland. Within such speculative works, the writing of geography and *geosophy* are often one and the same.[10] For my purposes here, Eugène Vinaver's description of the 'conquest of space' mobilised by the interlaced structures of the romance mode, together with his sense of how these recurrent narratives indi-

---

9 See, for example, David J. Baker, 'Charting Uncertainty in Renaissance Ireland', in *Representing Ireland: Literature and the Origins of Conflict, 1534–1660*, ed. Brendan Bradshaw, Andrew Hadfield, and Willy Maley (Cambridge: Cambridge University Press, 1993), pp. 76–92 and Bernhard Klein, *Maps and the Writing of Space in Early Modern England and Ireland* (Basingstoke: Palgrave Macmillan, 2001), pp. 171–87.
10 See John K. Wright, '*Terrae Incognitae*: The Place of the Imagination in Geography', *Annals of the Association of American Geographers*, 37.1 (1947), 1–15, p. 9. For this drive in the cartographic work of the mapmaker, Richard Bartlett, see Thomas Herron, 'Orpheus in Ulster: Richard Bartlett's Colonial Art', in *Ireland in the Renaissance, c. 1540–1660*, ed. Thomas Herron and Michael Potterton (Dublin: Four Courts Press, 2007), pp. 289–308. For the dynamic in Spenser's *View* see Joanne Woolway Grenfell, 'Significant Spaces in Edmund Spenser's *View of the Present State of Ireland*', *EMLS*, 4.2 (1998), 6.1–21.

cate a 'design still unfulfilled', offers another analogy for the attempts by Spenser and his contemporaries to subject Irish space to ever multiplying plots.[11] Through a use of shared motifs and a sense of teleology that persists in delaying closure, Spenser and his contemporaries create literary geographies that operate at a significant remove from their subject. Any 'proving ground' is encountered at an aestheticized distance and the land limned is characterised by the artifice of its representation.[12]

I take the phrase 'personal curvature' from the work of the historical geographer J.H. Andrews, who coined it to describe 'the subjective element in a cartographer's linework' in his book on the history of mapping Ireland,[13] and in the readings that follow, the making of spatial knowledge manifests as a vagrant undertaking, characterised by its unsettled and unsettling qualities. In the opening dialogic exchanges of Spenser's *View*, for example, the New English interlocutor Irenaeus famously speculates that 'the fatall destinie of that Lande' may 'proceed from the *very Genius* of the soile, or influence of the starres' (p. 43). By paying particular attention to the mutable textures of the Irish environment – its hydrographic features, soils, and shores – I examine how Spenser and his contemporaries sought to find a rhetoric of discovery that also acknowledged the frustrations of describing a landscape that was not fully understood: a process that disrupted ideas of empire-building modelled on successful classical precedents.[14] Bruce Avery's summary of the traditional critical observation, that when Spenser wrote of Ireland in *A View* he 'marred a political document with descriptions formed by a poetic consciousness', is useful in that it draws attention to the ways in which both poet and planter share a formal interest in matter and aesthetic control.[15] For Spenser, such interstices often play out in the

11 Eugène Vinaver, *The Rise of Romance* (Oxford: Clarendon Press, 1971), p. 81. For Spenser's engagement with a mutable landscape of intertextuality and rhetorical *topoi* see Julia Reinhard Lupton, 'Mapping Mutability: or, Spenser's Irish Plot', in *Representing Ireland*, pp. 93–115.
12 Kenneth Gross describes Ireland as 'the proving ground of the imagination's faith and fate' and the place, for Spenser, 'where nature, mind and culture fought unresolvable battles'. See *Spenserian Poetics: Idolatry, Iconoclasm, and Magic* (Ithaca: Cornell University Press, 1985), p. 80 and p. 79.
13 J.H. Andrews, *Shapes of Ireland: Maps and their Makers 1564–1839* (Dublin: Geography Publications, 1997), p. 31. For a map-minded reading of Spenser see Mercedes Camino, '(Un)folding the Map of Early Modern Ireland: Spenser, Moryson, Bartlett, and Ortelius', *Cartographica*, 34.4 (1997), 1–17, p. 2.
14 See Mark Dorrian, 'On Some Spatial Aspects of the Colonial Discourse on Ireland', *The Journal of Architecture*, 6.1 (2001), 27–51 and D.B. Quinn, 'Renaissance Influence in English Colonization', *TRHS*, 26 (1976), 73–93.
15 Bruce Avery, 'Mapping the Irish Other: Spenser's *A View of the Present State of Ireland*',

relationship between matter and metaphor:[16] a relationship that comes under increasing strain in the writing of Ireland's wetlands.

The importance of earthy imagery in *The Faerie Queene* takes on new resonance when read within the context of a material landscape notorious for its 'watery soyle' and treacherous coastline.[17] Jon A. Quitslund comments, for example, that Spenser often represents 'earth and water together as the substratum of animate life';[18] however, the contexts brought to bear on Spenser's poetry by the violence and labour involved in colonial plantation refigure cosmic archetypes as localised struggle. By anchoring readings in the kinds of environments that Mentz evocatively classifies as 'brown' – namely the shifting strands, muddy brinks, and bogs of Books V and VI – this chapter places particular emphasis on questions concerning the properties of unstable ground.[19] Through this focus, it seeks to complement two different strands of existing criticism: the first of which identifies connections between Spenser's narrative strategies and the visualising techniques of mapmaking and surveying, and the second of which concerns husbandry and habitation.[20] In particular, I consider the names, occlusions, and inundations that shape Spenser's view of Ireland and its propensity to go awry; after all, the rhetoric of unstable ground has the capacity to undermine both physical activities and argumentative foundations. The approach thus synthesises previous critical interests in the *techne* of colonial projecting and builds, in particular, on Thomas Herron's reading of the 'elemental violence' implicit in Spenser's '*plantation aesthetic*', wherein the 'civic well-being of the planter in Ireland coincides with his artistic ambition as a "maker"'.[21]

---

 *ELH*, 57.2 (1990), 263–79, p. 264.
16 See John Erskine Hankins, *Source and Meaning in Spenser's Allegory* (Oxford: Clarendon Press, 1971), pp. 228–97 and Eamon Grennan, 'Language and Politics: A Note on Some Metaphors in Spenser's *A View of the Present State of Ireland*', *Spenser Studies*, 3 (1982), 99–110.
17 Fynes Moryson, *An Itinerary* (London, 1617), Part III, p. 159.
18 Jon A. Quitslund, *Spenser's Supreme Fiction: Platonic Natural Philosophy and The Faerie Queene* (Toronto: University of Toronto Press, 2001), p. 165.
19 See Steve Mentz, 'Brown', in *Prismatic Ecology*, ed. Jeffrey Jerome Cohen (Minneapolis: University of Minnesota Press, 2013), pp. 193–212.
20 Linda Gregerson, for example, identifies the making of a 'new political ecology' in Spenser's work in 'Spenser's Georgic: Violence and the Gift of Place', *Spenser Studies*, 22 (2007), 185–201, p. 199.
21 See Thomas Herron, *Spenser's Irish Work: Poetry, Plantation and Colonial Reformation* (Aldershot: Ashgate, 2007), p. 11 and p. 85. See also his '"Goodly Woods": Irish Forests, Georgic Trees in Books 1 and 4 of Edmund Spenser's *Faerie Queene*', *Quidditas*, 19 (1998), 97–122.

## Surveying wetlands

For Spenser and others who came to Ireland from England, attempts to rationalise what were perceived to be defects in the Irish landscape posed the problem of transforming perceived chaos into order: wetland typically defies, as Barbara Hurd observes, 'all those grand "Let there be this" and "Let there be that" proclamations'.[22] As a result, the representation of this specific kind of ecotonal environment offers a figure for the anxiety of the colonist: an anxiety which pertains, as Bruce McCleod observes, to the sense that the 'inevitable cross-cultural and territorially uncertain character' of colonial society 'means that the colonizers' social order is in constant jeopardy'.[23] Indeed, descriptions of the country's perceived aberrance are startlingly formulaic: the alleged profundity of bogs and woodland collude to produce descriptions of a waterlogged landscape that exists as a kind of indeterminate world, resistant to precise physical definition, and which permeates the otherwise wholesome body of the planter.[24] Richard Stanihurst, for example, observes that the soil of Ireland 'is low and waterish, including diverse little Ilands, invironed with lakes and marrish. Highest hils have standing pooles in their tops. Inhabitants especialllie new come, are subject to distillations, rheumes and fluxes'.[25] A characteristic moistness appears to act on the bodily humours, aligning the constitution of the land's temporary residents with the instability of the terrain; travellers are changed by their sojourn in ways that imply physical perviousness and uncomfortable liquidity.[26] For John Dymmok, the country of Ireland 'lyeth very low, and therefore watrish, and full of marishes, boggs, and standing pooles, even in

---

22 Barbara Hurd, *Stirring the Mud: On Swamps, Bogs, and Human Imagination* (Boston: Beacon Press, 2001), p. 67.
23 McLeod, *The Geography of Empire*, p. 6. For 'anxiety' as a theme in Spenserian criticism see Herron, *Spenser's Irish Work*, pp. 17–30.
24 See R.A. Butlin, 'Land and People, c. 1600', in *A New History of Ireland: Early Modern Ireland 1534–1691*, ed. T.W. Moody, F.X. Martin, and F.J. Byrne (Oxford: Oxford University Press, 2009), pp. 142–67 (pp. 142–3).
25 Richard Stanihurst, 'A Treastise Conteining a Plaine and Perfect Description of Ireland', in *The Second Volume of Chronicles: Conteining the Description, Conquest, Inhabitation, and Troblesome Estate of Ireland; First Collected by Raphaell Holinshed* (London, 1586), sig. B1$^r$.
26 For the concept of 'geohumouralism' see Mary Floyd-Wilson, *English Ethnicity and Race in Early Modern Drama* (Cambridge: Cambridge University Press, 2003) and Mary Floyd-Wilson and Garrett A. Sullivan, Jr. 'Introduction: Inhabiting the Body, Inhabiting the World', in *Environment and Embodiment in Early Modern England*, ed. Mary Floyd-Wilson and Garrett A. Sullivan, Jr. (Basingstoke: Palgrave Macmillan, 2007), pp. 1–13.

the highest mowntaynes, which causes the inhabitants, but specially the sojoners there, to be very subject to rhewmes, catarrs, and flixes':[27] an echo that can be traced back to the common twelfth-century source text of both works, *The History and Topography of Ireland* by Gerald of Wales.[28]

As emblematic reductions of a variegated land, Ireland's amphibious and terraqueous qualities seem to mediate anxieties particular to the New English planters concerning the limitations of their control, over both self and environment. Stuart McLean explains that the English word for bog 'comes from the Irish *bogach*, meaning soft or marshy ground'; such places will not support the weight of a body and possess a 'seeming recalcitrance to human projects and designs'.[29] Boggy grounds may thus act on the mind and memory but in a way that does not provide respite or clarity. For Spenser, writing in his dedicatory sonnet 'To the right Honourable the Earle of *Ormond and Ossory*' that follows *The Faerie Queene*, the fertile geographical imaginary of classical Greece cannot be projected or overlaid on to such a 'saluage soyl' and 'barren field'. When Muses are absent, there is also no accompanying habitat for the imagination: 'Not one *Parnassus*, nor one *Helicone*/ Left for sweete Muses to be harboured'. In lieu of clear running water and named landmarks, Spenser's mind's eye is instead drawn to images of elemental confusion: a state with which the view from his house at Kilcolman would perhaps have made him familiar.[30]

In addition, the bog or quagmire has long carried the suggestion of transgressive immorality; indeed, indeterminate places have longstanding associations with ethical and intellectual confusion in the literary and theological imagination.[31] Psalm 69, for example, uses wetland to locate the condition of spiritual distress: to 'sticke fast in the deepe myre,

27 John Dymmok, 'A Treatice of Ireland', in *Tracts Relating to Ireland*, Vol. II (Dublin: The Irish Archaeological Society, 1843), p. 5.
28 See Gerald of Wales, *The History and Topography of Ireland*, trans. John O' Meara (London: Penguin, 1951; repr. 1988), p. 34. For a literary history of non-native authors 'writing' Ireland see Andrew Murphy, *But the Irish Sea Betwixt Us: Ireland, Colonialism, and Renaissance Literature* (Lexington: University Press of Kentucky, 1999).
29 Stuart McLean, '"To Dream Profoundly": Irish Boglands and the Imagination of Matter', *Irish Journal of Anthropology*, 10.2 (2007), 61–8, p. 61 and p. 65.
30 See Tadhg O'Keeffe, 'Plantation-era Great Houses in Munster: A Note on Sir Walter Raleigh's House and Its Context', in *Ireland in the Renaissance*, pp. 274–88 (p. 279 in particular).
31 More recently, Lowell Duckert has countered this in favour of a 'posthumanist wetland ethic'. See 'The Slough of Respond', *O-Zone: A Journal of Object-Orientated Studies*, 1 (2014), 110–17.

where no ground is', is to experience spiritual and existential despair.[32] Immersion is not baptismal but annihilating: a fevered association of mire and deep that creates all-encompassing oblivion. As in Book IX of John Milton's *Paradise Lost*, when Eve elects to follow her serpent-tempter towards the Tree of Knowledge and is there, like 'th' amazed night-wanderer', misled though 'bogs and mires',[33] the threat of being engulfed by the terrain figures an anxiety concerning the threat of the formless to overwhelm the subject. And when the physician Helkiah Crooke wanted to prepare his audience for the complexities of his analysis of the generation of life in *Mikrokosmographia* (1616), for example, he employed a rich metaphorical blend that culminated in an image of fathoming uncertain terrain. A descendent of the figurative tradition in which Spenser's questing knights also participate, the erstwhile reader is imagined as entering both hostile wetlandscape and tournament in hope of success:

> Verilie a knotty and snarled skaine to unreele; a thicket, wherein he that hasteth with bold rashnesse and temerity shall offend and stumble at every step; he that is diligent shall entangle himself, and he that is guided by blinde ignorance shall light upon pits and bogs; so that it will bee impossible for any man that enters into these Listes fairely to acquite himselfe. The further he wadeth in this River, the greater confluence of waters wil overtake him, the deeper must he sound if he will finde the bottome.[34]

The eye of the reader is tasked with navigating the maelstrom of orientational imagery, which creates a series of mutually informative mental spaces; the knotted skein that resembles Ariadne's clew of twine eventually transforms, via fenny depths and exposing tilts, into the pilot's lead and line.

A cognate confusion of inundation and generation can be found in the first book of *The Faerie Queene* when Spenser elaborates upon the condition of error in which the heavily armoured Redcrosse is mired. Errour's vomit is likened to the annual deluge of waters associated with the Nile: 'His fattie waues doe fertile slime outwell,/ And ouerflow each plaine and lowly dale': a flood that recedes to leave 'Huge heapes of mudd …, wherin there breed/ Ten thousand kindes of creatures' (I.i.21). The relationship between matter and thought is kept in constant play by the

---

32 *The Bible in English* (London, 1568), fol. 179ᵛ, Psalm 69:2.
33 John Milton, *Paradise Lost*, ed. Scott Elledge (New York: Norton, 1975), IX.640-2.
34 Helkiah Crooke, *Mikrokosmographia: A Description of the Body of Man* (London, 1615), sig. Z3ʳ.

allegory, and the immediacy of Redcrosse's sensory revulsion is accompanied by a more subtle kind of disorientation, surrounded as he is by the spontaneous generation of threatening, half-formed things.[35] The analogies Crooke employs, and the images found in Spenser's poetry, can thus be productively set alongside English writing about Ireland in order to demonstrate how closely associated images of thickets, bogs, and floods can be found within contexts that ostensibly have very little to do with describing the contours and peculiarities of a specific material landscape but which ground themselves in the bodily experience and mnemonic charge of material encounter and discomfort.[36] As a way of describing an intellectual challenge, Crooke's terms also perhaps provide a sense of why the Irish landscape appears in such formulaic rhetorical guises in colonial writings. It is no coincidence that Judith H. Anderson describes the 'duplicitous' interlocutors of *A View* as implicating themselves in a 'possibly bottomless miring' that 'lands us in cultural quicksand'.[37] The wetland ultimately offers a commonplace, or rhetorical *topos*, for 'matter out of place'.[38]

Wetland thus retains a sense of epistemological and literary experiment, generating the creation of moralised and marginalised geographies. In the description of Ireland found within the English translation of Mercator's *Historia Mundi*, for example, the author draws attention to the relationship of art, nature, form, and matter in the constitution of the country:

> The Countrie is shadowed with great woods. To speake in a word, although it be barren in some places by reason of Lakes, Bogs, and thicke Woods, yet it is every where full of Cattell, and Grasse, and at all times it abundantly requiteth the labour of the husbandman. Nature is so little beholding here to Art or Industrie, that the flourishing bankes of Rivers embrodered with flowers, the shadie Woods, greene Medowes, bending Hills, and Fields fit to

---

35 See Walter M. Kendrick, 'Earth of Flesh, Flesh of Earth: Mother Earth in *The Faerie Queene*', *RQ*, 27.4 (1974), 533–48. See also Hankins, *Source and Meaning in Spenser's Allegory*, p. 285.
36 See Herron, *Spenser's Irish Work*, pp. 127–43.
37 Judith H. Anderson, *Reading the Allegorical Intertext: Chaucer, Spenser, Shakespeare, Milton* (New York: Fordham University Press, 2008), p. 177.
38 Mary Douglas, *Purity and Danger: An Analysis of Concept of Pollution and Taboo* (London: Routledge, 2002), p. 44. The suggestive connection between Douglas's concept and wetlands is made by Rod Giblett in *Postmodern Wetlands: Culture, History, Ecology* (Edinburgh: Edinburgh University Press, 1996), p. 13. For how commonplaces 'permit a community to arrive at mutually agreeable conclusions in matters of uncertainty' see Catherine Nicholson, '*Othello* and the Geography of Persuasion', *ELR*, 40.1 (2010), 56–87, p. 68.

beare corne if they were tilled, do seeme to be angrie with the Inhabitants, because by their carelesnesse and negligence they suffer them to be rude and wilde.[39]

In the description of contoured shade, curving gradients, and waterways edged by the decorative embellishments of flora, a vision of an aesthetically ordered landscape emerges, in spite of the author's protestation that the country lacks 'art'.[40] The suggestion of a shaping mind and eye lingers, but this is confronted by the idea that the topography is itself rebellious and 'angrie' with its inhabitants, as if an innate aggressive fecundity requires transformation by a firmer hand. As an element of the composition, the presence of 'wetlandscape' challenges the sense of orderly landscaping established by Mercator's surveying eye: what remains is a paradoxical balance between the intrusion of 'barren' places and the promise of exaggerated profundity 'every where', as if established systems of classifying terrain no longer hold water.

Spenser repeatedly returns to the distinction between culture and dissolution, and form and formlessness, in *The Faerie Queene*. In Book III, which offers a reframing of the inundating textures of Errour's den, the muddy littoral of the Nile offers an image of fecund generation: after the flood, 'Infinite shapes of creatures men do fynd,/ Informed in the mud, on which the Sunne hath shynd' (III.vi.8). Spenser's choice of the word 'informed' implies both fashioning and instruction: the shaping of the creatures suggests the action of an 'intellectual trace'.[41] It is striking that, for early modern practitioners of cartography and surveying, the Nile and its associated agricultural practices had long served as the site of an object lesson in how fecundity is no substitute for formal resilience, and Egypt as the mythic locus for the founding of the art of geometry.[42]

---

39 Gerhard Mercator, *Historia Mundi: Or, Mercator's Atlas* (London, 1635), sig. F1$^v$–F2$^r$.
40 For a deconstruction of the colonial gaze see Paul Carter, *The Road to Botany Bay: An Exploration of Landscape and History* (New York: Knopf, 1988). In *Poetry, Space, Landscape: Toward a New Theory* (Cambridge: Cambridge University Press, 1995), Chris Fitter notes how 'landskip', or the consciously defined pictorial definition of space, was introduced into early modern English, 'imitating the painter's art of perspectival recession, balanced land-masses and chiaroscuro, in contrast with the old medieval carelessness about prospect' (see pp. 268–9). See also Denis Cosgrove and Stephen Daniels, 'Introduction', in *The Iconography of Landscape: Essays on the Symbolic Representation, Design and Use of Past Environments* (Cambridge: Cambridge University Press, 1988), pp. 1–10.
41 See Dorrian, 'On Some Spatial Aspects of the Colonial Discourse on Ireland', p. 29.
42 See Jess Edwards, *Writing, Geometry and Space in Seventeenth Century England and America: Circles in the Sand* (London: Routledge, 2006), p. 41. See also Peter Remien,

In a discussion of professional challenges in *The Surveyors Dialogue* (1607), for example, which elaborates upon the narrative expounded in both John Dee's *Mathematicall Praeface* (1570) and Thomas Digges's *A Geometrical Practise, named Pantometria* (1571), John Norden underscores the contingencies associated with the habitation and management of a changeable environment,[43] locating what Spenser calls the 'fattie waues' and 'fertile slime' of the Nile's banks as an archetypal site of human trial and error.[44] By moving from abstract macrocosm to local microcosm, Norden's dialogue situates the discussion of flooded land in relation to the writings of the classical geographer Ptolemy, and in the following extract, the surveyor finally begins to gain ground from his interlocutor, a sceptical tenant farmer:

**Surveyor**
As for description, it was used in Egypt by Ptolomy the King, who described the whole world. And where the River Nilus in Egypt overflowed the bancks (as at this day it doth about harvest) the violence of the inundations were such, as they confounded the marks and bounds of all the grounds that were surrounded, in such sort as none knew his own land: wherupon they devised to measure every mans land, and to plot it: so that afterwards always at the waters recesse, every man could finde out his owne land by the plot.

**Farmer**
Truly that was a most excellent invention, and I thinke it indeede a most necessary course to be held in some grounds that I know in England, which are subject to like confusion: many marsh lands neere the sea coast in Kent, Sussex, Essex, Suffolke, Lincolnshire, Cambridgeshire, and other Shires confining the Sea, or subject to great waters, and if they were thus plotted out as you say, I must needs confesse it were a good worke, howsoever these kind of grounds should be hereafter surrounded, increased or diminished by the force of Seas continuall rage, whereunto they are dayly subject.[45]

The farmer, who speaks from personal experience, is distrustful of the surveyor's methods. He typically voices a position, identified by Klein,

'Silvan Matters: Error and Instrumentality in Book I of *The Faerie Queene*', *Spenser Studies*, 27 (2013), 119–43, p. 120.
43 See Dee, sig. a2$^r$ and Digges, sig. A2$^v$.
44 See Dan Brayton, 'Shakespeare and Slime: Notes on the Anthropocene', in *Ecological Approaches to Early Modern English Texts: A Field Guide to Reading and Teaching*, ed. Jennifer Munroe, Edward J. Geiseweidt, and Lynne Bruckner (Farnham: Ashgate, 2015), pp. 81–9 and Mary Floyd-Wilson, 'Transmigrations: Crossing Regional and Gender Boundaries in *Antony and Cleopatra*', *Enacting Gender on the English Renaissance Stage*, ed. Viviana Comensoli and Anne Russell (Chicago: University of Illinois Press), pp. 73–96.
45 John Norden, *The Surveyors Dialogue* (London, 1607), sig. C2$^r$.

which considers the art of surveying as 'a form of territorial invasion, designed to dispossess people of their land'.[46] It is only when the surveyor persuasively reminds the farmer that the man who arrived to measure Jerusalem in the Old Testament was in fact no less than 'an Angell of God' that he begins to appreciate how a descriptive survey 'might after the winning of these surrounded grounds againe, truly reconcile them, and allot every man his own' (*The Surveyors Dialogue*, sig. C2$^{r-v}$). Particularly striking is how he relates the surveyor's narrative to a series of landscapes that he knows first-hand: marshlands that are 'subject to like confusion'. More than a marker of perplexity, his choice of the word 'confusion' itself catches at the material concerns that arise when a 'distinction of ... elements is lost by fusion, blending, or intimate intermingling': a resonance present in the word's latent etymology.[47]

For Dee, who describes the benefits of 'land measuring' in his *Mathematicall Praeface* in similar terms, the mathematical description of area and limit could offer only rational comprehension and pleasure: as a way of diffusing the chaos and violence resulting from unauthorised plotting, 'by Gods mercy, and mans Industrie', he writes, the 'perfect Science of Lines, Plaines, and Solides (like a divine Justicer,) gave unto every man, his owne' (sig. a2$^v$). As a way of measuring and allocating territory, applied mathematics is likened to divine judgement; yet, the analogy glosses over the relationship between methodical objectivity and the subjective desires associated with possession and use.[48] For Sir Thomas Smith, for example, who succeeded William Cecil as Elizabeth's Secretary of State in 1572, all Ireland required for its reformation was the labour of diligent husbandry: 'for there cannot be ... a more fertile soile thorowe out the world for that climate than it is, a more pleasant, healthful, ful of springs, rivers, great fresh lakes, fishe, and foule, and of moste commodious herbers ... it lacketh only inhabitants, manurance, and pollicie'.[49] By imagining Ireland as a land that 'lacketh ... inhabitants', Smith's writerly hand fashions an idealised landscape in which fecund soil is differentiated from fresh water, and perceived geographical aberrance from opportunity; in collaboration with the hand of the husbandman, a venturer 'shall goe to possesse a lande that floweth with milke

---

46 Klein, *Maps and the Writing of Space*, p. 112.
47 See 'confusion, n.' *OED Online*. Oxford University Press, June 2016 (last accessed 6 July 2016).
48 See Bernhard Klein, 'The Lie of the Land: English Surveyors, Irish Rebels and *The Faerie Queene*', *IUR*, 26.2 (1996), 207–25.
49 Sir Thomas Smith, *A Letter Sent by I.B. Gentleman* (London, 1572), sig. B1$^v$.

and hony', whereby the ambiguities associated with fluidity are forcibly rechannelled by the rhetoric and promises of biblical precedent.[50]

In a complementary rhetorical move by Stanihurst, the discourses of soil amendment are used both to address forms of agricultural practices unrecognisable to English eyes and to suggest a way of reforming what is perceived as a lack in the intellectual and devotional culture of the island's inhabitants.[51] A 'betle', or 'battle', soil is nourishing for use as pasture:

> Let the soile be as fertile and betle as anie would wish, yet if the husbandman will not manure it, sometime plow and eare it, sometime harrow it, sometime till it, sometime marle it, sometime delve it, sometime dig it, and sow it with good and sound corne, it will bring foorth weeds, bindcorne, cockle, darnell, brambles, briers, and sundrie wild shoots. So it fareth with the rude inhabitants of Ireland, they lacke universities, they want instructors, they are destitute of teachers, they are without preachers, they are devoid of all such necessaries as apperteine to the training up of youth.[52]

In the words of both Smith and Stanihurst, then, we see evidence of how colonising action was routinely associated with reshaping relationships between land, ethos, and opportunity: a trope that can be found in Homer's *Odyssey* in the critical description of the domain of the Cyclopes, 'who never plant with their own hands or plow the soil' and 'have no meeting place for council, no laws either', as well as in the prospecting approach to the offshore island that catches Odysseus's eye:

> No flocks browse, no plowlands roll with wheat;
> unplowed, unsown forever – empty of humankind –
> the island just feeds droves of bleating goats.
> ... No mean spot,
> it could bear you any crop you like in season.
> The water-meadows along the low foaming shore
> run soft and moist, and your vines would never flag.
> The land's clear for plowing. Harvest on harvest,
> a man could reap a healthy stand of grain –
> the subsoil's dark and rich.

---

50 Ibid., sig. D1ʳ. A similar likening of Ireland to the description of the promised land found in 'the eighth of Deuteronomy' is made by Sir John Davies in *A Discovery of the True Causes*. See *Ireland Under Elizabeth and James the First*, ed. Henry Morley (London: Routledge, 1890), pp. 213–42 (p. 341).
51 For a description of seasonal pastoral transhumance in Ireland ('booleying') see J.A. Watt, 'Gaelic Polity and Cultural Identity', in *A New History of Ireland, Volume II: Medieval Ireland 1169–1534*, ed. Art Cosgrove (Oxford: Oxford University Press, 2008), pp. 314–51 (pp. 331–2).
52 Richard Stanihurst, 'A Plaine and Perfect Description of Ireland', sig. B2ᵛ.

> There's a snug deep-water harbour there, what's more,
> no need for mooring-gear, no anchor-stones to heave,
> no cables to make fast. Just beach your keels, ride out
> the days till your shipmates' spirit stirs for open sea
> and a fair wind blows.⁵³

As Edward Casey observes, the word culture 'meant "place tilled" in Middle English, and the same word goes back to Latin *colere*, "to inhabit, care for, till, worship." To be cultural, to have a culture, is to inhabit a place sufficiently intensely to cultivate it'.⁵⁴ For Odysseus and his crew, the unmanaged fecundity of the isle offers temporary respite in which to reassert a land-based culture of hunting and feasting: however, if the perspective that initially reveals the island is that of careful labour and husbandry, the action then located there is that of unconcealed consumption. For Smith, as for Stanihurst and Spenser writing after him, Ireland was similarly fashioned as both 'wasteland' and promised land, and imagined, as Lupton observes, as 'a desert in order to defend its further wasting through systematic depopulation, geographic re-inscription, and georgic recolonisation'.⁵⁵ For all their instabilities and ambiguities, the fertile ecologies of Ireland were seen by the English as fundamentally generative, ultimately offering Spenser the scope to imagine work perceived as salvage.⁵⁶

## Surveying alluvial waters

Within the context of Book V's allegorical interest in degeneration, the challenge facing Artegall, who operates in a world 'runne quite out of square' (V.pro.1), seems to be to continue the work of the surveying angel, allotting to 'euery man his own'. As in the travails of those tasked with surveying the banks of the Nile, the thrust of Artegall's piecemeal labour is pitched against a cosmological battle in which the threat of formlessness and elemental indistinction unendingly resides.⁵⁷

---

53 Homer, *The Odyssey*, trans. Robert Fagles (London: Penguin, 2006), IX, lines 121, 125, 135–7, and 143–154.
54 Edward S. Casey, 'How to Get from Space to Place in a Fairly Short Stretch of Time: Phenomenological Prolegomena', in *Senses of Place*, ed. Steven Feld and Keith H. Basso (Santa Fe: SAR Press, 1996), pp. 13–52 (pp. 33–4).
55 Lupton, 'Mapping Mutability: or, Spenser's Irish Plot', p. 94.
56 For Spenser's play on the word 'saluage' and its 'connotations of law and land, being both littoral and literary' see Willy Maley, *Salvaging Spenser: Colonisation, Culture and Identity* (Basingstoke: Macmillan, 1997), p. 4.
57 For the threat levelled by the second canto's giant see Klein, *Maps and the Writing of*

In several episodes, including Artegall's encounter with the two sons of Milesio, Spenser evokes natural processes that are formalised in concepts found in Roman Law, namely *alluvion* and *avulsion*: alluvion, a gradual process whereby earthy matter suspended in water is transferred imperceptibly over time, contrasts with the trauma of avulsion, in which the form of littoral spaces is visibly and rapidly disturbed by part of a landmass being violently torn away by surrounding currents.[58] The force of avulsion, for example, can be likened to the threat of the second canto's giant: that is, to fill the encroaching sea with rocks in order to 'equalize againe' (V.ii.38) the relationship between land and water. Conversely, Spenser's earlier imitation of the opening of Lucretius's *De Rerum Natura* evokes the potential pleasures of alluvion; here, the goddess Venus oversees an enduring cosmology of playful interaction and balance, which eschews violent alteration in favour of temperate variation. When she spreads her

> ... mantle forth on hie,
> The waters play and pleasant lands appeare,
> And heauens laugh, and al the world shews ioyous cheare. (IV.x.44)

The goddess and the giant embody archetypal, even unexpectedly cognate, models of the way in which water and the continued forms of the 'daedale earth' (IV.x.45) can interact: processes which, the giant suggests, can be forcibly redesigned. The allegories of Book V, far from being obvious and clumsy, then, often hold together a variety of scales and perspectives.[59] The consequences of cosmic mutability play out within regional sites: a dynamic that Spenser also identifies in the behaviour of nations.

The immediate practical implications of alluvial movements are given voice by the Farmer in *The Surveyors Dialogue* when he attests to having seen the effects for himself:

> I know where great strife hath risen ..., where the sea hath woon and lost ground, and devoured the true bounds of which I am not alone witnes,

---

*Space*, pp. 168–9 and Anne Fogarty, 'Narrative Strategy in *The Faerie Queene*, Book VI', in *Edmund Spenser*, ed. Andrew Hadfield (London: Longman, 1996), pp. 196–210.

58 See *The Institutes of Justinian*, trans. John Baron Moyle, 5th edn (Oxford: Clarendon Press, 1913), pp. 38–9 and Robert D. Melville, *A Manual of the Principles of Roman Law Relating to Persons, Property and Obligations* (Edinburgh: Green, 1915), pp. 220–2. See also Andrew Zurcher, *Spenser's Legal Language* (Cambridge: Cambridge University Press, 2012), pp. 143–5.

59 Compare C.S. Lewis, *The Allegory of Love: A Study in Medieval Tradition* (New York: Oxford University Press, 1936; repr. 1958), pp. 348–9.

and it is dayly seene, the questions do rise by like casualties, where townes, houses, fields, woods, and much land hath been and are dayly devoured, and in some places augmented, Rivers by force turned out of their right courses, upon other confining lands; whereof time hath taken such hold, as the truth is now brought in question, to the stirring up of quarrels betweene parties, which if these places had been formerly laid out in plot, the doubt would be easily answered.[60]

In V.iv of *The Faerie Queene*, such 'great strife' is reflected in the brief history recounted to Artegall by Amidas and Bracidas: an interlude that has long been recognised as an allegory of an aspect of the relationship between England and Ireland, wherein the plotting of the narrative across two shape-shifting islands suggests 'an allegorical rendering of the English appropriation of Irish land', as Clare Carroll has argued.[61] Arriving in time to observe the fraternal quarrel escalate to violence, the Knight of Justice makes enquiries concerning the origin of the dissent:

> To whom the elder did this aunswere frame;
>    Then weete ye Sir, that we two brethren be,
>    To whom our sire, *Milesio* by name,
>    Did equally bequeath his lands in fee,
>    Two Ilands, which ye there before you see
>    Not farre in sea; of which the one appeares
>    But like a little Mount of small degree;
>    Yet was as great and wide ere many yeares,
> As that same other Isle, that greater bredth now beares.
>
> But tract of time, that all things doth decay,
>    And this deuouring Sea, that naught doth spare,
>    The most part of my land hath washt away,
>    And throwne it vp vnto my brothers share:
> So his encreased, but mine did empaire. (V.iv.7-8)

As Artegall discovers, surveying the state of the islands from the privileged perspective of a further shore, the movement of the silt and soil of the littoral appears to have happened abruptly, only to be relived as formalised gain and loss once the grievances are heard. The judgement Artegall goes on to make concerning the distribution of persons and assets ultimately defers to the action of the sea, which may 'dispose by his imperiall might,/ As thing at randon left, to whom he list' (V.iv.19).

---

60 John Norden, *The Surveyors Dialogue* (London, 1607), sig. C2ᵛ.
61 See Clare Carroll, 'Spenser and the Irish Language: The Sons of Milesio in *A View of the Present State of Ireland*, *The Faerie Queene*, Book V and the *Leabhar Gabhála*', *IUR*, 26.2 (1996), 281-90, p. 289.

In its representation of alluvial and avulsive movement, Spenser's tale of the two sons of Milesio may offer a complex fusion of the English, Roman, and Brehon laws of the sea, but it also offers a reflection on the relationship between two insular nations.[62] The geopolitical implications of the allegory come into greater focus when read alongside a moment in Sir John Hayward's *A Treatise of Union of the Two Realmes of England and Scotland* (1604), which advocates union between nations as a source of peace and Una-like goodness; 'all true testimonies doe agree', he writes, citing a litany of classical authorities, 'that the greatest perfection of glory, beautie, stabilitie or strength, is either occasioned by union, or therein found'.[63] Printed shortly after his release from prison following the death of Elizabeth I, the text uses an alluvial analogy to figure the risks, which Hayward downplays, of uniting the English and Scottish systems of government: he is, of course, thinking diplomatically, and in terms of a transaction of equals, rather than in terms of colonial conquest. He looks to the motions of the natural world to explain the complex idea of self-identity and endurance within formal alteration. Union and exchange can occur, he writes, 'so long as the people doe remaine the same, and loose no point of their libertie and honor':

> as a field remaineth the same which looseth upon one part by alluvion of waters, and winneth upon the other: or as it remaineth the same sea, which leaveth one part of earth, and possesseth another: or as it remaineth the same river which doth altogether change the channell.[64]

Hayward's insistence on the retention of continuity and integrity contrasts with Spenser's far more ambivalent use of alluvial figures and wetlandscapes throughout his poetic and political works. Although Hayward is typically highly attuned to the formal, political, and cultural problems of 'debateable' lands, his image of alluvion flows uncritically into an image of rivers changing channels.[65] In the writings of both Hayward and Spenser, then, the suggestive contemplation of wetland forms, of

---

62 See Roland M. Smith, 'Spenser's Tale of the Two Sons of Milesio', *MLQ*, 3 (1942), pp. 547–57.
63 John Hayward, *A Treatise of Union of the Two Realmes of England and Scotland* (London, 1604), sig. B1ᵛ.
64 Ibid., sig. H1ᵛ.
65 See Christopher N. Warren, *Literature and the Law of Nations, 1580–1680* (Oxford: Oxford University Press, 2015), p. 101. The term 'debateable lands' draws on two distinct etymologies, suggesting respectively conflict and pasture: see 'debatable, adj. and n.' *OED Online*. Oxford University Press, June 2018 (last accessed 1 August 2018) and 'battable, adj.1.' *OED Online*. Oxford University Press, June 2018 (last accessed 1 August 2018).

shifting currents informing the arrangement of land and water, stands in for a parallel narrative concerning the negotiations between states.[66] If diplomacy can contain alluvial process, then the effects of colonialism suggest avulsive force.

For Spenser, changeable hydrographic features tend to become focal points for thinking about different kinds of betrayal: an anxiety that stimulates discussions concerning control. By virtue of their arrival by the secret means of 'their hidden race' (IV.xi.40) at the river marriage in Book IV, for example, the Irish rivers tell of a world outside the carefully constructed artifice of *The Faerie Queene*: as Richard A. McCabe has pithily commented, channelling the words of Richard Helgerson: 'in chorographical terms "the land speaks", but in reading Spenser it is essential to remember that most Irish land "spoke" Gaelic'.[67] In spite of their fluidity and fecundity, the Irish waters are non-navigable to linguistic strangers. In Spenser's poem 'Colin Clouts Come Home Againe', the devious river Bregog, the lover of Mulla, poses a related linguistic problem: he is 'So hight because of this deceitfull traine,/ Which he with *Mulla* wrought to win delight' (118–19). By eschewing silence for fecund mythmaking, Spenser capitalises on the river's fluid ambivalence for his own purposes, thus continuing his fluxive and riverine conversations with Ralegh: Bregog's treacherous liaison, as previous critics have explained, may have been understood by Spenser's early readers as a representation of Ralegh's unauthorised marriage to Elizabeth Throckmorton, which was regarded by Elizabeth I as a betrayal and presaged his subsequent fall from favour.[68] Spenser's ability to synthesise etymologies has been noted by many critics and Bregog, named from the Irish word for a lie or deception, *bréag*, suits Spenser's crafty manipulation of the landscape owing to the space for play invited by the implied hydrographical lack of fixity.[69]

---

66 See Annabel S. Brett, *Changes of State: Nature and the Limits of the City in Early Modern Natural Law* (Princeton: Princeton University Press, 2011), pp. 221–4.
67 Richard A. McCabe, *Spenser's Monstrous Regiment: Elizabethan Ireland and the Poetics of Difference* (Oxford: Oxford University Press, 2002), p. 201.
68 See James Nohrnberg, 'Britomart's Gone Abroad to Brute-land, Colin Clout's Come Courting from the Salvage Ire-Land: Exile and the Kingdom in Some of Spenser's Fictions for "Crossing Over"', in *Edmund Spenser: New and Renewed Directions*, ed. J.B. Lethbridge (Madison: Fairleigh Dickinson University Press, 2006), pp. 214–85 (pp. 269–74).
69 See Willy Maley, 'Spenser's Languages: Writing in the Ruins of English', in *The Cambridge Companion to Spenser*, ed. Andrew Hadfield (Cambridge: Cambridge University Press, 2001), pp. 162–79. See also Joan Fitzpatrick, 'Marrying Waterways: Politicizing and Gendering the Landscape', in *Archipelagic Identities*, ed. Philip Schwyzer and Simon Mealor (Aldershot: Ashgate, 2004), pp. 81–91.

As Patrick Weston Joyce notes, place-names in Ireland are often closely associated with the character of the land and waterscape:

> *Brég* is an Irish word meaning a falsehood, and in various forms it is applied to rivers that are subject to sudden and dangerous floods or which flow through deep quagmires; signifying, in this application, deceitful or treacherous. ... Trawbreaga Bay at Malin in the north of Donegal is so called (Trawbreaga meaning the strand of falsehood or treachery) because the tide rises there so suddenly that it has often swept away people walking incautiously on the shore.[70]

For Spenser, Bregog's dissembling passage prompts imaginative if not physical appropriation: in the description of how the river's broken streams 'into the *Mullaes* water slide' (144), a subterranean coupling leaves no surface visible trace.[71] In the manipulation of topographical feature and toponymical matter, Spenser imitates the 'onomastic and aetiological tendencies' of '*dinnshenchas*': a tradition of writing place and name in Ireland that formed an important part of a literary, historical, and cultural education.[72] The name and nature of Bregog comes to stand for the poet as a figure of betrayal over which he, as poet and maker, has illusory control.[73]

The idea of 'walking incautiously on the shore' offers a prompt for thinking about the kind of writing that channels a desire to control passage across and around littoral, and potentially alluvial, spaces. A waterlogged interest in gaining traction, for example, can be found in the majority of early modern descriptions of Ireland written by Englishmen. In the *Itinerary* of Fynes Moryson, who served as a secretary to Lord Deputy Mountjoy, the terrain may not exhibit the same level of ethical

---

70 Patrick Weston Joyce, 'Spenser's Irish Rivers', in *The Wonders of Ireland and Other Papers on Irish Subjects* (London: Longmans, Green, and Co., 1911), pp. 72–114 (p. 111).
71 Andrews notes the difficulties rivers posed to English surveyors owing to the ways in which they accrued 'a bewildering variety of aliases' from the places through which they passed. See *Shapes of Ireland*, p. 16.
72 Gerry Smyth, *Space and the Irish Cultural Imagination* (Basingstoke: Palgrave, 2001), p. 48. Roland M. Smith argues that Spenser must have known the legends of the area he made his home. See 'Spenser's Irish River Stories', *PMLA*, 50.4 (1935), pp. 1047–56. The song of 'Crotta Cliach', the old name for the Galtee mountains in Munster, for example, tells of a place where 'a man of the fairies made music'. See *The Metrical Dindshenchas*, trans. Edward Gwynn, Vol. 3 (Dublin: Hodges Figgis, 1913), p. 225. For Spenser's engagement with bardic culture see Christopher Highley, *Shakespeare, Spenser and the Crisis in Ireland* (Cambridge: Cambridge University Press, 1997), pp. 20–39.
73 See Donald Cheney, 'Colin Clout's Homecoming: The Imaginative Travels of Edmund Spenser', *Connotations*, 7.2 (1997/98), 146–58, pp. 153–4.

and allegorical framing typically employed by Spenser, but the residue of inconstancy remains. Ireland is no *terra firma* but a place in which every aspect of the unsolid ground seems to hinder the safe passage of foreign travellers. As he writes:

> The land of Ireland is uneven, mountainous, soft, watry, woody, and open to windes and flouds of raine, and so fenny, as it has Bogges upon the very tops of Mountaines, not bearing man or beast, but dangerous to passe, and such Bogs are frequent over all Ireland. Our Marriners observe the sayling into to be more dangerous not onely because many tides meeting, makes the sea apt to swell upon any storme, but especially because they ever find the coast of Ireland covered with mists, whereas the coast of England is commonly cleare, and to be seene farre off.[74]

Even the weather colludes against the will of the English mariner, Moryson suggests, where dense vapours provide atmospheric cover for a country that keeps its secrets. Unlike in the vision of Rome with which this chapter opened, water seeps into spaces that are meant to be solid, causing anxiety and confusion, occluding places to walk and to make landfall in safety.

A similar articulation of coastal appropriation is notoriously found in *A View*. Spenser is alert to the fecundity of Ireland and the potentially strategic placement of the country's shores. It is:

> adorned with goodly woodes fitt for buildinge of howsses and shipps so comodiously as that if some princes in the worlde had them they woulde sone hope to be Lordes of all the seas and ere longe of all the worlde Allsoe full of verye good portes and havens openinge vppon Englande and Skotlande as invitinge vs to Come vnto them to see what excellente Comodities that Countrye Cane afforde, besides the soile it self moste fertile fit to yealde all kinde of fruite/ that shallbe committed thearevnto (p. 62).

A fructifying landscape emerges, dispossessed of all inhabitants, and redolent of the island on which Odysseus makes profitable landfall before facing Polyphemus. Navigable harbours gape in welcome and fertile soils promise full harvests and timber for the construction of habitation and shipping. The passage holds latent promise of movement and expansion, safe passage, and access to the materials that will facilitate future traversal and conquest: as Peter Remien pithily observes, the 'instrumental view of matter' posited here is a reminder to the reader that 'without an abun-

---

74 Fynes Moryson, *An Itinerary* (London, 1617), Part III, p. 159.

dant supply of timber for the construction of fleets of ships, Agamemnon, Odysseus, and Aeneas would remain forever landlocked'.[75] The poet-propagandist's sense that those in control of Ireland's natural resources could become 'lords of all the seas' is both an enticing challenge to Spenser's own monarch and a veiled threat that another might seize them first: a reminder that the powers of Catholic Spain also desired Ireland's assets and saw its proximity to England as a vantage point for invasion.[76]

The rhetorical opening up of the landscape to an imperialist eye participates in the relationship between cartography and conquest, and provides an example of the 'sanguine assurances' Hillary Eklund finds in colonial texts that ask their readers to see 'amphibious landscapes ... as pastoral and agrarian paradises ready for optimization'.[77] When Luke Gernon addressed his 'Discourse of Ireland' (c. 1620) to an anonymous friend, for example, his aim seemed to be to make his view present for the reader; evoking the bonds of homosocial friendship,[78] his rhetorical choices and mode of address charge his description with an eroticised immediacy:

> Ireland shall be my theame, not so much because I am resident there, as for this cause that it will be most appropryated to your love, for though you would not look into Ireland but for me, yett when you look after me, your imaginacion transports yourself into Ireland. Do you look that I should describe the clymat, the degrees, the scituation, the longitude, the latitude, the temperature, etc. Go look in your mapps, I must have a more quaynt and genuine devise.[79]

His address is initially teasing; it is for reasons of his own presence in Ireland that the country 'will be most appropryated' by his addressee's love. This flirtatious glimpse is gradually redirected as a penetrating gaze,

---

75 Remien, 'Silvan Matters', p. 127 and p. 128.
76 See Wallace T. MacCaffrey, *Elizabeth I: War and Politics, 1588–1603* (Princeton: Princeton University Press, 1992), p. 10.
77 Hillary Eklund, 'Wetlands Reclamation and the Fate of the Local in Seventeenth-Century England', in *Groundwork: English Renaissance Literature and Soil Science* (Pittsburgh: Duquesne University Press, 2017), pp. 149–70 (p. 156). See also Mercedes Camino, '"Methinks I See an Evil Lurk Unespied": Visualizing Conquest in Spenser's *A View of the Present State of Ireland*', *Spenser Studies*, 12 (1990), 169–94 and John Breen, 'The Empirical Eye: Edmund Spenser's *A View of The Present State of Ireland*', *The Irish Review*, 16 (1994), 44–52.
78 For the homosocial bonds of the English in Ireland see Highley, *Shakespeare, Spenser and the Crisis in Ireland*, pp. 117–26.
79 Luke Gernon, 'A Discourse of Ireland', in *Illustrations of Irish History and Topography, Mainly of the Seventeenth Century*, ed. C. Litton Falkiner (London: Longmans, Green, and Co., 1904), pp. 348–62 (pp. 348–9).

and by dismissing the kinds of mapping practices that purport to be objective reflections of the terrain displayed, Gernon finally promises to offer his reader a mode of imaginative transport; in imitation of an image of Europe that has impressed itself on his own imagination, he proposes a device that will depict Ireland 'in the lineaments of a naked woman'. The resulting account voyeuristically blends topography with the female form, whereby the literary cartographer's 'personal curvature' performs an expression of sexualised proclivity in which the reader is invited to share:

> This Nymph of Ireland, is at all poynts like a yong wenche that hath the greene sicknes for want of occupying. ... Her flesh is of a softe and delicat mould of earthe, and her blew vaynes trayling through every part of her like ryvoletts. ... And betwixt her leggs (for Ireland is full of havens), she hath an open harbor, but not much frequented.[80]

Gernon's choice of malady to describe what he perceives as the country's needs is particularly striking. Lesel Dawson writes of how the female affliction of green sickness, as distinct from lovesickness, was thought to occur as 'the result of a bodily dysfunction', the cure for which was a physical unblocking through intercourse.[81] Gernon's 'quaynt and genuine devise' is to build to an image of the nymph's genitals; the soft fertile soils and trailing rivers of Ireland make up her translucent flesh and Gernon imagines future successful conquest as a restoration and regulation of circulation and passage.[82] She is not intact, only in possession of a body 'not much frequented': as a woman already open to conquest, she performs the role of singular object of desire and site of multiple openings, all of which, in Gernon's vision, invite use.[83] The nymph's own desire is situated by the author at the level of unconscious physical

---

80   Gernon, 'A Discourse of Ireland', pp. 349–50.
81   Lesel Dawson, *Lovesickness and Gender in Early Modern English Literature* (Oxford: Oxford University Press, 2008), p. 52.
82   For the 'woman-as-land trope' see Joan Fitzpatrick, *Irish Demons: English Writings on Ireland, the Irish, and Gender by Spenser and his Contemporaries* (Lanham: University Press of America, 2000), pp. 21–3. For the scatological connections made between Irish geography and female anatomy see Bernhard Klein, 'Partial Views: Shakespeare and the Map of Ireland', *EMLS*, 4.2 (1998), 5.1–20 (6). For female liquidity and leakiness see Gail Kern Paster, *The Body Embarrassed: Drama and the Disciplines of Shame in Early Modern England* (New York: Cornell University Press, 1993), pp. 23–63.
83   A more aggressively pragmatic version of this argument, specifically concerning maritime trade and the movement of soldiers, is made by the anonymous author of the earlier work, 'A Discourse of Ireland' (c. 1599). See David B. Quinn, '"A Discourse of Ireland" (Circa 1599): A Sidelight on English Colonial Policy', *Proceedings of the Royal Irish Academy. Section C*, 47 (1941/1942), 151–66 (pp. 161–3).

demand and her disease is one that can be ameliorated only by admitting the arrivals at her borders. Ultimately, she is all wetland: a 'quaynt', rather than 'genuine', device indeed.

For Spenser's questing knights, whose restless forward motion is typically lauded, the act of making landfall is particularly charged. The memory of Guyon's voyages in Book II, and his arrival at false insular paradises ripe with tempting pleasures, underlies the voyaging of Artegall, whose movements are pervaded by the persistent resonance of his predecessor's failings. McCabe has remarked, for example, on how Gernon's expression of the 'louche eroticism of conquest' appears reversed in Spenser's fashioning of Book II's Bower of Bliss, where the temptations of a landscape shaped by fantasies of New World conquest threaten to overwhelm Spenser's protagonists.[84] In Book V, perhaps as a strategy of containment, Spenser anticipates the terms of Gernon's fantasy by fashioning an image of an aspect of Ireland in the form of a young virtuous woman, Irena, who embodies the goal of Artegall's quest and, as such, also functions as another shadowing of Gloriana. Spenser's allegory makes the association with the virgin monarch possible only by limiting its reach; as a figure who 'encompasses both the fluxive, seductive female body and Ireland' Irena resides, in McLeod's words, 'on the brink of unnaturalness', which suggests her potential to shadow treacherous or even pathological desires of her own.[85] The narrator emphasises how her movements are determined by others, and she ultimately remains a passive prize, awaiting rescue 'on th'appointed tyde' (V.xi.39).

In spite of the bitter return journey, which culminates in Artegall's shameful encounter with 'Enuie' and 'Detraction', the final cantos of Book V begin optimistically: his labour to 'worke *Irenaes* franchisement,/ And eke *Grantortoes* worthy punishment' (V.xi.36) is renewed and Spenser's narrative is back on course after 'other great aduentures .../ Had it forslackt' (V.xii.3). Having made his way to the sea shore and commandeered a ship, Artegall is ready for the voyage to Irena's land:

> Tho when they came to the sea coast, they found
>  A ship all readie (as good fortune fell)
>  To put to sea, with whom they did compound,

---

84 McCabe, *Spenser's Monstrous Regiment*, p. 138.
85 McLeod, *The Geography of Empire*, p. 59. As Kaara L. Peterson observes, desire 'in female virgins is understood as a pathology, in pointed contrast to the construction of desire in men as relatively chivalric and heroic'. See 'Fluid Economies: Portraying Shakespeare's Hysterics', *Mosaic*, 34.1 (2001), 35–59, p. 42. Quoted by Dawson in *Lovesickness and Gender*, p. 47.

> To passe them ouer, where them list to tell:
> The winde and weather serued them so well,
> That in one day they with the coast did fall;
> Whereas they readie found them to repell,
> Great hostes of men in order martiall,
> Which them forbad to land, and footing did forstall.
>
> But nathemore would they from land refraine,
> But when as nigh vnto the shore they drew,
> That foot of man might sound the bottome plaine,
> *Talus* into the sea did forth issew,
> Though darts from shore and stones they at him threw;
> And wading through the waues with stedfast sway,
> Maugre the might of all those troupes in vew,
> Did win the shore, whence he them chast away,
> And made to fly, like doues, whom the Eagle doth affray. (V.xii.4–5)

The description of the voyage itself is over quickly; there is no rough weather to delay the mariners' progress or atmospheric interference to occlude the place of arrival. In order to 'win the shore' as soon the depth makes human inhabitation possible, Talus meets the shallow seabed as if, for a moment, the iron man has the capacity to act as a plummet, or lead and line. The scale implied suggests Talus's manlike build; yet, the stanza's syntax frames him as a surrogate that replaces the vulnerable human bodies for whom the passage would be more fraught.[86] He resists the defensive assault mounted from the shoreline as if his presence is instrumental, eliciting the depth of water and gauging the safety of the approach. As Dee explains in his *General and Rare Memorials Pertayning to the Perfect Arte of Navigation* (1577), the physical and epistemological actions implied by such 'Sowndings, and Serchings' are practices of hydrographical expertise associated with possession and control (see sig. A4$^r$).

In his guise as a machine of war, Talus bears an uncanny resemblance to the kinds of armoured submarine figures found in illustrated editions of Vegetius's *De Re Militari* (see Figure 8).[87]

---

86 Jessica Wolfe coins the term 'inhumanism' in reference to Spenser's 'iron man'. See *Humanism, Machinery, and Renaissance Literature* (Cambridge: Cambridge University Press, 2004), p. 203.

87 See Michael West, 'Spenser, Everard Digby, and the Renaissance Art of Swimming', *RQ*, 26.1 (1973), 11–22, pp. 21–2. Highley has argued that the moment shadows the historical capture of the fort at Smerwick: a reading that elides Talus's 'amphibious force' with the seaborne actions of Sir Richard Bingham, 'the Flail of Connaught'. See *Shakespeare, Spenser and the Crisis in Ireland*, p. 120.

*Figure 8* Flavius Vegetius Renatus. 'Submarine Knight', in *Du Fait de Guerre* (*De Re Militari*) (Paris, 1536), p. cxiv.

He is notably indifferent to the fear identified by McCabe that manifests elsewhere in the poem, whereby 'the landscape ... may, at any moment, assimilate person to place through some bizarre stroke of Ovidian metamorphosis – as in the case of Fradubio and Fraelissa (1.2.30–44) – thereby realizing the colonists' deepest fears'.[88] Where Guyon and even Artegall have a more ambivalent relationship to water, the immersion enacted by Talus reinforces his impenetrable quality; the 'stedfast sway' of his movement through salt water emphasises his invulnerability to sexual, spiritual, and ethical uncertainty. Unlike the Redcrosse Knight, whose removal of armour in Book I is associated with moral looseness and liquidity, Talus's iron frame and flail remain watertight, his resolve not subject to dissolution or corrosion.[89] When read as a further instance of Talus's 'vnpittied spoyle', last seen at the end of the previous canto, in which a 'scattred crew/ Into the sea he droue quite from that soyle' (V.xi.65), the lingering vision is of irretrievable displacement and an avulsive dispersion of persons as well as place.[90] For a writer of epic allegorical romance, the metaphorical displacement, or *translatio*, implicit in the use of figurative language permeates and amplifies narrative movement.[91]

## Spatial freedom

The distinction Moryson makes between the insular neighbours, as described above, which compares the occluded coasts of Ireland with the open clarity of familiar English shores, figures an implicit contrariness that is made explicit in Spenser's *View*. Eudoxus's perception of Ireland's problems, for example, is articulated using vocabulary drawn from applied geometry: the 'realmes government', he explains, is 'evill plotted', and 'thoroughe other ouersight run more out of square to that disorder which it is now Come vnto'. Irenaeus's sense of the futility of replacing such ordinances with 'peaceable plottes to redresse the same' (p. 146) uses the language of surveying as if to criticise the integrity of

---

88 McCabe, *Spenser's Monstrous Regiment*, p. 57.
89 For Spenser's interest in the 'metaphoric implications of *dissolute*' see Harold L. Weatherby, 'Pourd out in Loosnesse', *Spenser Studies*, 3 (1982), 73–85.
90 Thomas Herron observes the echo of the scattered ships of the Armada. See 'The Spanish Armada, Ireland, and Spenser's *The Faerie Queene*', *New Hibernia Review*, 6.2 (2002), 82–105, p. 84. See also Michael West, 'Spenser's Art of War: Chivalric Allegory, Military Technology, and the Elizabethan Mock-Heroic Sensibility', *RQ*, 41.4 (1988), 654–704.
91 See Galbraith, *Architectonics of Imitation*, pp. 1–28, pp. 59–62, and pp. 72–4.

the initial projection. In addition, Eudoxus's complaint that disorder increases exponentially, 'like as to indirecte lynes', which 'the further they are drawen out, the further they goe asunder' (p. 146), presents an image that is cognate with *The Faerie Queene*'s monstrously deformed Ate, the 'mother of debate,/ And all dissention' (IV.i.19). Unrecognisable as Homer's swift divinity, whose 'feet are soft, and move/ Not on the earth',[92] Spenser's Ate is characterised by the 'contrarie' motion of her 'misplast' (IV.i.28) feet, which threatens to rend her malformed body in two. As more than an agent of delusion and folly in Spenser's fiction, she stands in for an emblem of the body politic on which Spenser's geopolitical allegories and desires can be mapped:[93] a misshapen and desexualised sister-image, perhaps, to Gernon's grotesque cartographical fantasy.

One of the first myths that Robert Payne wished to counter in a propaganda piece designed to encourage English interest in plantation, *A Brief Description of Ireland* (1589), was the rumour that 'there is great danger in travelling the countrie, and much more to dwell or inhabite there'.[94] As Smyth comments, 'spatial freedom – to be able to move freely across and between landscapes and territories – is a good indication of power'.[95] This plays out in Book V of *The Faerie Queene* in the way that Britomart's movements become increasingly associated with urgency and violence. On leaving the house of Dolon accompanied by Talus, she is confronted by Dolon's two surviving sons as they guard a fortified bridge over a river: the same 'perillous Bridge,/ On which *Pollente* with *Artegall* did fight' (V.vi.36). Galloping between them, she makes a passage as swift and destructive as lightning through a pair of oaks:

> As when the flashing Leuin haps to light
> Vppon two stubborne oakes, which stand so neare,
> That way betwixt them none appeares in sight;
> The Engin fiercely flying forth, doth teare
> Th'one from the earth, and through the aire doth beare;
> The other it with force doth ouerthrow,

---

[92] See Homer, *The Iliad*, trans. George Chapman, ed. Adam Roberts (Hertfordshire: Wordsworth, 2003), 19: 92–3 and 'Ate' in Jenny March, *Cassell Dictionary of Classical Mythology* (London: Cassell, 1998; repr. 2002), p. 76. For Ate as 'a walking trochee' see Debra Fried, 'Spenser's Caesura', *ELR*, 11.3 (1981), 261–80, p. 274.

[93] See Jonathan Goldberg, *Endlesse Worke: Spenser and the Structures of Discourse* (Baltimore: Johns Hopkins University Press, 1981), p. 98. See also Richard Neuse, 'Book IV as Conclusion to *The Faerie Queene*', *ELH*, 35.3 (1968), 329–53, pp. 336–7.

[94] Robert Payne, *A Brief Description of Ireland* (London, 1589), sig. A1ᵛ.

[95] Smyth, *Map Making, Landscapes and Memory*, p. 25. For the relationship between mobility, modernity, and surveillance see Tim Cresswell, *On the Move: Mobility in the Modern Western World* (New York: Routledge, 2006), pp. 12–21.

> Vppon one side, and from his rootes doth reare.
> So did the Championesse those two there strow,
> And to their sire their carcasses left to bestow. (V.vi.40)

Her passage marks an unusual moment in the poem's topography in that the bridge is one of the rare places that is encountered for a second time. The initial image of a dramatic natural phenomenon almost masks the subsequent simile that likens her assault to an act of engineered extirpation, in which dense ancient forest is cleared in order to create a passing place. Her violent ease here contrasts with Artegall's labours four cantos earlier, when he had to fight in the 'dangerous deepe' (V.ii.8) below the bridge with Pollente.[96] This previous fight only ends when Artegall beheads his opponent:

> But *Artegall* pursewd him still so neare,
>   With bright Chrysaor in his cruell hand,
>   That as his head he gan a litle reare
>   Aboue the brincke, to tread vpon the land,
>   He smote it off, that tumbling on the strand
>   It bit the earth for very fell despight,
>   And gnashed with his teeth, as if he band
>   High God, whose goodnesse he despaired quight,
> Or curst the hand, which did that vengeance on him dight. (V.ii.18)

The death of Pollente occurs in the movement from water to land. As a bridge-guardian, a role 'presided over by the gods Janus and Portunus',[97] he is killed at an ecotonal transition: a death that draws attention to boundaries in the natural world and to the legal and social borders demarcated by the man-made structure and the treacherous trapdoor leading to the river below.

The misuse of the bridge and the mode of Pollente's death at the brink suggests a kind of dishonour and sullying: within Spenser's allegory, as Quitslund writes, a proximity to muddy slime recalls the way in which an 'essential evil seems to reside within the element of earth when it symbolizes the mortal body' even though 'the same element properly tempered will be fruitful'.[98] By sinking his teeth into the waterlogged land, Pollente meets his demise in a manner that anticipates the subsequent death of

---

96 For Artegall's skill as a swimmer and Pollente's fear of drowning see Michael West, 'Spenser, Everard Digby, and the Renaissance Art of Swimming'.
97 W.H. Herendeen, 'Bridges', in *SEnc*, p. 111.
98 Quitslund, *Spenser's Supreme Fiction*, pp. 165–6. See also Kendrick, 'Earth of Flesh, Flesh of Earth: Mother Earth in *The Faerie Queene*', p. 546.

Munera, who, having had her metallic 'suppliant hands' and feet cut off and 'nayld on high' (V.ii.26), is thrown by Talus from a castle wall and left to drown in 'the durty mud' (V.ii.27). Although the motif has classical and biblical origins, its place in Spenser's poetry is also fully complicit in the historical realities of warfare.[99] In the case of both Pollente and Munera, the deaths fit a paradigm identified by Rod Giblett in his discussion of the wishes made by American soldiers in Vietnam to make a clean death:

> A filthy death ... in a wet land or in excrement, on the one hand, is feared as the ultimate horror by the heroic who desire a clean and proper death, and on the other hand is desired as the appropriate gesture by the anti-heroic who desire a filthy and improper death as the ultimate act of rebellion ... as a way of representing the truth about a shitty war.[100]

The threat of a muddied death was ever-present in Ireland, as Sir Thomas Smith observed: the men employed by the Lord Deputy, he writes, are 'alwayes constrayned, to march thorow the Bogges and rivers' and miserably tasked 'to apprehend the Rebelles bodies, following them thorowe Bogge, thorowe plaine'.[101] In Spenser's poem, Artegall's opponents are deliberately shamed as well as destroyed. Although they fulfil antagonistic roles in Spenser's plotting, the human cost they shadow and the strain they place on the workings of allegory are a reminder of the bloody and relentless struggle of the Munster wars and the violence of re-forming local custom while establishing the Munster settlement.[102] The progress of Artegall's rough justice, followed by Britomart's violent reshaping, channels the attempts at erasure and reformation advocated by the English administration to remake the Irish landscape and its people in its chosen image.

As Smyth notes, 'Spenser's use of mapping metaphors ... goes so deep as to imagine the process of the reformation of the Irish and Irish landscape as the equivalent of drawing a new map on a blank surface and

---

99 See Fitzpatrick, *Irish Demons*, pp. 101–28 and *FQ*, note to V.ii.18 (p. 518).
100 Giblett, *Postmodern Wetlands*, p. 134. R.B. Outhwaite describes the Nine Years' War, from the perspective of the English professional soldiers, as 'the most hated war of their era: England's Vietnam'. See 'Dearth, the English Crown and the "Crisis of the 1590s"', in *The European Crisis of the 1590s: Essays in Comparative History*, ed. Peter Clark (London: Allen & Unwin, 1985), pp. 23–43 (p. 32). For another example of the connection between mud and abjection in warfare see Santanu Das, 'Slimescapes', in *Touch and Intimacy in First World War Literature* (Cambridge: Cambridge University Press, 2008), pp. 35–72.
101 Sir Thomas Smith, *A Letter Sent by I.B. Gentleman*, sig. F2ʳ.
102 See Charles Stanley Ross, *The Custom of the Castle: From Malory to Macbeth* (Berkeley: University of California Press, 1997), p. 175.

remodelling the whole terrain, both natural and cultural'.[103] In articulating a desire to reform 'all that is worne out of fashion' (p. 146) in *A View*, Spenser imagines a wholesale remaking, whereby problems of government, imaged as divergent lines, could be brought to a newly established centre. For Spenser, a reformed Ireland was not necessarily a blank space but a plot of geometrically perfect roads and bridges that enabled ordered and safe passage for Elizabeth's agents. The author's terms seek control of the sightlines within the landscape by allowing no opportunity for deviation: as Irenaeus proposes, new roads should be 'laide open' through woodland only for 'all higeh waies' to be 'fenced and shutt vp on bothe sides'. Fords should be 'marred and split so as none mighte passe anie other waye'. A desire to lay things bare in clear sight is juxtaposed with a need for the protections made available by enclosure and fortification: 'in all stretes and narrowe passages as betwene Two Boggs or thoroughe anie depe forde or vnder anye mountaine side theare shoulde be some litle fortilage or woden Castle set which shoulde kepe and Comaunde that streighte' (p. 224). Irenaeus's suggestions do not confer a sense of 'spatial freedom' but rather its opposite: a landscape whose closure and restriction is designed to limit unregimented motion.

Spenser's plotting is designed to limit undesirable movement, characterised by Irenaeus's perception that, like Saxon England, Ireland's wastes and passing places are lawless, 'euerie Corner havinge a Robin hoode in it that kepte the woodes and spoilled all passengers and inhabitantes' (pp. 202–3). By the late sixteenth century this archetypal figure of transgression had developed several characteristic facets, defined in part by his relationship to the distinctive regional landscape of Sherwood Forest, from the mischievous folk-hero of fifteenth-century popular ballads and festive misrule to the politicised figure known for resisting authority. For Spenser, the singular 'Robin Hood', as a man of many guises, stands in for a people complicit in the perceived anarchic dimensions of the terrain, redolent of the greenwood and outlawry.[104] For the physician George Bate, who wrote a description of Cromwell's Irish wars in the next century, a similar motif recurs in his descriptions of the tendency of peoples of 'barbarous Nations' to avoid an invading gaze via their place-specific knowledge:

---

103 Smyth, *Map Making, Landscapes and Memory*, p. 45.
104 See Peter Stallybrass, 'Robin Hood, the Carnivalesque and the Rhetoric of Violence', in *The Violence of Representation: Literature and the History of Violence*, ed. Nancy Armstrong and Leonard Tennenhouse (London: Routledge, 1989), pp. 45–76.

they betake themselves to the Mountains, Desarts, Bogs and Rocks, according as the Countrey is naturally fortified, declare War against all other Mortals, and live by Rapine. ... They are a kind of land Pirats; who wandring amongst Lakes and Bogs, according to the light-footedness of the Nation, they safely skip over the Quagmires and loose ground, wherein strangers unacquainted with the places that follow them commonly stick.[105]

The characteristics of Bate's 'land Pirats' are recognisable in Artegall's Protean adversary Malengin, who dances like a wild goat in places 'where footing was so ill' (V.ix.15). The space and movements associated with his 'hollow caue' indicate that he is kin to Ate, for 'some doe say, it goeth downe to hell' and 'full of wyndings is', where 'none can backe returne, that once are gone amis' (V.ix.6). The guileful figure of the souterrain's inhabitant embodies the *genius loci* of the environment and his changeable cunning finds a parallel in Spenser description of the fleeting Irish rebel in *A View*: the 'flyinge enemye' who hides 'him self in woodes and bogges from whence he will not drawe forthe but into some streighte passage or perilous forde' (p. 151).[106] Once again, the later writers find common ground in the work of Gerald of Wales, who observes in *The Conquest of Ireland* that the eleventh-century Norman invasion only succeeded in part: 'for the soile and countrie in France is plaine, open, and champaine; but in these parts it is rough, rockie, full of hils, woods, and bogs'. Heavy armour cannot be worn 'where the fight and triall' is in such places and where the men have not been trained to fight adversaries who are 'verie nimble and quicke of bodie, and light of foot'.[107]

When offering a potential definition of the distinct connotations of 'space' and 'place', Doreen Massey writes of how the '"retreat to place" represents a protective pulling up of drawbridges and a building of walls

---

105 George Bate, *A Short Historical Account of the Rise and Progress of the Late Troubles in England* (London, 1685), pp. 53-4.
106 See Thomas Herron, 'Irish Den of Thieves: Souterrains (and a Crannog?) in Books V and VI of Spenser's *Faerie Queene*', *Spenser Studies*, 14 (2000), 303-17. As Andrew Hadfield argues, the solitary Malengin stands in for the many making up 'the salvage nation – who wait, ready to haunt those unlucky enough to encounter them'. See *Edmund Spenser's Irish Experience: Wilde Fruit and Salvage Soyl* (Oxford: Clarendon: 1997), p. 136.
107 Giraldus Cambrensis, 'The Second Booke the Conquest of Ireland', trans. John Hooker, in *The Second Volume of Chronicles: Conteining the Description, Conquest, Inhabitation, and Troblesome Estate of Ireland; First Collected by Raphaell Holinshed* (London, 1586), fol. 56. For Henry VIII's role, see Karl S. Bottigheimer, 'Kingdom and Colony: Ireland in the Westward Enterprise, 1536-1660', in *The Westward Enterprise: English Activities in Ireland, the Atlantic and America, 1480-1650*, ed. K.R. Andrews, N.P. Canny, and P.E.H. Hair (Liverpool: Liverpool University Press, 1978), pp. 45-64.

.... Place, on this reading, is the locus of denial, of attempted withdrawal from invasion/difference'.[108] The raised drawbridges and fortified walls of *The Faerie Queene*'s archaic landscape make it possible to utilise Massey's definitions as a gloss on the allegorical thresholds of Spenser's poem; yet, in both his poetry and his prose, Spenser writes not only of borders that are internal and man-made, built to shield that which is perceived as 'civilised' from 'the saluage cuntreis' (IV.xi.40) offered as its opposite, but also of natural topographies, exploited for defensive or legal gain.[109] By representing the movements between region and territory, perceived wilderness and home, Spenser creates a network of permeable thresholds. To evoke Dagmar Reichert's meditation on the epistemological poetics, or 'topo-logic' attraction of thinking spatially, Spenser creates traces of a 'dialectic between inside and outside' and a shadowed place in which 'identity and difference merge'.[110] His spatial metaphors have material contexts and consequences and, as such, rarely take up constant positions; in poetry, imagined boundaries are as vulnerable to penetration, if not more so, than those of the material world.

The labour associated with restricted movement and heavy arms, for example, is represented by Spenser in Book VI of *The Faerie Queene* in a series of images which combine the allegorical connotations of movement with an interest in physical stamina and the embodied experience of a distinct physical environment. As more than a meditation on the respective virtues of 'closed' and 'open' landscapes, the poem reflects on passing places and who has the ability to negotiate them.[111] Following the wounding of Serena by the Blatant Beast, for example, Sir Calidore may make energetic chase after his foe, but the cardiac exertion is too great and he is ultimately left behind, forced to 'gape and gaspe, with dread aghast,/ As if his lungs and lites were nigh a sunder brast' (VI.iii.26). Similarly, his surrogate Sir Calepine, who walks alongside his horse after courteously coming to Serena's aid, pushes at both physical and topographical limits in pursuit of a safe harbour:

> Now when as *Phoebus* with his fiery waine
> Vnto his Inne began to draw apace;

---

108 See Doreen Massey, *For Space* (London: Sage Publications, 2005), p. 6.
109 See Heather Dubrow, '"A Doubtful Sense of Things": Thievery in *The Faerie Queene* 6.10–6.11', in *Worldmaking Spenser: Explorations in the Early Modern Age*, ed. Patrick Cheney and Lauren Silberman (Kentucky: University Press of Kentucky, 2000), pp. 204–16.
110 Reichert, 'On Boundaries', p. 87.
111 See Fitter, *Poetry, Space, Landscape*, pp. 294–7 and p. 300.

> Tho wexing weary of that toylesome paine,
> In trauelling on foote so long a space,
> Not wont on foote with heauy armes to trace,
> Downe in a dale forby a riuers syde,
> He chaunst to spie a faire and stately place,
> To which he meant his weary steps to guyde,
> In hope there for his loue some succour to prouyde.
>
> But comming to the riuers side, he found
> That hardly passable on foote it was:
> Therefore there still he stood as in a stound,
> Ne wist which way he through the foord mote pas. (VI.iii.29–30)

The careful attempt that Calepine and Serena make in crossing the ford, 'strongly wading through the waues vnused' (VI.iii.33), in full sight of the swift-footed and mocking Turpine who refuses to help them, is thus a minor triumph over both physical obstruction and their lack of local knowledge. In the evolutionary movement between Book I's emblematic landscape and Book VI's textured environs, Turpine ultimately emerges, in something of an ironic inversion, as a species of Despair. In the landscape of psychomachia established in *The Faerie Queene*'s first book, for example, Redcrosse had found himself listening to Despair pose the following defence of how he has treated the suicidal Sir Terwin:

> Who trauailes by the wearie wandring way,
> To come vnto his wished home in haste,
> And meetes a flood, that doth his passage stay,
> Is not great grace to helpe him ouer past,
> Or free his feet, that in the myre sticke fast?
> Most enuious man, that grieues at neighbours good,
> And fond, that ioyest in the woe thou hast,
> Why wilt not let him passe, that long hath stood
> Vpon the banke, yet wilt thy selfe not pas the flood? (I.ix.39)

In Book I, the landscape evoked was that of Psalm 69, but in Book VI, the thinness of the allegory, or at least its vulnerability to penetration by a material landscape, seems to suggest that Spenser's reading of courtesy in human action is very much of the immediate world. Calepine and Serena need help to pass the flood but the lesson takes its primary significance from the challenge of the physical obstacle: an offer of help made to a traveller is in itself a kindness, or courtesy. For Calepine, courtesy thus dictates that he must bear the weight of his responsibilities with 'great grace': a reminder that 'human conduct', as William Howarth writes, cannot be severed 'from natural or biological conditions'.[112]

Turpine's refusal to provide the knight and his half-dead lady with lodging, and the violent escalation of action that leads to the wounding of Calepine, is juxtaposed with the deeds of the compassionate 'wyld man' (VI.iv.11) who eventually provides the knight and the lady with succour:

> ... he signes vnto them made,
> With him to wend vnto his wonning neare:
> To which he easily did them perswade.
> Farre in the forrest by a hollow glade,
> Couered with mossie shrubs, which spredding brode
> Did vnderneath them make a gloomy shade;
> There foot of liuing creature neuer trode,
> Ne scarse wyld beasts durst come, there was this wights abode.
>
> Thether he brought these vnacquainted guests;
> To whom faire semblance, as he could, he shewed
> By signes, by lookes, and all his other gests.
> But the bare ground, with hoarie mosse bestrowed,
> Must be their bed, their pillow was vnsowed,
> And the frutes of the forrest was their feast:
> For their bad Stuard neither plough'd nor sowed,
> Ne fed on flesh, ne euer of wyld beast
> Did taste the bloud, obaying natures first beheast. (VI.iv.13–14)

The gloomy glade recalls the den of Errour; yet, here, the habitation of a fecund place, which balances wildness with domesticity, connotes the possibility of retrenchment and liberty. The wyld man's vegetarian diet and knowledge of 'herbes to dresse ... wounds' (VI.iv.16) suggests a symbiosis of nature and culture; yet, as Patricia Palmer observes, as one of 'the indigenes of Book VI' he remains 'studiously excluded from the conversations of the civil'.[113] His kind gestures are cautiously accepted but they are those of a solitary figure and thus his spatial freedom does not connote an accompanying sense of political freedom: ultimately revealed as one 'borne of noble blood' (VI.v.2), he figures little more than as an image 'of colonial wish-fulfilment'.[114] For Serena and Calepine, respite is short-lived. Once again separated from his lady, Calepine merely rec-

---

112 William Howarth, 'Imagined Territory: The Writing of Wetlands', *NLH*, 30.3 (1999), 509–39, p. 515.
113 Patricia Palmer, *Language and Conquest in Early Modern Ireland* (Cambridge: Cambridge University Press, 2001), p. 119 and p. 120.
114 McCabe, *Spenser's Monstrous Regiment*, p. 242.

onciles himself to sustaining laboured progress 'through many a soyle' in search of her, travelling 'still on foot in heauie armes', and content to pause for sleep only until woken by the 'loud alarmes' (VI.viii.47) of the 'saluage nation' (VI.viii.35).

For Book V's Malengin, landscape can be used defensively, 'as if', to borrow Thomas Gainsford's appraisal, 'disobedience had a protection'.[115] Yet, as in the case of Book VI's 'saluage man' (VI.iiii.3), topographies that appear hostile to strangers can also be used by the allies of Spenser's knights for their strategic capacities: a marker of the poem's capacity to handle lasting ambivalence.[116] In the earlier exchange between Belge and Arthur in V.x, for example, Arthur's words of encouragement follow Belge's reluctant acknowledgement of the protective qualities of the terrain in which she finds herself. She has been deprived of her lands by Geryoneo and has been banished into 'moores and marshes …/ Out of the pleasant soyle, and citties glad' to which she has been accustomed (V.x.18). Her sojourn in the 'fennes for fastnesse' (V.x.18) is cause for lament; yet, it is these oozing, sodden spaces that have also been her saviour:

> Ay me (sayd she) and whether shall I goe?
> Are not all places full of forriane powres?
> My pallaces possessed of my foe,
> My cities sackt, and their sky-threatning towres
> Raced, and made smooth fields now full of flowres?
> Onely these marishes, and myrie bogs,
> In which the fearefull ewftes do build their bowres,
> Yeeld me an hostry mongst the croking frogs,
> And harbour here in safety from those rauenous dogs.
>
> Nathlesse (said he) deare Ladie with me goe,
> Some place shall vs recieue, and harbour yield;
> If not, we will it force, maugre your foe,
> And purchase it to vs with speare and shield:

---

115 Thomas Gainsford, 'Chapter XVII: The Description of Ireland', in *The Glory of England* (London, 1618), p. 144.
116 The remnants of Malengin's shattered body and subterranean dwelling are left latent as Artegall and Talus move on, becoming markers of desolation if not lasting destruction. See Christopher Burlinson, *Allegory, Space and the Material World in the Writings of Edmund Spenser* (Cambridge: D.S. Brewer, 2006), p. 143. See also Patricia Palmer's discussion of Spenser's Malengin and the elegies written in honour of Fiach Mac Hugh O'Byrne in *The Severed Head and the Grafted Tongue: Literature, Translation and Violence in Early Modern Ireland* (Cambridge: Cambridge University Press, 2013), pp. 139–40.

And if all fayle, yet farewell open field:
The earth to all her creatures lodging lends. (V.x.23-4)

Arthur's championing of Belge's cause offers a preview of the aid Artegall purports to bring to Irena, thus providing a composite image of wetlandscape that sits midway between allegory and the material landscape of Ireland and the Low Countries.[117] The fen is home to amphibious creatures that repel the lady's delicate sensibilities and within the allegory's network of correspondences, the fragile bodies of newts and frogs share something of a dangerous likeness with the slimy half-formed offspring of Errour.

The image of a space in which 'fearefull ewftes do build their bowres' unites the comfort of sustained dwelling with a sense that the territory claimed remains a site of fear. Belge's reaction is thus striking for its ambivalence and, as Hamilton observes, the stanza seems to imply a 'distinction ... between earth and bogs, which provide no lodging'.[118] The inhabitants of the 'myrie bog' may exist within what Arthur and Belge perceive to be an uncultured space, but they still have a place in a natural order, because the earth 'to all her creatures lodging lends': an acknowledgement that comes only after the suggestion that force and violent aggression should first be used to defend Belge's claim. Arthur's idea that land can be purchased 'with speare and shield' is a measure of the pitiless violence implicit in Spenser's idea of magnificence, and the extent to which the idea of peaceful habitation is an afterthought when 'all places' are 'full of forriane powres'. In the description of how Geryoneo's occupation of Belge's city has served to 'Shut vp her hauen' and 'mard her marchants trade' (V.x.25) we see echoes of Gernon's vision of restoring circulation to Ireland; the proper husbanding of the Low Counties, like that of Ireland, Spenser suggests, should be by Protestant rather than Catholic forces.[119] Homi K. Bhabha observes how our understanding of territory is itself 'etymologically unsettled' and 'derives from both *terra* (earth) and *terrēre* (to frighten)'; as such, 'the colonialist demand for narrative carries, within it, its threatening reversal: ... the *other* side of

---

117 For a similarly polyvalent wetlandscape see Todd Andrew Borlik, 'Caliban and the Fen Demons of Lincolnshire: The Englishness of Shakespeare's *Tempest*', *Shakespeare*, 9.1 (2013), 21–51. Borlik suggests that Caliban has one foot in imagined New World colonies and the other in the oozing fens of Lincolnshire.
118 *FQ*, note to V.x.24 (p. 581).
119 As Aaron Kitch observes, 'Spenser describes Arthur's ultimate triumph over Geryoneo' in terms of allowing 'ships to sail between Antwerp and other European ports'. See *Political Economy and the States of Literature in Early Modern England* (Farnham: Ashgate, 2009), p. 40.

narcissistic authority may be the paranoia of power'.[120] As a figure for occupied territory, Belge, and her fear of taking refuge in uncertain spaces, exposes Book V's narrator to cognitive dissonance, holding a mirror up to the conduct of the English in Ireland, even if the accusatory glimpse is short-lived.[121]

The challenging anxieties revealed by the writing of wetland is thus allied with the challenges of articulating the 'form-engendering and form-dissolving processes already at work in "nature" as much as in "culture"', as Stuart McLean observes.[122] In the closing paragraph of Spenser's *View*, Irenaeus concludes with a thought that demonstrates how subjective his attestation has been: 'Thus I haue *Eudox*: as brieflye as I coulde and as my remembraunce woulde serue me run thoroughe the state of that wholle Countrye bothe to let youe see what it now is and allsoe what it maie be by good Care and amendment' (p. 230). The invocation of memory and brevity as the frames of his testimony offers an indication of how Ireland was recalled in the mind and reconstructed in the plots and speculative visions of the Tudor and Stuart administrations.[123] As a final observation, Irenaeus's claim to have 'run thoroughe the state' is strangely misleading, for it is something of a static perspective that he offers: a textual trace that attempts to perfect a 'present view' of an inconstant land.[124] In his final speech, he explains that he has not delivered a finished description or 'a perfecte plott of [his] owne invencion' but a precis of that which he has 'learned and vnderstode ... by the Consvltacions and accions of euerye wise gouernour and Councellour' (p. 230). The last thought that he leaves to his audience is the hope that his travails have not been in vain. Considering the reader who follows in his footsteps, he hopes that he 'by the lighte of others foregoinge him maie followe after with more ease and happelye finde a fairer waie thearevnto then they which haue gone

---

120 Homi K. Bhabha, *The Location of Culture* (London: Routledge, 1994; repr. 2004), p. 142. Emphasis in original.
121 For how the 'narrative flies in the face of historical fact' see Andrew Fichter, *Poets Historical: Dynastic Epic in the Renaissance* (New Haven: Yale University Press, 1982), p. 199. For the problems of pity and pain in Book V see Patricia Palmer, 'Where Does It Hurt? How Pain Makes History in Early Modern Ireland', in *The Body in Pain in Irish Literature and Culture*, ed. Fionnuala Dillane, Naomi McAreavey, and Emilie Pine (Basingstoke: Palgrave Macmillan, 2016), pp. 21–38.
122 McLean, 'Irish Boglands and the Imagination of Matter', p. 65.
123 For the violence of 'colonial amnesia' see Willy Maley, '"The Name of the Country I Have Forgotten": Remembering and Dismembering in Sir Henry Sidney's Irish *Memoir* (1583)', in *Ireland in the Renaissance*, pp. 52–73.
124 See John P. Harrington, *The English Traveller in Ireland: Accounts of Ireland and the Irish through Five Centuries* (Dublin: Wolfhound Press, 1991), p. 15.

before' (p. 230). Like the unfortunate poet Bon/Malfont, who is found with his tongue 'Nayld to a post' in Mercilla's court (V.ix.25), Irenaeus finally reveals himself to be something of a Janus figure himself.[125] His authority rests at the feet of others and his claim to spatial freedom is more an articulate dream than a practical reality: an incomplete survey, of land perceived to be supportive of neither body nor argument, made in haste.

---

[125] See Roland Greene, 'The "Scriene" and the Channel: England and Spain in Book V of *The Faerie Queene*', *JMEMS*, 39.1 (2009), 43–64, p. 54. For Bon/Malfont as an image of Spenser himself see Hadfield, *Spenser's Irish Experience*, p. 165.

# 7

# Spenser's insular fictions

Dreaming of islands – whether with joy or in fear, it doesn't matter – is dreaming of pulling away, of being already separate, far from any continent, of being lost and alone – or it is dreaming of starting from scratch, recreating, beginning anew.[1]

Something about the insular beckons alluringly. It inspires a greater malleability to grand designs.[2]

The scattered islands encountered by Guyon in Book II of *The Faerie Queene* are not only one of the most imaginatively satisfying geographical features in the poem but also one of the strangest. The poet describes the islands as being 'not firme land, …/ But stragling plots, which to and fro doe ronne' (II.xii.11) and, in the generic welter of the epic romance, the description seems particularly loaded owing to the latent pun on 'plot' that links literary topography to narrative structure. The *wandring Islands* paradoxically plot, to borrow Lorna Hutson's term, the 'imprecise spatio-temporality' of romance narratives, in which ground shifts and landmarks are subject to the needs of the action.[3] As Spenser writes, a trespasser who 'once hath fastened/ His foot thereon, may neuer it recure,/ But wandreth euer more vncertein and vnsure' (II.xii.12). For a moment, the nature of the space, and the way one encounters it,

---

1 Gilles Deleuze, *Desert Islands and Other Texts, 1953–1974*, ed. David Lapoujade, trans. Michael Taormina (Cambridge, MA: Semiotext(e), 2004), p. 10.
2 Godfrey Baldacchino, 'Islands as Novelty Sites', *Geographical Review*, 97.2 (2007), 165–74, p. 166.
3 Lorna Hutson, 'Fortunate Travellers: Reading for the Plot in Sixteenth-Century England', *Representations*, 41 (1993), 83–103, p. 86. See also Martin Brückner and Kristen Poole, 'The Plot Thickens: Surveying Manuals, Drama, and the Materiality of Narrative Form in Early Modern England', *ELH*, 69 (2002), 617–48 and Julia Reinhard Lupton, 'Mapping Mutability: or, Spenser's Irish Plot', in *Representing Ireland: Literature and the Origins of Conflict, 1534–1660*, ed. Brendan Bradshaw, Andrew Hadfield, and Willy Maley (Cambridge: Cambridge University Press, 1993), pp. 93–115.

temporarily coincide. When offering a kind of shorthand for the discontinuous landscape of *The Faerie Queene*, Angus Fletcher has observed that 'the questing mind fills the area between the places, while the places – quite unreal as places we might have been to – are islands of hope in a landscape of wonder';[4] yet, insular space in Spenser's writing, as the *wandring Islands* demonstrate, rarely offers fixed points between which a reader can navigate. This final chapter brings together various strands of criticism concerned with the depiction of space in imaginative literature and offers an exploration of the role that insularity ultimately comes to perform in Spenser's writing. In the movement from coastline to wetland, as explored in Chapters 5 and 6 respectively, and finally to island, as explored here, Spenser's spaces hold material geography, narrative motion, and poetic and political ideology in tension; for all its promises, the writing of insular space provides the ecotonal and metafictional site at which Spenser's making finds its limits. By moving towards a reading of the Mutabilitie Cantos, via a discussion of *A View of the Present State of Ireland* and a fuller reading of 'Colin Clouts Come Home Againe', I offer a survey of the insular perspectives that the provisional end to *The Faerie Queene* fails to resolve.

In particular, this chapter responds to the idea that islands hold a privileged position in imaginative literature, and draws on the work of authors writing before, during, and after the Renaissance who address the qualities of insular space in ways that range widely across disciplines. Tom Conley, for example, has revealed the occurrence of 'an insular moment' in the cosmographical writing of Renaissance France,[5] and more recently, in her study of early modern Iberian romance, Simone Pinet has reflected on the ways in which the 'book of chivalry and the *isolario* or book of islands' share an interest in how 'to solve different problems of poetics and politics, of ethics and the articulation of fiction and truth'.[6] As these explorations suggest, isolated landmasses or worlds in microcosm offer ground-plots on which authors are free to create second natures or golden worlds: worlds improved or oppositional, or where

---

4 Angus Fletcher, *The Prophetic Moment: An Essay on Spenser* (Chicago: University of Chicago Press, 1971), p. 304.
5 See Tom Conley, *The Self-Made Map: Cartographic Writing in Early Modern France* (Minneapolis: University of Minnesota Press, 1997), pp. 167–201.
6 Simone Pinet, *Archipelagoes: Insular Fictions from Chivalric Romance to the Novel* (Minneapolis: University of Minnesota Press, 2011), p. xi and p. xxxiv. See also John R. Gillis, *Islands of the Mind: How the Human Imagination Created the Atlantic World* (New York: Palgrave Macmillan, 2004).

dreams are temporarily inseparable from reality.⁷ When placed within such European literary and cartographical contexts, then, the 'mental space' of Spenser's fictions can be reconfigured not only as a category in which representations of geography can be seen to allow, if not rely on, imaginative impositions, but also as one in which insular space, in particular, presents unique opportunities for posing philosophical and political questions.⁸

Both Thomas More's *Utopia* and William Shakespeare's *The Tempest* use paradoxically insular focal points to anchor travails that take place on simultaneously local and transatlantic scales; as geopolitical fantasies they are not without worldly ties, favouring island locations *en route* to the New World.⁹ As Roland Greene observes in an essay on *The Tempest*, 'insularity comes to stand for a kind of knowledge' in early modern literature, namely 'a distinctively partial knowledge that counters the totalities of institutions and regimes'.¹⁰ To be isolated, or insulated, is to be placed apart and made island-like. He imagines Shakespeare's Prospero as the embodiment of 'island logic': a protean figure who stages enchantments and encounters. On the mainland Prospero 'would be power itself', not the means by which its manifold structures can be viewed.¹¹ Yet, for all the promise of mental and physical activity, insularity also carries the threat of self-involvement and inertia. Spenser's contemporary Roger Ascham associated romance literature with the 'inchantementes of Circes' and it seems fitting that the ruling deity of the mode should be an

---

7  See Harry Berger, Jr., 'The Renaissance Imagination: Second World and Green World', in *Second World and Green World: Studies in Renaissance Fiction-making*, ed. John Patrick Lynch (Berkeley: University of California Press, 1988), pp. 3–40. See also Alfred K. Siewers, 'Spenser's Green World', *Early English Studies*, 3 (2010), 1–34.
8  See Chloë Houston, ed., *New Worlds Reflected: Travel and Utopia in the Early Modern Period* (Farnham: Ashgate, 2010). For the importance of insular and archipelagic space in the formation of an English national identity and vernacular see Catherine A.M. Clarke, *Literary Landscapes and the Idea of England, 700-1400* (Cambridge: D.S. Brewer, 2006); Philip Schwyzer and Simon Mealor, eds, *Archipelagic Identities: Literature and Identity in the Atlantic Archipelago, 1550-1800* (Aldershot: Ashgate, 2004); John Kerrigan, *Archipelagic English: Literature, History, and Politics, 1603-1707* (Oxford: Oxford University Press, 2008), pp. 48–51 in particular; and Catherine Nicholson, *Uncommon Tongues: Eloquence and Eccentricity in the English Renaissance* (Philadelphia: University of Pennsylvania Press, 2014), p. 9.
9  See, for example, Crystal Bartolovich, '"Baseless Fabric": London as a "World City"', in *The Tempest and Its Travels*, ed. Peter Hulme and William H. Sherman (London: Reaktion, 2000), pp. 13–26 and Steve Mentz, 'Isle of Tempests', in *Shipwreck Modernity: Ecologies of Globalization, 1550-1719* (Minneapolis: University of Minnesota Press, 2015), pp. 51–74.
10  Greene, 'Island Logic', in *The Tempest and Its Travels*, pp. 138–45 (p. 138).
11  Ibid., p. 139.

island-dweller in the early modern imagination.¹² For Ascham, as seen, the seductive power of vernacular romance could tempt a reader to withdraw into a world of violence and bawdry, and to succumb to a life of passive isolation. Furthermore, as Spenser discovered in his fashioning of the witch Acrasia, a literary descendent of Circe, and her island dwelling, the Bower of Bliss, the subversive perspectives put in play by collocations of islands offered poetic spaces not just of seduction but also of threatening transformation, which undermined his 'previous philosophy of allegorical tidiness'.¹³

Spenser's insular fictions epitomise a marvellous geography of shifting coasts and landmasses; their shores render a fluctuating littoral topography that mediates between the literary and the literal. Yet, to locate the abstract notion of insular space within a localised and historicised setting, it is impossible to think of the islands in Spenser's work without considering Ireland itself. Spenser's *A View of the Present State of Ireland* notoriously offered the author's English readers multiple views and imaginings of what Ireland is, was, and could be,¹⁴ demonstrating the capacity of insular space to hold alternative perspectives in tension. Indeed, as Bernhard Klein observes, when 'William Cuningham declared in his *Cosmographical Glasse* that "vnder the name of Englande, I comprehende *the whole Ilande* conteyning also Schotlande, & Irelande"' his 'casual reference to an all-inclusive English insularity hardly echoes widely shared assumptions about Britain's physical topography but indicates both the imaginary potential and the political relevance of early modern geographical thought'.¹⁵ In Spenser's own literary soundings of the Irish Sea, an equally disorientating example of archipelagic manipulation can be observed in the arrangement of the islands used to chart the shepherd's travels in Spenser's pastoral poem 'Colin Clouts Come Home Againe'. Spenser manipulates the reader's sense of scale and distance and the island that Colin calls 'home' shrinks perceptively after his revelation that there are more spacious lands across the waves.¹⁶

12 Roger Ascham, *The Scholemaster* (London, 1570), sig. Iii$^v$.
13 Judith Yarnall, *Transformations of Circe: The History of an Enchantress* (Chicago: University of Illinois Press, 1994), p. 128.
14 Bruce Avery, for example, remarks on the dialogue's extraordinary 'polyvocality'. See 'Mapping the Irish Other: Spenser's *A View of the Present State of Ireland*', *ELH*, 57.2 (1990), 263–79, p. 264.
15 Bernhard Klein, 'Partial Views: Shakespeare and the Map of Ireland', *EMLS*, 4.2 (1998), 5.1–20 (5).
16 See Bruce McLeod, *The Geography of Empire in English Literature, 1580–1745* (Cambridge: Cambridge University Press, 1999; repr. 2009), p. 65.

In the case of *The Faerie Queene*, as the poem progresses, the seductive and secluded island paradises of Acrasia and Venus are replaced with brusquer allegories that explore issues of land ownership and conquest. The 'two Ilands' belonging to the quarrelling sons of Milesio, as seen, anticipate the larger forces shaping the 'saluage Island' (VI.i.9), the realm of Irena, from which Artegall returns defeated.[17] Spenser may use islands to consider ideas in isolation; yet, like continental islands, these breakaway thoughts are connected to larger motions at work. The retrospective reading practices that the poem invites also encourage the impression that landmasses change their significance as the reader moves through the poem; the fluid temperament of allegorical correspondences means that the poet's 'stragling plots' are always in the process of realigning their implications. The sense that Spenser's islands eventually all seem to shadow Ireland suggests that any so called 'islands of hope' function in ways that are as treacherous as Phaedria's floating domain. Within the compass of an island's space, Spenser provided the measure of his larger project. The various islands seeded throughout his writing offer ground-plots on which to create wonders: dreams of tested and triumphant virtues, and dreams of reformation. Yet, their irresolvable insularity is also the final image he leaves to his readers: the impossibility of unified and immutable vision.

## Dreaming of islands

In his survey charting early modern efforts to map Ireland, J.H. Andrews remarks on the 'strange psycho-cartographical predilection' that delights in insularity:

> Islands have always held a fascination for the mapmaker. In the pre-scientific era of cartography he would exaggerate their size and colour them more brightly than anything else. He would also make a special point of discovering their names or if necessary of christening them himself. If there were no islands in his study-area an irresponsible cartographer might even invent some, or at least half-invent them by snipping peninsulas off the mainland. The roots of this strange psycho-cartographic predilection may lie in some kind of biological analogy: complete within its enclosure, the island can be likened to a self-sufficient organism capable of developing its own personality, whereas a peninsula can never be more than a dependent limb.[18]

---

17 See Clare Carroll, 'Spenser and the Irish Language: The Sons of Milesio, *A View of the Present State of Ireland*, *The Faerie Queene*, Book V and the *Leabhar Gabhála*', *IUR*, 26.2 (1996), pp. 281–90.

18 J.H. Andrews, *Shapes of Ireland: Maps and their Makers 1564–1839* (Dublin: Geography Publications, 1997), p. 1.

Andrews evokes the peculiar attraction of insular space, alluding to the curious way in which the cartographical history of islands has long been associated with a capacity for invention, as if miniature landmasses occasion a level of imaginative potential that overcomes that of desirable accountability. For Conley, such a fascination is epitomised by the sixteenth-century cartographic genre of the *isolario*, whose pages chart spaces 'where reality and fantasy are tested together, and where the subject continually invents his or her relation to the unknown'.[19] From *isolario* to monumental tome, then, this drive can be seen at work in an anecdote recalled by Sir Walter Ralegh in *The History of the World*, when he reminds his readers of the ways in which both historical and geographical records can be augmented by the conjectures of a covetous imagination:

> To which purpose I remember a pretie jest of *Don Pedro de Sarmiento*, a worthie *Spanish* Gentleman, who had beene employed by his King in planting a Colonie upon the Streights of *Magellan*: for when I asked him, being then my Prisoner, some question about an Island in those Streights, which me thought, might have done eyther benefit or displeasure to his enterprise, he told me merrily, that it was to be called the *Painters wives Island*; saying, That whilest the fellow drew that Map, his wife sitting by, desired him to put in one Countrey for her; that she, in imagination, might have an Island of her owne.[20]

The desire of the mapmaker's wife to be granted sole possession of the strategic site suggests the ease with which the colonising imagination supresses the implicit violence involved in its quotidian processes. The cartographical fiction of the '*Painters wives Island*' is a 'pretie jest' at odds with the historical circumstances shaping Ralegh's brief narrative intervention; as a retelling of a tale once related to him by Pedro Sarmiento de Gamboa, the cosmographer general of Peru and the man who helped shape Ralegh's dreams of the city of Eldorado, surface levity masks the costs involved in such enterprises.[21] The image of a directing agency leaning over the shoulder of the labouring craftsman, here a wife and a husband, adds a further subjective and interpersonal inflection to

---

19 Conley, *The Self-Made Map*, p. 178.
20 Walter Ralegh, *The History of the World* (London, 1614 [i.e. 1617]), Chapter 23, S. 4, p. 574.
21 See Roland Greene, *Unrequited Conquests: Love and Empire in the Colonial Americas* (Chicago: University of Chicago Press, 1999), pp. 191–3 and pp. 231–2; Matthew Steggle, 'Charles Chester and Richard Hakluyt', *SEL*, 43.1 (2003), 65–81, pp. 71–2; and Mary C. Fuller, *Voyages in Print: English Travel to America, 1576–1624* (Cambridge: Cambridge University Press, 1995), pp. 55–84.

Ralegh's comment concerning the performativity of ostensibly objective accounts.

Ralegh's question concerning the nature of the island's 'benefit or displeasure' to his interlocutor's 'enterprise' demonstrates how insular space allows the invention, manipulation, and play of relations. Such acts are not limited to purely visual or cartographical modes. As Greene observes, Ralegh's report of the conversation reveals the 'homology of fictions and islands', which demands 'a strategy of mediation between mainland and island, world and fiction, here and there'.[22] To offer a complementary example, by way of returning from the New World to Ireland, it is noteworthy that Sir Thomas Smith's ambitious plans to establish a colony in Ulster proposed to make strategic landfall on the Ards Peninsula. It is, he writes,

> a peece of ground as easie to be wonne, inhabited, safely kepte and defended, as any platte within the Realme of Ireland, being a reache of land (as it were of purpose bayed out from the mayne into the Sea, to wall in so muche of it as woulde make so faire and commodious a lake and herber as the haven of Strangford is) fasshioned like an Arme bente in the Elbowe, annexed no where to the mayne but at the one ende as the Arme to the shoulder.[23]

The subsequent description of how an invading force could advance gradually through the demi-island, having established 'a place for Artificers to lie safely in', offers a vision of occupation via gradual annexation.[24] And as something of a literary precursor, it is telling that More set his thought-experiment *Utopia* on a man-made island hewn from the mainland by King Utopos.[25] In More's island-origin story, insular space offers not only a fantasy of separation and inviolability but also an indication of the shaping influence of the imagination and the will. In the work of both authors, what was once a 'dependent limb' is violently transformed into a site from which to build a vision of a new social order.

## An islandish monarchie

The epic drive of Spenser's poem concerns the origin story and prophesised future of an island nation, whose ruling dynasty had origins on

22  Greene, *Unrequited Conquests*, p. 7.
23  I.B., *A letter sent by I.B. Gentleman* (London, 1572), sig. C1ᵛ.
24  See Herron, *Spenser's Irish Work*, p. 39 and pp. 47–50.
25  Sir Thomas More, *Utopia*, trans. Ralph Robinson (1551), in *Three Early Modern Utopias*, ed. Susan Bruce (Oxford: Oxford University Press, 1999; repr. 2008), pp. 1–148 (p. 50).

'the fruitful Ile/ Of Mona', or Anglesey, the birthplace of Henry VII: from this island, the narrative of Book III suggests, exiled majesty shall 'breake forth into bright burning flame' and 'the Briton blood their crowne againe reclaime' (III.iii.48).[26] The Tudors, Spenser suggests, remain the vessels of the *translatio imperii* inaugurated by Brutus's journey to find a new homeland, which is in itself an archetypal insular fiction:[27]

> At last by fatall course they driuen were
>   Into an Island spatious and brode,
>   The furthest North, that did to them appeare:
> Which after rest they seeking farre abrode,
> Found it the fittest soyle for their abode,
>   Fruitfull of all thinges fitt for liuing foode,
>   But wholy waste, and void of peoples trode (III.ix.49)

In his description of Brutus and his men making landfall, Spenser imagines a deserted island, on which no human foot has left a trace of cultured habitation. It is a savage place, of 'Geaunts broode' and barbarism, ready to be claimed by civil men brought there by 'fatall course'. The Trojan wanderer, as James Nohrnberg observes, was spurred thither following a dream vision in which he was visited by the goddess Diana, whose propulsive properties shadow those of Elizabeth I, as well as those of Gloriana in Arthur's dream.[28] As Milton would later write in his retelling of the same mythic past, the place that Brutus sought was a 'sea-girt' realm, 'far to the West';[29] a geographically peripheral place on the cusp of the known world.

The way in which Spenser's writing about Ireland echoes the fabled voyage of Brutus to an insular wasteland elides an ancient heroic narrative with one in the process of being aggressively written: as Joan Fitzpatrick observes, the state of ancient Britain, encountered by Brutus as a 'saluage wildernesse,/ Vnpeopled, vnmannurd, vnproud, vnpraysd' (II.x.5), 'bears resemblance to contemporary descriptions of Ireland and

---

26 See Donald Kimball Smith, *The Cartographic Imagination in Early Modern England* (Aldershot: Ashgate, 2008), p. 122. As Andrew Fichter argues, 'Henry is the agent of a spiritual as well as a political renovatio'. See *Poets Historical: Dynastic Epic in the Renaissance* (New Haven: Yale University Press, 1982), p. 178.
27 See David Galbraith, *Architectonics of Imitation in Spenser, Daniel and Drayton* (Toronto: University of Toronto Press, 2000), pp. 52–74.
28 See James Nohrnberg, 'Britomart's Gone Abroad to Brute-land, Colin Clout's Come Courting from the Salvage Ire-Land: Exile and the Kingdom in Some of Spenser's Fictions for "Crossing Over"', in *Edmund Spenser: New and Renewed Directions*, ed. J.B. Lethbridge (Madison: Fairleigh Dickinson University Press, 2006), pp. 214–85 (p. 214).
29 John Milton, *The History of England* (London, 1670), sig. C2r.

the Irish'.³⁰ For the purposes of crafting an epic past, it was on such a piece of land, which was once itself a dependent peninsula and 'of some thought/ By sea to haue bene from the *Celticke* mayn-land brought', that the 'warlike Britons' raised a 'mightie empire', naming the land Albion on the grounds of its most famous seamark (II.x.5–6). The landmass appears to achieve definition as its cultural, legal, and economic stability solidifies. And, in spite of the sceptical attitude Spenser presents elsewhere in *A View* concerning the legend's veracity, the narrative progression of savage wastes, salvation, and reformation comes to share similarities with the arguments presented by the same text for the necessity of conquest.³¹

For Spenser, the Irish landscape offered a place where histories, myths, and identities could be written and re-written, but in ways that were not always in keeping with the epic mode befitting Elizabethan dreams of expansion.³² David Quint, for example, observes the subversive quality of insular geographies when he comments upon Homer's decision to set the majority of the *Odyssey*'s adventures 'on islands that reinforce their self-enclosed nature'.³³ Such episodes, which fuse romance wanderings with the poetics of empire, indicate, as he writes, 'the possibility of other perspectives, however incoherent they may ultimately be, upon the epic victors' single-minded story of history'.³⁴ For Spenser's *Faerie Queene*, which falls somewhere between the neat binary of 'single-minded' epic and subversive romance, the resulting hybrid forms are heir to the island-logic of both poets and propagandists. And indeed, as Andrews writes, 'unlike Shakespeare's Illyria, Gaelic Ireland was no place for feeding one's knowledge of the town', where the allusion to the setting of Shakespeare's *Twelfth Night* recalls the audience's first glimpse of a safe harbour for the play's storm-tossed protagonists.³⁵ As a locus of both

30 Joan Fitzpatrick, *Irish Demons: English Writings on Ireland, the Irish, and Gender by Spenser and his Contemporaries* (Lanham: University Press of America, 2000), p. 77.
31 See Andrew Hadfield, *Edmund Spenser's Irish Experience* (Oxford: Clarendon, 1997), pp. 99–100; David Lee Miller, *The Poem's Two Bodies: The Poetics of the 1590 Faerie Queene* (Princeton: Princeton University Press, 1988), pp. 196–9; and Judith H. Anderson, *Reading the Allegorical Intertext: Chaucer, Spenser, Shakespeare, Milton* (New York: Fordham, 2008), pp. 156–7.
32 See Stephen Greenblatt, *Renaissance Self-Fashioning from More to Shakespeare* (Chicago: University of Chicago Press, 1980), pp. 185–6.
33 David Quint, *Epic and Empire: Politics and Generic Form from Virgil to Milton* (Princeton: Princeton University Press, 1993), p. 34.
34 Ibid., p. 34. For contrast, see Ayesha Ramachandran's description of the *Aeneid*'s 'teleological drive and its desire to consolidate a singular, unified nation against the multiplicity of the world beyond' in *The Worldmakers: Global Imagining in Early Modern Europe* (Chicago: University of Chicago Press, 2015), p. 107.
35 Andrews, *Shapes of Ireland*, p. 11.

conflict and sanctuary, the Illyrian shoreline acts as Andrews's shorthand for mapping the romance potential of unfamiliar terrain, and indicates Ireland's resistance to non-native fictions. The production of views, itineraries, and observations during this period remained vulnerable to the damning criticism levelled as far back as the twelfth century by Gerald of Wales at his predecessors, wherein veracity is compromised by distance: 'Neither would it be strange if these authors sometimes strayed from the path of truth, since they knew nothing by the evidence of their eyes, and what knowledge they possessed came to them through one who was reporting and was far away'.[36] Blank spaces on maps may be ground for invention, but they are also symptomatic of blindness and anxiety.[37] The simultaneous desire for geographical reformation and depopulation stemmed from the anxiety of English officials concerning their inability to travel freely and thus acquire a full measure of the terrain.[38]

When considered alongside Spenser's *View*, Spenser's 'stragling plots' provide a measure of what McLeod describes as the 'subversive, metaphoric nature of the relationship between colonist, colonial space, and the colonized' in his reading of early modern England's uncoordinated colonial system.[39] When Eudoxus proclaims that he 'will take the mapp of Irelande before me and make myne eyes in the meane while my Scollemasters to guide my vnderstandinge to iudge of your plott' (*A View*, p. 152), for example, Spenser's interlocutor emphasises the importance of *autopsy*, of 'seeing for oneself' in the acquisition of knowledge, even if the object gazed upon is a simulacrum.[40] The production of the map by the dialogue's English representative is a noteworthy event because it serves as a physical gesture that impacts upon the dialogue's organisation of spatial knowledge, introducing an empirical eye to ease the quantification of terrain.[41] Its use in invigorating the technical detail of Irenaeus's

---

36 Gerald of Wales, *The History and Topography of Ireland*, trans. John O' Meara (London: Penguin, 1951; repr. 1988), p. 35.
37 See David J. Baker, 'Charting Uncertainty in Renaissance Ireland', in *Representing Ireland*, pp. 76–92.
38 In an essay on the surveys of Robert Lythe, J.H. Andrews notes that 'two hard years in the field had left Lythe lame and almost blind'. See 'The Irish Surveys of Robert Lythe', *Imago Mundi*, 19 (1965), 22–31, p. 26.
39 McLeod, *The Geography of Empire*, p. 72.
40 See Frank Lestringant, *Mapping the Renaissance World: The Geographical Imagination in the Age of Discovery*, trans. David Fausett (Cambridge: Polity, 1994), p. 130. See also Denis Cosgrove, *Geography and Vision: Seeing, Imagining and Representing the World* (London: Tauris, 2008), p. 42.
41 Avery notes that it is the 'only non-verbal performance of either character'. See 'Mapping the Irish Other', p. 263.

argument illustrates how the 'major function of colonial cartography was to give tangible presence to what could only be imagined'.[42] Yet, this shift is far from stable; when faced with uncertainty, as Spenser's writings consistently demonstrate, invention 'fed with fancies vayne' is often seen to disguise the shortfall (see *Amoretti*, 'Sonnet LXXVIII', 12). Indeed, as Patricia Palmer observes, 'mapping the landscape of atrocity was a dangerous business', and the demise of Lord Mountjoy's mapmaker, Richard Bartlett, during the Nine Years' War offers a telling response to how intrusion was met:[43] as Sir John Davies pithily observed, 'when he came into Tyrconnell, the inhabitants took off his head, because they would not have their country discovered'.[44]

In spite of its proximity to England, then, as William J. Smyth comments, Ireland often appeared on maps and in written accounts as a threatening alternative world, resistant to full and accurate visualisation:

> Discontinuities, absences, errors and imaginative inventions were also an integral part of the sixteenth-century mapping heritage. Indeed, one could argue that the whole mapping drive over the century and a half between the 1530s and the 1680s was aimed at reducing these ambiguities and geographical anxieties, eliminating the errors and exorcising the ghosts of long-lost imagined islands and other fantastic landscape features and legends, so as to produce a more rational, 'scientific' view of Ireland, albeit one heavily coloured by anglo-centric lenses and concerns.[45]

Smyth's image of progress is striking, particularly in his sense that the attempts made by emergent sixteenth-century empiricists to exorcise the 'ghosts of long-lost imagined islands' were countered by the longevity of subjective and politically motivated spatial stories. Spenser's *View*,

---

42 See Zbigniew Bialas, 'Ambition and Distortion: An Ontological Dimension in Colonial Cartography', in *Borderlands: Negotiating Boundaries in Post-Colonial Writing*, ed. Monika Reif-Hulser (Amsterdam: Rodopi, 1999), 17–28, p. 19.
43 Patricia Palmer, *The Severed Head and the Grafted Tongue: Literature, Translation and Violence in Early Modern Ireland* (Cambridge: Cambridge University Press, 2013), p. 28. See also J.H. Andrews, *The Queen's Last Map-Maker: Richard Bartlett in Ireland, 1600–3* (Dublin: Geography Publications, 2008) and Bernhard Klein, *Maps and the Writing of Space in Early Modern England and Ireland* (Basingstoke: Palgrave, 2001), pp. 125–7.
44 Sir John Davies, 'Sir John Davys to Salisbury', in *Calendar of State Papers, Ireland, James I: 1608–1610*, ed. Charles W. Russell and John P. Prendergast (Nendeln: Kraus Reprint, 1974), p. 280. See also Mercedes Camino, '(Un)folding the Map of Early Modern Ireland: Spenser, Moryson, Bartlett, and Ortelius', *Cartographica*, 34.4 (1997), 1–17.
45 William J. Smyth, *Map Making, Landscapes and Memory: A Geography of Colonial and Early Modern Ireland, c. 1530–1750* (Cork: Cork University Press, 2006), p. 41.

as a participant in what Conley terms a body of 'cartographic writings', is infused with the same problems Mary B. Campbell observes in the writing of Christopher Columbus a century earlier, which uses 'inherited languages of pastoral and heroic romance and anagogical geography' in place of 'simply denotative discourse'.[46] Spenser's own proclivities are revealed through the use of analogy and metaphor given to the interlocutors of *A View*, which function as if shaping the world by the author's own readerly associations and touchstones.[47] As Irenaeus explains, for example, not only does sixteenth-century Ireland resemble Saxon England before the Norman Conquest, but the dress of the Irish horsemen is a direct import.[48] Spenser even directs his readers to evidence provided by Chaucer's *Tale of Sir Thopas*, where the robe worn by Sir Thopas, that 'was of syklatoun,/ That coste many a jane',[49] is called by Irenaeus 'the proper wede of the horsemen' in *A View*. He goes on to note that the Irish horseman appears 'as ye maye reade in *Chaucer* wheare he describeth: $S^r$ *Thopas* apparrell and armour when he wente to fighte againste the Geaunte' and that 'Checklaton is that kinde of gilden leather with which they vse to imbrother theire Irish Iackes' (p. 121).[50] Subject to the drifting 'plots' of the author, the island itself, 'a moste bewtifull and swete Countrie as anye is vnder heauen' that is 'sprinckled with manye swete Ilandes and goodlye lakes like little Inlande seas' (p. 62), seems to multiply under Spenser's metaphors and allusions to other times, other places, and other literary works.

---

46 Mary B. Campbell, *The Witness and the Other World: Exotic European Travel Writing, 400–1600* (Ithaca: Cornell University Press, 1988), p. 222.

47 See Eamon Grennan, 'Language and Politics: A Note on Some Metaphors in Spenser's *A View of the Present State of Ireland*', *Spenser Studies*, 3 (1982), 99–110 and Andrew Hadfield and Willy Maley, 'Introduction: Irish Representations and English Alternatives', in *Representing Ireland*, pp. 1–23 (p. 13).

48 Doreen Massey observes how modern politics downplays difference in favour of producing a narrative of development, thus rendering 'coexisting spatial heterogeneity as a single temporal series'. In the example she provides, this would mean that '"Africa" is not *different* from Western Europe, it is (just) behind. (Or maybe it is indeed only different *from*; it is not allowed its own uniqueness, its coeval existence)'; emphasis in original. See *For Space* (London: Sage Publications, 2005), p. 68.

49 Geoffrey Chaucer, *The Tale of Sir Thopas* in *The Riverside Chaucer*, pp. 212–17, lines 734–5.

50 For a more detailed reading of this allusion see A. Kent Hieatt, *Chaucer, Spenser, Milton: Mythopoeic Continuities and Transformations* (Montreal: McGill-Queen's University Press, 1975), pp. 20–2 and William Rhodes, 'Chaucer in Ireland: Archaism, Etymology, and the Idea of Development', in *Rereading Chaucer and Spenser: Dan Geffrey with the New Poete*, ed. Rachel Stenner, Tamsin Badcoe, and Gareth Griffith (Manchester: Manchester University Press, 2019).

## 'Colin Clouts Come Home Againe'

If one of the rhetorical tactics of *A View* is to emphasise the apparent temporal discrepancy between England and Ireland, it is spatial and cultural distance that comes to the foreground in Spenser's pastoral poem 'Colin Clouts Come Home Againe'. The poem was written to commemorate the journey made with Sir Walter Ralegh to England in 1589 to publish the first part of *The Faerie Queene*, and the pastoral persona adopted in the poem allows Spenser to feign what Seamus Heaney has called 'a lived, illiterate and unconscious' relationship to the land, which masks the 'learned, literate and conscious' mind at work in the writing of pastoral.[51] 'Home' for Colin is Ireland, but the poem's travails keep Spenser's literary ambitions and the nature of the perilous divide between the insular neighbours, England and Ireland, in constant motion. As Syrithe Pugh observes, the 'doubleness in each setting is given urgency by the troubling ambiguity over which constitutes "home" and which "exile", and what such labels might mean'.[52] Spenser famously fashions his identity as a poet in response to Virgilian pastoral, and in Virgil's first eclogue, the shepherd Meliboeus talks of abandoning the fields outside Rome for unfamiliar climes, the furthest of which in his mind's eye is the land of 'the Britons, wholly sundered from all the world'.[53] In the woodcut accompanying the 'Januarye' eclogue of Spenser's *Shepheardes Calender* (1579), an earlier incarnation of Spenser's Colin Clout persona casts a mournful glance over his shoulder at the city whose walled boundaries exclude him. Surveying his 'winterbeaten flocke' he breaks his pipe in despair, and the hoary landscape becomes a reflection of his mood: the 'barrein ground, .../ Art made a myrrhour, to behold [his] plight' (*SC*, 19–20). As Andrew Hadfield observes, 'no reader of Virgil in the light of Spenser's January eclogue could have failed to respond to the ironic reversal of Britain from the periphery of exile to the centre of "home"';[54]

---

51 Seamus Heaney, *Preoccupations: Selected Prose, 1968–1978* (London: Faber, 1980), p. 131.
52 Syrithe Pugh, *Spenser and Ovid* (Aldershot: Ashgate, 2005), pp. 178–9. See also See Richard A. McCabe, *Spenser's Monstrous Regiment: Elizabethan Ireland and the Poetics of Difference* (Oxford: Oxford University Press, 2002), pp. 3–4.
53 Virgil, *Eclogues; Georgics; Aeneid I–VI*, trans. H. Rushton Fairclough; revised by G.P. Goold (Cambridge, MA: Harvard University Press, 1916; repr. 2006), I.66, p. 29. For the estranged strains of Spenser's pastoral see Nicholson, *Uncommon Tongues*, pp. 100–23.
54 Andrew Hadfield, *Literature, Politics and National Identity: Reformation to Renaissance* (Cambridge: Cambridge University Press, 1994), p. 182. Spenser's 1594 marriage to Elizabeth Boyle produced a child named Peregrine: a name that identifies the child as a stranger sojourning in a strange land. As Jerome Turler observes, the word 'Peregrinus

for an Englishman such as Spenser, to write in and of Ireland even further to the west, was to write poetry as if seeking to limn the edges of the ancient inhabited world.[55]

The voyage of Colin Clout elevates the crossing of the Irish Sea to a voyage worthy of epic proportions; however, this energy is focused with microcosmic intensity on the space, physical and ideological, between islands. It is a fragile and much diminished reality that provides the undersong to the grandeur of his borrowed rhetoric, which moves between depicting a motion-sick journey across the Irish Sea and a mythological passage through a 'world of waters heaped vp on hie' (197). Spenser writes in imitation of Ovid's exile poetry, where to cross the perilous pathless ocean, to 'tempt that gulf, and in those wandring stremes/ Seek waies vnknowne' (210–11), seems an act of suicidal ambition.[56] Suspended for a moment, as he 'stood there waiting on the strond' (212), Colin surveys the monstrous vessel on which he will undertake the journey. As in *The Faerie Queene*, the coastal image figures the limit of a certain kind of knowledge: a natural frontier that censures further passage, but from which outward imaginative projections can be made. Journeys to coastal peripheries typically pre-empt Spenser's island encounters and this moment is no exception; Colin and the 'shepheard of the Ocean' leave *terra firma* behind in favour of a liquid realm of mountainous waters and that which lies beyond: a world of 'nought but sea and heauen' (227). As Paul Carter explains, the delineation of coastal space exhibits openness and potentiality, and islands occur when coastlines reveal their 'other side' and become 'detached'.[57] Islands turn the gaze back inwards again, betraying the limits of the cultural fantasies in which they partake.

Colin leaves the safety of his 'shepheards nation' (17) for a nation of islands in which sea and land meet: 'For land and sea my *Cynthia* doth deserue/ To haue in her commandement at hand' (262–3). Here, the holding command of Cynthia is subject to liquid unpredictability. On

... signifieth a straunger or traueiler' and 'descendeth from the worde *Peragrare* to wander'. See *The Traveiler* (London, 1575), sig. B1[r–v]. A copy of this book was given to Gabriel Harvey by Spenser. See Virginia F. Stern, *Gabriel Harvey: His Life, Marginalia and Library* (Oxford: Clarendon Press, 1979), p. 237. For further discussion of Spenser's children (where Sylvanus and Katherine were the offspring of his first wife) see Andrew Hadfield, *Edmund Spenser: A Life* (Oxford: Oxford University Press, 2012; repr. 2014), pp. 221–2.

55  See Julia Reinhard Lupton, 'Home-Making in Ireland: Virgil's *Eclogue* I and Book VI of *The Faerie Queene*', *Spenser Studies*, 8 (1990), 119–45.
56  See Pugh, *Spenser and Ovid*, p. 180.
57  Paul Carter, 'Dark with Excess of Bright: Mapping the Coastlines of Knowledge', in *Mappings*, ed. Denis Cosgrove (London: Reaktion, 1999), pp. 125–47 (p. 131).

such terms, the crossing of a watery threshold is an act that risks both body and soul:

> We *Lunday* passe; by that same name is ment
> An Island, which the first to west was showne.
> From thence another world of land we kend,
> Floting amid the sea in ieopardie,
> And round about with mightie white rocks hemd,
> Against the seas encroching crueltie. (270-5)

The description of Lundy and the isle beyond, 'Floting amid the sea in ieopardie', dramatises the unending elemental battle between the sea and the land. Here we see the making of geography, not only as the representational trace of a material and habitable world, but also as the manifestation of a moral lesson. For Gordon Braden, the perilous nature of even attempting to settle on an island is the driving and destabilising principle of 'Colin Clouts Come Home Againe', which by extension also informs Spenser's *View* and the final books of *The Faerie Queene*:

> Colin's advice is to stay home; but we hear more than once in *The Faerie Queene* how the sea even eats away at and changes the land, where we do our living. And how, in any case, do you avoid the lure of the sea when you live in a country where tides are felt sixty miles inland? How, indeed, when you live on an *island*?[58]

Braden conveys how precarious an island-dwelling existence can be; however, although he also evokes Artegall's observation that 'the primordial state of all dry land' is like being 'Hemd in with waters like a wall in sight' (V.ii.35), the implications of this observation are far greater than the critic acknowledges. Artegall's analogy is intended to speak of the shape of the cosmos itself, where 'The earth was in the middle centre pight,/ In which it does immoueable abide' (V.ii.35). In this brief moment the 'stedfast globe of earth' (I.viii.23) itself is imagined as an island, bounded by the waters of the *sphera aque*. As early as the fifth book of *The Faerie Queene*, Spenser shows Mutabilitie to be breaking her bounds.

From macrocosmic insular worlds to microcosmic echoes, Spenser's islands refract the unity of singular myth in order to play out the processes of mythmaking through recurrence and displacement. Lundy Island, which 'the first to west was showne', sits in the Bristol Channel about twelve miles from the North Devon coast. As well as being a

---

58 Gordon Braden, 'Riverrun: An Epic Catalogue in *The Faerie Queene*', *ELR*, 5.1 (1975), 25-48, p. 39. Emphasis in original.

seamark on the voyage between Ireland and England, Lundy, as Colin sights it, is a reminder of how otherworldly westward islands are a typical feature of the Irish tale-type known as *immram*, or 'voyage' literature, wherein archipelagic geographies span a continuum between earth and heaven, desert sea and garden.[59] Westward islands are also a feature of Arthurian geography, and in the sixth book of *The Faerie Queene* Spenser introduces the character of Tristram, son of King Meliogras, into Faery land from his birthplace on 'fertile *Lionesse*' (VI.ii.30), the fabled vanished land said to have been located between Cornwall and the Isles of Scilly. Echoing his representation of the youth of King Arthur, Spenser writes of Tristram's career as a squire, inventing a prelude to his role in the Matter of Britain: an introduction that is perhaps already darkened by Tristram's later exploits, as readers of Malory's *Morte d'Arthur* would forsee.[60] Spenser's brief mention of Lyonesse adds to the imagery of receding coastlines which, as in Book V's episode detailing the island-dwelling sons of Milesio, the 'deuouring Sea … hath washt away' (V.iv.8). In his *Britannia*, Camden records how the inhabitants of Cornwall suppose that the promontory 'heeretofore ran further into the Sea' and that according to fable 'the earth now covered there all over with the in-breaking of the Sea, was called *Lionesse*'.[61] Cornwall may be, as Bart van Es observes, the 'birthplace of the nation' and the locus of 'Britain's first settlement' in the fecund founding myths of early modern chorography;[62] yet, its vulnerable peripheries anchor narratives that are ever subject to what Richard Carew describes in his *Survey of Cornwall*

---

59 See Alfred K. Siewers, *Strange Beauty: Ecocritical Approaches to Early Medieval Landscape* (Basingstoke: Palgrave Macmillan, 2009), pp. 4–10. Lundy was believed to be a holy island by the Celts. See Charles Thomas, 'Lundy's Lost Name', in *Island Studies: Fifty Years of the Lundy Field Society*, ed. R.A. Irving, A.J. Schofield, and C.J. Webster (Bideford: Lazarus Press for The Lundy Field Society, 1997), pp. 29–37. Whether or not Spenser knew the St Brendan legend, which exists in several versions dating from the ninth century, he would have been aware of the legends of the Blessed or Fortunate isles from classical literature. See James Carney, 'Language and Literature to 1169', *A New History of Ireland, Volume I: Prehistoric and Early Ireland*, ed. Dáibhí Ó Cróinín (Oxford: Oxford University Press, 2005), pp. 500–9, and W.H. Babcock, 'St. Brendan's Explorations and Islands', *Geographical Review*, 8.1 (1919), 37–46. See also John R. Gillis, *Islands of the Mind*, pp. 29–41.
60 See Elizabeth M. Weixel, 'Squires of the Wood: The Decline of the Aristocratic Forest in Book VI of *The Faerie Queene*', *Spenser Studies*, 25 (2010), 187–213, pp. 194–200 in particular.
61 William Camden, *Britannia*, trans. Philemon Holland (London, 1610), sig. Q2$^r$.
62 Bart van Es, *Spenser's Forms of History* (Oxford: Oxford University Press, 2002), pp. 70–1. Van Es notes that the approach to Cornwall in Spenser's poem also performs 'the perspective of the chorographic muse' and that the place of disembarkation 'involves a transition from Spenser's to Ralegh's land' (pp. 69–70).

(1602) as 'the encroaching sea'.⁶³ As a piece of an island and a lost promontory made shake by the elements, Tristram's evocative birthplace dramatises the fragility of terrain that can be 'from the mayneland rift' (I.xi.54).

In Michael Drayton's *Poly-Olbion* (1612) Lundy is the beguiling subject of an ownership contest between England and Wales: an island-nymph 'That often had bewitcht the Sea-gods with her eye'.⁶⁴ As the personification of a pivotal space, she seems caught between mainland desires. For Colin, the 'wandring' island of Lundy acts as a seamark from the real world, spiting the constant threat of the eroding tide. Proudly added as an indicator of his narrative's veracity, the 'westward' sign asserts his eyewitness authority; yet, the ambiguous syntax Spenser uses to describe the 'Island, which the first to west was showne' hints at the paradoxes inherent in the shepherd-mariner's travels. The inclusion of a westward island is a knowing nod to literary and geographical convention; yet, Spenser writes as if Colin's description is a response to a first-time encounter, which has something of the *unheimlich* about it.⁶⁵ Lundy rests to the west if the origin of the journey is England, not Ireland, but offers the most westerly seamark of newly discovered terrain if the journey starts out from Irish soil. From Lundy the west coast of England can be 'kend' – or seen and known by the naked eye – on a clear day. In the mirror formed by the sea, the poet seems to imagine both return journey and maiden voyage, aligning the contours and placements of the isles to his subjective will.⁶⁶

In either case, the sense of the marvellous associated with the heightened westward movement demonstrates the longevity of medieval authorities.⁶⁷ In *The History and Topography of Ireland*, Gerald of Wales had emphasised Ireland's peripheral position: he wrote, of course, before America had come into view and before Mercator's projection had placed Europe snug and central at the heart of published maps. Framed thus, Ireland seemed to be at the periphery of civilisation,

---

63 Richard Carew, *The Survey of Cornwall* (London, 1602), sig. B3ʳ.
64 Michael Drayton, 'The Fourth Song', in *Poly-Olbion*, ed. John Selden (London, 1612), p. 56.
65 See Kenneth Gross, *Spenserian Poetics: Idolatry, Iconoclasm, and Magic* (Ithaca: Cornell University Press, 1985), p. 79.
66 See van Es, *Spenser's Forms of History*, pp. 71–3.
67 See Sir John Davies, *A Discovery of the True Causes*, in *Ireland Under Elizabeth and James the First*, ed. Henry Morley (London: Routledge, 1890), pp. 213–342. Davies claims, for example, that the 'manners of the mere Irish' still match 'the description made by Giraldus Cambrensis' (p. 218).

the last known land and western extremity before the pathless and uncharted ocean beyond:

> what new things, and what secret things not in accordance with her usual course had nature hidden away in the farthest western lands? For beyond those limits there is no land, nor is there any habitation either of men or beasts – but beyond the whole horizon only the ocean flows and is borne on in boundless space through its unsearchable and hidden ways.[68]

During the sixteenth century, the assumption of Ireland into a wider ranging 'westward enterprise', which sought to claim territories in the newly discovered Americas, may have brought the isle geographically closer but also served to position it ideologically further away.[69] A similar effect in miniature, then, can be observed in Spenser's treatment of Lundy. The isle appears in a way that exchanges mainland proximity for isolation on the threshold of 'another world of land'.

In 'Colin Clouts Come Home Againe', Spenser offers the reader a compressed and witty inversion of what would typically be expected from a travel narrative. Unexpectedly, it is the distant territory that offers Colin the pastoral idyll that is the natural habitat of the shepherd; at 'home' he is an exile in terms of both geography and genre, who has forgotten himself and 'base shepheard seemeth not' (618). By adopting the persona of Colin Clout, Spenser feigns a relationship between the speaking person and the land; however, as Jonathan Bate notes, shepherds 'do not write poems about their native hills' and 'do not exist in a self-conscious relationship to them'.[70] With a view that sees further than his native hill, Colin pipes a complicated tune that attempts to articulate a spatial relationship expressing archipelagic difference alongside identity. From his perspective, it is England that plays the role of the fortunate isle, as a new land to inspire wonder in his incredulous audience back home:

> There did our ship her fruitfull wombe vnlade,
> And put vs all ashore on *Cynthias* land.
> What land is that thou meanst (then *Cuddy* sayd)

---

68 Gerald of Wales, *The History and Topography of Ireland*, p. 30.
69 See Karl S. Bottigheimer, 'Kingdom and Colony: Ireland in the Westward Enterprise, 1536–1660', in *The Westward Enterprise*, ed. K.R. Andrews, N.P. Canny, and P.E.H. Hair (Liverpool: Liverpool University Press, 1978), pp. 45–64. For the idea that 'the Irish are too western and too eastern at one and the same time' see David Wallace, *Premodern Places: Calais to Surinam, Chaucer to Aphra Behn* (Oxford: Blackwell, 2004; repr. 2006), p. 193.
70 Jonathan Bate, *Romantic Ecology: Wordsworth and the Environmental Tradition* (London: Routledge, 1991), p. 88.

> And is there other, then whereon we stand?
> Ah *Cuddy* (then quoth *Colin*) thous a fon,
> That hast but seene least part of natures worke:
> Much more there is vnkend, then thou doest kon,
> And much more that does from mens knowledge lurke. (288–95)

Cuddy's questioning expression of surprise, following the revelation of the existence of a land other than the one he has inhabited all his life, emphasises the sense of meticulously crafted naivety associated with the pastoral mode. Convention suggests that pastoral poetry should be written from a sphere that is somehow counter to everyday life, a world of *otium*, not *negotium*; yet, an imagined existence in which Cynthia's name carries no meaning at all offers an extraordinary fusion of innocence and conscious refusal.

Colin's home, Spenser's Ireland, is thus redefined only in relation to the lands he has encountered to the east: Cynthia's land, Elizabeth's England. Colin explains the wonders he has seen using the rhetorical figure of *litotes*, processing the unfamiliar by eschewing what John Breen terms a waning 'mode of acquiring knowledge, ... based upon resemblance and finding affinities and similarities', in favour of identifying difference.[71] The two landmasses can only be perceived when informing on the other, their identities dependent on their juxtaposition:

> For there all happie peace and plenteous store
> Conspire in one to make contented blisse:
> Nor wayling there not wretchednesse is heard,
> No bloodie issues nor no leprosies,
> No griesly famine, nor no raging sweard,
> No nightly bodrags, nor no hue and cries;
> The shepheardes there abroad may safely lie,
> On hills and downes, withouten dread or daunger: ... (310–17)

They are either the same, or not the same; more complicated modes of variation are categories beyond the grasp of Colin and his homely audience. The shepherds only have Colin's word on which to base their image of a new world and he has described it in a way that appears to confirm only what they already know about their current location, perceived as a savage isle, surrounded by an 'encroaching' sea.

---

71 John Breen, '"Imaginatiue Groundplot": *A View of the Present State of Ireland*', *Spenser Studies*, 12 (1998), 151–68, p. 154.

*Constanter.* 129

THE raging Sea, that roares, with fearefull sounde,
And threatneth all the worlde to ouerflowe:
The shore sometimes, his billowes doth rebounde,
Though ofte it winnes, and giues the earthe a blowe
   Sometimes, where shippes did saile: it makes a lande.
   Sometimes againe they saile: where townes did stande.

So, if the Lorde did not his rage restraine,
And set his boundes, so that it can not passe:
The worlde shoulde faile, and man coulde not remaine,
But all that is, shoulde soone be turn'd to was:
   By raging Sea, is ment our ghostlie foe,
   By earthe, mans soule: he seekes to ouerthrowe.

And as the surge doth worke both daie, and nighte,
And shakes the shore, and ragged rockes doth rente:
So Sathan stirres, with all his maine, and mighte,
Continuall siege, our soules to circumuente.
   Then watche, and praie, for feare wee sleepe in sinne,
   For cease our crime: and hee can nothing winne.
                       R      *Dict.*

*Cicer. 2. Offic.*
Præclara est in omni vita æquabilitas, idemque vultus, eademque frons.

*Bern. in Epist.*
Perseuerantia est finis virtutum, & virtus sine qua nemo videbit deum.

*Figure 9* Geffrey Whitney. 'The Raging Sea', in *A Choice of Emblemes* (Leiden, 1586), fol. 129ᵛ.

## Coasting islands

Figure 9 shows an emblem of constancy taken from Geffrey Whitney's *A Choice of Emblemes* (1586). The viewer is positioned at a precarious cliff edge, looking out over the results of a process of ruin. The image shows a submerged city, where the waters of the deep have broken their bounds, and where fragile ships have been wrecked on a treacherous coastline: in the play of land and seascape, the waters have washed almost all traces of an inhabited, cultivated landscape away. What we are shown, by both image and text, is not an emblem of constancy at all, but one of inconstancy, and mutability: a representational gesture towards a material world that is tasked with bearing the weight of allegorical significance. As the increasingly alliterative verse below explains:

> The raging Sea, that roares, with fearefull sounde,
> And threatneth all the worlde to overflowe:
> The shore sometimes, his billowes doth rebounde,
> Though ofte it winnes, and gives the earthe a blowe
>    Sometimes, where shippes did saile: it makes a lande.
>    Sometimes againe they saile: where townes did stande.
>
> So, if the Lorde did not his rage restraine,
> And set his boundes, so that it can not passe:
> The worlde should faile, and man coulde not remaine,
> But all that is, shoulde soone be turn'd to was:
>    By raging Sea, is ment our ghostlie foe,
>    By earthe, mans soule: he seekes to overthrowe.
>
> And as the surge doth worke both daie, and nighte,
> And shakes the shore, and ragged rockes doth rente:
> So Sathan stirres, with all his maine, and mighte,
> Continuall siege, our soules to circumvente.
>    Then watche, and praie, for feare wee sleepe in sinne,
>    For cease our crime: and hee can nothing winne.[72]

What could have been a regional scene is remade as a universal site of strife. The land takes on divine significance as the soul of man, holding out against the wrath and tempest of Satan. In what is no longer an image of coastal erosion but a sixteenth-century reimagining of Noah's flood, natural contours have been washed away by a sudden rush of ethical significance. The anxiety at the heart of the stanzas, that 'the worlde should faile, and man coulde not remaine' is a cultural anxiety as well as a moral

---

72 Geffrey Whitney, *A Choice of Emblemes* (Leiden, 1586), fol. 129ᵛ.

one, where cultivated, inhabited, land speaks of labour that assumes endurance.

In his short essay on *Desert Islands*, Gilles Deleuze suggests that the reason why islands are often deserted in the imagination, and that this desertion 'must appear *philosophically* normal to us', is because 'humans cannot live, nor live in security, unless they assume that the active struggle between earth and water is over, or at least contained'.[73] In his writings on Ireland in both poetry and prose, Spenser manipulates the reader's sense of literal and figurative insularity in order to capture the instability of a plantation always in jeopardy of being washed away by forces greater than itself. In his reading of Deleuze, Alfred K. Siewers observes that islands are seen to function 'as a continual reminder of elements in flux, ... a "double movement" of earth and sea, of separation and creation (much like the shifting sands and horizons in the desert), which humans want to forget because of the unsettling ramifications for any discrete sense of identity'.[74] Spenser's *View*, after all, famously begins with Eudoxus's enquiry concerning the suitability of Ireland for plantation, to which he receives the response from Irenaeus that perhaps owing to 'the fatall destinie of that Land', all English plots and purposes result in failure (p. 43). Irenaeus's description of the natural world is consciously shaped; Spenser may name these forces as fate, as influences that are both cosmic and divine, and may lay them all at the feet of a particularly wretched *genius loci*, but the prevailing impression is of a mediated, emblematic landscape.[75] As Eudoxus replies, attempting, and failing, to grasp the situation fully: 'I allsoe harde it often wished, even of some whose greate wisdome in opinion shoulde seme to iudge more soundlye of so weightye a Consideracion, that all that Land weare a sea poole, which kinde of speache, is the manner rather of desperate men farre driven to wishe the vtter rvine of that which they Cannot redress' (p. 44). Eudoxus might push against rumour and superstition; yet, the fantasy of erasure and submergence to which he refers captures the implicit severity of Elizabethan colonial policy. An Ireland figured as blank expanse to be charted afresh, cleansed as if by another biblical deluge, lies latent within Spenser's *View* as a desirable precondition for conquest. As wetland gives way to open water, the strange image of drowned terrain offers an inverted kind of revelation: a defilement of the apocalyptic

---

73 Deleuze, *Desert Islands*, p. 9.
74 Siewers, *Strange Beauty*, p. 21.
75 Gross, *Spenserian Poetics*, p. 79 and pp. 82–4.

vision in which 'the first heaven, and the first earth were passed away, and there was no more sea'.[76]

Ortelius's 1573 re-edition of his atlas included a map of Ireland based on his friend Mercator's Irish map of 1564 and, as Andrews notes, Ortelius replaced 'Mercator's placid-looking sea-stipple with the most turbulent waves to be seen anywhere in the *Theatrum*'.[77] As a representation of hydrographical danger, Ortelius's waves share a heightened sense of worldly contingency with the turbulent images of navigation used by Spenser throughout his dialogue to make political arguments. The way in which the waters of Eudoxus's 'sea poole' reappear in later passages of *A View* suggests that Elizabeth's desperate agents should be careful in what they wish for. During the digression that accompanies Spenser's praise of Arthur Grey, Lord Deputy of Ireland, under whom Spenser served as secretary from 1580 to 1582, for example, the encroaching waters become a tempest, and through Spenser's sustained use of metaphor and simile, the political and legal dialogue becomes allegorical:

> Eudoxus: ... I do muche pittye the swete lande to be subiecte to soe manye evills, as everye daie I see more and more throwne vppon her and doe halfe begine to thinke that it is, as ye saide at the beginninge her fatall misfortune aboue all Countries that I knowe to be thus miserablye Tossed and turmoylled with these variable stormes of affliccions. But since we are thus farr entred into the Consideracion of her mishapps tell mee, Haue there bynne anye more suche Tempestes as yee terme them whearein she hathe thus wretchedlye bene wrecked. (p. 63)

Spenser's prose increasingly shares the alliterative argumentative style of the emblem book. And, as Irenaeus reports, Ireland has been left, 'like a shippe in a storme amiddest all the raginge surges vnruled and vndirected of anye, ffor they to whom shee was Comitted either fainted in theire labour or for sooke theire Chardge' (p. 63).

The rhetorical maelstrom then moves through fantasies of postdiluvian submergence to an image of the ship of state being piloted wisely though uncertain times, portraying Grey as a Christ-like figure who holds his course despite the storm of criticism:[78]

> But he like a moste wise Pilott kepte her Course Carefullye and helde her moste strongelye even against those roringe billowes that he safelye broughte her out of all, so as longe after, even by the space of xii or xiii

---

76 *The Bible* (London, 1576), Revelation 21:1, fol. 115ʳ.
77 Andrews, *Shapes of Ireland*, p. 51.
78 See Herron, *Spenser's Irish Work*, p. 62.

yeares shee rod at peace thoroughe his onelye paines and excellent endurance how euer envye liste to batter againste him. (p. 63)

Unlike Christ in Mark 4:35–40, Grey cannot afford to sleep at the head of his vessel. As William Bourne makes transparently clear in *A Regiment for the Sea*, for example, he who is fit to be the 'maister of ships in Navigation' ought to be 'such a one as can wel govern himselfe' in moments of difficulty and 'have capacitie howe for to handle or shift himselfe in foule weather or stormes'.[79] He must also 'cause himself both to be feared and loved'.[80] As Spenser's generous defence of Grey's actions after the massacre at Smerwick in 1580 shows, the line between fear and love, or brute force and friendship, was often hard to distinguish in English eyes.[81] As a favourite Renaissance image for the art of good government, the handling of the ship of state offered an image of controlled labour that occluded the discharge of accompanying violence.

In an attempt to reassert the influence of the English administration, for example, Spenser's Irenaeus advocates repositioning the seat of the Lord Deputy away from Dublin, 'beinge the outest Corner in the realme and leaste nedinge the awe of his presence'. Relocation to Athlone, he argues, would offer a more favourable perspective, 'in the middest of his Chardge', from which to observe the fullest measure of the population:

> he shoulde seate himselfe aboute Athie or theareaboutes vppon the skirte of that vnquiet Countrye so that he mighte sitt as it weare at the verye maine maste of his shipp where he mighte easelye ouerloke and somtimes ouerreache the moores/ the Butlers the dempsies the ketins the Connours/ Ocarroll Omoloy and all that heape of Irish nacions which theare lie hundredes togeather without anie to ouerawe them or Containe them in dewtie for the Irishmen I assure youe feares the gouernment no longer then he is within sighte or reache. (pp. 188–9)

Again, the Lord Deputy is imagined as a ship's pilot, this time gaining the raised perspective necessary to navigate the microcosmic ship of state through uncertain waters and the proximity to 'be sone at hande in anie place' (p. 188).[82] Yet, for all the suggestion of skilled labour and a master-

---

79 William Bourne, *A Regiment for the Sea* (London, 1574), sig. B3ʳ.
80 Ibid., sig. B3ᵛ.
81 See David Read, *Temperate Conquests: Spenser and the Spanish New World* (Detroit: Wayne State University Press, 2000), p. 14.
82 A comparable image is provided by Sir John Davies, who describes Alexander the Great's use of an animal hide to demonstrate the best place from which to govern an empire. When pressure was exerted on 'the middle of the hide' the rest lay 'flat and even'. See *A Discovery of the True Causes*, p. 313.

ful gaze, the repositioned mooring of the Lord Deputy at Athlone is ominously static; Spenser's ship of state exists in peril of being run aground. It is noteworthy that the description of the overthrow of the Munster Plantation that appears in an anonymous work written in 1598 figures the toppling of English governance as an unstoppable flood:

> As a huge sea bounded in with bankes, having once made a breache and passage sufficient open, overfloweth the underlyinge feildes of a suddaine: soe were we overrune before we hard of any breache made into oure quarters. It was no yeares worke: It was not a moneth in doinge: It was finyshed in a fewe houres: he that was abroade coulde not get home to save himselfe but was intercepted. He that was in a thatchte house had no leasure to shifte himselfe into a Castell for defence, but was slayne by the waye: he that was in the Contrie had no respite to flye into the Cittie. Every base Chorle layd hands on his next neighbour.[83]

No dialogue this, but a diatribe, the treatise resonates with the cadences of sermon literature and directs its most pointed criticism at a congregation of one: Elizabeth I herself. The reformation sought is not just of Ireland but also of Elizabeth's policies and her failing grip on the island's population, Gaelic Irish and Old English alike.

The tumultuous waters associated with Ireland in these texts heighten the effect of the navigational motifs and commonplaces in Spenser's poetry; in particular, the Legend of Courtesy returns repeatedly to similar images of breached banks, unstopped waters, and ill-piloted vessels. The fury of Sir Calidore's attack on Maleffort, for example, is likened to water's capacity to violate attempts to tame its flow:

> Like as a water streame, whose swelling sourse
>   Shall driue a Mill, within strong bancks is pent,
>   And long restrayned of his ready course;
>   So soone as passage is vnto him lent,
>   Breakes forth, and makes his way more violent. (VI.i.21)

Like Guyon and Artegall before him, Calidore is an intemperate man.[84] The moment shares similarities with Sir Walter Ralegh's images of rechannelled waters and failed labour in the '21th: and last booke of the Ocean to

---

83 Willy Maley, 'The Supplication of the Blood of the English Most Lamentably Murdered in Ireland, Cryeng out of the Yearth for Revenge (1958)', *Analecta Hibernica*, 36 (1995), 1–77 (p. 17). Maley suggests that the initials found at the end of the manuscript, T.C., could be those of the theologian Thomas Cartwright.

84 For Calidore as a man 'radically inadequate to his task' see Richard Neuse, 'Book IV as Conclusion to *The Faerie Queene*', *ELH*, 35.3 (1968), 329–53 (p. 352).

Scinthia' (see Chapter 5). In its images of lost fecundity, Ralegh's elegiac and fragmentary lyric mourns the withdrawal of an animating force from the landscape, and its replacement by indistinction; his Cynthia, his beloved, and his queen no longer maintain a dwelling presence. In Book VI of *The Faerie Queene*, a similar motif can also be found in Matilde's lamentation of her inability to provide her husband Sir Bruin with an heir; although he has defeated the giant Cormoraunt, named perhaps for his ravenous aquatic nature, by the nearby ford, Matilde fears that the control Sir Bruin enjoys over his lands is fated to wane, and 'like in time to further ill to grow,/ And all this land with endless losse to ouerflow' (VI.iv.30). Only a son, '*Be gotten, not begotten*' will 'drinke/ And dry vp all the water, which doth ronne/ In the next brooke, by whom that feend shold be fordonne' (VI.iv.32). For Matilde, whose maternal and geopolitical desires are put to rest by the arrival of Calepine and the foundling, the threat of water recedes with her grateful weeping. For Elizabeth, as absent monarch, there was no such easy solution.[85]

If Calepine's movements are determined by his weary limbs and heavy armour (see Chapter 6), then the progress of Sir Calidore, Spenser's eponymous Knight of Courtesy, is fashioned as an extension of Artegall's maritime labour. On meeting for the first time 'They knew them selues, and both their persons rad' (VI.i.4). Calidore's decision to relinquish the active life seems deliberately framed in the language of seafaring, where courtesy, the narrator implies, requires the same ability to manage contingency as temperance and justice.[86] In the battle between Artegall and Grantorto, for example, the narrator emphasises Artegall's defensive strategies: he bides his time, akin to the 'skilfull Marriner' who would strike 'his sayles, and vereth his mainsheat' when a storm approaches (V.xii.18), exchanging the pursuit of swift passage for that of relative steadfastness, as if understanding how to manage the force of the waters.[87] For Artegall, negotiating when to exert mastery over, and when to collaborate with, the sea is a project of endless labour, but for Calidore it is an exertion from which he has become tired:

> Since then in each mans self (said *Calidore*)
>   It is, to fashion his owne lyfes estate,
>   Giue leaue awhyle, good father, in this shore

---

85 For the Irish dimension of Spenser's many mirrors for Elizabeth see Andrew Hadfield, 'Another Look at Serena and Irena', *IUR*, 26.2 (1996), 291–302.
86 See Herron, *Spenser's Irish Work*, p. 186.
87 See Philip Edwards, *Sea-Mark: The Metaphorical Voyage, Spenser to Milton* (Liverpool: Liverpool University Press, 1997), p. 32.

> To rest my barcke, which hath bene beaten late
> With stormes of fortune and tempestuous fate,
> In seas of troubles and of toylesome paine,
> That whether quite from them for to retrate
> I shall resolue, or backe to turne againe,
> I may here with your selfe some small repose obtaine. (VI.ix.31)

When Calidore makes the decision to end his quest prematurely by making landfall on the shores of a pastoral world his actions result not in fecundity but wreck.[88] As one who had purported to 'tread an endlesse trace' (VI.i.6), his retreat to what he perceives to be a safe harbour marks him as one of those criticised by Spenser in *A View* as having 'fainted in theire labour or for sooke theire Chardge'.

In his definitions of literary chronotopes, Mikhail Bakhtin refers to the 'specific insular idyllic landscape' of pastoral poetry, emphasising the deliberate attempt of much pastoral writing to provide a 'sealed-off segment of nature's space'.[89] For Spenser, the pastoral world of which his shepherds sing seems only to exist in order to illustrate its fragility. The pastoral mode may be insular but its boundaries, as Calidore himself demonstrates, are penetrable.[90] Julia Reinhard Lupton has argued that 'Book VI of *The Faerie Queene* stands in bright relief against the disturbing greys of Book V's stone and iron, a welcome alleviation facilitated by pastoral as the genre of idealization and escape';[91] however, rather than providing an oppositional space to Book V, Book VI's narratives of husbandry, violence, and conquest suggest that earth, stone, and iron are precisely the foundations on which its pastoral spaces are built.[92] With this in mind, the proem to Book VI is often invoked as evidence that

---

88 For the apocalyptic implications of reframing 'pastoral harmony in a maritime environment' see Mentz, *Shipwreck Modernity*, p. 169. See also Harry Berger, Jr., 'The Renaissance Imagination: Second World and Green World', in *Second World and Green World*, ed. John Patrick Lynch (Berkeley: University of California Press, 1988), pp. 3–40 (p. 36) and Jerome S. Dees, 'The Ship Conceit in *The Faerie Queene*: "Conspicuous Allusion" and Poetic Structure', *Studies in Philology*, 72 (1975), 208–25, pp. 220–5.
89 Mikhail Bakhtin, 'Forms of Time and of the Chronotope in the Novel', in *The Dialogic Imagination*, ed. Michael Holquist, trans. Caryl Emerson and Michael Holquist (Austin: University of Texas Press, 1981; repr. 2002), pp. 84–258 (p. 103). In Anderson's words, the 'larger context of Book VI might be said to encompass its pastoral cantos, as they in turn encompass the vision on Mount Acidale, and as the entire book is encompassed by what is beyond and outside it'. See *Reading the Allegorical Intertext*, p. 104.
90 See Nohrnberg, 'Britomart's Gone Abroad to Brute-land', pp. 223–5.
91 Lupton, 'Home-Making in Ireland', p. 119.
92 See Benjamin P. Myers, 'The Green and Golden World: Spenser's Rewriting of the Munster Plantation', *ELH*, 76.2 (2009), 473–90 and Herron, *Spenser's Irish Work*, pp. 185–224.

Spenser's poem begins to cast an eye back across its textures in order to take account of its cumulative progress.[93] Here, the narrator begins to explain how the beauty and variety of the poem sustains the poet-traveller; no longer cast adrift, he has made secure landfall, allowing painful labour give way to ravishment:

> The waies, through which my weary steps I guyde,
>   In this delightfull land of Faery,
> Are so exceeding spacious and wyde,
> And sprinckled with such sweet variety,
>   Of all that pleasant is to eare or eye,
> That I nigh rauisht with rare thoughts delight,
>   My tedious trauell doe forget thereby;
> And when I gin to feele decay of might,
> It strength to me supplies, and chears my dulled spright. (VI.Pro.1)

The prospect seems secure until the reader is tasked with reflecting retrospectively on the ways in which Spenser's encompassing frames interact. The headway claimed by the narrator is troublingly analogous to that made by Calidore, who makes temporary landfall only to be thrown back into his quest in the final canto; in this canto's opening stanza, the narrator returns to the image of the storm-tossed ship, whose 'often stayd' (VI. xii.1) course becomes the compositional motif once more.[94]

Similarly, the shepherd Meliboe may offer Calidore simple hospitality but his subsequent imprisonment at the hands of a 'lawlesse people' (VI.x.39) and death in captivity evidences what Heather Dubrow has seen as 'the tragic permeability of this, though perhaps not all, pastoral worlds'.[95] If Ralegh can imagine the death of the pastoral world as an ecological disaster (see Chapter 5), then Spenser uses his final completed book of *The Faerie Queene* to imagine the massacre of its 'innocents', whose pastoral dwellings, in this instance, shadow the activities of the New English, as if all the members of this 'shepheards nation' were poet-planters like Spenser himself.[96] In Book VI of *The Faerie Queene*, the

---

93 See Patricia A. Parker, *Inescapable Romance: Studies in the Poetics of a Mode* (Princeton: Princeton University Press, 1979), p. 101.
94 For the narrator's relationship to the motions of the poem's characters see Paul J. Alpers, 'Narration in *The Faerie Queene*', *ELH*, 44.1 (1977), 19–39, pp. 30–1.
95 Heather Dubrow, '"A Doubtful Sense of Things": Thievery in *The Faerie Queene* 6.10–6.11', in *Worldmaking Spenser: Explorations in the Early Modern Age*, ed. Patrick Cheney and Lauren Silberman (Lexington: University Press of Kentucky, 2000), pp. 204–16 (p. 205).
96 For the idea of a 'pastoral empire' see Thomas Herron, 'New English Nation: Munster Politics, Virgilian Complaint, and Pastoral Empire in Spenser's "Colin Clouts Come Home Againe" (1595)', *Eolas*, 8 (2015), 89–122.

pressure of the transition between epic and pastoral plays out in ecotonal habitats gone awry; in the recurrent images of waters out of place, and mariners on dry land, Spenser reflects on the resilience of cultivating practices, embedding narratives concerning the endurance of individual and collective government. In so doing, the book as a whole returns on both microcosmic and macrocosmic levels to a motif found in Book I, in which Una, described as experiencing 'paines far passing that long wandring *Greeke*' (I.iii.21), finds what she thinks is a safe harbour, only to be met by the illusions and false promises of Archimago.[97]

When the consequences of Calidore's choices are framed in the above terms, the capture of Pastorella by brigands and her potential sale to pirates seems to figure, for Spenser, a rough kind of poetic justice. She may survive the massacre in which her fellow shepherds and shepherdesses are killed but her fate retains an insular focus. Earlier figurations of pastoral insulation solidify into the crannog-like island-stronghold of the brigands in canto xi:[98] a space that entices other outlaws, a 'sort of merchants', to engage in maritime trade. Hiding her 'constant mynd' (VI.xi.5) in order to please her captors with feigned favours, Pastorella is soon faced with this new seaborne threat:

> During which space that she thus sicke did lie,
>    It chaunst a sort of merchants, which were wount
>    To skim those coastes, for bondmen there to buy,
>    And by such trafficke after gaines to hunt,
>    Arriued in this Isle though bare and blunt,
>    T'inquire for slaues ... (VI.xi.9)

The 'bare and blunt' island is a far cry from the fantastic island loci of Phaedria and Acrasia, but redolent of Colin Clout's Ireland. Although Pastorella's eventual rescue by Calidore and the revelation of her noble identity seems to make good Spenser's promise to return the poem 'vnto one certaine cost' (VI.xii.1), *The Faerie Queene*, it seems, contains no such thing, particularly if, as Fitzpatrick argues, the shepherdess's role in Spenser's allegory has the capacity to shadow 'the land of Ireland itself'.[99] Donald Cheney has written of the resonant pastoral and romance motifs

---

97 For the 'failure of courtesy' and, consequently, Spenser's epic vision, see Neuse, 'Book IV as Conclusion to *The Faerie Queene*', p. 331.
98 See Thomas Herron, 'Irish Den of Thieves: Souterrains (and a Crannog?) in Books V and VI of Spenser's *Faerie Queene*', *Spenser Studies*, 14 (2000), 303–17.
99 Fitzpatrick, *Irish Demons*, p. 121.

employed by Spenser in the depiction of Pastorella's homecoming;[100] yet, the family reunion is framed by fragmentation. Pastorella's travails end uncannily at the castle of her long-lost birth parents, Sir Bellamoure and Claribell, who the narrator explains is the daughter of 'The Lord of *Many Ilands*' (VI.xii.4): a name that suggests multiplicity rather than unity, and gestures towards the idea that a singular safe harbour is not to be found either literally or metaphorically. It is too difficult to forget the number of fallen bodies that populate the penultimate canto of the book: casualties of different causes and estates whose stories are not fully resolved either by Calidore's resumed exercise of 'courtesie' (VI.xii.2) or by his failed attempt to silence the Blatant Beast.[101] During Calidore's retaliatory massacre, the ground is 'strowd with bodies' (VI.xi.49), mingling those of the shepherds with those of the 'theeues' (IV.xi.48). As Lupton remarks, the sense that 'the Brigants themselves might be victims of displacement is a possibility actively excluded by the poem';[102] yet, complicit with Colin Clout's revelation that there are other, stranger lands across the waters, the possibility of homecoming for any character loses its distinction within the multitudinous plots, inversions, and mirrorings put in motion by the violent energies of Spenser's insular fictions.

## Unperfected space

It is perhaps in the brief space afforded by the unfinished, 'vnperfite', seventh book of *The Faerie Queene* that the implications of Spenser's 'island logic' can be fully seen. First published a decade after Spenser's death in the 1609 folio edition by Matthew Lownes, the cantos juxtapose images of macrocosmic space with local landmarks visible from Spenser's estate on the Munster Plantation in Ireland.[103] The cantos provide an ambiguous and provisional end to the poem. As the headnote to the cantos reads: 'TWO CANTOS OF MUTABILITIE: Which, both for Forme and Matter, appear to be parcell of some following Booke of the FAERIE QVEENE, VNDER THE LEGEND OF Constancie'. It is as if they have broken off from the mainland of the rest of the poem. In

100 See Donald Cheney, 'Colin Clout's Homecoming: The Imaginative Travels of Edmund Spenser', *Connotations*, 7.2 (1997–1998), 146–58, pp. 156–8.
101 See Hadfield, *Edmund Spenser's Irish Experience*, p. 184.
102 Lupton, 'Home-Making in Ireland', p. 133.
103 As Patricia Coughlan observes, Galtymore (called Arlo-hill by Spenser) 'is the summit of the Galtee mountains, clearly visible, because of its height, from a long distance around, but in fact located some fifteen miles east of Kilcolman'. See 'The Local Context of Mutabilitie's Plea', *IUR*, 26.2 (1996), 320–41, p. 326.

particular, the use of the word 'parcell' recalls Dee's definition of chorography in his *Mathematicall Praeface* (see Chapter 4), which addresses the way in which the word can refer to a 'portion or piece of land, frequently one in separate occupation or ownership from those that surround it'.[104] Space becomes place, and narratives writ large on the cosmos are also inscribed on Irish soil; when Spenser locates the action on *Arlo-hill* – '(Who knowes not *Arlo-hill*?)' – he thus re-emphasises the importance of the poem's concern for the fixity of landmarks, and one's knowledge of them (VII.vi.36). Spenser's rhetorical question is, after all, a question of geographical knowledge, and of possessing the ability to locate and organise thought and meaning.

For Spenser, the cantos trace the horizon visible from his estate, lands that he could view but not master; the summit functions, as Patricia Coughlan writes, 'no longer purely as a *locus amoenus* in the tradition of classical poetry ... but also as Galtymore, the highest peak of a mountain range above a heavily wooded and enclosed valley – the Glen of Aherlow'.[105] As a literal and literary landmark, *Arlo-hill* serves to 'grapple, or moor, the visionary to the real world'.[106] It provides a brief image of *terra firma* on which to locate the visionary: the local and the cosmic are temporarily seen to coexist within the poem, collapsing differences in scale in order to stage an encounter between different ways of knowing and understanding. The specificity of the geography in the Mutabilitie Cantos provides an unexpected focal point to a cosmos that would otherwise be an abstraction; the leap from macrocosm to local geography positions Ireland, in E.A.F. Porges Watson's words, as 'a frontier, blurred but permeable, between different kinds of imaginative apprehension'.[107] Spenser's cosmos, with *Arlo-hill* placed at its centre, reveals the way in which the creative mind shapes its own perspective on the world.

As a site of re-beginning, *Arlo-hill* works as a mythically believable site for an apocalypse, because, as the highest point on the skyline, it

104 See 'parcel, n., adv., and adj., 5a', *OED Online*. Oxford University Press, June 2018 (last accessed 31 August 2018).
105 Ibid., p. 325.
106 A. Bartlett Giamatti, *Exile and Change in Renaissance Literature* (New Haven: Yale University Press, 1984), p. 82. As Linda Gregerson writes, it is 'one of those wonderful Spenserian sites where the floating world of mythic place is rudely reconfigured by the pull of the actual'. See 'Telling Time: Temporality in *The Faerie Queene*', Hugh MacClean Memorial Lecture, International Spenser Society, 7 January 2012, *Spenser Review*, 42.7, p. 3.
107 E.A.F. Porges Watson, 'Mutabilitie's Debateable Land: Spenser's Ireland and the Frontiers of Faerie', in *Edmund Spenser: New and Renewed Directions*, ed. J.B. Lethbridge (Madison: Fairleigh Dickinson University Press, 2006), pp. 286–301 (p. 295).

is prefigured for Spenser by biblical geography. Porges Watson, for example, remarks that *Arlo-hill* echoes the Mount of Contemplation in the first book of *The Faerie Queene*, recalling Sinai, the Mount of Olives and Parnassus.[108] In addition, the presence of great Dame Nature upon *Arlo-hill* strikes the narrator as an echo of the transfiguration of Christ upon Mount *Thabor* (VII.vii.7). Finally, it also echoes Ararat *in potentia*: a refuge for the time after *A View*'s diluvian waters have receded and left behind a deserted island ripe for reformation. For Deleuze, islands and mountains, 'or both at once', often figure archetypal sacred spaces in the geographical imagination; they are places where an ark, even a ship of state, could make landfall. They are 'the one place on earth that remains uncovered by water, a circular and sacred place, from which the world begins anew'.[109] For Spenser, *Arlo-hill* provides a final harbour for the 'weary vessell' of the poet (I.xii.42): a site of situated knowledge where the battle between land and sea is at once both over and perpetual.

Spenser may write that Ireland is a place 'Of wealths and goodnesse, far aboue the rest/ Of all that beare the *British* Islands name' (VII.vi.38); however, in the parenthetical story of Diana and Faunus, he explains how the Gods abandoned the holy-Island and left it a forsaken place under a 'heauy haplesse curse' (VII.vi.55), connecting the reaction of the virgin deity, and the indecorum of the laughing spectator who discovers her nakedness, to failed Elizabethan policy in Ireland.[110] His fecund mythmaking tells of endings resulting in failure and abandonment, of a once holy-Island now deserted; yet, it also imagines a future in which such myths can be rewritten, resisting narrative closure.[111] Again, as for Deleuze, the 'mythological life of the deserted island' implies 'not creation but re-creation, not the beginning but a re-beginning'.[112] The fantasies that Spenser's images attempt to hold together, of re-inscription and reformation, are precisely the issues that the 'Cantos of Mutabilitie' attempt to negotiate.

Ireland, of course, far from being deserted, was fertile, populated, and mythologically self-sustaining:[113] only English eyes viewed it in pola-

---

108 Ibid., pp. 299–300.
109 Deleuze, *Desert Islands*, p. 13.
110 See Herron, *Spenser's Irish Work*, pp. 158–63 and McCabe, *Spenser's Monstrous Regiment* (Oxford: Oxford University Press, 2002), pp. 260–4.
111 See Gross, *Spenserian Poetics*, p. 81 and p. 89. As Colin Burrow observes, 'Faunus, a Spenserian descendent of Actaeon, suffers no such terminal change'. See *Epic Romance: Homer to Milton* (Oxford: Clarendon, 1993), p. 144.
112 Deleuze, *Desert Islands*, p. 13.
113 See Brian J. Graham and Lindsay J. Proudfoot, eds, *An Historical Geography of Ireland* (London: Academic Press, 1993).

rised terms as either 'sweet' or 'waste'.[114] As Gordon Teskey observes, the true threat of Mutabilitie, which emerges as *The Faerie Queene* progresses, is the threat of endless dispersal and 'inchoateness': 'She contains every world that would struggle to displace this actual world were her genealogical power released, spawning worlds by the tens of thousands, like roe'.[115] Teskey's image is of Spenser's 'worldmaking' gone awry, in which the poet's unified image of Faery land can no longer contain 'the welter of innumerable adjacent worlds' and 'the confusion of alterity and diplomacy' that the poet imagines.[116] This is the culmination, perhaps, of what Gregerson identifies as Redcrosse's challenge in Book I, where the 'thinking in which he is trained through twelve cantos demands complex suspensions: multiple forms of citizenship, multiple forms of allegiance, multiple forms of ethical obligation, multiple modes of moving through time, both sacred and historical'.[117] Echoing the moment in *The Tempest* when the travellers debate how Carthage, a lost world, has become Tunis, a site of diplomatic relations and arranged marriages, the *oikos* is no longer steadfast. As Shakespeare's Antonio and Sebastian mockingly remark, the island on which they stand could be carried home like an apple, and Gonzalo, 'sowing the kernels of it in the sea' could 'bring forth more islands'.[118] The connection between islands and plantation is surely in the playwright's mind.[119] In Spenser's *Faerie Queene*, this is the power of Mutabilitie; she claims power, after all, over all Nature's creatures and 'this lower world' (VII.vii.47).

In the midst of the spatial dissonance, the presence of the island-mountain shows how the mythology of *The Faerie Queene* depends on examples taken from the poet's life in Ireland. Far from corrupting his imagination, as C.S. Lewis would have it, they sustain it.[120] By offering the potential of a raised perspective, exaggerated by the site's adoption as a seat of gods and titans, the view from *Arlo-hill* suggests the possibility of looking across the mutable coastlines, islands, and wetlands

---

114 For 'waste' as a key word in Spenser's *View* see Lupton, 'Mapping Mutability', p. 93.
115 Gordon Teskey, *Allegory and Violence* (Ithaca: Cornell University Press, 1996), p. 182.
116 Roland Greene, 'A Primer of Spenser's Worldmaking: Alterity in the Bower of Bliss', in *Worldmaking Spenser*, pp. 9–31 (p. 15).
117 Linda Gregerson, 'Spenser's Georgic: Violence and the Gift of Place', *Spenser Studies*, 22 (2007), 185–201, p. 198.
118 William Shakespeare, *The Tempest*, ed. Virginia Mason Vaughan and Alden T. Vaughan (London: Thompson, 1999; repr. 2003), II.i.93–4.
119 See Barbara Fuchs, 'Conquering Islands: Contextualizing *The Tempest*', *SQ*, 48.1 (1997), 45–62.
120 See C.S. Lewis, *The Allegory of Love: A Study in Medieval Tradition* (New York: Oxford University Press, 1936; repr. 1958), pp. 348–9.

beneath; a distancing, it seems, that facilitates abstraction. As this and the previous chapters have argued, Spenser's curious geographies constantly inform the depth and permeability of his allegories. In the case of Book VII, the implicit images of desertion in the two existing cantos illuminate the most ethically indefensible aspects of Spenser's writing and an explicit failure to acknowledge the violence involved in the cultivation of a colony: 'if poetry is finally the home which Spenser creates for himself', Lupton writes, 'it is an abode built with costs to others'.[121] The 'one certaine cost' (VI.xii.1), it seems, is no safe harbour, only a measure of distance and loss. The desertion of Ireland could only ever be a reprehensible fantasy, possible only after the implementation of schemes such as those considered by the anonymous author of 'A Discourse of Ireland' (c. 1599), 'whereby her Majesty shall make Ireland profitable unto her as England or mearely a West England',[122] and John Davies in his *A Discovery of the True Causes* (1612). Davies's reflection on Tudor policy in Ireland leads him to the observation that 'by consequence the conquest became impossible without the utter extirpation of all the Irish', where 'extirpation' from the Latin *exstirpare*, to tear up by the root, is the term he gives to his abortive dreams of depopulation.[123] Echoing Spenser, his predecessor as both poet and administrator in Ireland, Davies writes prose infused with metaphor, turning brutal truths into poetry. He recalls the desire for 'a mixed plantation of British and Irish', where 'the Irish were in some places transplanted from the woods and mountains into the plains and open countries', thus turning an entire people into a commodity. In praise of the blazing light of majesty brought by James VI and I to bear on Ireland, he writes of unruly forests becoming orchards of 'wild fruit trees' and of chaos realigning into order.[124]

For Spenser, the deliberate obfuscations enabled by the use of figurative language resulted in the source of his deepest and most self-referential poetic meditations but also left him with the irresolvable paradox that Ireland could never be both 'blessed' and the finest of the '*British* Islands'. As Greene supposes, 'the ethical challenge of island logic, of course, is in accepting someone else's'.[125] This challenge becomes

---

121 Lupton, 'Home-Making in Ireland', p. 141.
122 David B. Quinn, '"A Discourse of Ireland" (Circa 1599): A Sidelight on English Colonial Policy', *Proceedings of the Royal Irish Academy. Section C*, 47 (1941/1942), 151–66, p. 166.
123 Sir John Davies, *A Discovery of the True Causes*, p. 280. For a similar motif see 'A Discourse of Ireland', p. 164.
124 Ibid., pp. 339–40.
125 Greene, 'Island Logic', p. 144.

explicit in the 'Cantos of Mutabilitie': an impasse that the poem in its present state leaves unresolved. Spenser's islands are microcosmic, not heterocosmic.[126] As a way of plotting the archipelagic and multivalent relationship between England and Ireland, 'island logic' may have initially provided Spenser with 'places to go' but this strategy ultimately could not privilege England's myth of its impermeable singularity, try as it might. At his most triumphant, Dee may have asked the readers of his *General and Rare Memorials Pertayning to the Perfect Arte of Navigation*, 'And shall not we, have the Courage and skill, rightfully to enjoy the very Precinct of our own Naturall Ilandish walls, and Royallty of our Sea Limits, here, at home, and before our doores?', but his writings ultimately did little to bring his vision of an 'incomparable ilandish monarchie' to pass (sig. C3$^v$ and A2$^r$). To embrace the concept of '*British* Islands' fully, any Elizabethan island poetics would have had to admit something more vulnerable and fragmented: the image of a kingdom or kingdoms scattered like apple pips amongst the waves. This image would have had to allow for proximity, hybridity, and what Spenser would have thought of as cultural contagion, for the play of difference and all its transformations, and would have had to reconfigure the short-comings of insularity and all its implications.

---

126 For a 'heterotopian' reading see Anne Fogarty, 'Narrative Strategy in *The Faerie Queene*, Book VI', in *Edmund Spenser*, ed. Andrew Hadfield (London: Longman, 1996), pp. 196–210.

# Afterword

If, as one critic has suggested, the epic 'is built to evoke man's struggle to orient himself in time',[1] then it appears comparatively difficult to identify a single complementary literary mode that orients the imagination in space. The spatial imagination of sixteenth-century English literature is, as this study has demonstrated, simultaneously expansive and inward-looking, characteristically unsettled but in search of steadfastness, and as concerned with displacement as it is with strategies of orientation. It moves through different modes and genres, inviting multiple perspectival proclivities: the ideal sightlines of the cartographer are, after all, different from those of the surveyor, the chorographer, and the pilot. A regional landscape of open plains or managed wilderness makes claims on the viewer that differ from those made by the sea and the desert: the raised perspective, a marker of transcendent vision in Spenser's writing, cannot be sustained where typologies are resisted by the particularity, and idiosyncrasy, of the local. Strategies prompted by desire conflict with those of understanding. The art of mapping, as both scopic tool and literary metaphor, is a provisional and performative labour: a work of 'making' that occludes as much as it purports to discover.

The language of space is often self-reflexive and those wielding it frequently resort to a spatial form of reference that folds back on itself. In the work of several of the authors discussed in the preceding chapters, thought is figured as motion, particularly when matters are elusive and difficult to define. Although this study has focused on Edmund Spenser's epic allegorical romance *The Faerie Queene*, its intentionally digressive interests in the writings of spatial strategists such as William Cuningham, Lucas Waghenaer, and John Dee have been intended to catch at the tech-

---

1 Andrew Fichter, *Poets Historical: Dynastic Epic in the Renaissance* (New Haven: Yale University Press, 1982), p. 4.

nical skill required by the literary cosmographer and hydrographer; for all their stratagems of objectivity, the spaces written resist perfection and abstraction, ever exposed to contingent events. The anticipated reader is often cast as a participant, tasked with acts of fragile cognitive collaboration: a challenge undertaken, to return to the paratextual frames of *The Mariners Mirrour*, 'as it shall best like him selfe'.[2]

The reading of Spenser's work that I hope emerges from this study is one that does not seek to distinguish between the aspects of Spenser's writing that have historically divided critics; I have not been interested in whether his imagination was 'corrupted' by his work in Ireland but have instead sought to consider how the poet's making and so called 'mental space' was conditioned by his environment, both literal and literary.[3] The direction in which Spenser's imagination moves can be wayward, confronted by both the violence in which he was complicit and by disillusionment, but it is no less fecund. Reading the work of his equally complicit contemporaries, including the poetry of Sir Walter Ralegh, suggests that there are no ideal forms, only sustained attempts to give shape to the present relationship between self and world as it is perceived in a given moment. Epic certainly has its own ways of imagining space and motion but, as this study has shown, romance, allegory, and pastoral provide pliable structures that both frame, and are framed by, spatial thinking; their contradictions allow for spaces of tempering to be created, and for narratives to be told in multiple ways. If romance has emerged as the dominant mode in the study it is because it admits the others; although the literary foundations of romance run deep, the forms to which they give rise are not so much 'built' as constantly evolving. The ecotonal sites at which the second part of this study came to rest – coastlines, wetlands, and islands – invite composite readings: a single genre or strategy is insufficient to contain the potential for flux.

It has been beyond the scope of this study to address the literary geographies of Irish writings in any depth, even though the place-making strategies of *dindshenchas* offer a practice of binding place, name, and

---

2 Anthony Ashley, 'To ... Sir Christopher Hatton', in *The Mariners Mirrour* (London, 1588), sig. ¶1ʳ.
3 See C.S. Lewis, *The Allegory of Love: A Study in Medieval Tradition* (New York: Oxford University Press, 1958), p. 349 and Samuel Taylor Coleridge, *Coleridge's Miscellaneous Criticism*, ed. Thomas Middleton Raysor (London: Constable, 1936), p. 36. As Joan Fitzpatrick observes, 'Spenser himself suggests that a literary work is conditioned by the environment in which it has been produced'. See *Irish Demons: English Writings on Ireland, the Irish, and Gender by Spenser and his Contemporaries* (Lanham: University Press of America, 2000), p. 17.

memory in ways that both anchor and orientate; I mention the tradition here to evoke the gulf between the Edmund Spenser who lived and worked in Ireland and the utopian Spenser, capable of being at home within Irish literary customs, imagined by the Anglo-Irish poet Yeats.[4] Although my key intertexts have incorporated dialogue and multiple forms of preface and address, they have all been English in orientation. The spatial, it seems, is a descriptive category that emerges through biased and subjective exchanges, which for the purposes of this study have involved distinct cohorts of masculine conversationalists, readers, and interlocutors, from Cuningham's Spoudaeus and Philonicus, and the numerous addressees of the English translation of *The Mariners Mirrour*, to Spenser's Eudoxus and Irenaeus, Luke Gernon's epistolary intimate, and the many voices seeking, and typically failing to reach, the ear of Elizabeth I. If my readings have been focused on the rhetorical features of particular genres, the purpose has been to dispel the idea that the writing of space is an objective activity: as a labour that encompasses a 'simultaneity of stories-so-far' it is an act of persuasion that looks to find consent.[5]

For Spenser, many such conversations happen within the textures of *The Faerie Queene* itself; the poem refracts and internalises contemporary debates concerning how to live and act well, its multiple plains, bowers, and waters inwardly informing the labyrinthine scope of the work as a whole. In the readings I have presented, the language of space at some points supplies the subject of description and at others the method by which the subject can be described. Across all the texts discussed, it has been the characteristic tendency of the spatial to slip between the tenor and vehicle of figurative language that has provided a constant source of fascination, illuminating a capacity for 'making' that is present in the work of both poets and propagandists. The words of these authors configure ways of thinking in which world and self are not mutually constitutive, and which instead limn experience informed by the patterns, modes, and commonplaces of representing worldly encounter.

To return a final time to *The Faerie Queene*, then, it has often struck readers that the space of the Mutabilitie Cantos is different from that of the rest of the poem, owing to the notable absence of a knight wandering though the action.[6] Instead, the narrator's eye is elevated far above

---

4 See W.B. Yeats, *The Cutting of an Agate*, in *Essays and Introductions* (London: Macmillan, 1961; repr. 1980), p. 372.
5 Doreen Massey, *For Space* (London: Sage Publications, 2005), p. 9.
6 See Sheldon P. Zitner, '*The Faerie Queene*, Book VII', in *SEnc*, pp. 287–9 (p. 287).

the 'wide deepe wandring' to gaze upon a vision of time and space that exists as if in paradoxical processional simultaneity. The intrusion of the first-person perspective, which emerges in the description of Nature's garments 'when she on *Arlo* sat', leads the hapless narrator to comment that he shares in the state of Peter, James, and John when they 'their glorious Lord in strange disguise/ Transfigur'd sawe' (VII.vii.7). In this moment, which is recounted in the Synoptic Gospels, the face of Christ 'did shine as the Sunne, and his clothes were as white as the light', and he is accompanied by Moses and Elijah: the impulse, articulated by the disciple Peter, to build three 'tabernacles', or dwelling places, for these figures in glory, offers an archetypal image of situated incomprehension, in which Peter seeks to prolong a visionary encounter by creating space to rest.[7] For Spenser, in the pageant that follows the temporary emplacement of Nature, in which personifications of the seasons are followed by the months, then day and night, then hours, and then life and death, a strange vision of coexistent flux and fixity comes into focus. The sequential procession of the words on the page imitate the passage of time, where the form of the Spenserian stanza, with its eight lines of iambic pentameter followed by an alexandrine, continues to suggest a movement that halts before progressing. Within the canto, perhaps more so than anywhere else in the poem, the stanzas stand as 'miniature memory houses, perfect sacred spaces'.[8] Mutabilitie speaks, and Nature considers her judgement, in a curious lacunary space, only where all times 'were past' (VII.vii.47).

On top of *Arlo-hill*, time, in a last iteration, draws attention to its workings on the world. The power over the lower world that Mutabilitie claims is that of movement, an absence of steadfastness, so that 'nothing here long standeth in one stay' (VII.vii.47). Her argument, that all things 'within this wide great *Vniuerse*' are 'tost and turned by transuerse' (VII.vii.56), offers a superhuman perspective on spaces that evade emplotment in spite of the narrator's gesture towards a named landmark. And yet, the image of Nature's silent contemplation of her judgement emphasises the depth and breadth of Nature's own surveyed field of vision: 'with firme eyes affixt', she 'the ground still viewed' (VII.vii.57), foregrounding the poem's movement towards located stillness one final time. What is visible only within the compass of Nature's singular gaze is, of course, beyond the scope of narrator and reader. For us, all appears as a 'design

---

7 *The Bible* (London, 1576), Matthew 17:2–4, fol. 8ᵛ–9ʳ.
8 Angus Fletcher, *The Prophetic Moment: An Essay on Spenser* (Chicago: University of Chicago Press, 1971), p. 130.

still unfulfilled', in which questing imaginations are invited to speculate, invent, and desire.[9] In one final reconciliation of contrasts, Nature is herself '*a-topos*', vanishing at the canto's close, 'wither no man wist' (VII. vii.59). It is therefore apt that Spenser ends with an appeal to faith that could only be born out of worldliness and the memory of negotiating radical contingency: the concluding line of the fragmentary eighth canto, in which the author asks to be granted 'that Sabaoths sight' (VII.viii.2), expresses a final desire for his travails, and for the pricking of his pen, to be over.

---

9 See Eugène Vinaver, *The Rise of Romance* (Oxford: Clarendon Press, 1971), p. 81.

# Bibliography

### Primary reading

Alberti, Leon Battista, *On Painting and On Sculpture: The Latin Texts of De Pictura and De Statua*, trans. Cecil Grayson (London: Phaidon Press, 1972)

Allott, Robert, *Wits Theatre of the Little World* (London, 1599)

Anderson, Anthony, 'A Forme of Prayer for Sea Men', in *A Godly Sermon* (London, 1575)

Antoniszoon, Cornelis, *The Safegarde of Saylers, or Great Rutter* (London, 1584)

Ascham, Roger, *The Scholemaster* (London, 1570)

Bacon, Francis, *The Philosophical Works of Francis Bacon* (Routledge Revivals), ed. John M. Robertson (Oxford: Routledge, 1905; repr. 2011)

Bate, George, *A Short Historical Account of the Rise and Progress of the Late Troubles in England* (London, 1685)

*The Bible in English* (London, 1568)

*The Bible that is, the Holy Scriptures conteined in the Olde and Newe Testament* (London, 1576)

Bourne, William, *Inventions or Devises* (London, 1590)

Bourne, William, *A Regiment for the Sea* (London, 1574)

Browne, Thomas, *21st-Century Oxford Authors: Thomas Browne*, ed. Kevin Killeen (Oxford: Oxford University Press, 2014)

Bullinger, Heinrich, *Fiftie Godlie and Learned Sermons*, trans. H.I. (London, 1577)

Calvin, Jean, *The Institution of Christian Religion*, trans. Thomas Norton (London, 1561)

Cambrensis, Giraldus, 'The Second Booke the Conquest of Ireland', trans. John Hooker, in *The Second Volume of Chronicles: Conteining the Description, Conquest, Inhabitation, and Troblesome Estate of Ireland; First Collected by Raphaell Holinshed* (London, 1586)

Camden, William, *Britannia*, trans. Philemon Holland (London, 1610)
Camden, William, *Camden's Britannia* (London, 1695)
Carew, Richard, *The Survey of Cornwall* (London, 1602)
Chaucer, Geoffrey, *The Riverside Chaucer*, ed. Larry D. Benson and F.N. Robinson, 3rd edn (Oxford: Oxford University Press, 1987; repr. 2008)
Clairvaux, Bernard of, *Life and Works of Saint Bernard, Abbot of Clairvaux*, ed. John Mabillon, ed. and trans. Samuel J. Eales, Vol. IV (London: John Hodges, 1896)
Cortés, Martín, *The Arte of Navigation*, trans. Richard Eden (London, 1589)
Crooke, Helkiah, *Mikrokosmographia: A Description of the Body of Man* (London, 1615)
Cuningham, William, *The Cosmographical Glasse* (London, 1559)
Davies, Sir John, *A Discovery of the True Causes*, in *Ireland Under Elizabeth and James the First*, ed. Henry Morley (London: Routledge, 1890), pp. 213–342
Davies, Sir John, 'Sir John Davys to Salisbury', in *Calendar of State Papers, Ireland, James I: 1608–1610*, ed. Charles W. Russell and John P. Prendergast (Nendeln: Kraus Reprint, 1974), p. 280
Dee, John, *General and Rare Memorials Pertayning to the Perfect Arte of Navigation* (London, 1577)
Dee, John, *Mathematicall Praeface*, in *The Elements of Geometrie of the Most Auncient Philosopher Euclide of Megara*, trans. Henry Billingsley (London, 1570)
Dering, Edward, *A Brief and Necessary Instruction* (London, 1572)
Derricke, John, *The Image of Irelande* (London, 1581)
De Troyes, Chrétien, 'The Knight with the Lion', in *The Complete Romances of Chrétien de Troyes*, trans. David Staines (Bloomington: Indiana University Press, 1993)
Digges, Leonard and Thomas, *A Geometrical Practise, named Pantometria* (London, 1571)
Digges, Leonard and Thomas, *A Prognostication Everlastinge of Right Good Effecte* (London, 1576)
Drayton, Michael, *Poly-Olbion*, ed. John Selden (London, 1612)
Du Bellay, Joachim, *Les Antiquitez de Rome*, in *The Regrets, with, The Antiquities of Rome, Three Latin Elegies, and The Defense and Enrichment of the French Language*, ed. and trans. Richard Helgerson (Philadelphia: University of Pennsylvania Press, 2006)
Duchesne, Joseph, *A Breefe Aunswere of Josephus Quercetanus*

Armeniacus, Doctor of Phisick, to the Exposition of Jacobus Aubertus Vindonis, trans. John Hester (London, 1591)

Dymmok, John, 'A Treatice of Ireland', in *Tracts Relating to Ireland*, Vol. II (Dublin: The Irish Archaeological Society, 1843)

Erasmus, Desiderius, *Moriae Encomium* (Basel, 1515)

Erasmus, Desiderius, *The Praise of Folie*, trans. Thomas Chaloner (London, 1549)

Fraunce, Abraham, *The Third Part of the Countesse of Pembrokes Yuychurch* (London, 1592)

Gainsford, Thomas, 'Chapter XVII: The Description of Ireland', in *The Glory of England* (London, 1618)

Garcie, Pierre, *The Rutter of the Sea*, trans. Robert Copland (London, 1560)

Gernon, Luke, 'A Discourse of Ireland', in *Illustrations of Irish History and Topography, Mainly of the Seventeenth Century*, ed. C. Litton Falkiner (London: Longmans, Green, and Co., 1904), pp. 348–62

Guarino, Battista, 'A Program of Teaching and Learning', in *Humanist Educational Treatises*, ed. and trans. Craig W. Kallendorf (Cambridge, MA: Harvard University Press, 2002), pp. 260–309

Hakluyt, Richard, *The Principall Navigations, Voiages and Discoveries of the English Nation* (London, 1589)

Harvey, Gabriel, *Three Proper, and Wittie, Familiar Letters* (London, 1580)

Hayward, John, *A Treatise of Union of the Two Realmes of England and Scotland* (London, 1604)

Homer, *The Iliad*, trans. George Chapman, ed. Adam Roberts (Hertfordshire: Wordsworth, 2003)

Homer, *The Odyssey*, trans. Robert Fagles (London: Penguin, 2006)

Lhwyd, Humfrey, *The Breviary of Britayne*, trans. Thomas Twyne (London, 1573)

Lucretius, *De Rerum Natura*, trans. W.H.D. Rouse (London: William Heinemann, 1924; repr. 1943)

Maley, Willy, 'The Supplication of the Blood of the English Most Lamentably Murdered in Ireland, Cryeng out of the Yearth for Revenge (1958)', *Analecta Hibernica*, 36 (1995), 1–77

Marlowe, Christopher, *Hero and Leander* (London, 1598)

Mercator, Gerhard, *Historia Mundi: Or Mercator's Atlas Containing his Cosmographicall Description of the Fabricke and Figure of the World* (London, 1635)

*The Metrical Dindshenchas*, trans. Edward Gwynn, 5 vols (Dublin: Hodges Figgis, 1903–1935)

Middleton, Thomas, *A Game at Chess*, in *Women Beware Women and Other Plays*, ed. Richard Dutton (Oxford: Oxford University Press, 1999; repr. 2009)

Milton, John, *The History of England* (London, 1670)

Milton, John, *Paradise Lost*, ed. Scott Elledge (New York: Norton, 1975)

Montaigne, Michel de, *The Complete Essays*, ed. and trans. M.A. Screech (London: Penguin Books, 1993)

More, Sir Thomas, *Utopia*, trans. Ralph Robinson (1551), in *Three Early Modern Utopias*, ed. Susan Bruce (Oxford: Oxford University Press, 1999; repr. 2008), pp. 1–148.

Moryson, Fynes, *An Itinerary* (London, 1617)

Nashe, Thomas, *The Anatomy of Absurdity* (London, 1589)

Nashe, Thomas, *Nashes Lenten Stuffe* (London, 1599)

Nashe, Thomas, *Pierce Pennilesse his Supplication to the Devil* (London, 1592)

Nashe, Thomas, *The Unfortunate Traveller. Or, The Life of Jacke Wilton* (London, 1594)

Norden, John, *The Surveyors Dialogue* (London, 1607)

Ortelius, Abraham, *Theatrum Orbis Terrarum*, or *The Theatre of the Whole World*, trans. William Bedwell (London, 1606[08])

Ortúñez de Calahorra, Diego, *The Third Part of the First Booke, of the Mirrour of Knighthood*, trans. R.P. (London, 1586)

Ovid, *Metamorphoses*, trans. A.D. Melville (Oxford: Oxford University Press, 1986)

Payne, Robert, *A Brief Description of Ireland* (London, 1589)

Periegetes, Dionysius, *The Surveye of the World*, trans. Thomas Twyne (London, 1572)

Plato, *Protagoras*, trans. Stanley Lombardo and Karen Bell, in *Plato: Complete Works*, ed. John M. Cooper (Indianapolis: Hackett, 1997), pp. 746–90

Plato, *Theaetetus*, trans. M.J. Levett and Myles Burnyeat, in *Plato: Complete Works*, ed. John M. Cooper (Indianapolis: Hackett, 1997), pp. 157–234

Plato, *Timaeus*, trans. Donald J. Zeyl, in *Plato: Complete Works*, ed. John M. Cooper (Indianapolis: Hackett, 1997), pp. 1224–91

Ptolemy, *Ptolemy's Geography: An Annotated Translation of the Theoretical Chapters*, ed. J. Lennart Berggren and Alexander Jones (Princeton: Princeton University Press, 2000)

Puttenham, George, *The Art of English Poesy: A Critical Edition*, ed. Frank Whigham and Wayne A. Rebhorn (Ithaca: Cornell University Press, 2007)

Quinn, David B., '"A Discourse of Ireland" (Circa 1599): A Sidelight on English Colonial Policy', *Proceedings of the Royal Irish Academy. Section C*, 47 (1941/1942), 151–66

Ralegh, Sir Walter, *The History of the World* (London, 1614 [i.e. 1617])

Ralegh, Sir Walter, *The Poems of Sir Walter Ralegh: A Historical Edition*, ed. Michael Rudick (Tempe: Arizona Center for Medieval and Renaissance Studies, 1999)

Recorde, Robert, *The Pathway to Knowledge* (London, 1551)

Rogers, Thomas, *The Anatomie of the Minde* (London, 1576)

Shakespeare, William, *Shakespeare's Sonnets*, ed. Katherine Duncan-Jones (London: Arden Shakespeare, 2010)

Shakespeare, William, *The Tempest*, ed. Virginia Mason Vaughan and Alden T. Vaughan (London: Thompson, 1999; repr. 2003)

Sidney, Sir Henry, *A Viceroy's Vindication? Sir Henry Sidney's Memoir of Service in Ireland 1556–1578*, ed. Ciaran Brady (Cork: Cork University Press, 2002)

Sidney, Sir Philip, *The Defence of Poesy*, in *The Oxford Authors: Sir Philip Sidney*, ed. Katherine Duncan-Jones (Oxford: Oxford University Press, 1989; repr. 1992), pp. 212–50

*Sir Gawain and the Green Knight*, ed. J.R.R. Tolkien and E.V. Gordon, 2nd edn revised by Norman Davis (Oxford: Clarendon Press, 1967)

Smith, Sir Thomas, *A Letter Sent by I.B. Gentleman* (London, 1572)

Spenser, Edmund, *Edmund Spenser: The Shorter Poems*, ed. Richard A. McCabe (London: Penguin, 1999)

Spenser, Edmund, *The Faerie Queene*, ed. A.C. Hamilton, Hiroshi Yamashita, and Toshiyuki Suzuki (Harlow: Longman, 2001)

Spenser, Edmund, *A View of the State of Ireland*, ed. Andrew Hadfield and Willy Maley (Oxford: Blackwell, 1997; repr. 1998)

Spenser, Edmund, *The Works of Edmund Spenser: A Variorum Edition, X: The Prose Works*, ed. Rudolf Gottfried (Baltimore: Johns Hopkins University Press, 1949)

Stanihurst, Richard, 'A Treastise Conteining a Plaine and Perfect Description of Ireland', in *The Second Volume of Chronicles: Conteining the Description, Conquest, Inhabitation, and Troblesome Estate of Ireland; First Collected by Raphaell Holinshed* (London, 1586)

Turler, Jerome, *The Traveiler* (London, 1575)

Vegetius Renatus, Flavius, *Du Fait de Guerre* (*De Re Militari*) (Paris, 1536)
Vegetius Renatus, Flavius, *The Foure Bookes of Flavius Vegetius Renatus*, trans. John Sadler (London, 1572)
Virgil, *Eclogues; Georgics; Aeneid I–VI*, trans. H. Rushton Fairclough; revised by G.P. Goold (Cambridge, MA: Harvard University Press, 1916; repr. 2006)
Virgil, *The Whole .xii. Bookes of the AEneidos of Virgill*, trans. Thomas Phaer (London, 1573)
Waghenaer, Lucas Janzoon, *The Mariners Mirrour*, trans. Anthony Ashley (London, 1588)
Wales, Gerald of, *The History and Topography of Ireland*, trans. John O'Meara (London: Penguin, 1951; repr. 1988)
Watson, Henry, trans., *The Hystorye of Olyver of Castylle* (London, 1518)
Whitney, Geffrey, *A Choice of Emblemes* (Leiden, 1586)
Wilson, Thomas, *The Rule of Reason, Conteinyng the Arte of Logique* (London, 1551)
Worsop, Edward, *A Discoverie of Sundrie Errours and Faults Daily Committed by Lande-meaters* (London, 1582)

## Secondary reading

Abrams, M.H., *The Mirror and the Lamp: Romantic Theory and the Critical Tradition* (Oxford: Oxford University Press, 1953; repr. 1976)
Akbari, Suzanne Conklin, *Seeing Through the Veil: Optical Theory and Medieval Allegory* (Toronto: University of Toronto Press, 2004)
Albanese, Denise, *New Science, New World* (Durham: Duke University Press, 1996)
Alpers, Paul J., 'Narration in *The Faerie Queene*', *ELH*, 44.1 (1977), 19–39
Alpers, Paul J., *The Poetry of the Faerie Queene* (Princeton: Princeton University Press, 1967)
Anderson, Judith H., *Reading the Allegorical Intertext: Chaucer, Spenser, Shakespeare, Milton* (New York: Fordham University Press, 2008)
Anderson, Miranda, ed., *The Book of the Mirror: An Interdisciplinary Collection Exploring the Cultural Story of the Mirror* (Newcastle: Cambridge Scholars Press, 2007)
Andrews, J.H., 'The Irish Surveys of Robert Lythe', *Imago Mundi*, 19 (1965), 22–31
Andrews, J.H., 'Introduction', in J.B. Harley, *The New Nature of Maps:*

*Essays in the History of Cartography*, ed. Paul Laxton (Baltimore: Johns Hopkins University Press, 2001), pp. 1–32

Andrews, J.H., *The Queen's Last Map-Maker: Richard Bartlett in Ireland, 1600–3* (Dublin: Geography Publications, 2008)

Andrews, J.H., *Shapes of Ireland: Maps and their Makers 1564–1839* (Dublin: Geography Publications, 1997)

Andrews, K.R., *Elizabethan Seaman* (London: National Maritime Museum, 1982)

Andrews, K.R., N.P. Canny, and P.E.H. Hair, eds, *The Westward Enterprise: English Activities in Ireland, the Atlantic and America, 1480–1650* (Liverpool: Liverpool University Press, 1978)

Appelbaum, Robert, 'Anti-Geography', *EMLS*, 4.2 (1998), 12.1–17

Armitage, Christopher M., ed., *Literary and Visual Ralegh* (Manchester: Manchester University Press, 2013)

Armitage, David, 'The Elizabethan Idea of Empire', *TRHS*, 14 (2004), 269–77

Artese, Charlotte, 'King Arthur in America: Making Space in History for *The Faerie Queene* and John Dee's *Brytanici Imperii Limites*', *JMEMS*, 33.1 (2003), 125–41

Auerbach, Erich, *Mimesis: The Representation of Reality in Western Literature*, trans. Willard R. Trask (Garden City, NY: Doubleday, 1957)

Avery, Bruce, 'Mapping the Irish Other: Spenser's *A View of the Present State of Ireland*', *ELH*, 57.2 (1990), 263–79

Babcock, W.H., 'St. Brendan's Explorations and Islands', *Geographical Review*, 8.1 (1919), 37–46

Bachelard, Gaston, *The Poetics of Space*, trans. Maria Jolas (Boston: Beacon, 1964; repr. 1994)

Badcoe, Tamsin, '"The Compasse of that Islands Space": Insular Fictions in the Writing of Edmund Spenser', *Renaissance Studies*, 25.3 (2011), 415–32.

Badcoe, Tamsin, 'Mariners, Maps, and Metaphors: Lucas Waghenaer and the Poetics of Navigation', *Swiss Papers in English Language and Literature: Medieval and Early Modern Literature, Science and Medicine*, 28 (2013), 33–47.

Badcoe, Tamsin, '"The Porch of that Enchaunted Gate": Spenserian Influences and the Romance of Place in *Lamia* by John Keats', *Romanticism*, 17.3 (2011), 351–64

Baker, David J., 'Charting Uncertainty in Renaissance Ireland', in *Representing Ireland: Literature and the Origins of Conflict, 1534–*

*1660*, ed. Brendan Bradshaw, Andrew Hadfield, and Willy Maley (Cambridge: Cambridge University Press, 1993), pp. 76–92

Bakhtin, Mikhail M., 'Forms of Time and of the Chronotope in the Novel', in *The Dialogic Imagination*, ed. Michael Holquist, trans. Caryl Emerson and Michael Holquist (Austin: University of Texas Press, 1981; repr. 2002), pp. 84–258

Baldwin, Robert, 'John Dee's Interest in the Application of Nautical Science, Mathematics and Law to English Naval Affairs', in *John Dee: Interdisciplinary Studies in English Renaissance Thought*, ed. Stephen Clucas (Dordrecht: Springer, 2006), pp. 97–130

Barbour, Reid and Claire Preston, eds, *Sir Thomas Browne: The World Proposed* (Oxford: Oxford University Press, 2008)

Barnard, John, D.F. McKenzie, and Maureen Bell, eds, *The Cambridge History of the Book in Britain Volume 4: 1557–1695* (Cambridge: Cambridge University Press, 2002)

Barnes, Trevor J. and James S. Duncan, eds, *Writing Worlds: Discourse, Text, and Metaphor in the Representation of Landscape* (London: Routledge, 1992)

Bartolovich, Crystal, '"Baseless Fabric": London as a "World City"', in *The Tempest and Its Travels*, ed. Peter Hulme and William H. Sherman (London: Reaktion, 2000), pp. 13–26

Bate, Jonathan, *Romantic Ecology: Wordsworth and the Environmental Tradition* (London: Routledge, 1991)

Bates, Catherine, *Masculinity and the Hunt: Wyatt to Spenser* (Oxford: Oxford University Press, 2013)

Bath, Michael, *Speaking Pictures: English Emblem Books and Renaissance Culture* (Harlow: Longman, 1994)

Bawarshi, Anis S., *Genre and the Invention of the Writer: Reconsidering the Place of Invention in Composition* (Logan: Utah State University Press, 2003)

Bednarz, James P., 'The Collaborator as Thief: Ralegh's (Re)Vision of *The Faerie Queene*', *ELH*, 63.2 (1996), 279–307

Beer, Anna, '"Bellphebes Course is Now Observde No More": Ralegh, Spenser and the Literary Politics of the Cynthia Holograph', in *Literary and Visual Ralegh*, ed. Christopher M. Armitage (Manchester: Manchester University Press, 2013), pp. 140–65

Bellamy, Elizabeth J., *Dire Straits: The Perils of Writing the Early Modern English Coastline from Leland to Milton* (Toronto: University of Toronto Press, 2013)

Bellamy, Elizabeth J., 'Spenser's Faeryland and "The Curious Genealogy of India"', in *Worldmaking Spenser: Explorations in the Early Modern Age*, ed. Patrick Cheney and Lauren Silberman (Lexington: University Press of Kentucky, 2000), pp. 177–92

Bellamy, Elizabeth J., *Translations of Power: Narcissism and the Unconscious in Epic History* (Ithaca: Cornell University Press, 1992)

Bender, John B., *Spenser and Literary Pictorialism* (Princeton: Princeton University Press, 1972)

Benjamin, Walter, *The Origin of German Tragic Drama*, trans. John Osborne (London: NLB, 1977)

Bennett, Andrew, *Ignorance: Literature and Agnoiology* (Manchester: Manchester University Press, 2009)

Berger, Jr., Harry, 'Facing Sophists: Socrates' Charismatic Bondage in *Protagoras*', *Representations*, 5 (1984), 66–91

Berger, Jr., Harry, *Revisionary Play: Studies in the Spenserian Dynamics* (Berkeley: University of California Press, 1990)

Berger, Jr., Harry, *Second World and Green World: Studies in Renaissance Fiction-making*, ed. John Patrick Lynch (Berkeley: University of California Press, 1988)

Berger, Jr., Harry, 'The System of Early Modern Painting', *Representations*, 62 (1998), 31–57

Berry, Craig A., '"Sundrie Doubts": Vulnerable Understanding and Dubious Origins in Spenser's Continuation of the Squire's Tale', in *Refiguring Chaucer in the Renaissance*, ed. Theresa M. Krier (Gainesville: University Press of Florida, 1998), pp. 106–27

Berry, Philippa, *Of Chastity and Power: Elizabethan Literature and the Unmarried Queen* (London: Routledge, 1989)

Berry, Philippa and Margaret Tudeau-Clayton, *Textures of Renaissance Knowledge* (Manchester: Manchester University Press, 2003)

Betteridge, Thomas, ed., *Borders and Travellers in Early Modern Europe* (Aldershot: Ashgate, 2007)

Bhabha, Homi K., *The Location of Culture* (London: Routledge, 1994; repr. 2004)

Bialas, Zbigniew, 'Ambition and Distortion: An Ontological Dimension in Colonial Cartography', in *Borderlands: Negotiating Boundaries in Post-Colonial Writing*, ed. Monika Reif-Hulser (Amsterdam: Rodopi, 1999), 17–28

Bieman, Elizabeth, *Plato Baptized: Towards the Interpretation of Spenser's Mimetic Fictions* (Toronto: University of Toronto Press, 1988)

Blick, Fred, 'Spenser's *Amoretti* and Elizabeth Boyle: Her Names Immortalized', *Spenser Studies*, 23 (2008), 309–15

Blissett, William, 'Caves, Labyrinths, and *The Faerie Queene*', in *Unfolded Tales: Essays on Renaissance Romance*, ed. George M. Logan and Gordon Teskey (Ithaca: Cornell University Press, 1989), pp. 281–311

Blumenberg, Hans, *Shipwreck with Spectator: Paradigm of a Metaphor for Existence*, trans. Steven Rendall (Cambridge, MA: MIT Press, 1997)

Booth, Michael, '"Moving on the Waters": Metaphor and Mental Space in Ralegh's *History of the World*', in *Literary and Visual Ralegh*, ed. Christopher M. Armitage (Manchester: Manchester University Press, 2013), pp. 200–16

Borlik, Todd Andrew, 'Caliban and the Fen Demons of Lincolnshire: The Englishness of Shakespeare's *Tempest*', *Shakespeare*, 9.1 (2013), 21–51

Borris, Kenneth, *Allegory and Epic in English Renaissance Literature: Heroic Forms in Sidney, Spenser and Milton* (Cambridge: Cambridge University Press, 2000)

Borris, Kenneth, 'Platonism and Spenser's Poetic: Idealized Imitation, Merlin's Mirror, and the Florimells', *Spenser Studies*, 24 (2009), 209–68

Borris, Kenneth, *Visionary Spenser and the Poetics of Early Modern Platonism* (Oxford: Oxford University Press, 2017)

Bottigheimer, Karl S., 'Kingdom and Colony: Ireland in the Westward Enterprise, 1536–1660', in *The Westward Enterprise: English Activities in Ireland, the Atlantic and America, 1480–1650*, ed. K.R. Andrews, N.P. Canny, and P.E.H. Hair (Liverpool: Liverpool University Press, 1978), pp. 45–64

Braden, Gordon, 'Riverrun: An Epic Catalogue in *The Faerie Queene*', *ELR*, 5.1 (1975), 25–48

Bradshaw, Brendan, Andrew Hadfield, and Willy Maley, eds, *Representing Ireland: Literature and the Origins of Conflict, 1534–1660* (Cambridge: Cambridge University Press, 1993)

Brady, Ciaran, 'A Brief Note of Ireland', in *The Spenser Encyclopedia*, ed. A.C. Hamilton (Toronto: University of Toronto Press, 1990), pp. 111–12

Brayton, Dan, *Shakespeare's Ocean: An Ecocritical Exploration* (Charlottesville: University of Virginia Press, 2012)

Brayton, Dan, 'Shakespeare and Slime: Notes on the Anthropocene', in *Ecological Approaches to Early Modern English Texts: A Field Guide to Reading and Teaching*, ed. Jennifer Munroe, Edward J. Geisweidt, and Lynne Bruckner (Farnham: Ashgate, 2015), pp. 81–9

Breen, John, 'The Empirical Eye: Edmund Spenser's *A View of The Present State of Ireland*', *The Irish Review*, 16 (1994), 44–52

Breen, John, '"Imaginatiue Groundplot": A View of the Present State of Ireland', Spenser Studies, 12 (1998), 151–68
Brückner, Martin and Kristen Poole, 'The Plot Thickens: Surveying Manuals, Drama, and the Materiality of Narrative Form in Early Modern England', ELH, 69 (2002), 617–48
Burlinson, Christopher, Allegory, Space and the Material World in the Writings of Edmund Spenser (Cambridge: D.S. Brewer, 2006)
Burrow, Colin, Epic Romance: Homer to Milton (Oxford: Clarendon, 1993)
Burrow, J.A., '"Sir Thopas": An Agony in Three Fits', RES, 22 (1971), 54–8
Buisseret, David, The Mapmaker's Quest: Depicting New Worlds in Renaissance Europe (Oxford: Oxford University Press, 2003)
Butler, Chris, '"Pricking" and Ambiguity at the Start of The Faerie Queene', Notes and Queries, 55.2 (2008), 159–61
Butlin, R.A., 'Land and People, c. 1600', in A New History of Ireland: Early Modern Ireland 1534–1691, ed. T.W. Moody, F.X. Martin, and F.J. Byrne (Oxford: Oxford University Press, 2009), pp. 142–67
Buttimer, Anne, Geography and the Human Spirit (Baltimore: Johns Hopkins University Press, 1993)
Camino, Mercedes, '"Methinks I See an Evil Lurk Unespied": Visualizing Conquest in Spenser's A View of the Present State of Ireland', Spenser Studies, 12 (1990), 169–94
Camino, Mercedes, '(Un)folding the Map of Early Modern Ireland: Spenser, Moryson, Bartlett, and Ortelius', Cartographica, 34.4 (1997), 1–17
Campbell, Marion, 'Inscribing Imperfection: Sir Walter Ralegh and the Elizabethan Court', ELR, 20.2 (1990), 233–53
Campbell, Mary B., The Witness and the Other World: Exotic European Travel Writing, 400–1600 (Ithaca: Cornell University Press, 1988)
Campbell, Mary B., Wonder and Science: Imagining Worlds in Early Modern Europe (Ithaca: Cornell University Press, 1999)
Carey, Daniel, 'Travel and Sexual Fantasy in the Early Modern Period', in Writing and Fantasy, ed. Ceri Sullivan and Barbara White (London: Longman, 1999), pp. 151–65
Carney, James, 'Language and Literature to 1169', in A New History of Ireland, Volume I: Prehistoric and Early Ireland, ed. Dáibhí Ó Cróinín (Oxford: Oxford University Press, 2005), pp. 500–9
Carroll, Clare, 'The Construction of Gender and the Cultural and Political Other in The Faerie Queene 5 and A View of the Present State of Ireland:

The Critics, The Context, and The Case of Radigund', *Criticism*, 32.2 (1990), 163–92

Carroll, Clare, 'Spenser and the Irish Language: The Sons of Milesio in *A View of the Present State of Ireland, The Faerie Queene*, Book V and the *Leabhar Gabhála*', *IUR*, 26.2 (1996), 281–90

Carruthers, Mary, *The Book of Memory: A Study of Memory in Medieval Culture* (Cambridge: Cambridge University Press, 1990; repr. 2008)

Carruthers, Mary, *The Craft of Thought: Meditation, Rhetoric, and the Making of Images, 400–1200* (Cambridge: Cambridge University Press, 1998; repr. 2008)

Carruthers, Mary, ed., *Rhetoric Beyond Words: Delight and Persuasion in the Arts of the Middle Ages* (Cambridge: Cambridge University Press, 2010)

Carter, Paul, 'Dark with Excess of Bright: Mapping the Coastlines of Knowledge', in *Mappings*, ed. Denis Cosgrove (London: Reaktion, 1999), pp. 125–47

Carter, Paul, *The Road to Botany Bay: An Exploration of Landscape and History* (New York: Knopf, 1988)

Cartlidge, Neil, ed., *Boundaries in Medieval Romance* (Cambridge: D.S. Brewer, 2008)

Casey, Edward S., 'How to Get from Space to Place in a Fairly Short Stretch of Time: Phenomenological Prolegomena', in *Senses of Place*, ed. Steven Feld and Keith H. Basso (Santa Fe: SAR Press, 1996), pp. 13–52

Cavanagh, Sheila, *Wanton Eyes and Chaste Desires* (Indianapolis: Indiana University Press, 1994)

Cave, Terence, *Recognitions: A Study in Poetics* (Oxford: Clarendon Press, 1988)

Cawley, Robert R., *Unpathed Waters: Studies in the Influence of the Voyagers on Elizabethan Literature* (London: Frank Cass, 1940; repr. 1967)

Cheney, Donald, 'Colin Clout's Homecoming: The Imaginative Travels of Edmund Spenser', *Connotations*, 7.2 (1997–1998), 146–58

Cheney, Patrick, *Reading Sixteenth-Century Poetry* (Chichester: Wiley-Blackwell, 2011)

Cheney, Patrick, '"Secret Powre Unseene": Good Magic in Spenser's Legend of Britomart', *Studies in Philology*, 85.1 (1988), 1–28

Cheney, Patrick, 'Spenser's Completion of *The Squire's Tale*: Love, Magic and Heroic Action in the Legend of Cambell and Triamond', *Journal of Medieval and Renaissance Studies*, 15 (1985), 135–55

Cheney, Patrick and Lauren Silberman, eds, *Worldmaking Spenser: Explorations in the Early Modern Age* (Lexington: University Press of Kentucky, 2000)

Christian, Margaret, '"Waves of Weary Wretchedness": Florimell and the Sea', *Spenser Studies*, 14 (2000), 133–61

Clarke, Catherine A.M., *Literary Landscapes and the Idea of England, 700–1400* (Cambridge: D.S. Brewer, 2006)

Clifford, Gay, *The Transformations of Allegory* (London: Routledge and Kegan Paul, 1974)

Clifford-Amos, Terence, '"Certaine Signes" of "Faeryland": Spenser's Eden of Thanksgiving on the Defeat of the "Monstrous" "Dragon" of Albion's North', *Viator*, 32 (2001), 371–415

Clucas, Stephen, ed., *John Dee: Interdisciplinary Studies in English Renaissance Thought* (Dordrecht: Springer, 2006)

Cohen, Adam Max, *Shakespeare and Technology: Dramatizing Early Modern Technological Revolutions* (New York: Palgrave Macmillan, 2006)

Cohen, Jeffrey Jerome, ed., *Prismatic Ecology: Ecotheory Beyond Green* (Minneapolis: University of Minnesota Press, 2013)

Coleridge, Samuel Taylor, *Coleridge's Miscellaneous Criticism*, ed. Thomas Middleton Raysor (London: Constable, 1936)

Coles, Bryony and John, *People of the Wetlands: Bogs, Bodies and Lake-Dwellers* (London: Thames and Hudson, 1989)

Comito, Terry, 'Exile and Return in the Greek Romances', *Arion*, 2.1 (1975), 58–80

Conley, Tom, *An Errant Eye: Poetry and Topography in Early Modern France* (Minneapolis: University of Minnesota Press, 2011)

Conley, Tom, *The Self Made Map: Cartographic Writing in Early Modern France* (Minneapolis: University of Minnesota Press, 1996)

Cooper, Helen, *The English Romance in Time: Transforming Motifs from Geoffrey of Monmouth to the Death of Shakespeare* (Oxford: Oxford University Press, 2004)

Cooper, Helen, 'Romance after 1400', in *The Cambridge History of Medieval English Literature*, ed. David Wallace (Cambridge: Cambridge University Press, 2002), pp. 690–719

Corbett, Margery and Ronald Lightbown, *The Comely Frontispiece: The Emblematic Title-Page in England 1550–1660* (London: Routledge and Kegan Paul, 1979)

Cormack, Lesley B., 'Britannia Rules the Waves? Images of Empire in Elizabethan England', *EMLS*, 4.2 (1998), 10.1–20

Cormack, Lesley B., *Charting an Empire: Geography at the English Universities, 1580-1620* (Chicago: University of Chicago Press, 1997)
Cosgrove, Art, ed., *A New History of Ireland, Volume II: Medieval Ireland 1169-1534* (Oxford: Oxford University Press, 2008)
Cosgrove, Denis, *Apollo's Eye: A Cartographic Genealogy of the Earth in the Western Imagination* (Baltimore: Johns Hopkins University Press, 2001)
Cosgrove, Denis, *Geography and Vision: Seeing, Imagining and Representing the World* (London: Tauris, 2008)
Cosgrove, Denis, ed., *Mappings* (London: Reaktion, 1999)
Cosgrove, Denis, 'Prologue: Geography within the Humanities', in *Envisioning Landscapes, Making Worlds*, ed. Stephen Daniels, Dydia DeLyser, J. Nicholas Entrikin, and Douglas Richardson (Oxford: Routledge, 2011), pp. xxii–xxv
Cosgrove, Denis and Stephen Daniels, eds, *The Iconography of Landscape: Essays on the Symbolic Representation, Design and Use of Past Environments* (Cambridge: Cambridge University Press, 1988)
Coughlan, Patricia, 'The Local Context of Mutabilitie's Plea', *IUR*, 26.2 (1996), 320–41
Crane, Mary Thomas, 'Analogy, Metaphor and the New Science: Cognitive Science and Early Modern Epistemology', in *Introduction to Cognitive Cultural Studies*, ed. Lisa Zunshine (Baltimore: Johns Hopkins University Press, 2010), pp. 103–14
Crane, Mary Thomas, 'Surface, Depth, and the Spatial Imaginary: A Cognitive Reading of *The Political Unconscious*', *Representations*, 108.1 (2009), 76–97
Cresswell, Tim, *On the Move: Mobility in the Modern Western World* (New York: Routledge, 2006)
Cummings, R.M., *Spenser: The Critical Heritage* (London: Routledge and Kegan Paul, 1971)
Curry, Michael R., *The Work in the World: Geographical Practice and the Written Word* (Minneapolis: University of Minnesota Press, 1996)
Curtius, Ernst Robert, *European Literature and the Latin Middle Ages*, trans. Willard R. Trask (London: Routledge and Kegan Paul, 1953)
Daniels, Stephen, 'Geographical Imagination', *Transactions of the Institute of British Geographers*, 36.2 (2011), 182–7
Daniels, Stephen, Dydia DeLyser, J. Nicholas Entrikin, and Douglas Richardson, eds, *Envisioning Landscapes, Making Worlds: Geography and the Humanities* (Oxford: Routledge, 2011)

Das, Santanu, *Touch and Intimacy in First World War Literature* (Cambridge: Cambridge University Press, 2008)

Davis, Nick, *Stories of Chaos: Reason and its Displacement in Early Modern English Narrative* (Aldershot: Ashgate, 1999)

Dawson, Lesel, *Lovesickness and Gender in Early Modern English Literature* (Oxford: Oxford University Press, 2008)

Deacon, Richard, *John Dee: Scientist, Geographer, Astrologer and Secret Agent to Elizabeth I* (London: Frederick Muller, 1968)

De Certeau, Michel, *The Practice of Everyday Life*, trans. Steven Rendall (Berkeley: University of California Press, 1984)

Dees, Jerome S., 'Colin Clout and the Shepherd of the Ocean', *Spenser Studies*, 15 (2001), 185–95

Dees, Jerome S., 'The Narrator of *The Faerie Queene*: Patterns of Response', *Texas Studies in Literature and Language*, 12.4 (1971), 537–68

Dees, Jerome S., 'The Ship Conceit in *The Faerie Queene*: "Conspicuous Allusion" and Poetic Structure', *Studies in Philology*, 72 (1975), 208–25

De Girolami Cheney, Liana, 'Giorgio Vasari's *The Toilet of Venus*: Neoplatonic Notion of Female Beauty', in *Neoplatonism and Western Aesthetics*, ed. Aphrodite Alexandrakis and Nicholas J. Moutafakis (Albany: State University of New York Press, 2002), pp. 99–112

De Grummond, Nancy Thomson, *Etruscan Myth, Sacred History, and Legend* (Philadelphia: University of Pennsylvania Museum of Archaeology and Anthropology, 2006)

Deleuze, Gilles, *Desert Islands and Other Texts, 1953–1974*, ed. David Lapoujade, trans. Michael Taormina (Cambridge, MA: Semiotext(e), 2004)

DeNeef, A. Leigh, 'Timias', in *The Spenser Encyclopedia*, ed. A.C. Hamilton (Toronto: University of Toronto Press, 1990), pp. 690–1

Dening, Greg, 'Deep Times, Deep Spaces', in *Sea Changes: Historicizing the Ocean*, ed. Bernhard Klein and Gesa Mackenthun (New York: Routledge, 2004), pp. 13–35

Demaray, John G., *Cosmos and Epic Representation: Dante, Spenser, Milton and the Transformation of Renaissance Heroic Poetry* (Pittsburgh: Duquesne University Press, 1991)

Dixon, Sandra Lee, *Augustine: The Scattered and Gathered Self* (St Louis, Missouri: Chalice Press, 1999)

Dobin, Howard, *Merlin's Disciples: Prophecy, Poetry, and Power in Renaissance England* (Stanford: Stanford University Press, 1990)

Dobranski, Stephen B., *Readers and Authorship in Early Modern England* (Cambridge: Cambridge University Press, 2005)

Dolven, Jeff, *Scenes of Instruction in Renaissance Romance* (Chicago: University of Chicago Press, 2007)

Doob, Penelope Reed, *The Idea of the Labyrinth from Classical Antiquity through the Middle Ages* (Ithaca: Cornell University Press, 1990)

Doody, Margaret Anne, 'Marshes, Shores and Muddy Margins', in *The True Story of the Novel* (New Brunswick: Rutgers University Press, 1996), pp. 319–36

Dorrian, Mark, 'On Some Spatial Aspects of the Colonial Discourse on Ireland', *The Journal of Architecture*, 6.1 (2001), 27–51

Douglas, Mary, *Purity and Danger: An Analysis of Concept of Pollution and Taboo* (London: Routledge, 2002)

Dubrow, Heather, '"A Doubtful Sense of Things": Thievery in *The Faerie Queene* 6.10–6.11', in *Worldmaking Spenser: Explorations in the Early Modern Age*, ed. Patrick Cheney and Lauren Silberman (Kentucky: University Press of Kentucky, 2000), pp. 204–16

Duckert, Lowell, 'The Slough of Respond', *O-Zone: A Journal of Object-Orientated Studies*, 1 (2014), 110–17

Duckert, Lowell, 'Water Ralegh's Liquid Narrative: The Discoverie of Guiana', in *Literary and Visual Ralegh*, ed. Christopher M. Armitage (Manchester: Manchester University Press, 2013), pp. 217–41

Duffy, Eamon, *The Stripping of the Altars: Traditional Religion in England, c. 1400–c. 1580* (New Haven: Yale University Press, 1992)

Duncan, James and David Ley, eds, *Place / Culture / Representation* (London: Routledge, 1993)

Duncan, James and Derek Gregory, eds, *Writes of Passage: Reading Travel Writing* (London: Routledge, 1999)

Duncan-Jones, Katherine, 'The Date of Raleigh's "21th: And Last Booke of the Ocean to Scinthia"', *RES*, 21 (1970), 143–58

Dyas, Dee, *Pilgrimage in Medieval English Literature 700–1500* (Cambridge: D.S. Brewer, 2001)

Edgerton, Jr., Samuel Y., *The Renaissance Rediscovery of Linear Perspective* (New York: Harper and Row, 1975; repr. 1976)

Edwards, A.S.G., 'The Manuscript: British Library MS Cotton Nero A.x', in *A Companion to the Gawain-Poet*, ed. Derek Brewer and Jonathan Gibson (Cambridge: D.S. Brewer, 1997), 197–219

Edwards, Jess, *Writing, Geometry and Space in Seventeenth-Century England and America: Circles in the Sand* (London: Routledge, 2006)

Edwards, Philip, *Pilgrimage and Literary Tradition* (Cambridge: Cambridge University Press, 2006)

Edwards, Philip, *Sea-Mark: The Metaphorical Voyage, Spenser to Milton* (Liverpool: Liverpool University Press, 1997)
Edwards, Philip, *Sir Walter Ralegh* (London: Longmans, Green, 1953)
Eggert, Katherine, *Disknowledge: Literature, Alchemy, and the End of Humanism in Renaissance England* (Philadelphia: University of Pennsylvania Press, 2015)
Eklund, Hillary, 'Wetlands Reclamation and the Fate of the Local in Seventeenth-Century England', in *Groundwork: English Renaissance Literature and Soil Science* (Pittsburgh: Duquesne University Press, 2017), pp. 149–70
Eliade, Mircea, *The Sacred and the Profane: The Nature of Religion*, trans. Willard R. Trask (New York: Harper, 1957; repr. 1959)
Elkins, James, *The Poetics of Perspective* (Ithaca: Cornell University Press, 1994; repr. 1996)
Elliot, R.W.V., *The Gawain Country* (Ilkley: University of Leeds, 1984)
Ellrodt, Robert, *Neoplatonism in the Poetry of Spenser* (Geneva: E. Droz, 1960)
Enterline, Lynn, *The Rhetoric of the Body from Ovid to Shakespeare* (Cambridge: Cambridge University Press, 2000)
Erickson, Wayne, *Mapping The Faerie Queene: Quest Structures and the World of the Poem* (New York: Garland, 1996)
Erickson, Wayne, 'Spenser Reads Ralegh's Poetry in(to) the 1590 *Faerie Queene*', *Spenser Studies*, 15 (2001), 175–84
Escobedo, Andrew, *Nationalism and Historical Loss in Renaissance England* (Ithaca: Cornell University Press, 2004)
Ferguson, Margaret W., 'Saint Augustine's Region of Unlikeness: The Crossing of Exile and Language', in *Innovations of Antiquity*, ed. Ralph Hexter and Daniel Selden (London: Routledge, 1992), pp. 69–94
Fewster, Carol, *Traditionality and Genre in Middle English Romance* (Cambridge: D.S. Brewer, 1987)
Fichter, Andrew, *Poets Historical: Dynastic Epic in the Renaissance* (New Haven: Yale University Press, 1982)
Field, Rosalind, 'The King Over the Water: Exile-and-Return Revisited', in *Cultural Encounters in the Romance of Medieval England*, ed. Corinne Saunders (Cambridge: D.S. Brewer, 2005), pp. 41–53
Fitter, Chris, *Poetry, Space, Landscape: Toward a New Theory* (Cambridge: Cambridge University Press, 1995)
Fitzpatrick, Joan, *Irish Demons: English Writings on Ireland, the Irish, and Gender by Spenser and his Contemporaries* (Lanham: University Press of America, 2000)

Fitzpatrick, Joan, 'Marrying Waterways: Politicizing and Gendering the Landscape', in *Archipelagic Identities: Literature and Identity in the Atlantic Archipelago, 1550-1800*, ed. Philip Schwyzer and Simon Mealor (Aldershot: Ashgate, 2004), pp. 81-91

Fleck, Andrew, 'Early Modern Marginalia in Spenser's *Faerie Queene* at the Folger', *Notes and Queries*, 55.2 (2008), 165-70

Fletcher, Angus, *Allegory: The Theory of a Symbolic Mode* (Ithaca: Cornell University Press, 1964)

Fletcher, Angus, *The Prophetic Moment: An Essay on Spenser* (Chicago: University of Chicago Press, 1971)

Fletcher, Angus, *Time, Space, and Motion in the Age of Shakespeare* (Cambridge, MA: Harvard University Press, 2007)

Flint, Valerie I.J., *The Imaginative Landscape of Christopher Columbus* (Princeton: Princeton University Press, 1992)

Floyd-Wilson, Mary, *English Ethnicity and Race in Early Modern Drama* (Cambridge: Cambridge University Press, 2003)

Floyd-Wilson, Mary, 'Transmigrations: Crossing Regional and Gender Boundaries in *Antony and Cleopatra*', *Enacting Gender on the English Renaissance Stage*, ed. Viviana Comensoli and Anne Russell (Chicago: University of Illinois Press, 1999), pp. 73-96

Floyd-Wilson, Mary and Garrett A. Sullivan, Jr., eds, *Environment and Embodiment in Early Modern England* (Basingstoke: Palgrave Macmillan, 2007)

Fludernik, Monika, *Towards a 'Natural' Narratology* (London: Routledge, 1996)

Fogarty, Anne, 'The Colonisation of Language', in *Spenser and Ireland: An Interdisciplinary Perspective*, ed. Patricia Coughlan (Cork: Cork University Press, 1989), pp. 74-108

Fogarty, Anne, 'Narrative Strategy in *The Faerie Queene*, Book VI', in *Edmund Spenser*, ed. Andrew Hadfield (London: Longman, 1996), pp. 196-210

Foucault, Michel, 'Of Other Spaces', trans. Jay Miskowiec, *Diacritics*, 16.1 (1986), 22-7

Fowler, Alastair, *Renaissance Realism: Narrative Images in Literature and Art* (Oxford: Oxford University Press, 2003; repr. 2009)

Fowler, Alastair, 'The River Guyon', *MLN*, 75.4 (1960), 289-92

French, Peter J., *John Dee: The World of an Elizabethan Magus* (London: Routledge and Kegan Paul, 1972)

Fried, Debra, 'Spenser's Caesura', *ELR*, 11.3 (1981), 261-80

Fruen, Jeffrey P., 'The Faery Queen Unveiled? Five Glimpses of Gloriana', *Spenser Studies*, 11 (1994), 53–87

Frye, Northrop, *The Secular Scripture: A Study of the Structure of Romance* (Cambridge, MA: Harvard University Press, 1976)

Fuchs, Barbara, 'Conquering Islands: Contextualizing *The Tempest*', SQ, 48.1 (1997), 45–62

Fuchs, Barbara, *Romance* (New York: Routledge, 2004)

Fuller, Mary C., 'Ralegh's Fugitive Gold: Reference and Deferral in *The Discoverie of Guiana*', *Representations*, 33.1 (1991), 42–64

Fuller, Mary C., *Voyages in Print: English Travel to America, 1576–1624* (Cambridge: Cambridge University Press, 1995)

Galbraith, David, *Architectonics of Imitation in Spenser, Daniel, and Drayton* (Toronto: University of Toronto Press, 2000)

Genette, Gérard, *Paratexts: Thresholds of Interpretation*, trans. Jane E. Lewin (Cambridge: Cambridge University Press, 1997)

Giamatti, A. Bartlett, *Exile and Change in Renaissance Literature* (New Haven: Yale University Press, 1984)

Giblett, Rod, *Postmodern Wetlands: Culture, History, Ecology* (Edinburgh: Edinburgh University Press, 1996)

Gillies, John, *Shakespeare and the Geography of Difference* (Cambridge: Cambridge University Press, 1994)

Gillingham, John, 'The English Invasion of Ireland', in *Representing Ireland: Literature and the Origins of Conflict, 1534–1660*, ed. Brendan Bradshaw, Andrew Hadfield, and Willy Maley (Cambridge: Cambridge University Press, 1993), pp. 24–42

Gillis, John R., *Islands of the Mind: How the Human Imagination Created the Atlantic World* (New York: Palgrave Macmillan, 2004)

Gillis, John R., 'Not Continents in Miniature: Islands as Ecotones', *Island Studies Journal*, 9.1 (2014), 155–66

Ginzburg, Carlo, *Clues, Myths, and the Historical Method*, trans. John and Anne C. Tedeschi (Baltimore: Johns Hopkins University Press, 1989)

Goldberg, Benjamin, *The Mirror and Man* (Charlottesville: University of Virginia Press, 1985)

Goldberg, Jonathan, *Endlesse Worke: Spenser and the Structures of Discourse* (Baltimore: Johns Hopkins University Press, 1981)

Goodman, Jennifer R., *Chivalry and Exploration 1298–1630* (Woodbridge: Boydell Press, 1998)

Goodman, Nelson, *Ways of Worldmaking* (Hassocks: Harvester, 1978)

Gordon, Andrew and Bernhard Klein, eds, *Literature, Mapping and the Politics of Space in Early Modern Britain* (Cambridge: Cambridge University Press, 2001)

Gottfried, Rudolf, 'Irish Geography in Spenser's *View*', *ELH*, 6.2 (1939), 114-37

Grabes, Herbert, *The Mutable Glass: Mirror-Imagery in Titles and Texts of the Middle Ages and English Renaissance*, trans. Gordon Collier (Cambridge: Cambridge University Press, 1973; repr. 1982)

Graham, Brian J., and Lindsay J. Proudfoot, eds, *An Historical Geography of Ireland* (London: Academic Press, 1993)

Greenblatt, Stephen, *Renaissance Self-Fashioning from More to Shakespeare* (Chicago: University of Chicago Press, 1980)

Greenblatt, Stephen, *Sir Walter Ralegh: The Renaissance Man and His Roles* (New Haven: Yale University Press, 1973)

Greene, Roland, *Five Words: Critical Semantics in the Age of Shakespeare and Cervantes* (Chicago: University of Chicago Press, 2013)

Greene, Roland, 'Island Logic', in *The Tempest and Its Travels*, ed. Peter Hulme and William H. Sherman (London: Reaktion, 2000), pp. 138-45

Greene, Roland, 'A Primer of Spenser's Worldmaking: Alterity in the Bower of Bliss', in *Worldmaking Spenser: Explorations in the Early Modern Age*, ed. Patrick Cheney and Lauren Silberman (Lexington: University Press of Kentucky, 2000), pp. 9-31

Greene, Roland, 'The "Scriene" and the Channel: England and Spain in Book V of *The Faerie Queene*', *JMEMS*, 39.1 (2009), 43-64

Greene, Roland, *Unrequited Conquests: Love and Empire in the Colonial Americas* (Chicago: University of Chicago Press, 1999)

Gregerson, Linda, 'Protestant Erotics: Idolatry and Interpretation in Spenser's *Faerie Queene*', *ELH*, 58.1 (1991), 1-34

Gregerson, Linda, *The Reformation of the Subject: Spenser, Milton, and the English Protestant Epic* (Cambridge: Cambridge University Press, 1995)

Gregerson, Linda, 'Spenser's Georgic: Violence and the Gift of Place', *Spenser Studies*, 22 (2007), 185-201

Gregerson, Linda, 'Telling Time: Temporality in *The Faerie Queene*', Hugh MacClean Memorial Lecture, International Spenser Society, 7 January 2012, *Spenser Review*, 42.7

Gregory, Derek, 'Imaginative Geographies', *Progress in Human Geography*, 19.4 (1995), 447-85

Grenfell, Joanne Woolway, 'Do Real Knights Need Maps? Charting Moral, Geographical and Representational Uncertainty in Edmund

Spenser's *The Faerie Queene*', in *Literature, Mapping and the Politics of Space in Early Modern Britain*, ed. Andrew Gordon and Bernhard Klein (Cambridge: Cambridge University Press, 2001), pp. 224–38

Grenfell, Joanne Woolway, 'Significant Spaces in Edmund Spenser's *View of the Present State of Ireland*', *EMLS*, 4.2 (1998), 6.1–21

Grennan, Eamon, 'Language and Politics: A Note on Some Metaphors in Spenser's *A View of the Present State of Ireland*', *Spenser Studies*, 3 (1982), 99–110

Griffith, Gareth, 'Merlin', in *Heroes and Anti-Heroes in Medieval Romance*, ed. Neil Cartlidge (Cambridge: D.S. Brewer, 2012)

Gross, Kenneth, 'Green Thoughts in a Green Shade', *Spenser Studies*, 24 (2009), 355–71

Gross, Kenneth, 'The Postures of Allegory', in *Edmund Spenser: Essays on Culture and Allegory*, ed. Jennifer Klein Morrison and Matthew Greenfield (Aldershot: Ashgate, 2000), pp. 167–79

Gross, Kenneth, *Spenserian Poetics: Idolatry, Iconoclasm, and Magic* (Ithaca: Cornell University Press, 1985)

Guenther, Genevieve Juliette, *Magical Imaginations: Instrumental Aesthetics in the English Renaissance* (Toronto: University of Toronto Press, 2012)

Gwynn, Edward, *The Metrical Dindshenchas: General Introduction to the Dindshenchas*, Vol. 5 (Dublin: Hodges Figgis, 1935)

Hadfield, Andrew, 'Another Look at Serena and Irena', *IUR*, 26.2 (1996), 291–302

Hadfield, Andrew, *Edmund Spenser* (London: Longman, 1996)

Hadfield, Andrew, *Edmund Spenser: A Life* (Oxford: Oxford University Press, 2012; repr. 2014)

Hadfield, Andrew, *Edmund Spenser's Irish Experience: Wilde Fruit and Salvage Soyl* (Oxford: Clarendon: 1997)

Hadfield, Andrew, *Literature, Politics and National Identity: Reformation to Renaissance* (Cambridge: Cambridge University Press, 1994)

Hadfield, Andrew, *Shakespeare, Spenser and the Matter of Britain* (Basingstoke: Palgrave Macmillan, 2004)

Hadfield, Andrew and Willy Maley, 'Introduction: Irish Representations and English Alternatives', in *Representing Ireland: Literature and the Origins of Conflict, 1534–1660*, ed. Brendan Bradshaw, Andrew Hadfield, and Willy Maley (Cambridge: Cambridge University Press, 1993), pp. 1–23

Hadot, Pierre, *What is Ancient Philopsophy?*, trans. Michael Chase (Cambridge, MA: Harvard University Press, 2004)

Halliwell, James Orchard, ed., *The Private Diary of Dr. John Dee and the Catalogue of His Library of Manuscripts* (London: Camden Society, 1842)

Hamilton, A.C., 'Our New Poet: Spenser, "Well of English Undefyled"', in *A Theatre for Spenserians*, ed. Judith M. Kennedy and James A. Reither (Manchester: Manchester University Press, 1973), pp. 101–23

Hamilton, A.C., ed., *The Spenser Encyclopedia* (Toronto: University of Toronto Press, 1990)

Hamilton, A.C., *The Structure of Allegory in The Faerie Queene* (Oxford: Clarendon, 1961)

Hankins, James, *Plato in the Italian Renaissance*, Vol. 1 (Leiden: Brill, 1990)

Hankins, John Erskine, *Source and Meaning in Spenser's Allegory: A Study of The Faerie Queene* (Oxford: Clarendon Press, 1971)

Haraway, Donna, 'Situated Knowledges: The Science Question in Feminism and the Privilege of Partial Perspective', *Feminist Studies*, 14.3 (1988), 575–99

Hardie, Philip R., *The Last Trojan Hero: A Cultural History of Virgil's Aeneid* (London: I.B. Taurus, 2014)

Hardie, Philip R., *Virgil's Aeneid: Cosmos and Imperium* (Oxford: Clarendon Press, 2003)

Harley, J.B., 'Deconstructing the Map', in *Writing Worlds: Discourse, Text, and Metaphor in the Representation of Landscape*, ed. Trevor J. Barnes and James S. Duncan (London: Routledge, 1992), pp. 231–47

Harley, J.B., *The New Nature of Maps: Essays in the History of Cartography*, ed. Paul Laxton (Baltimore: Johns Hopkins University Press, 2001)

Harrington, John P., *The English Traveller in Ireland: Accounts of Ireland and the Irish through Five Centuries* (Dublin: Wolfhound Press, 1991)

Harvey, P.D.A., *Maps in Tudor England* (London: Public Record Office and the British Library, 1993)

Hazlitt, William, 'Lecture II: On Chaucer and Spenser', in *Lectures on the English Poets* (London: Taylor and Hessey, 1818), pp. 39–85

Heale, Elizabeth, 'Travailing Abroad: The Poet as Adventurer', in *Travels and Translations in the Sixteenth Century*, ed. Mike Pincombe (Aldershot: Ashgate, 2004), pp. 3–18

Heaney, Seamus, *Preoccupations: Selected Prose, 1968–1978* (London: Faber, 1980)

Hecht, Paul J. and J.B. Lethbridge, eds, *Spenser in the Moment* (Madison: Fairleigh Dickinson University Press, 2015)

Helgerson, Richard, 'The Folly of Maps and Modernity', in *Literature,*

*Mapping and the Politics of Space in Early Modern Britain*, ed. Andrew Gordon and Bernhard Klein (Cambridge: Cambridge University Press, 2001), pp. 241–62

Helgerson, Richard, *Forms of Nationhood: The Elizabethan Writing of England* (Chicago: University of Chicago Press, 1992)

Heng, Geraldine, *Empire of Magic: Medieval Romance and the Politics of Cultural Fantasy* (New York: Columbia University Press, 2003)

Heninger, Jr., S.K., *The Cosmographical Glass: Renaissance Diagrams of the Universe* (San Marino: Huntington Library, 1977; repr. 2004)

Heninger, Jr., S.K., *A Handbook of Renaissance Meteorology* (Durham, NC: Duke University Press, 1960)

Heninger, Jr., S.K., *Touches of Sweet Harmony: Pythagorean Cosmology and Renaissance Poetics* (San Marino: Huntington Library, 1974)

Henley, Pauline, *Spenser in Ireland* (Cork: Cork University Press, 1928)

Herron, Thomas, '"Goodly Woods": Irish Forests, Georgic Trees in Books 1 and 4 of Edmund Spenser's *Faerie Queene*', *Quidditas*, 19 (1998), 97–122

Herron, Thomas, 'Irish Den of Thieves: Souterrains (and a Crannog?) in Books V and VI of Spenser's *Faerie Queene*', *Spenser Studies*, 14 (2000), 303–17

Herron, Thomas, 'Irish Romance: Spenser's Prince Arthur and the *Hystorye of Olyuer of Castile* (c. 1518)', *Notes and Queries*, 51.3 (2004), 254–6

Herron, Thomas, 'Love's "Emperye": Raleigh's "Ocean to Scinthia," Spenser's "Colin Clouts Come Home Againe" and *The Faerie Queene* IV.vii in Colonial Context', in *Literary and Visual Ralegh*, ed. Christopher M. Armitage (Manchester: Manchester University Press, 2013), pp. 100–39

Herron, Thomas, 'New English Nation: Munster Politics, Virgilian Complaint, and Pastoral Empire in Spenser's "Colin Clouts Come Home Againe" (1595)', *Eolas*, 8 (2015), 89–122

Herron, Thomas, 'Orpheus in Ulster: Richard Bartlett's Colonial Art', in *Ireland in the Renaissance, c. 1540–1660*, ed. Thomas Herron and Michael Potterton (Dublin: Four Courts Press, 2007), pp. 289–308

Herron, Thomas, 'The Spanish Armada, Ireland, and Spenser's *The Faerie Queene*', *New Hibernia Review*, 6.2 (2002), 82–105

Herron, Thomas, *Spenser's Irish Work: Poetry, Plantation and Colonial Reformation* (Aldershot: Ashgate, 2007)

Herron, Thomas and Michael Potterton, eds, *Ireland in the Renaissance, c. 1540–1660* (Dublin: Four Courts Press, 2007)

Hieatt, A. Kent, *Chaucer, Spenser, Milton: Mythopoeic Continuities and Transformations* (Montreal: McGill-Queen's University Press, 1975)

Hieatt, A. Kent, 'Room of One's Own for Decisions: Chaucer and *The Faerie Queene*', in *Refiguring Chaucer in the Renaissance*, ed. Theresa M. Krier (Gainesville: University Press of Florida, 1998), pp. 147–64

Highley, Christopher, *Shakespeare, Spenser and the Crisis in Ireland* (Cambridge: Cambridge University Press, 1997)

Hile, Rachel E., 'The Limitations of Concord in the Thames-Medway Marriage Canto of *The Faerie Queene*', *Studies in Philology*, 108.1 (2011), 70–85

Hughes, Merritt Y., 'Spenser's Acrasia and the Circe of the Renaissance', *Journal of the History of Ideas*, 4 (1943), 381–99

Honig, Edwin, *Dark Conceit: The Making of Allegory* (Providence: Brown University Press, 1959; repr. 1972)

Horner, Joyce, 'The Large Landscape: A Study of Certain Images in Ralegh', *Essays in Criticism*, 5.3 (1955), 197–213

Houston, Chloë, ed., *New Worlds Reflected: Travel and Utopia in the Early Modern Period* (Farnham: Ashgate, 2010)

Howarth, William L., 'Imagined Territory: The Writing of Wetlands', *NLH*, 30.3 (1999), 509–39

Hulme, Peter and William H. Sherman, eds, *The Tempest and Its Travels* (London: Reaktion, 2000)

Hurd, Barbara, *Stirring the Mud: On Swamps, Bogs, and Human Imagination* (Boston: Beacon Press, 2001)

Hurd, Bishop Richard, *Hurd's Letters on Chivalry and Romance*, ed. Edith J. Morley (London: Henry Frowde, 1911)

Hutson, Lorna, 'Chivalry for Merchants; or, Knights of Temperance in the Realms of Gold', *JMEMS*, 26.1 (1996), 29–59

Hutson, Lorna, 'Fortunate Travellers: Reading for the Plot in Sixteenth-Century England', *Representations*, 41 (1993), 83–103

Iser, Wolfgang, *The Act of Reading: A Theory of Aesthetic Response* (Baltimore: Johns Hopkins University Press, 1978; repr. 1994)

Jameson, Fredric, 'Magical Narratives: Romance as Genre', *NLH*, 7.1 (1975), 135–63

Jerram, Leif, 'Space: A Useless Category for Historical Analysis?', *History and Theory*, 52.3 (2013), 400–19

Johnson, William C., *Spenser's Amoretti: Analogies of Love* (Lewisburg: Bucknell University Press, 1990)

Joyce, Patrick Weston, 'Spenser's Irish Rivers', in *The Wonders of Ireland*

*and Other Papers on Irish Subjects* (London: Longmans, Green, and Co., 1911), pp. 72–114

Judson, Alexander Corbin, *Spenser in Southern Ireland* (Bloomington: Principia Press, 1933)

Justice, Steven, 'Literary History and *Piers Plowman*', in *The Cambridge Companion to Piers Plowman*, ed. Andrew Cole and Andrew Galloway (Cambridge: Cambridge University Press, 2014), pp. 50–64

Kalas, Rayna, *Frame, Glass, Verse: The Technology of Poetic Invention in the English Renaissance* (Ithaca: Cornell University Press, 2007)

Kantorowicz, Ernst H., *The King's Two Bodies: A Study in Mediaeval Political Theology* (Princeton: Princeton University Press, 1957)

Keighren, Innes M., 'Geosophy, Imagination, and *Terrae Incognitae*: Exploring the Intellectual History of John Kirtland Wright', *Journal of Historical Geography*, 31.3 (2005), 546–56

Kendrick, Walter M., 'Earth of Flesh, Flesh of Earth: Mother Earth in *The Faerie Queene*', *RQ*, 27.4 (1974), 533–48

Kermode, Frank, *The Sense of an Ending: Studies in the Theory of Fiction* (Oxford: Oxford University Press, 1967; repr. 1977)

Kerrigan, John, *Archipelagic English: Literature, History, and Politics, 1603–1707* (Oxford: Oxford University Press, 2008)

Killeen, Kevin, *Biblical Scholarship, Science and Politics in Early Modern England: Thomas Browne and the Thorny Place of Knowledge* (Aldershot: Ashgate, 2009)

King, Andrew, *The Faerie Queene and Middle English Romance: The Matter of Just Memory* (Oxford: Clarendon, 2000)

King, Andrew, '"Well Grounded, Finely Framed, and Strongly Trussed up Together": The "Medieval" Structure of *The Faerie Queene*', in *Edmund Spenser: New and Renewed Directions*, ed. J.B. Lethbridge (Madison: Fairleigh Dickinson University Press, 2006), pp. 119–52

Kinzel, Ulrich, 'Orientation as a Paradigm of Maritime Modernity', in *Fictions of the Sea: Critical Perspectives on the Ocean in British Literature and Culture*, ed. Bernhard Klein and Gesa Mackenthun (Aldershot: Ashgate, 2002), pp. 28–48

Kitch, Aaron, *Political Economy and the States of Literature in Early Modern England* (Farnham: Ashgate, 2009)

Klein, Bernhard, 'Imaginary Journeys: Spenser, Drayton, and the Poetics of National Space', in *Literature, Mapping and the Politics of Space in Early Modern Britain*, ed. Andrew Gordon and Bernhard Klein (Cambridge: Cambridge University Press, 2001), pp. 204–23

Klein, Bernhard, 'The Lie of the Land: English Surveyors, Irish Rebels and *The Faerie Queene*', *IUR*, 26.2 (1996), 207–25

Klein, Bernhard, 'Mapping the Waters: Sea Charts, Navigation, and Camões's *Os Lusíadas*', *Renaissance Studies*, 25.2 (2011), 228–47

Klein, Bernhard, *Maps and the Writing of Space in Early Modern England and Ireland* (Basingstoke: Palgrave Macmillan, 2001)

Klein, Bernhard, 'Partial Views: Shakespeare and the Map of Ireland', *EMLS*, 4.2 (1998), 5.1–20

Klein, Naomi Reed, *Maps of Medieval Thought: The Hereford Paradigm* (Woodbridge: Boydell Press, 2001)

Knapp, James A., *Image Ethics in Shakespeare and Spenser* (New York: Palgrave Macmillan, 2011)

Knapp, Jeffrey, *An Empire Nowhere: England, America, and Literature from Utopia to The Tempest* (Berkeley: University of California Press, 1992)

Knight, Stephen, *Merlin: Knowledge and Power Through the Ages* (Ithaca: Cornell University Press, 2009)

Koeman, Cornelis, *The History of Lucas Janszoon Waghenaer and his Spieghel der Zeevaerdt* (Lausanne: Sequoia, 1964)

Koyré, Alexandre, *From the Closed World to the Infinite Universe* (Baltimore: Johns Hopkins University Press, 1957)

Krier, Theresa M., *Refiguring Chaucer in the Renaissance* (Gainesville: University Press of Florida, 1998)

Lachavanne, Jean-Bernard and Raphaëlle Juge, eds, *Biodiversity in Land-Inland Water Ecotones* (Paris: UNESCO; New York and Carnforth: Parthenon, 1997)

Lakoff, George and Mark Johnson, *Metaphors We Live By* (Chicago: University of Chicago Press, 1980)

Lambert, Ladina Bezzola, *Imagining the Unimaginable: The Poetics of Early Modern Astronomy* (Amsterdam: Rodopi, 2002)

Lee, Judith, 'The English Ariosto: The Elizabethan Poet and the Marvellous', *Studies in Philology*, 80.3 (1983), 277–99

Lees-Jeffries, Hester, 'From the Fountain to the Well: Redcrosse Learns to Read', *Studies in Philology*, 100.2 (2003), 135–76

Lefebvre, Henri, *The Production of Space*, trans. Donald Nicholson-Smith (Oxford: Blackwell, 1991)

Le Goff, Jacques, *The Birth of Purgatory*, trans. Arthur Goldhammer (Aldershot: Scholar Press, 1981; repr. 1990)

Le Goff, Jacques, *The Medieval Imagination*, trans. Arthur Goldhammer (Chicago: University of Chicago Press, 1985; repr. 1992)

Leslie, Michael, 'Spenser, Sidney and the Renaissance Garden', *ELR*, 22.1 (1992), 3–36
Lestringant, Frank, *Mapping the Renaissance World: The Geographical Imagination in the Age of Discovery*, trans. David Fausett (Cambridge: Polity, 1994)
Lethbridge, J.B., ed., *Edmund Spenser: New and Renewed Directions* (Madison: Fairleigh Dickinson University Press, 2006)
Lethbridge, J.B., 'Raleigh in Books III and IV of *The Faerie Queene*: The Primacy of Moral Allegory', *Studia Neophilologica*, 64 (1992), 55–66
Levinson, Stephen C., *Space in Language and Cognition: Explorations in Cognitive Diversity* (Cambridge: Cambridge University Press, 2003)
Lewis, C.S., *The Allegory of Love: A Study in Medieval Tradition* (New York: Oxford University Press, 1936; repr. 1958)
Lewis, C.S., *The Discarded Image: An Introduction to Medieval and Renaissance Literature* (Cambridge: Cambridge University Press, 1964)
Lewis, C.S., *English Literature in the Sixteenth Century Excluding Drama* (Oxford: Clarendon Press, 1954; repr. 1959)
Lim, Walter S.H., *The Arts of Empire: The Poetics of Colonialism from Ralegh to Milton* (Newark: University of Delaware Press, 1998)
Linton, Joan Pong, *The Romance of the New World: Gender and the Literary Formations of English Colonialism* (Cambridge: Cambridge University Press, 1998)
Lionarons, Joyce Tally, 'Magic, Machines, and Deception: Technology in the *Canterbury Tales*', *The Chaucer Review*, 27.4 (1993), 377–86
Livingstone, David N., *The Geographical Tradition: Episodes in the History of a Contested Enterprise* (Oxford: Blackwell, 1993)
Logan, George M. and Gordon Teskey, eds, *Unfolded Tales: Essays on Renaissance Romance* (Ithaca: Cornell University Press, 1989)
Lupton, Julia Reinhard, 'Home-Making in Ireland: Virgil's *Eclogue* I and Book VI of *The Faerie Queene*', *Spenser Studies*, 8 (1990), 119–45
Lupton, Julia Reinhard, 'Mapping Mutability: or, Spenser's Irish Plot', in *Representing Ireland: Literature and the Origins of Conflict, 1534–1660*, ed. Brendan Bradshaw, Andrew Hadfield, and Willy Maley (Cambridge: Cambridge University Press, 1993), pp. 93–115
MacCaffrey, Isabel G., *Spenser's Allegory: The Anatomy of Imagination* (Princeton: Princeton University Press, 1976)
MacCaffrey, Wallace T., *Elizabeth I: War and Politics, 1588–1603* (Princeton: Princeton University Press, 1992)

Macfarlane, Robert, *The Old Ways: A Journey on Foot* (London: Penguin, 2012)

Maley, Willy, '"The Name of the Country I have Forgotten": Remembering and Dismembering in Sir Henry Sidney's Irish *Memoir* (1583)', in *Ireland in the Renaissance, c. 1540–1660*, ed. Thomas Herron and Michael Potterton (Dublin: Four Courts Press, 2007), pp. 52–73

Maley, Willy, *Salvaging Spenser: Colonisation, Culture and Identity* (Basingstoke: Macmillan, 1997)

Maley, Willy, 'Spenser's Languages: Writing in the Ruins of English', in *The Cambridge Companion to Spenser*, ed. Andrew Hadfield (Cambridge: Cambridge University Press, 2001), pp. 162–79

Maley, Willy, '"To Weet to Work Irenaes Franchisement": Ireland in *The Faerie Queene*', *IUR*, 26.2 (1996), 303–19

Man, Paul de, 'The Rhetoric of Temporality', in *Interpretation: Theory and Practice*, ed. Charles S. Singleton (Baltimore: Johns Hopkins University Press, 1969), pp. 173–209.

Mann, Jenny C., *Outlaw Rhetoric: Figuring Vernacular Eloquence in Shakespeare's England* (Ithaca: Cornell University Press, 2012)

March, Jenny, *Cassell Dictionary of Classical Mythology* (London: Cassell, 1998; repr. 2002)

Marin, Louis, 'Frontiers of Utopia: Past and Present', *Critical Inquiry*, 19 (1993), 397–420

Martin, Carol A.N., 'Authority and the Defense of Fiction: Renaissance Poetics and Chaucer's *House of Fame*', in *Refiguring Chaucer in the Renaissance*, ed. Theresa M. Krier (Gainesville: University Press of Florida, 1998), pp. 40–65

Martin, Catherine Gimelli, 'Spenser's Neoplatonic Geography of the Passions: Mapping Allegory in the "Legend of Temperance", *Faerie Queene*, Book II', *Spenser Studies*, 24 (2009), 269–307

Massey, Doreen, *For Space* (London: Sage Publications, 2005)

Mazzio, Carla, *The Inarticulate Renaissance: Language Trouble in an Age of Eloquence* (Philadelphia: University of Pennsylvania Press, 2009)

Mazzola, Elizabeth, *The Pathology of the English Renaissance: Sacred Remains and Holy Ghosts* (Leiden: Brill, 1998)

McCabe, Richard A., *The Pillars of Eternity: Time and Providence in The Faerie Queene* (Blackrock: Irish Academic Press, 1989)

McCabe, Richard A., *Spenser's Monstrous Regiment: Elizabethan Ireland and the Poetics of Difference* (Oxford: Oxford University Press, 2002)

McCabe, Richard A., 'Translated States: Spenser and Linguistic Colonialism', in *Edmund Spenser: Essays on Culture and Allegory*, ed.

Jennifer Klein Morrison and Matthew Greenfield (Aldershot: Ashgate, 2000), pp. 67–88

McGurk, John, *The Elizabethan Conquest of Ireland: The 1590s Crisis* (Manchester: Manchester University Press, 1997)

McLean, Stuart, '"To Dream Profoundly": Irish Boglands and the Imagination of Matter', *Irish Journal of Anthropology*, 10.2 (2007), 61–8

McLeod, Bruce, *The Geography of Empire in English Literature, 1580–1745* (Cambridge: Cambridge University Press, 1999; repr. 2009)

McRae, Andrew, 'Fluvial Nation: Rivers, Mobility and Poetry in Early Modern England', *ELR*, 38.3 (2008), 506–34

McRae, Andrew, *Literature and Domestic Travel in Early Modern England* (Cambridge: Cambridge University Press, 2009)

Melville, Robert Dundonald, *A Manual of the Principles of Roman Law Relating to Persons, Property and Obligations* (Edinburgh: Green, 1915)

Mentz, Steve, 'After Sustainability', *PMLA*, 127.3 (2012), 586–92

Mentz, Steve, *At the Bottom of Shakespeare's Ocean* (London: Continuum, 2009)

Mentz, Steve, 'Brown', in *Prismatic Ecology: Ecotheory Beyond Green*, ed. Jeffrey Jerome Cohen (Minneapolis: University of Minnesota Press, 2013), pp. 193–212

Mentz, Steve, *Shipwreck Modernity: Ecologies of Globalization, 1550–1719* (Minneapolis: University of Minnesota Press, 2015)

Michael, Erika, *The Drawings by Hans Holbein the Younger for Erasmus' 'Praise of Folly'* (New York: Garland, 1985)

Michelet, Fabienne L., *Creation, Migration, and Conquest: Imaginary Geography and Sense of Space in Old English Literature* (Oxford: Oxford University Press, 2006)

Miller, David Lee, *The Poem's Two Bodies: The Poetics of the 1590 Faerie Queene* (Princeton: Princeton University Press, 1988)

Miller, Shannon, *Invested With Meaning: The Raleigh Circle in the New World* (Philadelphia: University of Pennsylvania Press, 1998)

Miller, T.S., 'Writing Dreams to Good: Reading as Writing and Writing as Reading in Chaucer's Dream Visions', *Style*, 45.3 (2011), 528–48

Mitchell, W.J.T., 'Preface to the Second Edition of *Landscape and Power*: Space, Place and Landscape', in *Landscape and Power*, ed. W.J.T. Mitchell (Chicago: University of Chicago Press, 2002), pp. vii–xii

Mitchell, W.J.T., 'Spatial Form in Literature: Toward a General Theory', *Critical Inquiry*, 6 (1980), 539–67

Mohsen, Emilien, *Time and the Calendar in Edmund Spenser's Poetical Works* (Paris: Publibook, 2005)

Monmonier, Mark S., *Coast Lines: How Mapmakers Frame the World and Chart Environmental Change* (Chicago: University of Chicago Press, 2008)

Monmonier, Mark S., *How to Lie with Maps* (Chicago: University of Chicago Press, 1991)

Montiglio, Silvia, *Wandering in Ancient Greek Culture* (Chicago: University of Chicago Press, 2005)

Montrose, Louis, 'Spenser and the Elizabethan Political Imaginary', *ELH*, 69.4 (2002), 907–46

Moody, T.W., F.X. Martin, and F.J. Byrne, eds, *A New History of Ireland: Early Modern Ireland 1534–1691* (Oxford: Oxford University Press, 2009)

Moore Smith, G.C., ed., *Gabriel Harvey's Marginalia* (Stratford-Upon-Avon: Shakespeare Head Press, 1913)

Morrison, Jennifer Klein and Matthew Greenfield, eds, *Edmund Spenser: Essays on Culture and Allegory* (Aldershot: Ashgate, 2000)

Mullally, Evelyn, *The Artist at Work: Narrative Technique in Chrétien de Troyes* (Philadelphia: American Philosophical Society, 1988)

Munro, Lucy, *Archaic Style in English Literature, 1590–1674* (Cambridge: Cambridge University Press, 2013)

Murphy, Andrew, *But the Irish Sea Betwixt Us: Ireland, Colonialism, and Renaissance Literature* (Lexington: University Press of Kentucky, 1999)

Murrin, Michael, *The Allegorical Epic: Essays in its Rise and Decline* (Chicago: University of Chicago Press, 1980)

Murrin, Michael, 'The Rhetoric of Fairyland', in *The Rhetoric of Renaissance Poetry From Wyatt to Milton*, ed. Thomas O. Sloan and Raymond B. Waddington (Berkeley: University of California Press, 1974), pp. 73–95

Murrin, Michael, *The Veil of Allegory: Some Notes Toward a Theory of Allegorical Rhetoric in the English Renaissance* (Chicago: University of Chicago Press, 1969)

Murtaugh, Daniel M., 'The Garden and the Sea: The Topography of *The Faerie Queene*, III', *ELH*, 40.3 (1973), 325–38

Myers, Benjamin P., 'The Green and Golden World: Spenser's Rewriting of the Munster Plantation', *ELH*, 76.2 (2009), 473–90

Nellist, Brian, 'The Allegory of Guyon's Voyage: An Interpretation', *ELH*, 30.2 (1963), 89–106

Neuse, Richard, 'Book VI as Conclusion to *The Faerie Queene*, *ELH*, 35.3 (1968), 329–53

Newcomb, Lori Humphrey, *Reading Popular Romance in Early Modern England* (New York: Columbia University Press, 2002)

Nicholson, Catherine, 'Othello and the Geography of Persuasion', *ELR*, 40.1 (2010), 56–87

Nicholson, Catherine, *Uncommon Tongues: Eloquence and Eccentricity in the English Renaissance* (Philadelphia: University of Pennsylvania Press, 2014)

Nicolson, Marjorie Hope, *The Breaking of the Circle: Studies in the Effect of the 'New Science' upon Seventeenth-Century Poetry* (New York: Columbia University Press, 1960)

Nievergelt, Marco, *Allegorical Quests from Deguileville to Spenser* (Cambridge: D.S. Brewer, 2012)

Nohrnberg, James, *The Analogy of The Faerie Queene* (Princeton: Princeton University Press, 1976)

Nohrnberg, James, 'Britomart's Gone Abroad to Brute-land, Colin Clout's Come Courting from the Salvage Ire-Land: Exile and the Kingdom in Some of Spenser's Fictions for "Crossing Over"', in *Edmund Spenser: New and Renewed Directions*, ed. J.B. Lethbridge (Madison: Fairleigh Dickinson University Press, 2006), pp. 214–85

Nohrnberg, James, 'Raleigh in Ruins, Raleigh on the Rocks: Sir Wa'ter's Two Books of Mutabilitie and their Subject's Allegorical Presence in Select Spenserian Narratives and Complaints', in *Literary and Visual Ralegh*, ed. Christopher M. Armitage (Manchester: Manchester University Press, 2013), pp. 31–88

Núñez, Rafael and Kensy Cooperrider, 'The Tangle of Space and Time in Human Cognition', *Trends in Cognitive Sciences*, 17.5 (2013), 220–9.

O'Keeffe, Tadhg, 'Plantation-era Great Houses in Munster: A Note on Sir Walter Raleigh's House and Its Context', in *Ireland in the Renaissance, c. 1540–1660*, ed. Thomas Herron and Michael Potterton (Dublin: Four Courts Press, 2007), pp. 274–88

O'Neill, Timothy, *Merchants and Mariners in Medieval Ireland* (Dublin: Irish Academic Press, 1987)

Oram, William A., 'Spenserian Paralysis', *SEL*, 41.1 (2001), 49–70

Oram, William A., 'What Did Spenser Really Think of Sir Walter Ralegh When He Published the First Installment of *The Faerie Queene*?', *Spenser Studies*, 15 (2001), 165–74

Orgel, Stephen, 'Margins of Truth', in *The Renaissance Text: Theory,*

Editing, Textuality, ed. Andrew Murphy (Manchester: Manchester University Press, 2000), pp. 91–107

Orgelfinger, Gail, 'Introduction', in *The Hystorye of Olyuer of Castylle* (New York: Garland Publishing, 1988), pp. ix–xxxvi

Ortony, Andrew, ed., *Metaphor and Thought* (Cambridge: Cambridge University Press, 1979; repr. 1980)

Osgood, Charles G., 'Comments on the Moral Allegory of *The Faerie Queene*', *MLN*, 46.8 (1931), 502–7

Outhwaite, R.B., 'Dearth, the English Crown and the "Crisis of the 1590s"', in *The European Crisis of the 1590s: Essays in Comparative History*, ed. Peter Clark (London: Allen & Unwin, 1985), pp. 23–43

Owen, Hywel Wyn and Richard Morgan, *Dictionary of the Place-Names of Wales* (Llandysul: Gomer, 2007)

Owens, Judith, *Enabling Engagements: Edmund Spenser and the Poetics of Patronage* (Montreal: McGill-Queen's University Press, 2002)

Padrón, Ricardo, 'Mapping Imaginary Worlds', in *Maps: Finding Our Place in the World*, ed. J. R. Akerman (Chicago: University of Chicago Press, 2007), pp. 255–88

Palmer, Patricia, *Language and Conquest in Early Modern Ireland: English Renaissance Literature and Elizabethan Imperial Expansion* (Cambridge: Cambridge University Press, 2001)

Palmer, Patricia, *The Severed Head and the Grafted Tongue: Literature, Translation and Violence in Early Modern Ireland* (Cambridge: Cambridge University Press, 2013)

Palmer, Patricia, 'Where Does It Hurt? How Pain Makes History in Early Modern Ireland', in *The Body in Pain in Irish Literature and Culture*, ed. Fionnuala Dillane, Naomi McAreavey, and Emilie Pine (Basingstoke: Palgrave Macmillan, 2016), pp. 21–38

Park, Katherine, 'Bacon's "Enchanted Glass"', *Isis*, 75.2 (1984), 290–302

Parker, Patricia A., *Inescapable Romance: Studies in the Poetics of a Mode* (Princeton: Princeton University Press, 1979)

Parker, Patricia A., *Shakespeare from the Margins: Language, Culture, Context* (Chicago: University of Chicago Press, 1996)

Parry, Glyn, 'John Dee and the Elizabethan British Empire in its European Context', *The Historical Journal*, 49.3 (2006), 643–75

Parry, Joseph D., 'Phaedria and Guyon: Travelling Alone in *The Faerie Queene*, Book II', *Spenser Studies*, 15 (2001), 53–77

Paster, Gail Kern, 'Becoming the Landscape: The Ecology of the Passions in the Legend of Temperance', in *Environment and Embodiment in Early Modern England*, ed. Mary Floyd-Wilson and Garrett A. Sullivan, Jr. (Basingstoke: Palgrave Macmillan, 2007), pp. 137–52

Paster, Gail Kern, *The Body Embarrassed: Drama and the Disciplines of Shame in Early Modern England* (New York: Cornell University Press, 1993)

Paster, Gail Kern, *Humouring the Body: Emotions and the Shakespearean Stage* (Chicago: University of Chicago Press, 2004)

Patch, Howard Rollin, *The Other World: According to Descriptions in Medieval Literature* (Cambridge, MA: Harvard University Press, 1950)

Patterson, Lee, '"What Man Artow?" Authorial Self-Definition in *The Tale of Sir Thopas* and *The Tale of Melibee*', *Studies in the Age of Chaucer*, 11 (1989), 117–75

Paxman, David B., *Voyage into Language: Space and the Linguistic Encounter, 1500–1800* (Aldershot: Ashgate, 2003)

Perec, Georges, *Species of Spaces and Other Pieces*, ed. and trans. John Sturrock (London: Penguin, 1997; repr. 1999)

Peters, Jeffrey N., *Mapping Discord: Allegorical Cartography in Early Modern French Writing* (Newark: University of Delaware Press, 2004)

Peterson, Kaara L., 'Fluid Economies: Portraying Shakespeare's Hysterics', *Mosaic*, 34.1 (2001), 35–59

Piehler, Paul, *The Visionary Landscape: A Study in Medieval Allegory* (London: Edward Arnold, 1971)

Pinet, Simone, *Archipelagoes: Insular Fictions from Chivalric Romance to the Novel* (Minneapolis: University of Minnesota Press, 2011)

Porges Watson, E.A.F., 'Mutabilitie's Debateable Land: Spenser's Ireland and the Frontiers of Faerie', in *Edmund Spenser: New and Renewed Directions*, ed. J.B. Lethbridge (Madison: Fairleigh Dickinson University Press, 2006), pp. 286–301

Porter, Philip W. and Fred E. Lukermann, 'The Geography of Utopia', in *Geographies of the Mind: Essays in Historical Geosophy*, ed. David Lowenthal and Martyn J. Bowden (New York: Oxford University Press, 1976), pp. 197–223

Powrie, Sarah, 'Spenser's Mutabilitie and the Indeterminate Universe', *SEL*, 53.1 (2013), 73–89

Pratt, Mary Louise, *Imperial Eyes: Travel Writing and Transculturation* (London: Routledge, 1992; repr. 1998)

Prendergast, Thomas A., *Poetical Dust: Poets' Corner and the Making of Britain* (Philadelphia: University of Pennsylvania Press, 2015)

Prendergast, Thomas A., 'Spenser's Phantastic History, *The Ruines of Time*, and the Invention of Medievalism', *JMEMS*, 38.2 (2008), 175–96

Pugh, Syrithe, 'Acrasia and Bondage: Guyon's Perversion of the Ovidian Erotic in Book II of *The Faerie Queene*', in *Edmund Spenser: New and Renewed Directions*, ed. J.B. Lethbridge (Madison: Fairleigh Dickinson University Press, 2006), pp. 153–94

Pugh, Syrithe, *Spenser and Ovid* (Aldershot: Ashgate, 2005)

Putter, Ad, *An Introduction to The Gawain Poet* (London: Longman, 1996)

Putter, Ad, 'The Landscape of Courtly Romance', in *Sir Gawain and the Green Knight and French Arthurian Romance* (Oxford: Clarendon Press, 1995; repr. 2001)

Quilligan, Maureen, *The Language of Allegory: Defining the Genre* (Ithaca: Cornell University Press, 1979; repr. 1992)

Quilligan, Maureen, *Milton's Spenser: The Politics of Reading* (Ithaca: Cornell University Press, 1983)

Quinn, D.B., 'Renaissance Influence in English Colonization', *TRHS*, 26 (1976), 73–93

Quint, David, *Epic and Empire: Politics and Generic Form from Virgil to Milton* (Princeton: Princeton University Press, 1993)

Quitslund, Jon A., *Spenser's Supreme Fiction: Platonic Natural Philosophy and The Faerie Queene* (Toronto: University of Toronto Press, 2001)

Rabkin, Eric S., 'Spatial Form and Plot', *Critical Inquiry*, 4 (1977), 253–70

Rajan, Balachandra, *The Form of the Unfinished: English Poetics from Spenser to Pound* (Princeton: Princeton University Press, 1985)

Ramachandran, Ayesha, *The Worldmakers: Global Imagining in Early Modern Europe* (Chicago: University of Chicago Press, 2015)

Rambo, Elizabeth L., *Colonial Ireland in Medieval English Literature* (Selinsgrove: Susquehanna University Press, 1994)

Rathborne, Isabel E., *The Meaning of Spenser's Fairyland* (New York: Columbia University Press, 1937)

Read, David, *Temperate Conquests: Spenser and the Spanish New World* (Detroit: Wayne State University Press, 2000)

Reichert, Dagmar, 'On Boundaries', *Environment and Planning D: Society and Space*, 10.1 (1992), 87–98

Reif-Hulser, Monika, ed., *Borderlands: Negotiating Boundaries in Post-Colonial Writing* (Amsterdam: Rodopi, 1999)

Reiss, Timothy J., *Knowledge, Discovery, and Imagination in Early Modern Europe: The Rise of Aesthetic Rationalism* (Cambridge: Cambridge University Press, 1997)

Relihan, Constance C., *Cosmographical Glasses: Geographic Discourse, Gender, and Elizabethan Fiction* (Kent, OH: Kent State University Press, 2004)

Remien, Peter, 'Silvan Matters: Error and Instrumentality in Book I of *The Faerie Queene*', *Spenser Studies*, 27 (2013), 119–43

Rhodes, William, 'Chaucer in Ireland: Archaism, Etymology, and the Idea of Development', in *Rereading Chaucer and Spenser: Dan Geffrey with the New Poete*, ed. Rachel Stenner, Tamsin Badcoe, and Gareth Griffith (Manchester: Manchester University Press, 2019), pp. 98–112

Rigolot, François, 'The Renaissance Fascination with Error: Mannerism and Early Modern Poetry', *RQ*, 57.4 (2004), 1219–34

Roche, Jr., Thomas P., *The Kindly Flame: A Study of the Third and Fourth Books of Spenser's Faerie Queene* (Princeton: Princeton University Press, 1964)

Rosenfeld, Colleen Ruth, *Indecorous Thinking: Figures of Speech in Early Modern Poetics* (New York: Fordham University Press, 2018)

Ross, Charles Stanley, *The Custom of the Castle: From Malory to Macbeth* (Berkeley: University of California Press, 1997)

Roszak, Theodore, *Where the Wasteland Ends: Politics and Transcendence in Postindustrial Society* (Berkeley: Celestial Arts, 1989)

Rouse, Robert, 'Walking (between) the Lines: Romance as Itinerary / Map', in *Medieval Romance, Medieval Contexts*, ed. Rhiannon Purdie and Michael Cichon (Cambridge: D.S. Brewer, 2011), pp. 135–48

Rudick, Michael, 'Three Views on Ralegh and Spenser: A Comment', *Spenser Studies*, 15 (2001), 197–203

Ruvoldt, Maria, *The Italian Renaissance Imagery of Inspiration* (Cambridge: Cambridge University Press, 2004)

Russell, John L., 'The Copernican System in Great Britain', in *The Reception of Copernicus' Heliocentric Theory*, ed. Jerzy Dobrzycki (Dordrecht: Reidel, 1972), pp. 189–239

Sadowski, Piotr, 'Spenser's "Golden Squire" and "Golden Meane": Numbers and Proportions in Book II of *The Faerie Queene*', *Spenser Studies*, 14 (2000), 107–31

Said, Edward W., *Culture and Imperialism* (London: Vintage, 1994)

Said, Edward W., *Orientalism* (London: Penguin, 1978; repr. 2003)

Salamon, Linda Bradley, 'The Imagery of Roger Ascham', *Texas Studies in Literature and Language*, 15.1 (1973), 5–23

Sanchez, Melissa E., *Erotic Subjects: The Sexuality of Politics in Early Modern English Literature* (Oxford: Oxford University Press, 2011)

Sanford, Rhonda Lemke, *Maps and Memory in Early Modern England: A Sense of Place* (New York: Palgrave, 2002)
Santore, Cathy, 'The Tools of Venus', *Renaissance Studies*, 11.3 (1997), 179–207
Saunders, Angharad, 'Literary Geography: Reforging the Connections', *Progress in Human Geography*, 34.4 (2010), 436–52
Saunders, Corinne J., *The Forest of Medieval Romance: Avernus, Broceliande, Arden* (Cambridge: D.S. Brewer, 1993)
Scafi, Alessandro, *Mapping Paradise: A History of Heaven on Earth* (Chicago: University of Chicago Press, 2006)
Schilder, Günter, *The Netherland Nautical Cartography from 1550 to 1650* (Lisboa: Instituto de Investigação Científica Tropical, 1984)
Schoenfeldt, Michael C., *Bodies and Selves in Early Modern England: Physiology and Inwardness in Spenser, Shakespeare, Herbert, and Milton* (Cambridge: Cambridge University Press, 1999)
Schwyzer, Philip, *Archaeologies of English Renaissance Literature* (Oxford: Oxford University Press, 2007)
Schwyzer, Philip and Simon Mealor, *Archipelagic Identities: Literature and Identity in the Atlantic Archipelago, 1550–1800* (Aldershot: Ashgate, 2004)
Seelig, Sharon Cadman, '"Speake, That I May See Thee": The Styles of Sir Thomas Browne', in *Sir Thomas Browne: The World Proposed*, ed. Reid Barbour and Claire Preston (Oxford: Oxford University Press, 2008), pp. 13–35
Sherman, William H., *John Dee: The Politics of Reading and Writing in the English Renaissance* (Amherst: University of Massachusetts Press, 1995)
Short, John Rennie, *Making Space: Revisioning the World, 1475–1600* (New York: Syracuse University Press, 2004)
Shuger, Debora K., *Habits of Thought in the English Renaissance: Religion, Politics, and the Dominant Culture* (Toronto: University of Toronto Press, 1997)
Siewers, Alfred K., 'Spenser's Green World', *Early English Studies*, 3 (2010), 1–34
Siewers, Alfred K., *Strange Beauty: Ecocritical Approaches to Early Medieval Landscape* (Basingstoke: Palgrave Macmillan, 2009)
Silberman, Lauren, *Transforming Desire: Erotic Knowledge in Books III and IV of The Faerie Queene* (Berkeley: University of California Press, 1995)
Smith, Donald Kimball, *The Cartographic Imagination in Early Modern*

*England: Rewriting the World in Marlowe, Spenser, Raleigh and Marvell* (Aldershot: Ashgate, 2008)

Smith, Helen and Louise Wilson, eds, *Renaissance Paratexts* (Cambridge: Cambridge University Press, 2011)

Smith, Jonathan M., 'Geographical Rhetoric: Modes and Tropes of Appeal', *Annals of the Association of American Geographers*, 86.1 (1996), 1–20

Smith, Pamela H., *The Body of the Artisan: Art and Experience in the Scientific Revolution* (Chicago: University of Chicago Press, 2004)

Smith, Roland M., 'Spenser's Irish River Stories', *PMLA*, 50.4 (1935), pp. 1047–56

Smith, Roland M., 'Spenser's Tale of the Two Sons of Milesio', *MLQ*, 3 (1942), pp. 547–57

Smyth, Gerry, *Space and the Irish Cultural Imagination* (Basingstoke: Palgrave, 2001)

Smyth, William J., *Map Making, Landscapes and Memory: A Geography of Colonial and Early Modern Ireland, c. 1530–1750* (Cork: Cork University Press, 2006)

Snyder, Susan, 'Guyon the Wrestler', *Renaissance News*, 14.4 (1961), 249–52

Sobecki, Sebastian I., *The Sea and Medieval English Literature* (Cambridge: D.S. Brewer, 2008)

Soja, Edward W., *Postmodern Geographies: The Reassertion of Space in Critical Social Theory* (London: Verso, 1989; repr. 1999)

Spearing, A.C., *Medieval Dream-Poetry* (Cambridge: Cambridge University Press, 1976)

Spiller, Elizabeth, *Science, Reading, and Renaissance Literature: The Art of Making Knowledge, 1580–1670* (Cambridge: Cambridge University Press, 2004; repr. 2007)

Spirn, Anne Whiston, *The Language of Landscape* (New Haven: Yale University Press, 1998)

Stallybrass, Peter, 'Robin Hood, the Carnivalesque and the Rhetoric of Violence', in *The Violence of Representation: Literature and the History of Violence*, ed. Nancy Armstrong and Leonard Tennenhouse (London: Routledge, 1989), pp. 45–76

Stanbury, Sarah, *Seeing the Gawain Poet: Description and the Act of Perception* (Philadelphia: University of Pennsylvania Press, 1991)

Steadman, John M., *The Hill and the Labyrinth: Discourse and Certitude in Milton and His Near-Contemporaries* (Berkeley: University of California Press, 1984)

Steggle, Matthew, 'Charles Chester and Richard Hakluyt', *SEL*, 43.1 (2003), 65–81

Stenner, Rachel, Tamsin Badcoe, and Gareth Griffith, eds, *Rereading Chaucer and Spenser: Dan Geffrey with the New Poete* (Manchester: Manchester University Press, 2019)

Stern, Paul, *Knowledge and Politics in Plato's Theaetetus* (Cambridge: Cambridge University Press, 2008)

Stern, Virginia F., *Gabriel Harvey: His Life, Marginalia and Library* (Oxford: Clarendon Press, 1979)

Stevens, John E., *Medieval Romance: Themes and Approaches* (London: Hutchinson, 1973)

Stillman, Robert E., '"Words Cannot Knytt": Language and Desire in Ralegh's *The Ocean to Cynthia*', *SEL*, 27.1 (1987), 35–51

Sullivan, Jr., Garrett, *Sleep, Romance and Human Embodiment* (Cambridge: Cambridge University Press, 2012)

Summers, David A., *Spenser's Arthur: The British Arthurian Tradition and The Faerie Queene* (Lanham: University Press of America, 1997)

Sutton, James M., *Materializing Space at an Early Modern Prodigy House: The Cecils at Theobalds, 1564–1607* (Aldershot: Ashgate, 2004)

Szönyi, György E., 'Paracelsus, Scrying and the *Lingua Adamica*: Contexts for John Dee's Angel Magic', in *John Dee: Interdisciplinary Studies in English Renaissance Thought*, ed. Stephen Clucas (Dordrecht: Springer, 2006), pp. 207–29

Taylor, E.G.R., *The Haven Finding Art: A History of Navigation from Odysseus to Captain Cook* (London: Hollis and Carter, 1956)

Taylor, E.G.R., *Late Tudor and Early Stuart Geography 1583–1650* (London: Methuen, 1934)

Taylor, E.G.R., 'A Letter Dated 1577 from Mercator to John Dee', *Imago Mundi*, 13.1 (1956), 56–68

Teskey, Gordon, *Allegory and Violence* (Ithaca: Cornell University Press, 1996)

Teskey, Gordon, 'From Allegory to Dialectic: Imagining Error in Spenser and Milton', *PMLA*, 101.1 (1986), 9–23

Teskey, Gordon, 'Notes on Reading *The Faerie Queene*: From Moment to Moment', in *Spenser in the Moment*, ed. Paul J. Hecht and J.B. Lethbridge (Madison: Fairleigh Dickinson University Press, 2015), pp. 217–34

Thomas, Charles, 'Lundy's Lost Name', in *Island Studies: Fifty Years of the Lundy Field Society*, ed. R.A. Irving, A.J. Schofield, and C.J. Webster (Bideford: Lazarus Press for The Lundy Field Society, 1997), pp. 29–37

Tonkin, Humphrey, 'Spenser's Garden of Adonis and Britomart's Quest', *PMLA*, 88.3 (1973), 408–17
Trinkaus, Charles, 'Protagoras in the Renaissance: An Exploration', in *Philosophy and Humanism: Renaissance Essays in Honour of Paul Oskar Kristeller*, ed. Edward P. Mahoney (Leiden: E.J. Brill, 1976), pp. 190–213
Tuan, Yi-Fu, *The Hydrologic Cycle and the Wisdom of God: A Theme in Geoteleology* (Toronto: University of Toronto Press, 1968)
Turchi, Peter, *Maps of the Imagination: The Writer as Cartographer* (Texas: Trinity University Press, 2004)
Turner, Henry S., *The English Renaissance Stage: Geometry, Poetics, and the Practical Spatial Arts 1580–1630* (Oxford: Oxford University Press, 2006; repr. 2010)
Unger, Richard W., *Ships on Maps: Pictures of Power in Renaissance Europe* (Basingstoke: Palgrave Macmillan, 2010)
Van Es, Bart, *Spenser's Forms of History* (Oxford: Oxford University Press, 2002)
Vermette, Rosalie, 'Terrae Incantatae: The Symbolic Geography of Twelfth-Century Arthurian Romance', in *Geography and Literature: A Meeting of the Disciplines*, ed. William E. Mallory and Paul Simpson-Housley (Syracuse: Syracuse University Press, 1987), pp. 145–60
Vernant, Jean-Pierre, *Myth and Thought Among the Greeks*, trans. Janet Lloyd with Jeff Fort (New York: Zone, 2006)
Viktus, Daniel, 'The New Globalism: Transcultural Commerce, Global Systems Theory, and Spenser's Mammon', in *A Companion to the Global Renaissance: English Literature and Culture in the Era of Expansion*, ed. Jyotsna Singh (Chichester: Wiley-Blackwell, 2009), pp. 31–49
Villeponteaux, Mary, 'Displacing Feminine Authority in *The Faerie Queene*', *SEL*, 35.1 (1995), 53–67
Vinaver, Eugène, *The Rise of Romance* (Oxford: Clarendon Press, 1971)
Wallace, David, *Premodern Places: Calais to Surinam, Chaucer to Aphra Behn* (Oxford: Blackwell, 2004; repr. 2006)
Walsham, Alexandra, *The Reformation of the Landscape: Religion, Identity, and Memory in Early Modern Britain and Ireland* (Oxford: Oxford University Press, 2011)
Warren, Christopher N., *Literature and the Law of Nations, 1580–1680* (Oxford: Oxford University Press, 2015)
Waters, David W., *The Art of Navigation in England in Elizabethan and Early Stuart Times* (New Haven: Yale University Press, 1958)

Watt, J.A., 'Gaelic Polity and Cultural Identity', in *A New History of Ireland, Volume II: Medieval Ireland 1169–1534*, ed. Art Cosgrove (Oxford: Oxford University Press, 2008), pp. 314–51

Weatherby, Harold L., 'Pourd out in Loosnesse', *Spenser Studies*, 3 (1982), 73–85

Weisl, Angela Jane, *Conquering the Reign of Femeny: Gender and Genre in Chaucer's Romance* (Cambridge: D.S. Brewer, 1995)

Weiss, Allen S., 'Preface: Gardens of the Imagination', in *Mirrors of Infinity: The French Formal Garden and Seventeenth Century Metaphysics* (New York: Princeton Architectural Press, 1995), pp. 8–19

Weixel, Elizabeth M., 'Squires of the Wood: The Decline of the Aristocratic Forest in Book VI of *The Faerie Queene*', *Spenser Studies*, 25 (2010), 187–213

Werth, Tiffany Jo, *The Fabulous Dark Cloister: Romance in England after the Reformation* (Baltimore: Johns Hopkins University Press, 2011)

West, Michael, 'Spenser, Everard Digby, and the Renaissance Art of Swimming', *RQ*, 26.1 (1973), 11–22

West, Michael, 'Spenser's Art of War: Chivalric Allegory, Military Technology, and the Elizabethan Mock-Heroic Sensibility', *RQ*, 41.4 (1988), 654–704

Whitehead, Christiania, *Castles of the Mind: A Study of Medieval Architectural Allegory* (Cardiff: University of Wales Press, 2003)

Whitfield, Peter, *The Charting of the Oceans: Ten Centuries of Maritime Maps* (London: British Library, 1996)

Williams, Elizabeth, 'England, Ireland and Iberia in *Olyver of Castylle*: The View from Burgundy', in *Boundaries in Medieval Romance*, ed. Neil Cartlidge (Cambridge: D.S. Brewer, 2008), pp. 93–102

Williams, Kathleen, 'Spenser: Some Uses of the Sea and the Storm-tossed Ship', in *Research Opportunities in Renaissance Drama*, XIII–XIV, ed. S. Schoenbaum (Evanston: Northwestern University Press, 1970–71), pp. 135–42

Williams, Kathleen, *Spenser's Faerie Queene: The World of Glass* (London: Routledge and Kegan Paul, 1966)

Williams, Kathleen, 'Venus and Diana: Some Uses of Myth in *The Faerie Queene*', *ELH*, 28.2 (1961), 101–20

Williams, Wes, *Pilgrimage and Narrative in the French Renaissance: 'The Undiscovered Country'* (Oxford: Clarendon, 1998)

Wilson Knight, G., 'The Spenserian Fluidity', in *Elizabethan Poetry: Modern Essays in Criticism*, ed. Paul J. Alpers (Oxford: Oxford University Press, 1967), pp. 329–44

Wofford, Susanne Lindgren, 'Britomart's Petrarchan Lament: Allegory and Narrative in *The Faerie Queene* III, iv', *Comparative Literature*, 39.1 (1987), 28–57

Wofford, Susanne Lindgren, *The Choice of Achilles: The Ideology of Figure in the Epic* (Stanford: Stanford University Press, 1992)

Wofford, Susanne Lindgren, 'Gendering Allegory: Spenser's Bold Reader and the Emergence of Character in *The Faerie Queene* III', *Criticism*, 30.1 (1988), 1–22

Wolfe, Jessica, *Humanism, Machinery, and Renaissance Literature* (Cambridge: Cambridge University Press, 2004)

Woodcock, Matthew, *Fairy in The Faerie Queene: Renaissance Elf-Fashioning and Elizabethan Myth-Making* (Aldershot: Ashgate, 2004)

Woods, William F., *Chaucerian Spaces: Spatial Poetics in Chaucer's Opening Tales* (Albany: State University of New York Press, 2008)

Woolway, Joanne, 'Spenser and the Culture of Place', Guest Lecture: University of Oslo, 17 April 1996. Archived by *EMLS* at http://extra.shu.ac.uk/emls/iemls/conf/texts/woolway.html (last accessed 2 June 2016)

Wright, John K., *The Geographical Lore of the Time of the Crusades: A Study in the History of Medieval Science and Tradition in Western Europe* (New York: American Geographical Society, 1925)

Wright, John K., '*Terrae Incognitae*: The Place of the Imagination in Geography', *Annals of the Association of American Geographers*, 37.1 (1947), 1–15

Yarnall, Judith, *Transformations of Circe: The History of an Enchantress* (Chicago: University of Illinois Press, 1994)

Yates, Frances A., *The Art of Memory* (Chicago: University of Chicago Press, 1966)

Yates, Frances A., *Astraea: The Imperial Theme in the Sixteenth Century* (London: Routledge and Kegan Paul, 1975)

Yates, Frances A., *Giordano Bruno and the Hermetic Tradition* (London: Routledge, 2002)

Yates, Frances A., *The Occult Philosophy in the Elizabethan Age* (London: Routledge, 1979)

Yates, Julian, *Error, Misuse, Failure: Object Lessons from the English Renaissance* (Minneapolis: University of Minnesota Press, 2003)

Yeats, W.B., *The Cutting of an Agate*, in *Essays and Introductions* (London: Macmillan, 1961; repr. 1980)

Zurcher, Andrew, *Edmund Spenser's The Faerie Queene: A Reading Guide* (Edinburgh: Edinburgh University Press, 2011)

Zurcher, Andrew, 'Printing *The Faerie Queene* in 1590', *Studies in Bibliography*, 57 (2005), 115–50

Zurcher, Andrew, *Spenser's Legal Language: Law and Poetry in Early Modern England* (Cambridge: Cambridge University Press, 2012)

# Index

Alberti, Leon Battista 87, 90
allegory 5, 8, 18, 38, 41, 43, 58, 64–96
Allott, Robert 157
analogy 13, 17, 58–9, 78, 87, 91, 106, 127, 169–70, 183, 192, 199, 206, 211, 214, 219, 245, 252, 255, 268
Andrews, J.H. 20, 206, 221n.71, 245–6, 249–50, 263
Antoniszoon, Cornelis 88
Ariosto, Lodovico 43, 94, 139n.22
Arthur, King 110, 112–15, 119, 123, 131, 168, 180, 256
Ascham, Roger 123, 131–2, 243–4
Ashley, Anthony 46–50, 55, 57, 145, 277

Bacon, Francis 1, 8, 167
Bakhtin, Mikhail 97n.4, 267
Bate, George 232–3
*Bible, The* 64, 69, 70, 78–81, 113, 210, 235, 263, 279
bogs 207–11, 222, 231–3, 237–9
Bourne, William 150, 197–8, 264
bridges 139, 229–34
*Brief Note of Ireland, A* 126
Browne, Thomas 61–2, 92
Bruno, Giordano, 191
Brutus legend 248–9
Bullinger, Heinrich 170

Calvin, Jean 154n.71
Camden, William 155–8, 256
Carew, Richard 6n.23, 256–7

cartography 12, 20, 50, 52, 146–7, 152, 206, 212, 223–4, 245, 251, 276
castles 69, 89–90, 156, 172, 179, 183, 231–2, 270
catoptromancy 149–51
Chaucer, Geoffrey 9, 99
works of:
*House of Fame* 73–8, 86, 92
'Legend of Ariadne' 87
*Merchant's Tale* 107n.48
*Squire's Tale* 101, 116, 141–2
*Tale of Sir Thopas* 97, 119–21, 252
chorography 19, 133–60, 170, 256, 271
Clairvaux, Bernard of 198–9
coastlines 14, 20–1, 38, 46–56, 59, 90, 93, 118, 133–7, 151–60, 163–201, 225–8, 254–9, 260–1, 269, 277
Coleridge, Samuel Taylor 15–16, 277
commonplaces 7, 62, 104, 106, 138, 194, 205, 211, 265, 278
Cortés, Martín, 192
cosmography 10, 13, 16–19, 25–60, 133–60, 163, 170, 242, 244, 246, 277
Crooke, Helkiah 210–11
Cuningham, William 17–19, 26–59, 136, 145–6, 158, 163–4, 170, 244, 276, 278

Daedalus myth 39–44, 57, 89, 217
Davies, Sir John 215n.50, 251, 257n.67, 264n.82, 274

De Certeau, Michel 19n.75, 69n.34, 71, 76, 139
Dee, John 20, 136, 149–51, 167–71, 191–3, 199, 276
  works of:
  *General and Rare Memorials Pertayning to the Perfect Arte of Navigation* 176–85, 226, 275
  *Mathematicall Praeface* 45–6, 88, 128, 149, 155, 169–70, 213–14, 271
Deleuze, Gilles 241, 262, 272
Dering, Edward 123
De Troyes, Chrétien 65–7n.22, 99
Digges, Leonard and Thomas, 104n.32, 213
*Dinnshenchas* 221, 277
Dousa, Janus 47, 53–5
Drayton, Michael 257
dream visions 32–5, 64, 68, 73–8, 92, 120–1, 157, 241, 248
drift 19, 27, 65–7, 102, 118, 119–32, 171, 252, 268
Du Bellay, Joachim 202–3
Duchesne, Joseph 106
Dymmok, John 208–9

ecotones 6–7, 21, 208, 230, 242, 269, 277
Elizabeth I 27, 41, 105, 150, 168, 176–9, 183–5, 191–201, 204, 248, 259, 265–6, 278
epic 5, 6–7n.24, 8, 10, 18, 37–8, 46, 53, 122, 127, 136, 139, 170, 184, 199, 247–9, 269, 276–7
Erasmus, Desiderius 65–7
error 4, 7, 15, 18, 38–44, 45, 51, 57–8, 62–3, 77, 126–8, 132, 210, 213, 251

Fraunce, Abraham 191

Garcie, Pierre 91
Genre 2, 6, 16, 21, 57, 128, 136n.9, 165, 258, 276–8
geography 1–21, 25, 31, 36, 56, 64, 67, 71, 101, 103, 106, 113, 124, 138–9, 146, 148–9, 154–5, 160, 169, 205–6, 213, 242–3, 246, 251–2, 271
geohumouralism 208n.26
geometry 31, 39, 90–1, 97, 126, 133, 149, 202, 212–13, 228
geosophy 15n.63, 102, 205
Gernon, Luke 223–5, 229, 238, 278
Grey, Arthur (Lord Grey de Wilton) 263–4
Guarino, Battista 83n.83

Hakluyt, Richard 114, 152
Harvey, Gabriel 9, 119
Hatton, Sir Christopher 27, 50
Hayward, John 219
Holbein, Hans (the Younger) 65–7
Homer 36, 94–5, 132, 215, 229, 249
Hurd, Bishop Richard 101–2
hydrography 16, 20, 47, 56–7, 156, 163–71, 178, 181–2, 189, 192, 199, 206, 220, 226, 263, 277

Ireland 10–21, 109, 113–19, 126, 140, 160, 167, 175, 181–2, 188, 191, 193, 199, 202–40, 241–78
islands 11, 52, 92, 107, 114, 128, 158, 181, 215–22, 241–77

Kilcolman 209, 270n.103

Langland, William 68
Lefebvre, Henri 5n.18, 11n.46, 19n.75, 142n.33
Leland, John 155
Llwyd, Humfrey 157
Lucretius 174n.33, 195, 217
Lundy 255–8

Marlowe, Christopher 197n.92
Massey, Doreen 20, 233–4, 252n.48, 278
memory 3, 12, 16–18, 62, 73–85, 104, 146, 155–60, 194–7, 201, 209, 239, 278–9

Mercator, Gerhard 52, 211–12, 257, 263
Middleton, Thomas 181–2
Milton, John 210, 248
mirrors 26–8, 35, 41, 49, 52–4, 59, 116, 140–51, 155, 158, 163, 168, 184
More, Sir Thomas 107, 243, 247
Moryson, Fynes 221–2, 228
mountains 31, 81, 90, 110n.54, 197, 221n.72, 222, 232–3, 270n.103, 271–3, 279
mud 194, 199, 207, 210–12, 230–1

Nashe, Thomas 121–5, 131, 160, 197n.92
navigation 3, 10, 12–13, 17, 26, 36–8, 45–60, 86–95, 109, 118n.76, 127, 140, 148, 163–71, 176–83, 192, 226, 263–5, 275
Neoplatonism 68, 144
Norden, John 213–14, 217–18

ocean 9, 28n.16, 36–7, 45, 54–6, 156, 169–71, 175, 188, 191, 193–7, 202–3, 258
*Olyver of Castylle* 100, 115–19
Ortelius, Abraham 9, 36–7, 146–7, 263
Ortúñez de Calahorra, Diego 98
Ovid 36, 228, 254

paratexts 25, 29, 35, 46–7, 55, 59, 146, 159, 165, 277
pastoral 5, 194, 215n.50, 223, 244, 252–3, 258–9, 267–9, 277
Payne, Robert 229
Perec, Georges 1, 133, 155, 158
Periegetes, Dionysius 8–9, 190
pilgrimage 4, 64–8, 72, 81, 121
Plantin, Christophe 47
Plato 61–2, 67–9, 106n.42, 107, 147
 works of:
  *Cratylus* 166
  *Protagoras* 68, 92–3
  *Theaetetus* 18, 68, 77–80
  *Timaeus* 30

plotting 6, 50, 73, 100–1, 119, 125–32, 147–8, 154, 202–6, 213–14, 218, 228, 231–2, 239, 241–5, 250, 252, 279
portolan charts 133
prayer 44, 110, 173
prophecy 75, 136–7, 140, 145–6, 151, 156–8, 183, 191
Proteus myth 167, 171, 201n.100
psychomachia 65, 108, 235
Ptolemy 144, 156, 213
Puttenham, George 38–9, 44, 127

Ralegh, Sir Walter 20, 106n.43, 167–9, 171, 188, 192–201, 220, 246–7, 253, 265–8, 277
Recorde, Robert 25, 97–8
rivers 163–5, 179, 188–90, 194, 198–9, 210–14, 219–24, 229–31
roads 65n.22, 67, 71, 97n.4, 232
Rogers, Thomas 61, 131
romance 5, 8, 18–19, 97–132, 136–60, 170, 186–7, 205, 241–4, 249–52, 277
ruins 72, 123–4, 261

seabed 54–6, 226
Shakespeare, William 113, 194–5, 201n.100, 243, 249, 273
Sidney, Sir Henry 239n.123
Sidney, Sir Philip 25, 30–1, 96, 105n.40, 127, 158
*Sir Gawain and the Green Knight* 100, 110–13, 125
Smith, Sir Thomas 214–16, 231, 247
Spenser, Edmund
 works of:
  *Amoretti* 144, 165–6, 187, 195, 251
  'Colin Clouts Come Home Againe' 21, 193, 198, 220, 242, 244, 253–9, 268n.96
  *Faerie Queene, The* figures and places in:
   Acrasia 11, 86–7, 92, 94–6, 128–9, 132, 137, 244–5, 269
   Amidas and Bracidas (sons of Milesio) 217–19, 245, 256

Spenser, Edmund (*cont.*)
  works of:
    *Faerie Queene, The* figures and
      places in:
      Amoret 46, 187
      Archimago 44, 59, 67, 74–5,
        80–1, 86–7, 129, 159, 269
      Arlo-Hill 270n.103, 271–3, 279
      Artegall 109, 115, 132, 135–6,
        140, 147, 153–4, 189–90,
        204–5, 216–18, 225, 228–33,
        237n.116, 238, 245, 255,
        265–6
      Arthur 25, 37, 69–80, 89, 115,
        136–7, 187, 237–8, 248
      Ate 229, 233
      Belge 204, 237–9
      Belphoebe 152n.62, 154, 187, 192
      Blatant Beast 49, 118n.78, 234,
        270
      Bower of Bliss 86, 92–6, 128–31,
        171, 225, 244
      Britomart 6, 19, 46, 109, 132,
        135–60, 171–6, 183, 187,
        189–99, 204–5, 229–31
      Bruin and Matilde 108n.49,
        109n.50, 266
      Calepine 108–13, 118, 125, 132,
        234–6, 266
      Calidore 109n.50, 186, 234,
        265–70
      Cambel and Triamond 188
      Castle of Alma 89–90, 179
      Duessa 59
      Errour 43–4, 80, 210–12, 236,
        238
      Faery land 76, 102–7, 109, 140,
        152, 157, 256, 268, 273
      False Florimell 142, 172
      Faunus 272
      Florimell 135, 172, 184–6
      Fradubio and Fraelissa 228
      Garden of Adonis 143, 171n.25,
        172
      Geryoneo 204, 237–8
      Giants 216–7n.57, 217, 266
      Glauce 135, 151, 158, 175, 190–1
      Gloriana 37, 75–9, 129, 225, 248
      Guyon 64, 71n.40, 81–96, 109,
        118, 128–32, 137, 140, 171,
        189, 225, 228, 241, 265
      House of Pride 58, 71
      Ignaro 69–71, 79
      Irena 132, 204, 225, 238, 245
      Malengin 204, 233, 237
      Marinell 171–2, 176, 184, 190
      Meliboe 268
      Merlin 19, 135–60, 166, 183
      Mount of Contemplation 81,
        90, 272
      Mutabilitie 255, 273, 279
      Nature 272–3, 279–80
      Orgoglio's Castle 69, 79–80
      Palmer 82–3, 86, 88–9, 95–6,
        128–30
      Phaedria 11, 131n.123, 185, 245,
        269
      Proteus 171, 186, 189, 194
      Redcrosse Knight 41–4, 58, 67,
        69, 71–2, 75, 78–86, 90, 108–9,
        115, 138, 140, 210–11, 228,
        235, 273
      Ryence 141, 148, 154n.74
      Saluage Man 236–7
      Scudamour 46, 187–88
      Serena 234–6
      Talus 204, 226–31, 237n.116
      Timias 187–8, 192
      Turpine 235–6
      Una 42–4, 129, 138, 219, 269,
      Venus 54, 135, 143–4, 217, 245
      Verdant 95–6
      Wandring Islands 241–2
      Wandring Wood 41–3, 71, 108–9
    'Letter of the Authors, A' 8, 25–7,
      38, 46, 59, 115, 124, 192
    'Ruines of Rome, The' 202
    *Shepheardes Calender, The* 253
    *View of the Present State of Ireland*
      12, 20–1, 114, 181, 205–7, 211,
      222, 228, 232–3, 239, 242, 244,
      249–55, 262–3, 267, 272
    'Virgil's Gnat' 126
Stanihurst, Richard 208, 215–16

surveying 20, 90, 126–8, 205, 207, 211–21, 228–9, 250n.38, 276

tides 20, 38, 52, 159, 165–9, 184–201, 221–2, 255–7

Turler, Jerome 243–4n.54

Vegetius Renatus, Flavius 153–4, 174, 226–7

Virgil (Vergilius Publius Maro) 36, 126, 153–4, 190, 253–4

Waghenaer, Lucas Janzoon 17–19, 26–9, 45–57, 134–6, 144–5, 156, 165, 174, 184, 200, 276–8

Wales 139–41, 152, 154–60, 257

Wales, Gerald of (Giraldus Cambrensis) 156, 209, 233, 250, 257–8

walking 61, 71–3, 79–91, 118, 221–2, 229, 234–6

Watson, Henry 115, 118–19

Whitney, Geffrey 260–1

Wilson, Thomas 104–5

woods 41–3, 71, 99, 108–9, 129, 208, 211, 222, 232–3, 271, 274

Worsop, Edward 128

Wright, John K. 14–15, 98, 205n.10

Yeats, William Butler 11, 278

EU authorised representative for GPSR:
Easy Access System Europe, Mustamäe tee 50,
10621 Tallinn, Estonia
gpsr.requests@easproject.com

www.ingramcontent.com/pod-product-compliance
Lightning Source LLC
Chambersburg PA
CBHW050201240426
43671CB00013B/2207